THE ROYAL AIR FORCE AND
TWO WORLD WARS

THE ROYAL AIR FORCE
— AND —
TWO WORLD WARS

SIR MAURICE DEAN, KCB, KCMG

Foreword by Marshal of the RAF
Sir Arthur T. Harris, Bt, GCB, OBE, AFC, LLD

CASSELL
LONDON

CASSELL LTD.
35 Red Lion Square, London WC1R 4SG
and at Sydney, Auckland, Toronto, Johannesburg,
an affiliate of
Macmillan Publishing Co., Inc.,
New York.

First published 1979

ISBN 0 304 30042 X

Filmset in Great Britain by
Northumberland Press Limited
Gateshead, Tyne and Wear
Printed and bound by
Richard Clay (The Chaucer Press) Ltd,
Bungay, Suffolk

Contents

Maps

Now all the youth of England are on fire,
And silken dalliance in the wardrobe lies:
Now thrive the armourers, and honour's thought
Reigns solely in the breast of every man.

William Shakespeare, *King Henry V*, Act II, Prologue

Foreword

by Marshal of the Royal Air Force Sir Arthur T. Harris,
Bt, GCB, OBE, AFC, LLD

Maurice Dean can be best described by those fortunate enough to have known him as an official and a friend, as the very antithesis of that type of Civil Servant—if such existed—so unkindly described by Winston Churchill as neither Servant nor Civil.

RAF officers unfortunate enough to be extracted from the active flying side of the Service, and condemned for their sins or their attainments to a period of incarceration in the Air Ministry, invariably found 'Maurus', as he was affectionately known by most of them, a tower of strength on which to lean and a guide and mentor in their faltering inexperienced steps through the Corridors of Power to their encounters with other Ministers, Ministries and those who served therein.

A brilliant scholar and mathematician he was a 'natural' for appointment as an Assistant Principal, and the Royal Air Force was fortunate indeed that he was appointed to the Air Ministry, wherein he spent the greater part of his career.

From 1929 to 1946 as an Assistant Principal and eventually Assistant Under-Secretary of State, he bore much if not most of the brunt as the Air Ministry fought politically to defend the Royal Air Force from destruction by the Army and Navy and then, practically, to make good the ravages of those Years of the Locust which had left the country—as usual—unwilling, unfit and unable to defend itself against an obvious and steadily increasing military threat.

As political panic succeeded political panic, Expansion Scheme after Expanded Expansion Scheme obtained grudging and belated approval, with all that that meant in chaos and clear-up for those immediately involved; and it was on Maurice Dean's broad shoulders, amongst too few others, that the task of keeping the whole vast organisation running smoothly, if at all, descended.

In 1946 he became Deputy Secretary, Control Office for Germany and

Austria and after a few periods elsewhere in the Foreign Office, Ministry of Defence, Treasury and Board of Trade he became Permanent Under-Secretary of State in the Air Ministry from 1955 to 1963, Second Secretary to the Treasury to 1964, then Joint Permanent Under-Secretary of State, Department of Education and Science and, finally, Permanent Secretary, Ministry of Technology to 1966. Thereafter he held a number of civilian appointments until 1972 when, one had hoped, he decided to take it easy at long last.

However, he spent his remaining years and energies in the production of this much needed history of the Royal Air Force, an invaluable guide to all who may need facts and not fancies on a much disputed subject.

Few Servants, Civil or otherwise, have served England better than Maurice Dean.

Arthur. T. Harris MRAF

12 June 1978

Introduction

This book is an attempt at a short history of the Royal Air Force from its earliest days until the end of the Second World War. My reason for writing it is that as an Air Ministry civil servant I was closely associated with the Force during half that period. Thus I got to know at first hand many of those who, over fateful years, made that history from the Royal Air Force point of view. So I decided that before it was too late I would endeavour to set out how the story looked to me as a close, sympathetic, but not uncritical observer. Of course such an attempt involves a major exercise in compression and this brings problems of its own. The aim has been to produce a perspective, highly individual of course, but still a perspective. For basic data in writing this book I have relied partly on official records in the Public Record Office and elsewhere, partly on personal recollections and contacts, and partly on a fairly extensive study of the wide literature now available on various aspects of the history of the Royal Air Force. A bibliography will be found at the end of the book. Among many publications which I have found helpful I would like to express a special sense of indebtedness to the following:

The War in the Air 1914–1918 by Sir Walter Raleigh and H. A. Jones; *Trenchard* by Andrew Boyle; *The Defence of the United Kingdom* by Basil Collier; *The Royal Air Force 1939–1945* by Denis Richards and Hilary St George Saunders; *The Strategic Air Offensive against Germany 1939–1945* by Sir Charles Webster and Noble Frankland; *Hankey, Man of Secrets* by Captain S. W. Roskill: *The Narrow Margin* by Derek Wood and Derek Dempster; *The Struggle for Europe* by Chester Wilmot; and an Air Ministry pamphlet, *The Rise and Fall of the German Air Force 1933–1945*. In dealing with Enigma, Colonel Gustave Bertrand's *Enigma* and the BBC Radio 3 broadcasts by Peter Calvocoressi (see Bibliography) were most helpful.

I should like to thank the friends who have helped me by reading one or more chapters of the book in draft. They include Air Chief Marshal Sir Harry Broadhurst, J. M. Bruce of the Royal Air Force Museum, the late Air Chief Marshal Sir Ralph Cochrane, Dr Noble Frankland, Air Marshal Sir Edward Gordon-Jones, Vice-Admiral Sir Peter Gretton, Air Marshal Sir Christopher Hartley, General Sir Ian Jacob, Denis Richards, Air Marshal Sir Geoffrey Tuttle and Sir Richard Way. My special thanks are due to Marshal of the Royal Air Force Sir Arthur Harris, Air Chief Marshal Sir Donald Hardman, Sir Peter Masefield and Sir Folliott Sandford who have read the whole text and provided invaluable comments. Finally, I am deeply indebted to Group Captain Haslam of the Air Historical Branch, Ministry of Defence, who has provided indispensable help throughout. No-one will suppose that these distinguished men necessarily agree with what I have said; indeed, far from it. The views expressed are of course my own responsibility. I have given ranks and titles as they were at the time of events described; subsequent ranks of those mentioned can be found in the Index.

Finally, I want to express my thanks to those who helped me prepare this book for publication: Miss Roslyn Nothnagel, Mrs John Dean, Toby Buchan of Cassell, and my wife, who also made the Index.

The author and publishers are grateful to the following for permission to quote material in copyright: Lady Blackett and Greenwood Press Inc., *Studies of War* by professor P. M. S. Blackett; John S. D. Eisenhower for the estate of President Dwight D. Eisenhower; Lady Portal for the estate of Marshal of the RAF Viscount Portal of Hungerford. Transcripts of Crown Copyright material in the Public Record Office and from Hansard appear by permission of the Controller, Her Majesty's Stationery Office.

PART ONE

1

The Origins of the Royal Flying Corps

Kill Devil Hill

Man's desire to fly goes back to the mists of antiquity. The practical achievement belongs to the last 200 years. There were always, or nearly always, two schools of thought, the lighter-than-air fanciers and the flying-machine fanciers. The lighter-than-air school was first off the mark with a line of development starting with the Montgolfier brothers in 1783 and extending through the work of the airship pioneers to Count Zeppelin in the early years of this century; to the flight of the British airship *R34* from Britain to America and back in 1919; to the *Graf Zeppelin*, the *R100*, the *R101* and the very large airships like the *Hindenburg*. With the loss of *R101* in 1930 and of the *Hindenburg* in 1937 airship development fell into decline. Today there are signs of a revival of interest, but whether or not this leads to anything, the record of lighter-than-air stands secure for all time, with the 144 ocean crossings of the *Graf Zeppelin* by the time she was decommissioned in 1937 as perhaps the greatest landmark.

The flying machine was intrinsically the more difficult problem. After all, if you take a large envelope and fill it with, say, hydrogen it will float. Make it big enough and it will carry a load. Give it ballast and a gas valve and it will go up or down, give it a rudder and a motor and it can be navigated. Over-simplification, of course, but the train of thought is plain to see. But how do you get a flying machine into the air? The obvious answer is 'like a bird', but this line of thought has serious limitations. Flapping mechanisms so far have given little help to man. The answer came as the result of two converging schools of thought. One was the development of the glider, that is to say, of an arrangement of wings not unlike the modern glider which a man could employ for unpowered gliding flights from, say, a hill. The names of Otto Lilienthal (1848–1896) of Germany and of Percy Pilcher (1866–

1899) of Britain, both of whom made great advances in the art, are specially honoured and remembered. Both, alas, lost their lives in gliding accidents. The other line of advance was the model aeroplane (or aerodrome as it was sometimes called) which was powered but of course unmanned; with this development the names of Sir George Cayley (1773–1857) in Britain and of Professor Langley (1834–1906) of the Smithsonian Institution in the United States will always be associated. The fusion of these two schools of thought, respectively manned/un-powered and powered/unmanned, was the unique achievement of the Wright brothers, though Pilcher might have got there first had he survived.

The story of the Wright brothers, Wilbur and Orville, is a fascinating one. They had set up in Dayton, Ohio, as cycle manufacturers and so had acquired in a fairly homely way some knowledge of engineering. Inspired by the achievements of Lilienthal and Pilcher they decided to build their own glider. To test it they went to Kill Devil Hill, four miles south of Kitty Hawk, North Carolina, where the Weather Bureau had said that strong and constant winds could be expected and where the Postmaster had said that the sandhills (created by the winds) were round and soft. Their trials and experiments extended over four seasons before the final triumph and during this period many hundreds of test glides were made. As a result, and with the help of a small 'do-it-yourself' wind tunnel, they steadily improved their design. In particular, they coupled the movements of the vertical tail to the wing warping mechanism which they developed to give lateral stability, and so simplified control. In 1903 they built a new machine and fitted it with an 8 hp motor. The new machine flew on its first test. The first practical heavier-than-air machine had been born. The date was 17 December 1903; Wilbur was thirty-six and Orville thirty-one. It is a long way from Dayton, Ohio, to Kitty Hawk where the Wright brothers had a temporary camp. Between 1899 when they first became hooked on flying and the end of 1903 when they reached their goal their experiments must have been practically a full-time occupation, and the cost must have been sub-stantial. One wonders who looked after the cycle business over this period.

The pioneers

After their triumph in December 1903 the Wright brothers returned to Dayton. They built several new machines and made many flights until October 1905 when for three years they disappeared from view in order to protect their invention. Their achievements at this stage were not widely understood either in their native land or abroad. As a result, in France a process of re-invention was soon in full swing. Santos Dumont made the first flight of a heavier-than-air machine in France in October 1906 and the work of the other great French pioneers, Blériot, Farman and Delagrange followed. But in August 1908 Wilbur Wright appeared in France and out-flew them all with a flight of over two hours. From this moment onwards the progress of aviation in France was very rapid indeed. Even in Germany, where there was much emphasis on airship design, steady progress was made with flying machines. In Britain matters proceeded at a slower pace. The first man to fly a heavier-than-air machine in Britain was A. V. Roe, first at Brooklands in June 1908 and later on the marshes of the River Lea near London. The reaction of the authorities to the latter flights was in the best British tradition. They sent for the police.

Another pioneer was S. F. Cody. Cody, an American who later acquired British nationality, was a good deal larger than life. A member of a theatrical company which specialised in Wild West shows, he developed a deep and effective interest in man-lifting kites. Later, he came to Britain and became Chief Instructor in kiting at HM Balloon Factory— surely an unusual recruit to the Civil Service. At Farnborough, Cody built himself an aeroplane modelled on the design of Glenn Curtiss in the United States and made many flights on Laffan's Plain, where the Balloon Factory was located. A metal replica of the tree to which Cody tethered his machine is preserved at Farnborough as a revered relic; the tree was used to measure the thrust of the aircraft by means of a spring balance. Cody had a small shed at Farnborough into which his aircraft could be squeezed, and one of his early helpers in manoeuvring the 'Cathedral' into its lair was Lieutenant Arthur Harris.

The tide was now rising swiftly and the manufacture of aeroplanes proceeded briskly. Roe departed to Manchester to build his famous trainer and Geoffrey de Havilland, Thomas Sopwith, Sir George White and the Short brothers, Eustace, Horace and Oswald, began their long and illustrious careers as aircraft designers. Truly, as Sir Walter Raleigh has remarked, it was an age of ferment. To use a flying metaphor, after a rough and ragged start the idea took off. Apart from making aeroplanes, the early manufacturers also trained pilots and this was important when, around 1911, the British Government began to take a serious interest in the military aspects of aviation. It was beyond question an exciting time. After 500,000 years or so of life, man had learned to fly. The event proved attractive to many brave and original spirits.

Military aviation

This book does not seek to do more than describe some aspects of the history of the Royal Air Force, but this short account of the early history of aviation is necessary to set the scene.

What interest did the British Government take in these events? Until 1911 the answer was—very little. Thus, between 1906 and 1908 they thrice refused to buy the Wright brothers' patents, wisely perhaps, because they subsequently purchased the rights for a modest sum. It is seldom wrong for governments to adopt a cautious approach, especially in military or commercial matters. In Britain, military experiments with balloons began at Woolwich Arsenal in 1878. Well, this was cautious enough, as the military aspect of balloons goes back at least to the Peninsular War. In 1882 a small military balloon establishment was created at Chatham and supplied the balloons used in various military expeditions. In 1890, this establishment was promoted to the status of a unit of the Royal Engineers and in 1892 it moved to Farnborough. Here was created the Balloon Factory, the lineal parent of the Royal Aircraft Establishment, becoming progressively His Majesty's Balloon Factory, the Army Aircraft Factory, the Royal Aircraft Factory and finally the Royal Aircraft Establishment. It was in the Balloon Factory from around 1910 onwards that most of the Army's developments in military aviation were concentrated. The Factory produced a number of experimental aeroplanes, the BE (Blériot experimental) series, the FE (Farman experimental) series, the RE (Reconnaissance experimental) series and the SE (Scout experimental) series, and these were developed as the years moved on. The Factory also produced a number of airships for the Army. The Navy steered as far clear of the Factory as possible, working directly with the aviation industry, notably with Short Brothers, Sopwith and with Vickers.

A landmark in the history of the Royal Air Force was the creation of the Air Battalion of the Royal Engineers in the spring of 1911. This organisation gathered into one piece the modest investment of the Army in military aviation—the Balloon Factory, a handful of men and perhaps a dozen aeroplanes. The life span of the Battalion was brief, a year perhaps. It was also inglorious, lacking both money and ideas. It was a landmark all the same in the eventful journey from the small unit in Woolwich Arsenal in 1878 or so towards the birth of a new fighting service in 1918.

Using all the advantages of hindsight, it is difficult to admire the achievements of the British Government in the field of aviation policy around this time. Look at the situation as it emerged towards the end of 1911. The military value of aviation was no novelty, it had been exploited in various ways for a hundred years. And now, for eight years, men had been flying heavier-than-air machines. The inference for military reconnaissance and artillery spotting was clear enough. The lessons had been learned well enough in France and Germany where considerable military air forces were in being. What was the situation in Britain? The elements of a successful and progressive industry existed owing little to Government orders and much to the enthusiasm of private individuals. There was the Air Battalion, including the chrysalis of a great idea in the shape of the Balloon Factory. But the rest, apart from a few splendid men, was a pathetic affair. The Navy was, if possible, in greater disarray. Their airship policy (which was important reconnaissance-wise) was in ruins. They had started late and fell straight into the troubles that Germany had surmounted years before. And in terms of aeroplanes, their achievements were minuscule. This neglect of military and naval aviation might have been understandable if the international scene had been tranquil. But this was far from being so. There was considerable tension between Britain and Germany and a naval re-armament race had begun. And 1911 was the year of the Agadir crisis when, as the result of conflicting policies in Morocco, Britain and Germany moved un-pleasantly close to war. So Britain was certainly slow off the mark in a field of obvious importance. This did not necessarily mean that the Government was wrong. After all, if you go to a roulette table and place a handsome stake you are right if your number turns up, otherwise wrong. But beyond question Britain was taking serious risks at a danger-ous time. These reflections, or something like them, came home to roost with the British Government towards the end of 1911.

The Royal Flying Corps

In November 1911 the Prime Minister, Asquith, appointed a Sub-Committee of the Committee of Imperial Defence under Lord Haldane 'to consider the future development of aerial navigation for naval and military purposes, and the measures which might be taken to secure to this country an efficient aerial service'. The Sub-Committee worked fast and its chief recommendations, which were accepted, were:

The creation of a British aeronautical service to be regarded as one and to be designated 'The Flying Corps', the Corps to consist of a Naval Wing, a Military Wing and a Central Flying School for the training of pilots.

The detailed working out of these proposals was entrusted to a small technical body of three persons, Brigadier-General David Henderson, Captain F. H. Sykes and Major D. S. H. MacInnes. Henderson was the leader, and his work in laying down the basic lines of development coupled with his distinguished leadership of the Royal Flying Corps at the outbreak of war entitles him to be called 'the Father of the Royal Air Force', a title often and quite erroneously attributed to Lord Trenchard. The idea of creating 'a British Aeronautical Service to be regarded as one' was bold and attractive, but it gave rise to obvious difficulties. To start with, was it intended to create a new service independent of the Army and Navy? The answer, clearly, was 'no'. Then the question arises, was the new service to be part of the Army or part of the Navy, or was it to be divided between them, in which case how could it be regarded as one? And who was to administer it? The answer to these questions is not clear. The new Corps was constituted by Royal Warrant, dated 13 April 1912, and the initial orders were issued by the Army Council. But the Admiralty soon established a new Department to supervise the Naval Wing and in practice military and naval aviation developed separately from the start. Even the name became split, the Military Wing becoming in practice the Royal Flying Corps and the Naval Wing soon turning itself into the Royal Naval Air Service. And from the start there were two Central Flying Schools, one at Upavon for Army pilots and the other at Eastchurch for the Navy. These arrangements were destined to cause great difficulties later.

2

Problems of Controlling Military and Naval Air Forces

The Royal Flying Corps at war

Two years or so after the Royal Flying Corps was formed, Britain was locked in a life and death struggle for existence. The First World War had begun. How did the Royal Flying Corps fare? We have seen that military aviation had been gravely neglected by the Asquith Government. Both air services were far inferior in strength to their German counterparts. Fortunately, the balance was to some degree restored by the French who entered the war with a strong air force.

The first squadrons of the Royal Flying Corps accompanied the British Expeditionary Force to France in August 1914. They were employed initially on reconnaissance, later on artillery spotting, later still on air fighting and bombing. These increasing tasks reflect the increasing sophistication of aircraft equipment. To start with aircraft could only fly. Later, they learned to communicate, to fire guns, to drop bombs. At the outbreak of war, four squadrons in all, Nos 2, 3, 4 and 5 went to France accompanied by a most essential Aircraft Park, and under the overall command of Henderson. From the beginning, their relations with the Army were close and harmonious. An intimate relationship developed between General Headquarters and Royal Flying Corps Headquarters, between Army and Royal Flying Corps Wing or Brigade and so down the line. This relationship persisted until the end of the war, by which time the Royal Flying Corps in its new guise, the Royal Air Force, was incomparably the greatest air force in the world. It was an improbable and perhaps a lucky end to Governmental faltering in 1912.

In this brief sketch of Royal Air Force history it is unnecessary to tell the story of Army/Royal Flying Corps relationships in detail. But some broad comments are in order. The four squadrons of the Royal Flying Corps that went to France in August 1914 took between them sixty-three aeroplanes, 105 officers and 755 other ranks. The aeroplanes were a mixed bag of BE2s, FE8s, Blériots, Avros and Henri Farmans. All the engines were French. Left behind, in the care of Lieutenant-Colonel Hugh Trenchard, were 116 aeroplanes, mainly junk, forty-one officers and a few hundred airmen. These modest forces were minute compared with the national air forces of France, Germany and indeed Italy. The years of neglect had taken their toll. It seems to be a British characteristic. Yet, four years later, the Royal Air Force was, beyond comparison, the most powerful Air Force in the world with a first line strength of some 2,600 aeroplanes and some 300,000 officers and men. It had always been on the offensive and had finally won for itself a position of unchallenged supremacy. How had this transition been achieved? First, perhaps, credit must be given to the responsible states-men, soldiers and sailors. They had been blind enough in all conscience up to August 1914. Thereafter, no target was big enough, and indeed many targets laid down were hopelessly unrealistic. Among the states-men, Lord Kitchener, perhaps, deserves special praise. He had an under-standing of the scale of magnitude of the forces involved which proved of great service to his country. 'Double this!' said Kitchener as Secretary of State for War when an early air programme was put in front of him. Of course, this kind of decision can be overdone, but without it in this instance the Royal Air Force would not have triumphed in 1918. Then there was Henderson, who led the Royal Flying Corps to battle in 1914 and returned to guide its destinies as Director-General of Military Aviation in Whitehall until 1917. Statesmen and soldiers are mentioned first because unless they had shown the way nothing could follow. But pieces of paper in the sense of air expansion programmes sanctioned take you only so far. If the pieces of paper are missing, disaster can follow, but if they are available, much more is necessary. In the air services, the programmes had to command airframes, engines, equipment of all kinds and, last, but not least, people.

The equipment/people relationship is basically that of the hen and the egg. Without adequate equipment, the bravest can accomplish little. Without brave people, equipment has no value. Which matters most? People, surely, it may be thought, but it is a tight complex.

So far as people were concerned, the air services were exceptionally fortunate. For many thousands of years men had endeavoured by various means, often subtle, to kill each other on chosen occasions on land and on sea. In 1903, with the achievements of the Wright brothers, this geometry acquired a third dimension. Strong indeed were the com-pulsions that these new ideas exercised over the minds of men. Brave and original spirits appeared, as if from nowhere, learned to fly in the most curious and dangerous ways and were around when Britain went to war in 1914. Among them was Trenchard, whose name is perhaps the greatest in this story and whose greatest gifts to his country were surely his unconquerable spirit and his ability to inspire the young. Trenchard's ideas were dominated by the offensive. He planted this idea in the mind of Britain's air service and it has remained there ever since. On balance it has served our country well. As a principle of war it arose at least in part from the consideration that pilots did not have to share the misery of life in the trenches. Accordingly, when they gave battle they gave everything they had. On the material front miracles were in the end achieved, at any rate as far as airframes were concerned, as the following figures will demonstrate:

Output of Aircraft (Britain)[1]

1914	211
1915	2,093
1916	6,099
1917	14,168
1918	Around 2,000 per month

These achievements were not realised without great convulsions of organisation which affected the whole structure of the air services. This story is told later. But figures are one thing, successful aeroplanes another. What happened? Well, of course, in 1914, the Royal Flying Corps was for practical purposes non-existent. By 1916, in the Battle of the Somme, British military aircraft had the edge. Later, with the Fokker and the Albatros the Germans recovered technical superiority. And so the tide of battle swung backwards and forwards. But, in the end, Britain triumphed. Quality swung backwards and forwards, numbers went steadily up. Most honoured, among British military aircraft in the First World War must be remembered: the Sopwith Camel fighter; the Handley Page 0/400 bomber; the Bristol F2 fighter; the SE 5A fighter; the Avro 504 trainer. Among the collection of early aeroplanes at the Royal Air Force Museum are a Blériot dating from 1912 looking not so very different from the first craft to fly the Channel in 1909, and a Vickers Vimy bomber dating from 1918. The latter is called 'Triple First', recording the first ever flight across the Atlantic by Captain Alcock and Lieutenant Brown (which ended in Ireland with enough fuel to carry the aircraft to Russia), by Captain Ross Smith and Lieutenant

Keith Smith to Australia, and to the Cape by Wing Commander Pierre Van Ryneveld and Flight Lieutenant Quintin Brand. How much had been accomplished under the stress of war in those six short years.

On the engine front the story is more patchy. At the outbreak of war Britain was dependent upon French designs. By early 1917, when responsibility for aircraft supplies was transferred from the Admiralty and War Office to the Ministry of Munitions and large expansion programmes were laid down, engines to some forty designs were under construction. It was decided to concentrate on eight: the Sunbeam Arab, the Beardmore-Halford-Pullinger (BHP), the Hispano-Suiza, the Rolls-Royce, the Royal Aircraft Factory 4A, the Clerget (130 hp), the Le Rhône (110 hp), the Bentley Rotary, the Wolseley Viper. The Sunbeam Arab, the BHP and the British-made Hispano turned out to be failures. The Clerget and the Le Rhône which were French designs gave good service as did the Royal Aircraft Factory 4A. The Bentley Rotary was a success but production suffered as the result of a substantial diversion of resources in favour of the ABC Dragonfly, which proved a failure. The greatest success was achieved by Rolls-Royce which company, as in the Second World War, made a magnificent contribution to victory. For this success much credit must go to the Admiralty for the early encouragement it gave. In 1917 the United States produced the Liberty engine which was a great success but naturally enough Britain had great difficulty in obtaining adequate supplies, with the result that many DH 9A bombers went short.

One factor which contributed to the success of the Royal Air Force towards the end of the war was a superb method of training flying instructors developed by an instructing genius, Major R. R. Smith Barry at the School of Special Flying, Gosport. The essence of the instruction was that an aeroplane is a rational piece of machinery and that for every characteristic of its behaviour there is an explanation and, when necessary, a remedy. Accordingly, the pilot was fully instructed in all the tricks an aeroplane can get up to, some hair-raising, and how to overcome them. The pilot was also taught, of course, the elements of good flying. Smith Barry was greatly helped in his work by the excellent qualities of the aircraft on which he relied, which was the Avro 504 trainer fitted with the Gnôme Monosoupape rotary engine.* The excellence of the Gosport School created a tradition of superb aviation training which remains with the Royal Air Force today.

* The odd name 'Monosoupape' raises not a flicker of surprise from early aviators. It means 'one valve'.

Spinning[2]

One of the manoeuvres taught at Gosport from 1917 onwards was the spin. This was a condition in which the aircraft got into a steep dive in the shape of a helix giving the pilot the impression that the aircraft was nose-down with its axis nearly vertical. Many pilots were killed in the early days from inability to recover from a spin, which could be started accidentally. In the course of the First World War the aerodynamics of the spin were explained, the remedy discovered, and pilots instructed in the technique of getting out of a spin once they had got into it. So far as the elevators are concerned the solution is the opposite of what might be expected in that the stick is eased forward, a manoeuvre which might be expected to increase the angle of dive. There is a legend that the first man to conquer the spin was Dr F. A. Lindemann, later Lord Cherwell, and this legend has given rise to a minor puzzle which over the years has attracted some interest. The following are facts:

At various dates between April 1914 and July 1916 a number of pilots recovered from intentional spins

In August 1916 Major F. W. Goodden, a Farnborough test pilot, spun an FE 8 three times to the left and three times to the right and wrote a report on the results

In June, July and August 1917, Lindemann carried out a series of spinning tests on BE 2s and FE 2s at Farnborough and wrote up the results

The legend is that before Goodden's flights in 1916 Lindemann produced the theory of the spin, learned to fly, took up a BE 2 and spun it both ways to prove his theory, this at a time when spinning was for practical purposes considered bound to be fatal. Later he learned to fly officially at the Central Flying School. There is no written contemporary evidence of these spins which, it is said, Lindemann treated as confidential. This account was supported by Colonel O'Gorman who was Superintendent at Farnborough at the time and it is said that O'Gorman's account was shown to Lindemann who said that it was true. It was, however, treated with reserve by some of Lindemann's scientific colleagues at Farnborough. The question of dates must clearly be regarded as in dispute though they certainly seem to support the 1917 theory. What cannot be disputed is that Lindemann, with his umbrella and his bowler hat and his poor eyesight, made a contribution to aviation which was brave, scientifically distinguished and timely. Other scientists at Farnborough who learned to fly at this time were Professor George Thomson, later a Nobel Laureate, and Henry Tizard of whom more will be heard later in this story. Here was established the beginnings of that happy bond between the academic scientist and the fighting pilot which was to prove immensely fruitful twenty years later.

The Royal Naval Air Service

At this point in our story it is necessary to outline the fortunes of the Royal Naval Air Service from the time at which it came into being, in fact if not in name, with the formation of the Royal Flying Corps in 1912.

The Royal Naval Air Service had four main responsibilities:

Reconnaissance and gunnery spotting for the Fleet
Anti-submarine and anti-minelaying patrols
Air defence of Britain
Bombing and torpedo-bombing

The devices available at various times to sustain these duties were: rigid airships, non-rigid airships, aircraft carriers, seaplanes, seaplane carriers, flying boats, lighters and balloons. The techniques used were a good deal more complex than those confronting the Royal Flying Corps and the tasks were more extensive. The complexity of the techniques arose from the fact that naval aircraft had not only to operate over the sea but also as a regular matter to accompany warships to sea and to alight and take off from the sea. The nature of the sea being what it is there were formidable problems. Some of the problems indeed were never solved during the First World War. The neglect of military aviation which has already been discussed in connection with the Royal Flying Corps had grave consequences also for the Royal Navy. These consequences were compounded by the fact that up to a fairly advanced date in the First World War the Admiralty were slow to recognise the potentialities of military aviation, especially in the matter of rigid airships.

It is convenient to discuss the development of the Royal Naval Air Service by reference to its various weapons.

Rigid Airships

Over the period (very roughly) 1900 to 1930 airships had certain major advantages over aeroplanes in the matter of range and load carrying capacity. This fact was fully exploited by Germany. Between 1900 and

1914 under the inspired direction of Count Zeppelin airship development was pressed vigorously ahead amid much patriotic support. There were wrecks and crashes aplenty, but on the outbreak of war Germany had an airship fleet in being and the know-how to develop and enlarge it. In consequence, Germany was for a period enabled to bomb British cities at will,* a fact of secondary importance except for the unfortunate victims, but which had major effects on British policy. The main advantage for Germany was in respect of reconnaissance for the German High Seas Fleet. Airship design had of course been among the interests of the Royal Aircraft Factory but when the Royal Flying Corps was formed in 1912 the Admiralty took over responsibility for lighter-than-air craft. So far as rigid airships were concerned the Admiralty record was unfortunate. In September 1911 the *Mayfly*, a prototype naval airship of 700,000 cubic feet capacity built by Vickers at Barrow, broke her back before she flew. The Admiralty, thereupon, closed down rigid airship development. It was quickly restarted and a new rigid (the *R9*) commissioned, but this development was also cancelled in March 1915. Re-started after the departure of Winston Churchill as First Lord, the *R9* first flew in November 1916 and joined the Fleet in the following year. Other rigids were ordered and *R23*, *R24* and *R25* made their trial flights in the autumn of 1917. In September 1916, however, the Zeppelin *L33*, hit by anti-aircraft fire, came down in Britain in a condition which enabled the design to be copied. Alas, the first British rigid to German design was not ready until the war had ended. The second ship in this class, the *R34*, flew from England to the United States and back in July 1919.

Non-rigids

The Admiralty record in regard to non-rigids is scarcely better. In 1912, when the development of airships was handed over to the Navy, they inherited a few non-rigids, mostly eccentric, from the Army. The Admiralty looked on them coldly and little happened until the spring of 1915 when the importance of the non-rigid airship for anti-submarine patrol was belatedly recognised. On the orders of the First Sea Lord, Lord Fisher, a class of non-rigids was conjured up more or less overnight by grafting the body of a BE2C aeroplane on to the envelope of a

---

* By the autumn of 1916, German airships had become vulnerable to military aircraft and the airship attack on British cities petered out. One of the problems for the defending aircraft was of course the fact that for them the techniques of night flying were in their infancy.

Willows airship. The development period was short but unusual. In the words of the Official Historian:

> The firms best able to make the envelope were waterproof garment manufacturers, whose workers, used as they were to patterns, could at first make little of drawings. For the making of the cars, too, firms of no airship experience had, with few exceptions, to be called upon. Indeed, a majority of the cars were made to Kingsnorth drawings by a firm whose previous experience had been confined to fitting out shops. [3]

This improvisation worked well and the SS non-rigid, soon superseded by the Coastal type non-rigid, did a valuable job. A string of airship stations appeared round Britain, of which Pembroke, Pulham, Howden, Longside, Mullion, East Fortune are examples. The non-rigids watched the submarine tracks and although they could rarely sink a U-boat by their own resources, anti-submarine bombs being primitive, they provided a reliable source of intelligence. Having a wireless they could summon destroyers, which made the U-boats keep their heads down.

Aircraft

Where aircraft were concerned the instincts of the Admiralty were conservative and, for the most part, successful. They regarded the Royal Aircraft Factory with a degree of reserve which may or may not have been merited. They preferred to deal direct with well established aircraft manufacturing companies, notably with Shorts, Sopwith and Vickers, and the Handley Page series of twin-engine bombers, the mainstay of long-range bombing, initially resulted from the Navy's request for a 'bloody paralyser of an aeroplane'. On the whole, they were good pickers. Further, being interested in the possibility of aircraft lifting torpedoes and the like, they encouraged the development of powerful engines, notably by Rolls-Royce. On the whole, the influence of the Admiralty on aircraft and engine design was highly successful, and from time to time land-based forces benefited handsomely from their activities.

It was a natural move for the Admiralty to fit as many as possible of their aeroplanes with floats, and a string of seaplane stations was established round the East Coast, notably at Eastchurch, the Isle of Grain, Calshot, Felixstowe, Yarmouth and Cromarty. It is, however, an unfortunate fact that the sea and aircraft do not make a good mix. Seaplanes are happy enough on inland or sheltered waters. On the open sea, when conditions are at all rough, as they often are, strains are imposed on aircraft and their floats that are hard or impossible to bear. This consideration limited and still limits the operational use of seaplanes. From very early days plans were developed to provide seaplanes with a floating base at sea. Some seaplane carriers like the *Empress*, the *Engadine* and the *Riviera*, which were converted cross-Channel steamers, provided storage plus facilities for hoisting seaplanes out and in. Others like the *Ark Royal* (a converted tramp steamer) and the *Campania* (a converted Cunarder) embodied facilities for flying off. (The business of flying on was much more complex and was not attempted until August 1917 on the *Furious*.) These facilities were inevitably somewhat makeshift, probably because the construction of purpose-built ships would have been costly in time and shipyard space. But the situation also reflects reservations on the part of the Admiralty, at any rate in the early stages of the war, as to the value of aircraft. Land-based aeroplanes were used by the Navy for bomber operations (especially from Dunkirk), for air defence (particularly during the period when the Navy was responsible for the air defence of Britain), and (in a disappointingly minor way) for the launching of torpedoes.

Flying Boats

The flying boat, though not conspicuously seaworthy when in contact with the sea, has many advantages over the seaplane, though of course it is much more expensive and much heavier. The Navy devoted some effort to developing flying boats, and the considerable degree of success which they achieved may be judged from the fact that by the end of the war the Felixstowe Fury was in service, powered by five 360 hp motors, mounting four guns and with an all-up weight of 15 tons. Naval flying boats gave an excellent account of themselves in the First World War. With these developments the name of Colonel J. C. Porte, who in September 1915 took command of the Felixstowe Naval Air Station, is especially honoured and remembered. Invalided from the Navy in 1911 he joined the honourable band of aircraft pioneers, helped in the United States to design the Glenn Curtiss flying boat, rejoined the Navy in 1914 and later improved the Curtiss boats when they came to Felixstowe. He died soon after the end of the war, aged thirty-five, but few have given more to the service of aviation in the course of a short and illness-stricken life.

Lighters, Balloons and Gun Turrets

The list of weapons available to the Royal Naval Air Service can be rounded off by a reference to lighters, balloons and gun turrets. Lighters were towed by warships and used to carry seaplanes with some success, the limiting factor being as always the weather. Balloons were towed by warships with considerable success, enabling observers to be mounted to a height of 1,500 feet or so with great advantages to the field of vision. Finally, it was found possible to mount launching platforms on the gun turrets of selected warships. The turret was turned into the 'felt' wind and a seaplane could be launched. Thus, bit by bit, the Navy won its eyes.

Naval Air Operations

In any study of Royal Naval Air Service operations a number of conflicting factors become evident. The Admiralty's negative approach to naval aviation, at least until 1915 or so, has much to answer for. Nevertheless, it is impossible not to admire the ingenuity and persistence with which the very difficult problems of naval aviation were tackled, and also, of course, the spirit of the aircrews, which was magnificent.

How much was achieved? The answer must surely be not enough. Once the non-rigid airships and the flying boats got going, anti-submarine patrols were pretty efficient. A number of Zeppelins were destroyed by gunfire or bombs. A modest dividend attended the naval bombing operations from Dunkirk. Reconnaissance for the Fleet improved as the war went on and the various devices discussed earlier were adopted. At Jutland, the most spectacular naval engagement of the war, naval air reconnaissance, what there was of it, was a disaster. The essence of the battle was an attempt by the German High Seas Fleet to draw the Battle Cruiser Squadrons of the Grand Fleet into an engagement on terms favourable to Germany. The plan was that the German battle cruisers under Admiral Hipper should show themselves off the coast of Norway and then retreat, pursued by Admiral Beatty and the British battle cruisers which would run straight into the German High Seas Fleet plus plenty of U-boats. The plot failed, as they say, because the British Admiralty was aware that the High Seas Fleet was putting to sea whereas the German Admiralty were not aware that the Grand Fleet was similarly bound. So here was Admiral Jellicoe presented with the first and only real chance throughout the war of bringing the High Seas Fleet to battle under conditions favourable to Britain. The event misfired. The fleets never met in a decisive engagement. Britain missed the chance of a memorable naval victory. Why? Many thousands of words have been devoted to this topic. The Battle of Jutland was a controversial issue for many years after the event, but several points stand out. Until an advanced stage Jellicoe, though he knew that the German Fleet was at sea, did not know where to look for it. 'Where is the enemy's battle fleet?' he signalled to Beatty at 18.01 hours on 31 May 1916. Beatty replied at 18.14 hours, Jellicoe deployed his Fleet at 18.15 hours and the engagement began at 18.17 hours, Jellicoe having cleared harbour nearly a day earlier. Later, after a confused series of engagements, the German Fleet was able to slip home by passing to the north of the Grand Fleet, then steaming south on its night dispositions. Why did the commanders of these great Fleets lack such super-essential intelligence? Firstly and without doubt because of weather conditions. Surface craft have limited range of vision at the best of times and the visibility at Jutland was often poor. Moreover, it favoured the Germans who could observe our ships silhouetted against the western sky. Great feats were performed on both sides by scouting ships. But what about aircraft? The Germans had their Zeppelin fleet, invaluable in the normal way for fleet reconnaissance, but useless at Jutland for weather reasons. Britain had the *Campania* which was part of the Grand Fleet at Scapa Flow, and the *Engadine*, a primitive seaplane carrier which was stationed with the Battle Cruiser Force in the Firth of Forth. Soon after German warships were first spotted by the Royal Navy, Beatty ordered a seaplane reconnaissance. The results, useful but not critical, never reached the Commander-in-Chief, one of many distressing communications failures at Jutland. The *Campania*'s story is more sad. The signal to sail never reached her and she cleared harbour some three hours after the main fleet. A fast ship, she could have made up for this late start but Jellicoe, no doubt thinking of possible U-boat attacks on an unescorted ship, ordered her back to harbour in the middle of the night. And so the poor dog had none. It is true to say that after Jutland interest in naval air reconnaissance rapidly improved and by 1918 many warships carried their own seaplane.

German air raids on Britain

During the First World War Britain was attacked from the air by Zeppelins and by German aircraft. The Zeppelins dropped 196 tons of bombs and killed 557 people. German aircraft dropped 73 tons of bombs and killed 857 people. Material damage, estimated in monetary terms, was put at just under £3,000,000.[4] The scale of damage and the civilian casualties were thus trivial compared with the losses suffered in the main theatres of war. The other consequences were not so trivial. The Admiralty became responsible for air defence in 1914 as a direct consequence of the fact that on the outbreak of war the Royal Flying Corps moved every serviceable aircraft to France. It was a tiresome distraction for that hard pressed Department. Later on, the Army and the Royal Flying Corps were able to take over. The Zeppelin threat quickly disappeared when effective incendiary ammunition became available, but no such simple remedy was at hand to deal with the German Gotha bombers and by 1918 a fairly substantial defence effort was deployed in response to the modest threat of German aeroplanes. It is true to say, however, that the Zeppelins' greatest enemy was the weather, while the long-range bombers suffered greater casualties from accidents than they did from British defence measures.

There was also the morale aspect, and this was somewhat surprising. In the Second World War Britain experienced air attack on a level at least one hundred times as intense as in the First World War, and the civilian population stood up to it pretty well. In the First World War there was a great outcry. Royal Flying Corps officers moving to their airfields east of London were liable to bě mobbed. When the Gothas bombed the centre of London in broad daylight without interference public reactions approached panic dimensions. Thus, on 7 July 1917, twenty-one Gothas dropped about 3 tons of bombs on London killing some fifty-seven people. Hilary St George Saunders describes the sequel thus:

> In an atmosphere of excitement amounting almost to panic the Cabinet met that same afternoon. It was a Saturday, and Ministers on their hasty way to Downing Street had ample evidence of the general public's indignation. Sir William Robertson, Chief of the Imperial General Staff, who was present, has left it on record that the agitation displayed at the Cabinet meeting itself was such that 'one would have thought the whole world was coming to an end'. In a letter written two days later to Haig he vividly describes the scene 'I could not', he said, 'get in a word edgeways.'[5]

Within four days of this raid General Smuts had been commissioned to write his famous report on air defence and air organization. That report will be discussed later, but the point is made here that these small scale German raids had a profound effect on British overall defence policy. Whether they should have done is another matter.

The problem of aircraft supply

Reference has already been made to the dramatic increase in the production of aircraft and engines from 1916 onwards. The apportionment of production and of capacity gave rise to acute differences between the Admiralty and War Office. On the supply front and again on many other aspects of air policy, an increasing need was demonstrated for some machinery of co-ordination. This machinery was established in five distinct phases:

The appointment of the Joint War Air Committee under Lord Derby in February 1916

The appointment of the First Air Board under Lord Curzon in May 1916

The appointment of the Second Air Board under Lord Cowdray in January 1917

The appointment of the War Priorities Committee and of the Air Policy Committee under Smuts in October 1917

The formation of the Air Council in January 1918

The Joint War Air Committee was the first manifestation of public disquiet about the state of the naval and military air services, triggered off by the appearance of the Fokker aeroplane on the Western Front in the autumn of 1915. The so-called 'Fokker Scourge' came about as the result of a single technical innovation—the fitting of an interrupter gear permitting the machine gun to fire forward through the airscrew arc, where previously it had been necessary to carry a gunner armed with a gun on a movable mounting, with all its attendant problems of deflection shooting. It is a measure of the importance of this device that so mediocre an aircraft as the Fokker monoplane could, for several months until Allied technology caught up, enjoy almost complete immunity from other aircraft.

The competition of two services for available air resources, though defended in some quarters as a healthy rivalry, was in fact a matter for concern, as was indeed the inevitable failure to define a logical division of duties and responsibilities. The Joint War Air Committee, which was given no executive powers, soon failed. Its Chairman, Derby, then Secretary of State for War, hit the nail on the head in his letter of resignation to Asquith when he remarked that the two air services could not be brought closer together unless they were amalgamated and that, while he thought amalgamation was inevitable in the end, the step was too difficult in wartime.

The failure of the Joint War Air Committee has the air of an irresistible force faced with an immovable object. The Admiralty and the War Office, for reasons which were logical and sensible, regarded their respective air services as integral parts of the Royal Navy and the Army, which indeed is what in practice they were. Consequently, they would admit no interference in regard to the management of these services. That was the immovable object. The irresistible force was provided by the rising volume of Parliamentary and other criticism which saw grave objections to the existing set-up, citing among other matters the muddle over air supply and the failure to co-ordinate air policy. The critics returned to the charge again and again. Each time they won a little ground. The formation of the Air Ministry early in 1918, whether or not it was a useful step, became inevitable in political terms from the moment of the failure of Derby's Committee. It was the only end to the argument. Maybe it was the right decision, maybe not, but that was the way things were going.

When the Joint War Air Committee foundered, Lord Curzon, Lord President of the Council, stepped into the breach. In the words of the Official History, 'He explored all possibilities, especially the formation of an Air Ministry and a separate Air Service.'[6]

There descended the anger of the War Office and the Admiralty. The War Office, its views no doubt moderated by the wise and experienced voice of Henderson, made some sensible comments. The Admiralty exploded, and their views, expressed through Balfour, then First Lord, were those of total rejection. It is right to feel some sympathy with the Admiralty. The future is difficult to foresee and when times become tumultuous we all, and rightly, fight for what we think is right. Still, viewed with the eyes of hindsight, a comfortable friend, Balfour went too far. The First Air Board was nevertheless set up in May 1916 under the Chairmanship of Curzon. It had no executive powers and no powers to determine policy, a mere talking shop. It achieved little except to stoke the fires of controversy, especially *vis-à-vis* the Admiralty. The controversy spilled over into the War Committee and in Lloyd George's war memoirs there is a hair-raising account of how far those redoubtable debaters, Curzon and Balfour, were prepared to go. The First Air Board survived until the fall of the Asquith Government in December 1916 when one of the first acts of Lloyd George's administration was to replace it with a body of wider powers. It was surely great weakness on the part of Asquith to allow such a state of affairs to continue for so long at a time of great anxiety about the efficiency of the Royal Flying Corps, an anxiety exemplified by the appointment of a judicial committee under Mr Justice Bailhache to investigate charges of maladministration.

The Second Air Board met for the first time on 3 January 1917. Its President was Cowdray a civil engineering contractor on the grand scale and an entrepreneur of the highest ability. The success of the Board under his leadership derived in part from his own personal qualities but also from four other factors. These were:

The addition to the Board of a Fifth Sea Lord with powers and authority similar to those of Henderson, the Director-General of Military Aviation. Hitherto, responsibility for the Royal Naval Air Service had been parcelled out among the Sea Lords.

The assumption by the new Air Board of responsibility for design of aircraft and engines. Responsibility for manufacture remained with the Ministry of Munitions. The Board was also responsible for allocation of resources.

The concentration of all the Departments connected with the Board including the representatives of the Ministry of Munitions and the military and naval air executives in a single building, the old Hotel Cecil in the Strand.

The genius of William Weir as Controller of Aeronautical Supplies.

The new organisation came into being none too soon. The Royal Flying Corps in France was still suffering from grave deficiencies in numbers and quality of aircraft, and their casualties were heavy. Partly because of German aircraft at the time, partly because of the need to use barely-trained pilots, and partly through the costly offensive policy dictated by Trenchard, British losses in the spring of 1917 were incredibly heavy. During what became known as 'Bloody April' the life expectancy of a front line Royal Flying Corps pilot was estimated to average eight days.

Throughout 1917, the Air Board began to realise that their achievements in the field of aircraft production and allocation, impressive as they were, did not go far enough. There was the question of overall policy in regard to the operational employment of naval and military aircraft. Who was looking after that? The answer plainly was no-one.

3

The Birth of the Royal Air Force

The Smuts Report

Cowdray, whose services to the Royal Air Force have never perhaps received the recognition they deserved, saw the difficulties plainly enough. He recognised that the existing organisation was inadequate. He believed that the Air Board should be given its own policy staff, he believed that an independent air service was inevitable in the long run and that planning for this new service should be started forthwith. He emphatically did not believe that any change in the administration of the naval and military air services was possible in time of war. Unknown to him, however, the War Cabinet at their meeting on 11 July 1917, partly at any rate under the stimulus of the daylight raid on London on 7 July, had instructed the Prime Minister and General Smuts to examine 'The air organisation generally and the direction of aerial operations'. The resulting report, dated 17 August 1917, was in effect written on the undivided responsibility of Smuts. The report is the most remarkable document in the history of the Royal Air Force. It recommended that an Air Ministry should be formed as soon as possible and plans worked out for the creation of a third fighting service into which the Royal Flying Corps and the Royal Naval Air Service would be absorbed.

> And the day may not be far off, [said the General] when aerial operations with their devastation of enemy lands and destruction of industrial and populous centres on a vast scale may become the principal operations of war to which the older forms of military and naval operations may become secondary and subordinate...

The apocalyptic character of the report was surely due to Smuts, but the idea of a new Department of State and a third fighting service was scarcely original. As we have seen, the idea can be traced back at least to the failure of Derby's Joint War Air Committee in the spring of 1916.

More recently it had been urged upon Smuts by Henderson in a cogently argued memorandum dated 19 July 1917.

Within a week of the signature of Smuts' report the War Cabinet accepted it in principle and an Air Organisation Committee under Henderson was established to work out the multitudinous details of creating a new service and embodying the two existing air services within it. By his memorandum of July 1917 and his brilliant creative work in planning the foundations of the Royal Air Force, Henderson redoubled his claims to be regarded as the greatest contributor to the formation of that service.

The decision to form a third fighting service was beyond question an act of momentous consequence to Britain in the long run. In the short run the effects were fairly modest. Smuts' report was in fact based on several assumptions which turned out to be seriously wrong. To start with, he was advised by the Air Board that a massive surplus of aircraft would be developed in 1918 and subsequently, over and above what was needed by the Army and Navy. This surplus, he believed, should be devoted to a direct strategic assault on Germany. In fact, the surplus, if surplus there was, was a small one. Smuts also believed that on the Western Front on land stalemate had been reached. He would indeed have been a genius if he had foreseen that, after the great crisis in the spring of 1918, the German Army was to be decisively defeated, the Hindenburg Line breached and Germany brought to her knees. Britain owes much to Smuts. His memory must always remain a deeply honoured one. But the main benefits of his famous report were reserved for future years. At the time the report was inevitably controversial.

October 1917, the month of committees

In July 1917 the Cabinet had agreed that the Royal Flying Corps and the Royal Naval Air Service should be doubled in size. By the autumn it became clear that under existing priorities these plans could not be fulfilled, and indeed that there were grave difficulties in keeping up with the original programmes. On 8 October 1917 the Cabinet established an immensely powerful War Priorities Committee under Smuts to clear the way for all military programmes. The other members were Sir Eric Geddes, First Lord of the Admiralty; Derby, Secretary of State for War; Cowdray, President of the Air Board; and Churchill, Minister of Munitions.

On the wider front, the War Cabinet, having taken their momentous

decision to form a new fighting service, had got cold feet. Sir Douglas
Haig, consulted after the decision was taken, was as always correct but
predictably hostile. At the War Cabinet meeting on 15 October mis-
givings were expressed and, in the words of the Official Historian, it
was decided

> to make a somewhat cautious announcement in Parliament that a
> Bill would be introduced to co-ordinate the air services and provide
> for the eventual setting up of an Air Ministry. It was further decided
> that an Air Policy Committee of the War Cabinet should be formed
> under the Chairmanship of Lieutenant-General Smuts to advise the
> Cabinet pending the establishment of an Air Ministry.[1]

Truly, October 1917 was the month of committees. Parliament, however,
was in no mood for vacillation and in response to its pressure the Air
Force (Constitution) Bill was approved by the War Cabinet early in
November. The Bill became law on 29 November. Orders in Council
were issued defining the composition and duties of the Air Council
and it was soon possible to announce that the new service would come
into being on 1 April 1918. The great day had dawned.

Early days in the Air Ministry

New Departments of State do not spring up every day. Old Departments
are split up or re-vamped from time to time. Bits of Departments are
sometimes promoted to full Departments. But a brand new Department
of State is something special. In order to survive, a new Department
has certain vital needs which must be met, including a policy, a staff,
an office and a reasonably friendly environment. When Harold Wilson
formed the Ministry of Technology in 1964 he omitted to provide for
any of these needs and the survival of that sorely tried Department
was something of a miracle. The Air Ministry in December 1917 was
scarcely better endowed. *Ex hypothesi* it inherited little in the way of
policy, indeed the creation of policy was one of its tasks. It inherited
a small staff from the Air Board. Suggestions for a place of work for
the new Ministry verged on the exotic, including as they did the County
Hall, the office of the Metropolitan Water Board, the Victoria and Albert
Museum and the British Museum. Pushed hither and thither, the new
Ministry finally fetched up with the Ministry of Munitions in the old
Hotel Cecil. Like the Ministry of Technology many years later,
it had few friends.

To do justice to the general environment in which the new Ministry found itself when the Air Council met for the first time on 3 January 1918, it is necessary to look for a moment at the general political scene and at the prevailing relations between the responsible Ministers, particularly Lloyd George, and the Army. They could scarcely have been worse. Haig was a man of gigantic moral stature, capable of bearing a burden of responsibility which passes comprehension. Without Haig the Allied front in France could well have collapsed in 1917 when the French Army crumbled into mutinies. Only the British Army, on the offensive in Passchendaele and elsewhere, magnificent and tragic, stood between the Germans and the sea. Had Haig faltered in his plan to take pressure off the French all would have been lost. No doubt Haig had the faults of his qualities as well as the qualities of his faults. Was he the best possible Commander-in-Chief? The point was hotly disputed from 1916 onwards and the debate continues today. Lloyd George would have dismissed him had he dared and he might have been right. But it was never a serious possibility. Haig's enormous prestige with the British public and the Palace were in themselves enough to rule out such an act. Furthermore, it is doubtful in the extreme if the Conservative Ministers in the Coalition Government, Curzon, Bonar Law, *et al.*, would have acquiesced in such a step. Relations between Ministers and fighting men were polarised. Ministers were disillusioned with soldiers and sailors and regarded them for the most part with profound distrust. They had a case. Soldiers and sailors were disillusioned with Ministers and regarded them for the most part with profound distrust. They had a case. Neither side had a monopoly of the truth; both were partly wrong and partly right. It is worth noting that it is perhaps because Churchill had first-hand experience of this hateful and harmful quarrel between statesmen and fighting men that, after he came into power, and to the immense advantage of the nation at large, no such polarisation disfigured Whitehall and there were far fewer and less damaging politico/military disputes. These comments are scarcely a diversion. What was true of the leaders was true of their subordinates and it is at this point that we rejoin the troubled history of the Air Ministry in its very early days. Haig distrusted Ministers, believed in aircraft in support of the Army (thought them perhaps a bit like cavalry), did not believe (to put it mildly) in the formation of an Air Ministry or in the severance of the military and naval air services from the Army and Navy. It is a good working assumption that for all practical purposes Trenchard's views were identical. It is important to remember this background when we come to consider what happened to Trenchard when he was summoned to London in December 1917 and invited to become Chief of the Air Staff in the about-to-be-formed Air Council.

The first Secretary of State for the Royal Air Force turned out to be Lord Northcliffe's younger brother, Lord Rothermere. The obvious candidate for the post was Cowdray, a man of great experience who had presided over the Air Board with great success. Lloyd George decided to offer the post to Northcliffe. No doubt Lloyd George's aim was to silence a formidable critic who was also chief proprietor of *The Times* though it is said, too, that he was taking revenge for an attack on him by one of Cowdray's newspapers. Anyway, Northcliffe, in a contemptuous and insulting letter which he printed in *The Times*, rejected the offer. Lloyd George thereupon offered the post to Rothermere. Rothermere was also a newspaper proprietor but a man cast in a less exotic mould than his formidable brother. He had acquired a great reputation for financial acumen. Rothermere accepted the post and decided to appoint Trenchard as his first Chief of Staff.

According to Andrew Boyle's account,[2] which is based on first-hand evidence, Trenchard was summoned to London and then confronted with Northcliffe and his brother. They intended to establish the third fighting service of course; this was no more than giving effect to firm Government policy which had been settled and announced. They also intended to attack Haig and Sir William Robertson, the Chief of the Imperial General Staff, and it is implied that they had hoped to use Trenchard in this campaign. This is surprising. The quarrel between Lloyd George on the one hand and Haig and Robertson on the other was a matter of public knowledge. Trenchard was well known as a trusted confidant and friend of Haig. Whatever else may be said of Northcliffe and Rothermere they were not fools. To approach Trenchard in this way was both clumsy and foolish. Boyle comments:

> Boiling with the bewildered wrath of a political innocent, Trenchard realised too late that he had been lured into a web of intrigue by a pair of scoundrels invincibly confident that everyone had his political price.

The reference to 'scoundrels' is hard to follow. Whatever may be said about Northcliffe, Rothermere was a man of ability and integrity. He was Secretary of State. Under our political system he was the boss and as the boss he had every right, within fairly wide limits, to choose his own methods.

It would have been logical for Trenchard to beg leave to refuse the proposed appointment. In fact, after consulting Haig, he accepted. Two reasons may have weighed with him. He may have wondered who would get the job if he refused it. He may have felt that he could better serve Haig in Whitehall than in France. Anyway, he accepted. The full composition of the Air Council was as follows:

Lord Rothermere, Secretary of State for the Royal Air Force; Major J. L. Baird, Under-Secretary of State; Lieutenant-General Sir David Henderson, Vice-President of the Air Council; Major-General Sir Hugh Trenchard, Chief of the Air Staff; Rear-Admiral Mark Kerr, Deputy Chief of the Air Staff; Commodore Godfrey Paine, Master-General of Personnel; Major-General W. S. Brancker, Controller-General of Equipment; Sir William Weir, Director-General of Aircraft Production in the Ministry of Munitions; and Sir John Hunter, Administrator of Works and Buildings.

The appointment of Trenchard as Chief of the Air Staff at this stage must be regarded in the light of hindsight as a serious error of judgement. For all his prestige, Trenchard suffered two fatal disabilities in the role. The Air Ministry was created as a matter of fully debated and accepted public policy to form a new fighting service and to embody in it the Royal Flying Corps and the Royal Naval Air Service. Whatever his subsequent views (and it is fascinating to reflect on when his change of heart occurred), Trenchard did not accept this policy. So much is abundantly clear from the otherwise differing accounts of Boyle and Lord Beaverbrook.[3] The job of officers however senior, like the job of civil servants, is to serve Ministers. So Trenchard was in a false position from the start. Secondly, Trenchard resented his Minister's policy of seeking advice not only from his main advisors but also from elsewhere. This was Rothermere's undoubted right and the exercise of this right was not unusual before 1918 or since. Of course a certain amount of tact is necessary. Anyway, it was the straw that broke Trenchard's back. On 19 March 1918, after little more than two months in the Hotel Cecil, he placed his resignation in the hands of the Secretary of State. Needless to say, serving officers, being subject to military discipline, have no right to resign, whether in peace or war. Trenchard asked to be relieved of his duties and it was up to his Minister to decide. It is difficult at this distance of time to assess Trenchard's motives. He may have found the whole situation intolerable. The Hotel Cecil was an unhappy place.

Weak departments lacking every advantage are unhappily situated when the pressure is on. The Hotel Cecil was under pressure—pressure from Ministers, pressure from the Army, pressure from the Navy, pressure from the Press. One may be sure that, being last in the queue, it was badly served for staff. Not for nothing was the Hotel Cecil called 'Bolo House',[4] 'Bolo Pasha' having been the code name of a German agent whose job was to spread alarm and despondency among the troops in France. He was caught and executed by the Allies. It is perhaps more likely that Trenchard judged that by standing firm on his principles as he saw them he could bring about the removal of Rothermere. Rothermere, after due consultations with Lloyd George and others, decided to accept Trenchard's resignation and to appoint Major-General Frederick Sykes from the Supreme War Council at Versailles in his place. The changes, which were announced on 15 April 1918, caused a considerable sensation. They seemed to round off the story of the earlier dismissals of Jellicoe and Robertson. There were speedy reactions. Henderson, Vice-President of the Air Council, resigned, being unwilling to work with Sykes. Baird, Under-Secretary of State, told the Prime Minister that he could not support Rothermere. Two Members of Parliament formerly on Trenchard's staff, Sir John Simon and Lord Hugh Cecil, said they would attack the Government and did so in a debate on 29 April. Their action was deeply resented by many. These developments were too much for Rothermere. Crushed by the intolerable burden of sorrow at the loss of two sons on active service he collapsed under his weight of responsibility and resigned on 25 April. He had done his best to serve his country well and his name should always be respected by the Royal Air Force.

Rothermere was succeeded by Weir, who carried out the Secretary of State's duties with immense competence until the end of the year. His first task was to deal with Trenchard who, according to his biographer, had removed himself in civilian clothes to a seat in Green Park. Trenchard had been invited by Rothermere to resume the command of the Royal Flying Corps in France, a post held at the time by Sir John Salmond. Trenchard declined and tried to resist the alternative suggestions put forward by Weir. He must surely have been hoping by his resistance to compel Weir to dismiss Sykes. Weir was not a man to be trifled with. In effect he ordered Trenchard to accept the command of the long range bombing forces being built up in France. Trenchard complied. Strangely, perhaps, this episode was the beginning of a firm friendship between Weir and Trenchard. Weir's firm and skilful handling of this awkward problem was neither the first nor the last of his many great services for the Royal Air Force.

The Independent Force

So Trenchard went to Nancy to take over from Lieutenant-Colonel Cyril Newall the command of the bomber force in that area. With the encouragement of Weir he then began, to the great advantage of Britain, a direct exchange of views with the Secretary of State, by-passing Sykes. When serving Rothermere, Trenchard had found such actions intolerable. Thus, Trenchard, defending his resignation, had this to say in March 1918:

> As will be seen I ventured to point out that the Chief of Staff was not allowed to carry out his work unfettered and without outside interference and that the Secretary of State had encouraged the intervention of various people without responsibility in decisions concerning operations and the means of carrying them out.[5]

A clearer statement of an untenable constitutional doctrine could scarcely be made. When Sykes became Chief of the Air Staff it was different. Circumstances alter cases. Be that as it may, Trenchard went to Nancy. The forces placed at his disposal over the next six months were far smaller than had been planned in 1917. They never amounted to more than ten squadrons. The essence of the Independent Force was that it was to be independent. 'Independent of what?' asked a French general, 'Independent of God?' The question, very French of course, was a good one. In the event it was independent of no-one. It was domiciled in France and came under the authority of the French State, and so under Marshal Foch. Haig was Foch's subordinate. John Salmond, the commander of the Royal Flying Corps in France (or whatever it was called after 1 April 1918) was part of Haig's command structure. Finally and in a subdued sense it was subordinate perhaps to the Air Council in their modest quarters in Bolo House. The Independent Force was entangled in the web. The Government, the Secretary of State and all the others huffed and puffed. It profited little. Eyes were bent not on the Independent Force but on the transformation of the war on land. Germany had cracked. The road to Berlin was open. It was a most unexpected development. If Smuts had been told in August 1917 that a year later the British Army would have breached the Hindenburg Line he would perhaps have laid down his pen.

The Independent Force played a full and honourable part. It bombed Germany or German airfields or intervened in the land battle in response to what all concerned including Foch considered important. There is no reason to suppose that the strategy and tactics were not first class. Nevertheless, it was all on a modest scale. Had the Independent Force never existed the result of the war would have been the same. This does not mean that lives were thrown away, far from it. The sacrifices, the action, were part of the supreme Allied effort which brought Germany to her knees, but the Independent Force did not dominate the scene. Had the war continued after 1918 it might have been a different matter. Happily it did not arise. In November 1918 Germany was finished.

The Armistice

And so the war ended. The British air services, insignificant when war began, had grown not without their troubles to a position of unchallenged supremacy. The Royal Air Force had been created, one of the most important events in the history of British arms. Events from the autumn of 1917 did not develop as Smuts expected and the benefits of creating a third fighting service in the First World War were negligible or perhaps negative. The Royal Naval Air Service and for that matter the so-called Independent Force went on after April 1918 much as before. But if the Royal Air Force had not been formed in 1918 either it would never have been formed at all, which would have been disastrous in the long term, or it would have been formed under duress in 1939 or 1940, which would have been just as bad. Smuts built even better than he knew.

Looking back over four momentous years certain names stand apart. Smuts, the man of vision; Henderson, the Father of the Royal Air Force who did more than anyone to create the air service; Trenchard and John Salmond who, by their special qualities of leadership in dreadful days in France, impressed the fighting service of the air with a stamp and quality which it has never lost; Weir the man of affairs whose wisdom was of immense service to the Royal Air Force then and later; and finally Sykes, effectively the first Chief of the Air Staff, who endured much and achieved much in the dark recesses of 'Bolo House'. And above all shines the spirit of the air crews, the youth of Britain in a new element.

4

The Uncertain Years 1919–1935

The struggle for survival 1919–1925

Soon after the end of the war Lloyd George held his famous Coupon election and returned to power in charge of an administration of Conservatives and 'Coupon' Liberals with a large majority over the unfortunate 'Squiffites' and the Labour Party. Weir, who had no desire to be a peace-time Minister, retired on 13 December, much to the consternation of Sykes. A month later Churchill was appointed to the twin offices of Secretary of State for War and Secretary of State for Air. 'You can take the Air with you', said Lloyd George, 'I am not going to keep it as a separate Department.'[1] So soon had Lloyd George tired of his child. Lloyd George's remark could be taken as indicating an intention to dismantle the Air Ministry. In fact it meant much more. During much of the next decade the whole existence of the Royal Air Force was in deadly peril.

One of Churchill's first acts was to replace Sykes by Trenchard, thus reversing the events of March 1918. Sykes was made Controller of Civil Aviation. This was hard on Sykes and it is perhaps surprising that he tolerated the situation. Demobilisation was of course the order of the day and the Royal Air Force was speedily run down from its wartime strength of 280 squadrons to a force one-tenth that size, mostly abroad. Its chances of survival around its first anniversary in the spring of 1919 were minimal. The reasons for this rather remarkable state of affairs were complex. After all, the formation of a new fighting service is a remarkable event by any test, but to follow that event by dissolving the new body within a year would have been sensational. The reasons were these, or something like them:

Government indifference. When the Royal Air Force was formed the war was expected to continue for some years. The collapse of Germany seven months after the formation of the Royal Air Force gave the new service no chance to show what it could do over and beyond what had been accomplished by the Royal Flying Corps and the Royal Naval Air Service. The mind of Lloyd George was far away from the trifling problems of the Royal Air Force. Bonar Law, when he succeeded as Prime Minister in the autumn of 1922, was no better. 'Off with its head' was his formula when he appointed Sir Samuel Hoare as Secretary of State on 2 November 1922.*

The hostility of the Army and Navy. This took two forms: a straight request for the return of the Royal Flying Corps and the Royal Naval Air Service to their respective parents, or such a return coupled with the disappearance of the Royal Air Force and the Air Ministry. Both ideas came to much the same thing. By the summer of 1923 Government indifference had evaporated, but Army and Navy hostility, which continued for most of a decade, was much deeper rooted. In Royal Air Force circles the story is often told in pantomime terms, with the Royal Air Force as the beleaguered maiden, the Army and Navy as the Dragon and its mate, and Trenchard as St George. There are distinct elements of truth in this fantasy. To start with, in the early Twenties, the Royal Air Force was indeed actively disliked by the older services. They considered it an upstart and its officers for the most part socially impossible. This was a part, if only a small one, of the cross that Trenchard and others had to bear. The Royal Air Force was an innovation and the way of innovators in Britain is hard. The first instinct is to ignore, the second to despise, the third to attack. But the Army and Navy also had a case for the return of their lost legions; indeed the justice of this case was admitted later with the return of the carrier-borne Fleet Air Arm to the Navy in 1937 and of some small elements of the Royal Air Force to the Army after the Second World War. So the story is not to be told in terms of goodies and baddies. The problem was partly one of timing, though this, for sure, could not have been foreseen at the time. Had the Army and Navy won their case in the early Twenties the Royal Air Force would have collapsed with results which would have been disastrous twenty years later.

To tell the history of the Royal Air Force's struggle for survival in the Twenties in detail would be tedious. In the round, there were two great economy campaigns; the Geddes Committee in August 1921 and onwards, and the Colwyn Committee in 1925. Both Committees received

---

* Churchill ceased to be Secretary of State for Air on 5 April 1921 when he was succeeded by Captain Frederick Guest. Guest continued as Secretary of State until the fall of Lloyd George's Government in October 1922.

advice, which they did not accept, that the way to economy lay over the grave of the Royal Air Force. At many dates between 1919 and 1925 and notably in 1923 the Army and Navy proposed major surgery. Such surgery, whatever its professional merits, would have been fatal to the Royal Air Force, which because of massive demobilisation would have been too weak to survive it.

Why did the Royal Air Force survive? It was surely against the odds. Several reasons suggests themselves. First, luck, the most important military virtue. Churchill, appointed to dissolve the Royal Air Force, had some sympathy for it. Further, he was confronted by an Army in mutiny against demobilisation muddles. One problem at a time. Secondly, the record of the Royal Air Force overseas, which was quite a sales point. Most of the tiny Air Force which existed in 1919 was located overseas, in Iraq, in Egypt (where Trenchard had established the Royal Air Force to use his memorable phrase 'in a small way and on a very low level')[2] in Palestine and in India. With no military textbooks to guide them the Royal Air Force quickly developed a system of air control in wild and communications-less territory which proved far more effective and far less expensive in lives and material than the older military methods. The classical method of dealing with rebellious tribes had been developed by the Army, notably on the North-West Frontier of India. Here was a mountainous, trackless, bare territory, mainly without roads, where the tribes eked out a bare existence with minimal support from Mother Nature. The conditions made the men, and for that matter the women and children, tough, hardy and hungry. From time to time the tribes wearied of this existence and mounted a lightning raid on some lush town in the plain, speedily decamping with a quantity of loot. The Government of India, arising in its wrath, would dispatch a punitive column into the hills. According to the standard practice this column would be ambushed, thus providing the tribes with a fight, an event close to their hearts, and large quantities of captured military equipment. After a delay of some months while the necessary preparations were made, a large military expedition would be mounted. A considerable battle then ensued which the Army usually won. Political officers were then sent within the tribal territory, roads were built with tribal labour, promises of future good behaviour were buttressed by suitable allowances to tribal chiefs, and so on. In a word, jobs and money flowed in and life for a time became tolerable. Later, over the years, demands for economy would arise, allowances would be withdrawn and conditions would revert to normal. After a bit, therefore, the tribes would revolt

again and the natural cycle would be resumed. The advent of the aeroplane made possible a different method of control. This was effected
not by bombing the women and children, as the critics of air control
usually asserted, but by the destruction by bombing of forts and other
military objects and by inhibiting the movements necessary for the
harvesting of crops and so on after the issue of warning notices. Because
so much of the Royal Air Force was overseas Trenchard was able to
exploit these new methods with considerable success. The operations
in Somaliland in 1919 showed the way. The Cairo Conference of March
1921 entrusted the defence of the new Arab kingdoms of Jordan and
Iraq to the Royal Air Force. And in May 1923 Salmond achieved a
tremendous victory over the Turks and Kurds who were threatening
Mosul. The significance of these events was not lost on statesmen at
home and Trenchard was able to argue convincingly with the various
economy committees that the Royal Air Force was a potential money-
saver. The argument was sound but the theory of air substitution made
many enemies for the Royal Air Force, not least in India.

The third factor was the influence of Weir. The Royal Air Force had
a firm friend in Weir and he demonstrated this friendship both during
his time as Secretary of State and on many occasions thereafter. In 1923,
when the Admiralty's claim for the return of the Fleet Air Arm had
reached the dimensions of a domestic crisis, with the First Sea Lord
(Beatty) threatening to resign, the Government set up a Committee under
Lord Salisbury to examine:

Co-ordination between the three services

The relations between the Navy and the Royal Air Force as regards
the control of Fleet Air Work

The corresponding relations between the Army and the Air Force

The second subject was handled by a Sub-Committee of three; Balfour,
Weir and Lord Peel, the Secretary of State for India. Although Balfour
had on several occasions expressed sympathy for the Royal Air Force
the dominant figure in the Sub-Committee was Weir. The Sub-
Committee decided not to detach the Fleet Air Arm from the Royal Air
Force and this decision was endorsed by the main Committee.[3] So the
crisis passed and the Royal Air Force lived to fight another day. The
man responsible was Weir.

The final factor was the influence of Trenchard. This was the greatest
factor of all and it was interlocked with the others. At some date between
March 1918 when he left the post of Chief of the Air Staff, and

January 1919 when he returned to that office, Trenchard had become convinced of the need for the third fighting service. In the ensuing ten years he planned its destinies and fought its battles with the strength of a giant. Like his former chief, Haig, Trenchard was not in the ordinary sense a clever man but he was certainly a very great one, one of the greatest of his generation. To look first at his faults, Trenchard was essentially a man with a one-track mind. He saw the truth as it was revealed to him and he saw it clearly. What was not revealed to him he did not see and therefore it did not exist. To the Army and Navy he must have been an infuriating colleague. But these points were the faults of his qualities. He had a vision of the new service and he carried the vision to reality despite appalling difficulties and despite the bitter opposition of the Army and Navy. He was a prophet and a giant among men. And despite his inarticulate quality he could and did carry conviction with the Ministers of his day. He certainly saved the Royal Air Force from destruction in times when in any other man's hands it would have fallen. Of course he was not always right. No man is. But he was indestructible. His qualities of massive strength were matched by deep humanity. He was loved as well as feared. And in addition to his abrasive side he had attractive personal idiosyncrasies. 'Give me the file about the world', he would roar. Everyone knew which one he meant.

Slow progress 1925–1931

In November 1919 Trenchard, with the encouragement of Churchill, produced a plan for the peace-time Royal Air Force which was published as a White Paper.[4] The Royal Air Force was to be independent, of course, though the elements concerned with naval and army work might later be returned to their parent services. It was to contain a substantial proportion of commissioned short-term pilots, a cadet training college for the permanent officers, an auxiliary element, a school for apprentices and so on. Above all it was to be small and therefore cheap, an important point at this stage of its destiny. Its main emphasis was on high standards, high standards of training for sure but also a strong orientation towards research into all the technical factors that are necessary in an efficient air force—aircraft, engines, navigation, armament, photography. This plan was fulfilled only in part. Responsibility for the failure can only in part, perhaps only in minor part, be laid at Trenchard's door. Trenchard was a prophet and the way of prophets is usually hard. For the first six post-war years Trenchard was concerned not so much with giving effect to his plan as with defending the Royal Air Force, with remarkable success, against attempts, various, to blow the whole project sky high. Occasionally events aided him. In the early years the Royal Air Force was minuscule, a breeze could have blown it away and nearly did so on several occasions. Sometimes a favourable breeze arrived. So it was in 1922 when Lloyd George's Government started to feel concern about the risk of air attack from France. Not very likely perhaps, even though there was some tension around. Still, the French had a striking force of some 600 machines while the Home Defence Air Force was still at its modest level of three squadrons. And so it happened that on 3 August 1922 Lloyd George announced the Government's intention to raise the strength of the Home Defence Air Force to 500 machines at a net additional cost to Air Estimates of £1.1m annually. The Royal Air Force had been given its first expansion programme. As happens so often in this story, the respite was of short duration. Three months later Lloyd George had gone, never again to return to office, and his successor was contemplating abolishing the service altogether. The very violence of the reaction against the Royal Air Force proved its salvation. It led to the appointment of the Salisbury Committee in 1923 which repealed the death sentence and established a new and enlarged programme for the Force. This was the famous scheme for fifty-two Royal Air Force squadrons for home defence 'to be created with as little delay as possible', announced to Parliament on 26 June 1923. Once again the Royal Air Force had a charter. It was decided to work for the completion of the plan by 1928. In fact the expansion soon lost its momentum. There were many reasons for this. To start with there was no obvious enemy in sight. Despite Lloyd George's fears in 1922 war with France was generally regarded as unthinkable and no other major power was in a position to attack our shores. The 'Ten Year Rule' (no major war for ten years) was still in force and no-one applied it more firmly than Churchill as Chancellor of the Exchequer from 1924 to 1929.* The Treaty of Locarno, signed in London in December 1925, bound the Western powers to keep the peace and to unite against the aggressor. Peace was in the air. 'There is no echo of Locarno in these Estimates', said Clement Attlee when Hoare asked for £16m for the Royal Air Force in the Air

---

* Churchill could be depended upon to be hell-bent on any project which lay immediately under his hand. Thus in 1927 he took on a full scale battle with the Admiralty to reduce Naval Estimates in the interests of a rating relief plan to the tune of £30m which he as Chancellor had taken under his aegis.

Estimates debate of February 1926. In fact there was. The Cabinet, acting under the influence of the Locarno talks had already decided to delay the completion of the fifty-two squadron plan by no less than five years, and this decision was mentioned in Hoare's speech. Finally, there was the financial stringency. This theme ran steadily throughout the Twenties and Thirties and was intensified when the economic depression began to take its grip in 1929. As the result of all these factors Air Estimates were kept well below the £20m mark over the period. It is easy enough to understand the argument; no enemy in sight, money as always tight, so run the Royal Air Force on a lean budget and be ready to expand if and when real danger appears. The argument was sound but it was pushed too far. Failure to invest at a reasonable rate over the period 1922–1931 was a source of real weakness when expansion began after yet further delays in 1934. Over this decade Britain was the leader and the centre of a great empire and with great responsibilities for its defence. Britain tried to run its Empire on the cheap.

For ten years Trenchard laboured to create the peace-time Royal Air Force, in such time, that is to say, as he could spare from resisting attempts at winding up or mutilation. In the main his development plan was highly successful. He carried over into peace-time the matchless spirit of the Royal Flying Corps and the Royal Naval Air Service. He created a cohesive and gallant force devoted to their country and not less to Trenchard personally. The highest standards of training and performance were maintained. But there were also weaknesses, some due to financial restrictions, some not. One of the most serious failures was that over the period 1919–1934 the quality of the fighting equipment of the Royal Air Force steadily deteriorated. The equipment of the Royal Air Force in 1929 when Trenchard departed was not so very different from what it had been ten years earlier. For bombers there were Handley Page Hyderabads, Vickers Virginias and Victorias, Fairey 111F's, Westland Wapitis, De Havilland DH9A's, Hawker Horsleys, Avros. For fighters, Armstrong-Whitworth Siskins and Gloster Gamecocks, for army co-operation, Bristol Fighters. For a force dedicated to the offensive, the quality of its offensive weapons was abysmal being mostly of wartime pattern. Worse still, there was the failure to develop the science of navigation, the apparatus for which in 1929 was rudimentary in the extreme. Experience in the Middle East and in India provided little background for operations in Europe, being often acquired in conditions of excellent visibility against no opposition. Development in defensive weaponry was no better. Fighters were slow, guns were of war-time design, and the acoustic mirrors designed to locate hostile aircraft were not only technically primitive but were also useless operationally since they could be completely masked by the low-flying aeroplane.

There was also the question of doctrine. The Trenchard doctrine was to put the maximum effort into offensive operations and the minimum (mainly to propitiate weak-kneed politicians and civilians) into defence. This doctrine was developed by Trenchard in the First World War, applied by him during his term as Chief of Staff and pressed by him on all concerned up to and during the Second World War. There is much force in this doctrine. Any fighting service that concentrates on defence and ignores the offensive will surely fail. But the absolute doctrine as laid down by Trenchard was simply not true and it was used to support theories which could not be sustained. Thus even in the mid-Thirties the Air Staff were pursuing the notion that there should be some fixed numerical ratio between fighters and bombers. In Salisbury's fifty-two squadron scheme in 1923 the ratio was fixed at one to two in favour of bombers. What should it be in the Thirties? In fact no such ratio is meaningful, the requirements of defence being determined by the area to be defended and the nature of the probable attack, the size of the needed bomber force depending on quite different considerations. As the result of the Trenchard doctrine air defence was neglected until the mid-Thirties and it is something of a miracle that a considerable air defence system was invented and put into service in the following five years to meet the supreme call in the summer of 1940. Another consequence of the doctrine was that when Trenchard handed over in 1929 no single Royal Air Force fighter squadron was located abroad. This resulted partly from the Trenchard doctrine and partly from the fear that fighter squadrons might fall into the clutches of garrison commanders. When the Abyssinian crisis arrived fighters had to be hastily shipped abroad from Britain. Also rejected, or never considered, was the idea that bombers should be escorted by long range fighters.

These were some of the disabilities of the Royal Air Force up to and, for different reasons, beyond 1931. Financial stringency was one causal factor, political indifference or hostility another. Yet a third was the dominance of Trenchard's strategic doctrines, not all of which were well founded.

The years of the locust 1931–1935

The title of this section is taken from Chapter 5 of the first volume of

Churchill's account of the Second World War. The words are taken from the Book of Joel (2:25) and were used by Sir Thomas Inskip when Minister for Co-ordination of Defence to describe the period. In the Revised Standard Version of the Bible the passage reads: 'I will restore to you the years which the swarming locust has eaten, the hopper, the destroyer and the cutter, my great Army which I sent among you.'

Two questions arise. Who were the locusts? And what did they eat? The second question is easy. The locusts ate the years from 1931, when the first presage of German militancy appeared, until 1935 which is the earliest possible date from which it can be argued, however tenuously, that the British Government took the threat seriously. It is a significant period. War broke out in 1939. In 1931 eight years remained for preparation. In 1935, only four. Clearly, dreadful risks were taken. The locusts were surely the British people. All the political parties were culpable and the electorate not less so. These were the years when Britain was hell-bent for collective security and prepared to accept incalculable risks in that cause. In 1925, a commission had been established under the aegis of the League of Nations to study the drafting of an agreement to limit armaments. The Conference finally met in 1932. It lingered on until 1934 but effectively it fell apart in 1933 when the situation in Germany was such as to render the exercise manifestly unreal. In 1932 Britain discarded her tiny re-armament effort, which was not resumed until 1934. The loss of time and the associated loss of momentum were significant. Under the Treaty of Versailles the disarmament of Germany was to be followed by a reduction in the armed forces of the Allies. This fact, coupled with a claim by Germany to parity, put the death mark on the Disarmament Conference. Before this happened Britain, who saw in disarmament the triple possibilities of political advantage, increased security and added economy, did everything in its power to lead the Conference to success. On 17 November 1932 Simon proposed the abolition of all military air forces and the prohibition of bombing from the air.[5] The proposal came to nothing owing to the difficulty of deciding what to do about civil aviation. In March 1933,[6] in a desperate attempt to save the Conference, the British delegation proposed that a Permanent Disarmament Conference should be established to work out a scheme for the abolition of military aviation and the international control of civil aviation. Meanwhile, a numerical limit was set for military aircraft in the participating states. Tentatively the upper limit was envisaged as 500 aircraft for the major powers. No mention was made of Germany. Germany would have none of it. The proposals of the British Government which were thus rejected contained the famous reservation in favour of 'bombing for police purposes in outlying parts'. This reservation attracted some notoriety but in practice had no effect on the outcome. All concerned knew quite well that it would be discarded without ceremony when necessary. The last flicker of disarmament occurred early in 1934, by which time German air rearmament was running strongly. In January 1934 Simon proposed that if the Permanent Disarmament Commission had not decided within two years to abolish military aviation, the participating powers should be entitled to possess military aircraft and that in the ensuing eight years such adjustments would be made as would give Germany numerical parity with the other powers. Germany was prepared, on paper at least, to discuss this. Predictably, France would have none of it. By now, surely, the chips were down. Late in 1933, a Defence Requirements Committee had been established under the aegis of the Committee of Imperial Defence to review and determine our worst defence deficiencies. It was a formidable Committee, having as its Chairman Sir Maurice Hankey, Secretary of the Cabinet, and as Members Sir Robert Vansittart, Head of the Foreign Service; Sir Warren Fisher, Head of the Treasury; and the Heads of the three fighting services. In the spring of 1934 they came up with proposals which, so far as the Royal Air Force was concerned, would have added some forty squadrons over the next five years, with a strong emphasis on strengthening our position *vis-à-vis* Japan. Ministers accepted the proposals as to the number of squadrons but as to disposition they favoured an increased emphasis on home defence. So Scheme A* was announced to Parliament in July 1934. It involved increasing the Royal Air Force by forty-one squadrons including four squadrons already announced in the 1934 Estimates. Thirty-three of the new squadrons were for Home Defence and the remainder for the Fleet Air Arm and for work overseas. The programme raised the Salisbury target (not then, of course, completed) to seventy-five squadrons. The other squadrons were for the Fleet Air Arm and for overseas. The programme was to be spread over five years. The additional cost to Air Votes was of the order of £2m annually. Even now Britain was not taking its problems seriously.

---

* This was the first of a series of expansion schemes which stretched forward until October 1938. Omitting those which were never approved, they were:

    Scheme A, submitted July 1934; C, March 1935; F, November 1935; L, April 1938; M, October 1938

Three schemes, respectively H, J, and K, failed to receive approval over the period November 1935 to April 1938.

5

The Problem of Parity

The approach of the Second World War

Chapter 4 carried our story to the point in July 1934 when the Government declared its intention to deal, in what seemed an excessively timid way, with the very worst of our defence deficiencies at that time. In this chapter we shall trace in outline the main events that led to the outbreak of war in September 1939 and discuss the response of the Government to these events in so far as they relate to the strengthening of the Royal Air Force.

A brief comment is necessary at this point on the nature of the government of Britain over the vital period 1935–1945. In the summer of 1931 Ramsay Macdonald's Labour administration found itself confronted with the British end of the economic crisis then besetting the whole of the Western world. The highlights for the British Cabinet were first high unemployment, mounting towards but never quite making the three million figure, and pressure on the pound sterling then worth $4.86 US or thereabouts and freely convertible into gold. On the advice of the Treasury and the Bank of England attempts were made to support the pound. As has happened so often since, they proved both expensive and fruitless. Soon the reserves were running out and international bankers were calling for a sign that Britain would put its house in order by cuts in state spending. Macdonald and some of his Cabinet colleagues were willing to play but in the event the Labour Government split. A Coalition Government was formed consisting of the Conservative Party, a small group of Labour Ministers including Macdonald, Snowden and Thomas, and a few Liberals. Macdonald was the new Prime Minister and one of his earliest acts was to devalue the pound. It dropped by 30 per cent in terms of the dollar. 'Nobody told us we could do this', said Lord Passfield.[1] The new Administration was in some sense a National Government, the qualification arising from the fact that the main force of the Labour Party was in Opposition. It became truly national in style when Churchill became Prime Minister in 1940 and formed a War Cabinet of four Ministers apart from himself, namely Chamberlain and Halifax for the Conservatives and Attlee and Greenwood for the Labour Party. There were also thirty Ministers of cabinet rank, sixteen Conservatives, five Labour Party, five non-party, two National Liberals, one National Labour and one solitary undiluted Liberal. Not for the last time the Liberals seem to have got the sticky end.

In Chapter 4 we traced the history of British air re-armament as far as the summer of 1934. By this time Hitler had succeeded Hindenburg as Reich Chancellor and was now in total control *de jure* as well as *de facto*. German re-armament, in the clearest breach of the Treaty of Versailles, was running strongly and was clearly aiming at some not too distant climax. Churchill believed that this was the first of a series of calculated steps of aggression, culminating no doubt in a challenge to Britain, France and perhaps the United States. It seems more likely that Hitler was resolved on a re-armed Germany which, by threats various, would shake the democratic trees and discover what fruits would descend. If the results were disappointing other methods were to hand, at any rate as far as his Eastern frontier was concerned. There is certainly no evidence that initially Hitler had any intention to pick a quarrel with Britain. Meanwhile Britain at large was in a mood for disarmament, which she was fighting hard for in Geneva, and collective security, whatever that elusive phrase may have meant apart from leaving the burden of enforcement to others. In February 1933 the Oxford Union decided that they would no longer fight for King and Country. At the East Fulham by-election in October 1933 the Labour candidate won with a majority of 5,000 and a swing of 19,000 votes. The result was widely interpreted as a victory for pacifism. In June 1935 the results of the notorious Peace Ballot organised by the League of Nations Union were announced. Over eleven million householders responded and the vote was solid for disarmament and collective security. The response to the last question on the ballot paper—whether the aggressor should be stopped by war if necessary—was divided but there was a majority in favour of war. So much for the mood of Britain.* What about the action? In October 1935 Mussolini, with whom Britain was trying to promote friendly relations as a counterpoise to Hitler, invaded Abyssinia. The Hoare–Laval Pact under which Abyssinia would have been partitioned was indignantly repudiated on the highest moral plane by Britain. Hoare

* British problems in the Far East are discussed in Chapter 17.

was sacked and five months later Haile Selassie lost not half his empire but all of it. Economic sanctions were imposed on Italy but stopped short of oil, the inclusion of which was deemed hazardous to peace. In March 1936, a Saturday, Hitler moved German armed forces into the Rhineland in gross violation of the Treaty of Versailles. Britain and France raised no finger. Germany could surely occupy its own backyard.* Later that year civil war broke out in Spain and massive military intervention was soon the order of the day, by Germany and Italy in favour of Franco and by Russia in favour of the Republican Government. The Spanish Civil War became something of a touchstone in British politics, being represented by the Left as heroic resistance to Fascism and the negation of appeasement. In fact it was tricky stuff for British politicians, the majority of whom, Conservative or Labour, shrank from marching shoulder to shoulder with the Communists. In the face of these developments it was not difficult to foresee that Hitler would resolve to see how far he could go. How much would Britain and France tolerate? Austria was invaded in March 1938 after Chancellor Schuschnigg had been given the treatment at Berchtesgaden. The union of Germany and Austria was forbidden under the Treaty of Versailles. No reaction. What next? Hitler had already resolved on 'self-determination' in Czechoslovakia, a state created by the Treaty of Versailles and whose minority groups included three million Germans. It was protected by strong natural features, a well-equipped army of thirty-six divisions, and a highly efficient arms industry. Its independence was guaranteed by France and Russia. There was a clear risk that if Hitler attacked, France would be drawn in and Britain too, fighting (horror of horrors) on the side of Russia. A few months after the occupation of Austria Hitler precipitated a full scale crisis over Czechoslovakia whose ability to defend itself had, of course, been gravely compromised by the occupation of Austria, which exposed the whole of her southern frontier. Chamberlain, who had succeeded Baldwin as Prime Minister in May 1937, resolved to persuade Hitler to settle the outstanding differences over Czechoslovakia by negotiation, even though the price to be paid by Czechoslovakia might include the loss of the Sudetenland and with it the strategic frontier. In September 1938, without consulting Russia, he flew to Berchtesgaden and made Hitler an offer on these lines. Hitler accepted and in return promised to hold back his troops for a week, which anyway was part of his time-

---

* There seems to be some doubt whether this comment should be attributed to Lord Lothian or to one of his taxi-drivers or, indeed, to one of Eden's: see Middlemas and Barnes, *Baldwin. A Biography*, p. 916.

table. The British and French then concussed the unfortunate Czechs into accepting this drastic surgery, but when Chamberlain flew back to Germany Hitler had raised the stakes. Chamberlain returned to London and for some days at the end of September there was an atmosphere of crisis in Britain. Trenches were dug, gas masks issued and the Fleet and Auxiliary Air Force mobilised. On 28 September the Foreign Office announced that if Czechoslovakia were attacked Britain would stand by France and Russia. At the last moment the tension was relieved by the promise of a four-power conference in Munich, organised by Mussolini. At this conference terms far more severe than those discussed at Berchtesgaden were agreed. The Czechs were informed of these terms and left to their fate. Russia was not consulted. A wave of hysterical relief swept over Britain, though in fact Chamberlain had been cheated and bounced. It is doubtful if Britain and France would have fought if the test had come. In March 1939 what was left of Czechoslovakia disintegrated.

What next? It is an extraordinary story. In February 1939 Britain resolved to build a Continental Army of thirty-two divisions, a total much greater than that which had been planned so far. A little late in the day it might be thought, with war as it turned out just seven months away. Still, there were those lost Czech divisions to be thought about. This done, and with the liquidation of Czechoslovakia in his thoughts, Chamberlain resolved to make a stand. Hitler had a long list of grievances resulting from the re-creation of the Polish state under the Treaty of Versailles, among them the severance of Danzig (formerly the capital of West Prussia) and the creation of a Polish Corridor, separating East Prussia and Brandenburg to give Poland access to the sea. Chamberlain resolved that the line should be drawn here. On 31 March 1939 he promised Poland the immediate support of the French and the British in the event that their independence was threatened. This promise must surely be regarded as one of the most astounding acts in the history of Britain. What, it might reasonably be asked, did Britain and France propose to do to assist Poland, if Germany attacked her? The answer surely was very little. In the event that Britain and France had found themselves at war with Germany the most likely outcome would have been the collapse of Poland and France, leaving Britain in a siege position facing the masters of Europe.* And indeed this is what happened.

* Of course the French were protected by the Maginot Line but this only extended from Switzerland to the Luxembourg frontier and could be outflanked by a German attack through Belgium, France and Holland. Allied dispositions on the Western Front in 1939/40 were made on the assumption that this was how the attack would come.

The declaration made, it became essential to attempt some kind of understanding with Russia. This aim was pursued in a leisurely way but blossomed into military conversations in August 1939. The conversations were a farce. Asked how Britain intended to defend Poland the British Mission had nothing to say. On one occasion Marshal Voroshilov, asked to arrange a meeting, excused himself on the grounds that he was going duck shooting. But Russian minds were attuned otherwise than to ducks. On 23 August the Nazi–Soviet Pact was signed. Britain and France had been isolated. Hitler issued an ultimatum to Poland and Britain urged the Poles to negotiate. When they refused Hitler invaded Poland. The date was 31 August. Even now Chamberlain and Lord Halifax hoped to avoid war. Once again Mussolini was ready to propose a conference as at Munich, and Chamberlain was willing to play. But the House of Commons, suddenly and strangely aroused, would have none of it. Chamberlain's temporising statement was coldly received.

'Speak for England, Arthur', said Leo Amery to Greenwood, acting leader of the Labour Party. And Greenwood spoke, later informing Chamberlain that unless war were declared next morning it would be impossible to hold the House.[2] Next morning Britain was at war.* An astounding story. Just as astounding was the folklore to which it gave rise. The legend grew or was developed that politicians at this time were divided broadly into two groups. One group consisted of the Appeasers, the Men of Munich, prominent among them Baldwin, Chamberlain, Halifax, Simon and Hoare. The other group comprised the firm-eyed resisters of aggression. They included the sturdy Left, of course, but also a few Conservative figures, notably Eden. The Appeasers had betrayed the country. By failing to resist aggression they had led Britain into war. They had compounded this appalling error by failure to re-arm. Baldwin's crime, according to Churchill, was that he had failed to arouse

---

* The mood of the House of Commons had in fact been changing fast. When the House met on the evening of Saturday 2 September 1939 they were expecting Chamberlain to tell them that pursuant to our treaty obligations to Poland, British and French ultimata had been delivered to Germany. When this news was not forthcoming the mood of the House grew deeply hostile. When the House met again on Sunday morning to hear Chamberlain report that Britain had declared war on Germany the mood was one of relief, based no doubt on the conviction that a dishonourable betrayal had been scorned. In the defence departments there was another reason for relief. No-one doubted that war was coming but at least on Sunday 3 September Britain faced it on the alert with her eyes open and did not find herself bundled into war as the result of an unheralded crisis and march-in in the course of a public holiday. Hitler gave us at least 11 days clear warning. After the Nazi–Soviet pact on 23 August few, Beaverbrook apart, doubted that the chips were down.

Britain to the dangers surrounding her, that he failed to re-arm and that he put Party before Country. These fairy tales have little relation to the facts. Chamberlain tried to avoid war and he was right to do so. He tried to make a bargain with Hitler and he had been cheated. He supported re-armament (as we discuss later) though he was over-constrained by economic considerations. Baldwin, despite all that the Left could do to hinder him, had given Britain its first real re-armament programme in 1936. He was almost certainly the only statesman on either side of the House who could have done this. Churchill's version of the facts is grossly wrong. The fact is that at all relevant times until, say, late 1938 the mood of Britain was against national armaments. Baldwin, sensitive as always to public opinion, may well have misjudged the international situation. Nevertheless he provided Britain with its most important re-armament programme, namely that announced in the 1936 White Paper. The Labour Party over the crucial period 1935–1938 was divided not as is customary into two groups but into four. There were first the out-and-out pacifists like George Lansbury and the extreme Left, notably Sir Stafford Cripps and Bevan, who wanted an alliance with Russia and a Popular Front. Both sections were opposed to British re-armament. The orthodox Labour Party was for the most part divided between those like Attlee who wished to oppose the defence estimates and those like Dalton who merely wished to abstain from voting on them.[3] Dalton as Chairman of the Labour Party put the matter to the vote in the Parliamentary Executive in July 1937. The majority in favour of abstention as opposed to opposition was small (forty-five to thirty-nine). Churchill's pre-war record was sound enough but from 1929 to 1939 he carried no Ministerial responsibility, a circumstance of immense value to him when he returned to office on the outbreak of war. Churchill gives an emotional account of the moment in February 1938 when he learned of Eden's celebrated resignation: 'There seemed one strong young figure standing up against long dismal drawling tides of drift and surrender, of wrong measurements and futile impulses.'[4] Fine writing no doubt, but surely too strong by half. The motive for Eden's resignation seems to have been increasing and reasonable annoyance with Chamberlain at the latter's habit of conducting foreign affairs without reference to the Foreign Secretary. There is little evidence that except in his dislike of Chamberlain and all his ways Eden's approach would have been much different from that of the Conservative Party at large.[5] The fact is that over the period 1935–1938 Britain was in no mood for war,[6] though she feared it might happen. In the event Britain was thrown into war by a miscalculation over the probable consequences of the Polish guarantee and a gradual change of heart on the part of Britain itself and of the House of Commons at a time when, in the military sense, Britain was largely unprepared.

Parity

This brief sketch of British foreign policy over the years 1935–1939 provides a background to the decisions over the same period on the future development of the Royal Air Force.

British policy in regard to the strength of the Home Defence Air Force* was first laid down in 1923. In June that year, as part of the discussions which led to the Salisbury Report, the principle was established and accepted by the Cabinet and announced to Parliament that

> British air power must include a Home Defence Air Force of sufficient strength adequately to protect us against air attack by the strongest air force within striking distance of this country.[7]

The principle was re-affirmed in the Air Estimates debate in July 1934 as the underlying basis of Scheme A† and in November 1934 when Baldwin said that the British Government was determined 'in no conditions to accept any position of inferiority with regard to what Air Force may be raised in Germany in the future.' That was plain enough, though it was unfortunate that the plan of air re-armament adopted was quite inadequate to fulfill the pledge, and was indeed little more than a façade.

The principle of maintaining equality in the air with Germany came to be called 'parity'. It is not a very satisfactory term and it was used at first in the sense of counting numbers of first line aeroplanes. This is not a scientific approach. It would be more realistic to say that two countries have achieved air parity if, when the test comes, their air forces can meet each other on equal terms. It should thus reflect not only numbers and quality but also sources of production, quality of training and special geographical considerations. Be that as it may, the concept was used as a rough and ready test. And the melancholy fact stands out that parity with Germany was an accepted and publicly proclaimed policy in 1934 and 1935, that in subsequent years it was unostentatiously abandoned on financial and economic grounds, and that when war broke

---

* ie The aggregate strength of all Royal Air Force Squadrons in the United Kingdom whatever their function—fighter, bomber, maritime, etc.
† See p. 42.

out in 1939 the Home Defence Air Force was far inferior in size to the Luftwaffe. Two principal factors were responsible for this sorry story. First, Britain, despite the pronouncements of Ministers, was not in the mood for the kind of re-armament measures necessary to keep pace with Hitler's Germany. Second, Britain, at any rate until Munich, was haunted by the memories of the economic crisis of 1931 and the Cabinet were determined to ration expenditure to a figure consistent with maintaining and strengthening the economic position of the country. Indeed as late as the summer of 1938 Chamberlain believed that the major dangers facing Britain were economic. In this he was supported by the Chancellor of the Exchequer, Simon, who on 29 July 1938, a month or so before the Czechoslovakia crisis, had this to say in a letter to the Prime Minister:[8]

July 29 1938

My dear P.M.,

I have been trying, during a large part of today, to get an agreed accommodation with Kingsley Wood over the £10 millions' worth of new schemes which he is pressing for, and which he accompanied by a light hearted warning that it will be £40 millions before he has finished his plans. After much negotiation I have agreed to go further than in my former letter, and I enclose you a copy of the new letter written in an effort to meet him. I hope you will think I have now done all I can and all I *should*.

I am very much concerned at this hand-to-mouth method of air expansion, without any survey and conclusion as to what our war potential can be. It seems to me that we must boldly scotch the idea of a pledge of parity as meaning the German figures however they grow. It is impossible: it is unnecessary: and it is quite inconsistent with rationing, which K.W. fights shy of. This is making the next Budget quite unmanageable.

I hope you will have a good holiday. No man ever deserved it more. And (except for finance) our situation is good.

Yours ever

John Simon

Thus in the economic sense neither the Government nor, it must be admitted the country, was yet ready to pay the price. 'If you don't like the heat', said President Truman in a memorable phrase, 'stay out of the kitchen.' Britain during these years of destiny disliked the heat but could not stay out of the kitchen.

It must not be supposed that to attach these major political considerations to the question of air re-armament is to yoke two matters of unequal weight. During these years, air re-armament was one of the great political issues in Britain. Speakers in major air debates were commonly Prime Ministers or their deputies. Churchill, as is common in this part of his memoirs, gets the story wrong. Looking back he comments:

> It would have been possible in 1933 or even in 1934, for Britain to have created an air power which would have imposed the necessary restraints on Hitler's ambition, or would perhaps have enabled the military leaders of Germany to control his violent acts. More than five whole years had yet to run before we were to be confronted with the supreme ordeal. Had we acted even now with reasonable prudence and healthy energy, it might never have come to pass. Based upon superior air power Britain and France could safely have invoked the aid of the League of Nations, and all the States of Europe would have gathered behind them. For the first time the League would have had an Instrument of Authority.[9]

The departure from reality is surely complete. Britain in 1934, led by Macdonald, Baldwin, Churchill, Attlee, going over to a semi-war economy to create an air power behind which the League of Nations and the states of Europe would have fallen in line? With the Peace Ballot a year away? What the military leaders of Germany would have done must necessarily remain obscure, though it is not difficult to arrive at an estimate.

What Britain would have done is less obscure. No political party existing in 1934 would have adopted Churchill's policy. Had they done so they would have been destroyed.

Still, these were big issues, and Churchill deals with them at length in his memoirs. In November 1934 he challenged the adequacy of the Government's programme of air re-armament. This programme, it will be remembered, aimed at preserving parity with Germany. Churchill said:

> I assert, first, that Germany already, at this moment, has a military air force—that is to say, military squadrons, with the necessary ground services, and the necessary reserves of trained personnel and material—which only awaits an order to assemble in full open combination; and

that this illegal air force is rapidly approaching equality with our own. Secondly, by this time next year, if Germany executes her existing programme without acceleration, and if we execute our existing programme on the basis which now lies before us without slowing down, and carry out the increases announced to Parliament in July last, the German military air force will this time next year be in fact at least as strong as our own, and it may be even stronger. Thirdly, on the same basis—that is to say, both sides continuing with their existing programmes as at present arranged—by the end of 1936, that is, one year further on, and two years from now—the German military air force will be nearly 50 per cent stronger, and in 1937 nearly double. All this is on the assumption, as I say, that there is no acceleration on the part of Germany, and no slowing-down on our part.[10]

Baldwin said in reply:

It is not the case that Germany is rapidly approaching equality with us. I pointed out that the German figures are total figures, not first-line strength figures and I have given our own first-line figures and said they are only first-line figures, with a considerably larger reserve at our disposal behind them.

Even if we confine the comparison to the German air strength and the strength of the Royal Air Force immediately available in Europe, Germany is actively engaged in the production of service aircraft, but her real strength is not 50 per cent of our strength in Europe today. As for the position this time next year, if she continues to execute her air programme without acceleration, and if we continue to carry out at the present approved rate the expansion announced to Parliament in July—I would ask the House to remember that we deliberately said nothing at that time as to the rate of expansion—so far from the German military air force being at least as strong as, and probably stronger than, our own, we estimate that we shall still have in Europe a margin —in Europe alone—of nearly 50 per cent. I cannot look farther forward than the next two years.

Mr Churchill speaks of what may happen in 1937. Such investigations as I have been able to make lead me to believe that his figures are considerably exaggerated. All that I would say is this, that His Majesty's Government are determined in no conditions to accept any position of inferiority with regard to what air force may be raised in Germany in the future.[11]

There was plenty of room for confusion in a public discussion of these matters and Churchill and Baldwin took full advantage of it. Most of Churchill's figures, derived perhaps from inspired leakages from Germany via France were exaggerated. His instinct that Britain was doing too little was sound. Baldwin's arithmetic was better. His instinct that Britain was doing enough, based surely on Air Ministry advice from whatever source, was certainly wrong.

The next major development occurred in March 1935 when in the course of a visit to Germany to discuss a proposed Air Pact, Simon and Eden were informed by Hitler that the German Air Force had already achieved parity with Britain and that the future policy was to achieve parity with France. So far as the size of the existing German Air Force was concerned this statement was incorrect. The error perhaps arose from confusing total numbers of aircraft with first line strength, that is to say military aircraft in formed units, and it may or may not have been intentional. So far as future plans were concerned Hitler's statement was accurate enough. This information was made public on 3 April 1935 and caused a very considerable sensation both in the Cabinet and elsewhere. The Air Ministry set to work to produce a new expansion plan and their proposals were reviewed by a specially appointed Sub-Committee of the Cabinet under Sir Philip Cunliffe-Lister, the Colonial Secretary. The Air Staff on this as on other occasions were reluctant to accept a rate of expansion which they thought would dilute the Royal Air Force unduly and intensify the flow of sub-standard aircraft. Under pressure from Ministers, however, they produced a new scheme of expansion known as Scheme C, aimed to raise the first line strength of the Home Defence Air Force to 1,500 by March 1937. It was estimated that this programme would give Britain parity with the German Air Force at that date.

The new plan was announced to Parliament in May 1935 and in the course of the debate Baldwin, then Lord President of the Council, made a most extraordinary statement. Speaking of the estimates of German air strength which he had given to the House in the previous November he said:

> First of all, with regard to the figure I gave in November of German aeroplanes, nothing has come to my knowledge since that makes me think that figure was wrong. I believed at that time it was right. Where I was wrong was in my estimate of the future. There I was completely wrong ... We were completely misled on that subject...

Naturally enough, this statement was greeted with applause by Baldwin's critics, notably Churchill. It is difficult to know why Baldwin took this line. Perhaps he had decided not to trust the Air Staff's figures and to rely on the information given by Hitler which, as we have seen, was incorrect. Anyway, he incurred much political odium quite unnecessarily.

Scheme C was certainly an improvement on the unworthy measures announced in the summer of the previous year, but it was in no sense a satisfactory programme being mainly directed to the shop window. Little provision was made for reserves. The level of Air Estimates in 1935 still remained at about the £30m mark. Even in those days not much could be bought with such a sum. No doubt this fact was not lost on Germany.

It is interesting to consider why a better expansion plan was not adopted at this stage. Scheme C was prepared under the supervision of Cunliffe-Lister, who a month later succeeded Lord Londonderry as Secretary of State for Air. There was certainly no lack of political wisdom and authority on Cunliffe-Lister's part. Still, at the end of the day, politics is about what people think and what people were thinking about at this stage was disarmament and collective security. And Cunliffe-Lister,* at this point Secretary of State for the Colonies, no doubt had to learn a new trade. He was an apt pupil. Another factor was Air Staff policy which at this stage and later was opposed to over-rapid expansion. The Chief of the Air Staff, Air Chief Marshal Sir Edward Ellington, like his predecessors Trenchard and Salmond, despite splendid qualities knew little about aviation as it existed world-wide in the mid-Thirties. After years of penury it was certainly hard for the Air Ministry to think in terms of large sums of money. And above all perhaps it was not easy to swallow the idea of an early renewal of war with Germany. It was difficult in the mid-Thirties to believe that in four short years Britain would be fighting for her life, and it could be argued that had Britain ordered a mass of reserve aircraft in 1935 they would have been largely junk because of the absence of modern designs, though of course the industry would have been strengthened by the corresponding injection of cash.

The inadequacy of Scheme C was quickly realised and not only by the Air Ministry. There was a general realisation that Britain had to re-arm seriously and the necessary plans were prepared. Baldwin, by this time Prime Minister, accepted this but decided that no announcement

---

* He went to the House of Lords as Lord Swinton soon after taking office as Secretary of State for Air.

must be made before the General Election which was held in November 1935. 'I give you my word that there will be no great armaments', he said in the Guildhall shortly before the Election. Well, 'great' is not a word of precision. Still, having won the Election, Baldwin in the Defence White Paper of February 1936[12] gave Britain its first coherent defence policy for twenty years. Politics is the art of the possible. By this act Baldwin deserved, but did not receive, the profound gratitude of Britain. So far as the Royal Air Force was concerned the result was Scheme F. This provided for a Home Defence Air Force of 124 squadrons by March 1939, and it was the longest lived of all expansion schemes. Sir Kingsley Wood, then Secretary of State for Air, was able to tell the House of Commons in March 1939 that in a few weeks the Scheme would be completed as planned. Other notable features of the Scheme were the substitution of medium bombers for light bombers, the provision of a full scale of reserves and the first steps towards a system of 'shadow' factories.

In May 1937 Baldwin retired from public life and was succeeded as Prime Minister by Chamberlain. In the following two years several schemes of additional expansion for the Royal Air Force were prepared but none was adopted. The reason lay largely in the area of financial stringency. The story is an odd one and the moral it carries is to beware of economic and financial predictions. In 1937 Simon, who had succeeded Chamberlain as Chancellor of the Exchequer, consulted the Treasury gurus and the Bank of England and established two remarkable precepts which have scarcely received from historians the attention they deserve. The first precept was that defence costs could no longer be financed from the annual budget but must be met in part from a Defence Loan. The second precept fixed the size of the loan at the sum of £400m and the size of the Defence Budget at £1,500m spread over five years. The loan was to be repaid in subsequent years out of normal defence votes, ie from the money voted by Parliament to meet the cost of the various Defence Estimates. In other words there was to be a once-for-all capital expenditure on armaments which thereafter were to last for ever. A quaint concept. There were precedents for a Defence Loan going back to the Naval Defence Act of 1889 but the relevance of such matters to the dark days of 1937 was obscure. The size of the loan was determined by the consideration that it was the largest burden which the economy could stand without undesirable inflation. Nevertheless the loan was doubled in 1938 and increased again in 1939. Chamberlain held closely to this economic principle. After the occupation of Austria further measures of expansion were decided on but the money was provided only after considerable hesitations on the part of the Prime Minister and the Chancellor. Still, the pace was speeding up. In March 1938 the services were freed from the requirement that their orders must not upset civilian trade. After Munich a larger programme of air expansion was adopted with a special emphasis on fighters and heavy bombers. In February 1939 the Cabinet authorised the production of aircraft to the limit, late in the day for sure but better late than never. The months sped past and Britain was now at war. The first line strength of the Home Defence Air Force (stretched well beyond what the Air Staff believed was wise) stood at 1,400 or so, that of the Luftwaffe at some 3,500 plus 500 transports.[13] What had happened to parity?

The end of Lord Swinton

Swinton was beyond question the greatest Secretary of State for Air. A. J. P. Taylor, in his immensely readable volume in the Oxford University Press English History, had this to say:

> Londonderry, also discredited by his defence of the bombing aeroplane, was replaced at the air ministry by Cunliffe-Lister, once called Lloyd-Graeme, soon to be called Lord Swinton and soon also to be as discredited as his predecessor.[14]

All historical writing is subjective and this passage is surely no exception. Londonderry's defence of the bomber was reasonable enough but a minor affair. The Royal Air Force in 1935 was a major political issue and Londonderry, despite his undoubted courage and enthusiasm, had neither the political stature nor the experience to handle it. Moreover, he was a peer. Swinton was a different matter. For three momentous years he gave immense services to Britain and to the Royal Air Force, ably supported by many hands but not least by ex-Secretary of State Weir. In May 1938 he was sacked. Why? At Swinton's memorial service Lord Butler in his address quoted Churchill as saying of Swinton and himself:

> We were both sacked for the two best things we ever did. I was sacked for the Dardanelles ... you were sacked for building the Air Force that won the Battle of Britain and they couldn't undo what you had done.

It was an excellent Churchillian remark, though it must be admitted that Churchill was one of those who did their best to encompass Swinton's downfall. But Churchill's remark covers only some of the facts. Swinton was not a man to suffer fools gladly, a somewhat dangerous point. Swinton moved to the House of Lords within months of his appointment, a grave political error. Political battles are settled in the House of Commons and at this time the strength of the Royal Air Force was a great political issue. And it did not help that Baldwin had given London-derry as one of the reasons for his dismissal the fact that it was essential for the Air Minister to be in the Commons. These are important points but Swinton was fired for a different reason. By May 1938 criticism of the Air Ministry had reached crisis proportions. Something had to be done and Chamberlain really had little choice but to move Swinton, even though he was demonstrably the best man for the job. The criticisms were partly of the kind inevitable in the early days of a gigantic expansion programme conducted in an immense hurry. Not enough of this, not enough of that, and so on. At the back of it all there was the question of parity. In the spring of 1938 there was grave public concern over this issue which simply expressed the question whether Britain was keeping pace with Germany in air re-armament. It was widely recognised by this time that Britain was not in fact keeping pace because the Government was unwilling to face the political and economic price. Swinton, a loyal Conservative Minister if ever there was one, was the fall guy. He lived to render other great services to his country.[15] We return to this subject in Chapter 8.

1938 or 1939?

The question is often raised whether Britain should have faced Germany with an ultimatum in September 1938. Some commentators have declared that had she done so the German generals would have been given the opportunity they needed to stand up to Hitler and maybe dislodge him. This can only be a speculation and it seems a highly unlikely one. The strong presumption must be that the ultimatum would have been ignored as it was in September 1939. Would the French have marched? They just did in 1939. In 1938 it was less likely. In the material sense Britain's inferiority to Germany in the air decreased over the period September 1938 to September 1939. Aircraft production, for example, at the latter date had nearly caught up with the German output. The following figures[16] of military aircraft production speak eloquently of what was happening:

	1938		*1939*	
	Germany	*Britain*	*Germany*	*Britain*
Combat Types	3,350	1,393	4,733	3,731
Other	1,885	1,434	3,562	4,209
Total	5,235	2,827	8,295	7,940

In other words British production of military aircraft was 54 per cent of that of Germany in 1938 and 96 per cent in 1939. In terms of combat types the comparable figures are 42 per cent and 79 per cent. In 1938, to take another illustration, the re-equipment of Fighter Command had barely begun. The radar chain was half completed. Of the forty-five fighter squadrons deemed necessary at that time only twenty-nine were mobilisable and all but five of these were obsolete. The five modern fighter squadrons could not fire their guns above 15,000 feet owing to freezing problems. A year later Fighter Command mobilised thirty-five fighter squadrons of which twenty-six were equipped with Hurricanes and Spitfires. Of course German re-armament continued apace during 1938 and 1939 but the relative position was improving in Britain's favour and there can be no real doubt that Britain was better placed to fight in September 1939.

6

Air Re-armament 1935–1939

Air Defence

> I think it is well also for the man in the street to realise that there is no power on earth that can prevent him from being bombed. Whatever people may tell him, the bomber will always get through. The only defence is offence, which means you have to kill more women and children more quickly than the enemy if you want to save yourselves.

The speaker was Baldwin, the place was the House of Commons and the date was 10 November 1932. As to Baldwin's remark it might be said, to use a Churchillian phrase, that it would be difficult to state the opposite of the truth with greater precision. Baldwin was expressing the standard Air Staff doctrine of the time, based largely on the views of Trenchard. Baldwin had an unhappy knack much to his disadvantage of coining memorable phrases remembered long after and often out of context. 'The bomber will always get through' was one such phrase. 'We were completely misled' (when we were not) in 1935 was another. 'I cannot think of anything that would have made the loss of the election from my point of view more certain' was a third. This was Baldwin's way of stating the unremarkable fact that public opinion in Britain in 1933 was solidly against re-armament and that any attempt to launch re-armament at that time would have been counter-productive. Churchill called it putting party before country which emphatically it was not.

The dramatic change in the dominance of the bomber came in 1935, characteristically as the result of chance. In January of that year the Air Ministry established a Committee for the Scientific Survey of Air Defence. Its chairman was Henry Tizard, Rector of Imperial College London and Chairman of the Aeronautical Research Committee. Its members were H. E. Wimperis, Director of Scientific Research at the Air Ministry (who first suggested the formation of the Committee),

Professor A. V. Hill (a Nobel Laureate from University College London who had been active in defence research matters in the First World War), and Patrick Blackett, then Professor of Physics at Manchester University and later also a Nobel Laureate. The Secretary was A. P. Rowe, a scientist later to become Director of the famous Telecommunications Research Establishment. An impressive Committee. The appointment of Tizard to this post at this stage was a major event in our history. It led of course to radar and the first effective system of air defence, but the significance of the appointment went deeper than this. Blackett, in his Tizard Memorial Lecture at the Institute of Strategic Studies in February 1960, remarked on three other consequences. First, he said Tizard's work inaugurated an era of rapidly growing intimacy between senior officers of the armed forces and the scientists in Government research establishments. In Blackett's words the second result was:

> The creation of mutual confidence and understanding between serving officers and university scientists; so that, when need arose, and it did arise very soon, many of the best academic workers flocked out of the universities into radar stations and later into service experimental establishments, where they became a vital part of the brilliantly creative, and sometimes obstreperous, teams whose work had so profound an effect on the waging of the war.[1]

The other result, again in Blackett's words, was:

> the recognition that scientifically-trained research workers had a vital part to play not only (as of course was traditional) in the weapons and gadgets of war but also in the actual study of operations. It was due to Tizard's personal initiative as early as 1936, before, in fact radar data on approaching aircraft were available, that civilian scientists were attached to the fighter station at Biggin Hill to study the art of controlled interception, as it would have to be done, when a year or two later the radar chain would become operational. This experiment seems to have been the first official recognition that the actual operations of modern war are so complicated and change so fast that the traditional training of the serving officers and personnel is inadequate.[2]

Blackett's words are quoted intact because they express the consequences of a new and remarkable relationship between scientists and military men. Let us follow up for a moment Blackett's reference to the Biggin Hill experiments. Here in 1936 is an embryonic radar chain, later to produce information about approaching aircraft detailing height, bearing, distance. Problem: to position fighters to intercept. Requirement: an organisation to handle large amounts of incoming information, to reject what is false, to add a little rapid trigonometry and to process the results into concise orders to fighter pilots. It is not as easy as it sounds. Tizard's part extended beyond his chair-borne role to personal experience as a flying observer in the experiments. The effect was profound. It was the fulfilment of a story which began twenty years before when Tizard, as a young Oxford scientist disguised as a Royal Flying Corps pilot, was investigating the air defence problems of the First World War.

The terms of reference of the Committee for the Scientific Survey of Air Defence were 'To consider how far recent advances in scientific and technological knowledge can be used to strengthen the present methods of air defence against hostile aircraft.' The anonymous draftsman of these terms deserves our gratitude. It has been well said that a problem once stated is half-solved. In preparation for the first meeting of the Committee on 28 January 1935, Wimperis felt that a new attempt should be made to assess the value of so-called 'death rays'. In other words, can we make a black box which can direct a ray of electromagnetic energy in any required direction resulting hopefully in the elimination of enemy personnel or material? Is there anything in this idea, said Wimperis, a question which must surely have been asked many times before? It seemed unlikely enough. Wimperis consulted Robert Watson-Watt, Head of the Radio Research Station of the National Physical Laboratory. Predictably, he said no, but he had something to add. This concerned the possibility of detecting, as opposed to destroying, a hostile aircraft by means of radio waves. He caused some calculations to be made by his staff. Assuming that an aeroplane when illuminated by short wave radiation with a wave length about twice its span acts like a thick wire of the same length, how much energy will be reflected back and what are the chances that it can be measured on a cathode ray oscillograph? The techniques for measuring the time taken for a radio pulse to make a return journey were at this time well understood through studies of the ionosphere and otherwise. The results of the calculations were impressive. Yes indeed, the reflection should be measurable on a cathode ray oscillograph. The Committee invited Watson-Watt to press on. A few practical tests were completed and the principle of radar was born. It is surprising that nobody in Britain had thought of this before. The fact that a metal surface will reflect electromagnetic radiation is as old as Hertz (1857–1894). And by November 1936, when the first television service opened in

Britain, there were sometimes tell-tale flickers on the screen when aircraft passed over. It was really a question of the enquiring mind asking the right question at the right time. Similar ideas had developed in Germany and by 1938 the German Freya device was capable of detecting aircraft at a distance of 90 kilometres. The same ideas were also being developed at around the same time in the United States.

The Air Defence Committee continued to work on all the possible methods of combating the bomber. In July 1935, at the suggestion of Churchill, Professor F. A. Lindemann was added to its membership. The appointment was not a success. Meetings became controversial and unproductive and the Secretary of State had to re-constitute the Committee without Lindemann. This he did, adding Appleton and Professor T. R. Merton instead of Lindemann. These disagreements between Lindemann and the Committee were odd. Tizard and Lindemann, originally friends, were for whatever reason not on good terms at this stage. Still, the differences in the Committee were about priorities. Lindemann, a better scientist than Tizard, was in a minority of one. Lindemann wanted lower priority for radar and more work on infra-red detection and miscellaneous parachute and piano-wire devices aimed to put small bombs in the path of approaching bombers. One such device, called 'Mutton' is amusingly described in Harris' book *Bomber Offensive*.[3] There were no two ways about it. Lindemann was wrong. Later, as in 1917, he gave great services to Britain.

Airborne radar was developed from the autumn of 1935 but here progress was slower, partly for reasons of priorities and partly because of the difficulty of accommodating apparatus of sufficient power within the restricted space of an aeroplane. The breakthrough came with the development of an improved form of the magnetron valve. In the spring of 1939 Watson-Watt persuaded a number of high-level physicists to spend their long vacations at radar stations. Among them were Professors Oliphant and Randall and Doctor Boot from the University of Birmingham who, in the course of the next six months, produced the resonant cavity magnetron which was soon developing astounding power in a device a few inches in size. The application of the improved magnetron to night air defence will be discussed in a later chapter.

So far as the fighter force was concerned the planned strength was raised step by step from the thirty-five squadrons envisaged in 1935 to a final peace-time plan for forty-nine squadrons. There were to be eight more fighter squadrons, four to accompany the Army to France and four for maritime defence. Of the forty-nine squadrons planned for air defence thirty-five were ready on the outbreak of war, including sixteen Hurricane squadrons and ten Spitfire squadrons. The rest were Blenheims, Gladiators, Hinds and Gauntlets.

In the matter of the choice of fighter aircraft Britain was on the whole exceptionally fortunate. When re-armament began the standard fighter was a conventional biplane like the Hawker Fury with a fixed under-carriage, a speed of say 220 mph, an armament of two machine guns, synchronised to fire through the airscrew arc. There were still some conservative voices at the Air Ministry when it came to defining the specifications for fighter replacements. As it turned out, however, re-equipment policy was influenced by two events which owed little to official action. In October 1934 Sir MacPherson Robertson sponsored an air race from London to Melbourne, the so-called MacRobertson Race. It was won by a wooden aircraft called the Comet built specially for the race by De Havillands. Piloted by C. W. A. Scott and T. Campbell Black the Comet flew the necessary 11,300 miles in just under seventy-one hours. Second in the race was a standard Douglas DC2 air-liner* belonging to Royal Dutch Airlines which arrived soon after the Comet having made all its scheduled stops. These events, highlighting as they did the advantages of the sophisticated monoplane, made a deep impression on the Air Ministry and helped to mould subsequent decisions. The design techniques embodied in the Comet laid the foundations for the war-time Mosquito, one of the most successful aircraft ever built. The other event was the Schneider Trophy for which the Royal Air Force competed on several occasions and which was won for Britain permanently in 1931 with the Supermarine Rolls-Royce S6B. The project was helped by a generous grant from Lady Houston. This aircraft, designed by R. T. Mitchell, the Chief Designer for Supermarine, later established a record speed of 407.5 mph. This design led in turn to the Spitfire, also designed by Mitchell, and influenced the ideas of Sydney Camm who designed the redoubtable Hawker Hurricane. These designers were the inspiration of the fighter specifications F5/34 and F36/34 issued by the Air Ministry in 1934. The Hurricane first flew in November 1935 and the Spitfire in March 1936. The Air Ministry issued production orders straight from these prototypes. The fact that these fighters each carried eight Browning machine guns mounted in the wings and not as was customary a smaller number mounted in the fuselage was due to the genius of Air Commodore Ralph Sorley, who pressed this highly

* The DC2 was the forerunner of the DC3—the Dakota—which became the standard transport aircraft of the Second World War, and for many years after.

novel idea on the designers and on the Air Ministry with most fortunate consequences. The other monoplane fighter commissioned at this time was the two-seater Defiant fitted with a four-gun turret. This turned out to be a disappointment. The rest of the air defence system was made up of anti-aircraft guns, searchlights, balloons, the Observer Corps, and the blackout. Ack-ack defences, guns and lights, were pretty primitive in 1939. Manned by the Territorial Army they rated only a back seat in the re-armament programme. Technologically too they were a long way behind, though this was no fault of the Army's. Priority had gone elsewhere. Later on, when radar had been applied effectively and the proximity fuse developed it was a different story, especially against the flying bomb. For what they are worth, and they are worth little, here are some figures:

	Planned	Available September 1939
Anti-aircraft guns	2,232	695
Light anti-aircraft	2,000	253
Lights	4,128	2,700

The defence preparations of the late Thirties included a substantial number of balloons, no less than 1,450 in fact. These were kite balloons, meaning that they had an aerodynamic structure and flew into wind. They carried a steel cable to a height of 5,000 feet or so and constituted a threat to low-flying aircraft attacking precise targets. Britain ought to have been good at balloons, having been interested in their military aspects for sixty years. In fact there were plenty of problems. Hydrogen cylinders used for inflating the balloons proved temperamental. Storms wrecked balloons, or worse sent them loose across country over high voltage transmission lines. Sometimes they were a threat to our own planes, sometimes they upset sensitive gun-laying radar, but on the whole they did a good and useful job throughout the war. Naturally, living in small detachments they tended to go native. The balloon crew under the Foreign Secretary's window kept chickens on the sacred Foreign Office grass. They protected the chickens and possibly the balloon as well with barbed wire.

The Royal Observer Corps, to give it the title by which it was finally known, was a peculiarly British institution. It was a civilian organisation organised and paid by the Air Ministry and directed by a senior Royal Air Force officer. It consisted of a vast number of civilian posts manned by civilians highly trained in spotting aircraft, hostile or otherwise, estimating numbers, height and course and feeding the results into the defence network. Equipment was simple, a telephone, a primitive theodolite, binoculars. The services of the Royal Observer Corps, though not on a high technological plane and largely unsung, were of inestimable value to air defence.

Finally, there was the blackout. Car headlights were dimmed, houses black-curtained, blast furnaces damped off, street lights minimal. Britain, especially in the winter, crept around with its gas masks and its little electric torches. No doubt the overall effect was valuable. Of course when London was bombed in September 1940 and the great fires in the London docks were still burning twenty-four hours later the advantages of diminished street lights in the face of fires visible fifty miles away was small. Still, overall, the blackout played its part. Some minor aspects are worth recording. Home Office experts (the blackout being, reasonably enough, Home Office territory) observing test blackouts from captive balloons were surprised to find that they could hear the British Broadcasting Corporation sound programme in their cage at a height of several thousand feet without the advantage of a radio receiver. They deduced subtle electronic effects, but in fact in their super-quiet environment they simply heard the noise coming up from the town below. In the Twenties and no doubt earlier small boys used to make telephones by connecting two small cardboard boxes by a taut piece of string, say 100 yards long. They worked, and the balloon cables acted in much the same way, bringing the sound up to the observers. When German air attacks coincided with a London fog things really got difficult. The homeward bound groped their way by sense of touch, helped from time to time by the light of a friendly incendiary bomb. In the First World War the lake in St James's Park was drained to prevent its being used by German pilots to identify the centre of Government. In the Second World War the lake remained, bringing pleasure to many. It would be tempting to deduce that the change in policy arose from a more cynical view of the value of Whitehall. In fact the shape of the River Thames as seen from the air is so unmistakable that the presence or absence of water in the lake made little difference.

Bomber Command

When British re-armament began in 1935 the bomber force was part of a unified air defence command called Air Defence of Great Britain,

ADGB for short. Around 1936 the decision was taken to divide ADGB into two and there emerged Fighter Command under Air Marshal Sir Hugh Dowding and Bomber Command under Air Marshal Sir John Steel. It is difficult to evaluate the success of this decision. One advantage to Fighter Command was the freedom given to press ahead with sophisticated techniques of air defence, an opportunity of which everyone from Dowding downwards took full advantage. The disadvantages were mostly for Bomber Command. As we shall see, they did not get the advantages they could have got from radar and lacking the training opportunities of a unified command they did not learn as quickly as they should have done how vulnerable bombers would prove to be in daylight against modern fighters.

The bombers with which ADGB was equipped were mostly light bombers like the Hawker Hart or night bombers like the Handley Page Heyford. The Hart was a single-engine two-seater which had a top speed of 200 mph or so, a range of 500 miles and a bomb load of 500 pounds. Its strategic purpose was obscure. From British bases it could reach few targets in France and none in Germany. It did, however, embody some shrewd ideas about economic production. Virtually the same aeroplane served as a fighter (the Fury), an Army co-operation plane (the Audax), and a Fleet Air Arm plane (the Nimrod). The Heyford was a twin-engined night bomber with a top speed of 137 mph a bomb load of 1,500 pounds and a range of 750 miles. All these aircraft were biplanes with fixed undercarriages. Even the British fighters of this date could not have caught contemporary airliners like the Italian Savoia or the American Douglas DC2. Britain had slipped. Clearly new types of bombers had to be ordered in a hurry. The first bomber to be ordered in substantial numbers when re-armament began was the Fairey Battle, a single-engined monoplane with retractable undercarriage, a range of 1,000 miles and a bomb load of 1,000 pounds. The Battle was a child of its time being basically a Hart/Hind replacement of which the prototype was first ordered in June 1934 when, for Britain at least, monoplanes and retractable undercarriages were rarities. It first flew in March 1936. The Battle was one of the two bomber types produced in the shadow factories. The other bomber so produced was the Bristol Blenheim. Originally ordered as an executive plane by Rothermere and called 'Britain First', this twin-engined monoplane designed and built by Bristol was capable of cruising at 210 mph. It was rapidly modified and pressed into service as a military aircraft and gave good service as a bomber and as a stop-gap night fighter. The next generation of bombers of reasonably modern vintage (all twin engined) consisted of the Armstrong Whitworth Whitley which made its first appearance in 1937, the Handley Page Hampden and the Vickers Wellington which came forward in 1938. These bombers carried the main burden of Bomber Command until 1942 when Stirlings, Halifaxes and Manchesters began to appear. These last types came from an Air Staff specification laid down in 1936 which sought to create the first true strategic bomber in the sense that it should have range and bomb load adequate for all needs, good defensive qualities and enough cabin space to carry all the necessary equipment. The specification was also coloured by the Air Staff's thought that if they could not compete with the German Air Force in numbers they might still do so in terms of bomb load. The Stirling, a four-engined bomber made by Shorts was not a success. The Halifax, also with four engines, made by Handley Page, though not outstanding, gave good service. The Avro Manchester, which was a failure with its two Rolls-Royce Vulture engines, became a triumphant success when, contrary to the wishes of Beaverbrook and the Ministry of Aircraft Production, it was re-engined with four Merlins as the Lancaster.

Bomber Command was from the outset organised in Groups. From its headquarters at High Wycombe it controlled No 1 Group headquarters forming at Benson, No 2 Group headquarters at Wyton (Blenheims), No 3 Group headquarters at Mildenhall (Wellingtons), No 4 Group headquarters at Linton-on-Ouse (Whitleys), No 5 Group headquarters at Grantham (Hampdens), and No 6 Group headquarters at Abingdon (Operational Training Units). From first to last the organisation of Bomber Command was superb and coped magnificently with the highly complex task of handling anything up to 1,000 bombers at night over our tiny island. Other aspects of preparations for the strategic bombing offensive were less satisfactory. In order to bomb a given target a chain of requirements must be met. First, the bomber aircraft must possess the necessary range and load-carrying capacity. Secondly, the bomber must be capable of resisting or evading enemy defences to an appropriate extent. Thirdly, the bomber must be able to navigate to its target. Fourthly, having arrived over its target the bomber must be able to release its bomb accurately. Finally the bomb, having hit the target, must perform satisfactorily. The Royal Air Force being a service dedicated to the offensive it would be reasonable to suppose that each of these vital requirements would have been closely studied and prepared for. It is sad indeed to relate that in respect of each and every requirement there were grave defaults. Let us look at the requirements in turn. Royal

Air Force Bombers in service in 1935 and 1936 had grotesquely inadequate range. This defect was largely overcome in the Hampden, Whitley, Wellington generation and completely overcome in the Stirling, Halifax, Lancaster generation. In regard to defence there were serious miscalculations. When put to the test the bombers could not defend themselves from fighter attack by day and had to turn over to night bombing, for which at that time they were largely unprepared. Long range fighters were not provided. The navigation techniques on which Bomber Command relied at the outbreak of war were primitive in the extreme. They amounted to 'dead reckoning' navigation (DR), a little radio direction finding which faded as distance from base increased, plus, if the weather was suitable, visual and astro observations. Of course if the target was visible and easily identifiable, as when attacking a coastal port or any target near a large expanse of water or in clear moonlight good results could be obtained. But if visibility was low or nil, as it often was, DR could produce errors of up to fifty miles. Means to provide the necessary navigational accuracy were developed with great success but they were not really available until more·than two years after the outbreak of war. The story in regard to bombsights was similar. Over the target bombers may want to manoeuvre, so gyroscopically stabilised sights and a small computer are essential to compensate for the various inherent bombing errors. Such a bombsight was finally produced, owing much to the genius of Blackett, but it was not available in service until 1942. The United States had such a sight much earlier but could not be prevailed upon to part with it. Perhaps they were right. Finally, as the supreme irony, the bombs. All that bravery, all that endurance, to deliver the bomb! It is sad to relate that by and large the bombs used by the Royal Air Force in 1939 were unsuited to their tasks, had a serious record of malfunction and were filled with indifferent explosives.

Most of these defects were overcome in the course of the war, but the question why they arose at all must be faced. The inability of bombers to defend themselves against fighters in daylight could perhaps have been determined in peace-time trials. The inability to navigate at night was partly at least obscured by the absence of blackout conditions. The development of sophisticated navigation and bombsight equipment raised questions of priorities *vis-à-vis* Fighter Command. Least easy to understand perhaps were the shortcomings of the bombs. After all, it is not a difficult matter to drop a bomb and see what happens. There was a history of serious shortcomings of bomb performance in the First World War. Here perhaps the shortage of armament testing facilities in our small island made itself felt. Of course these defects have to be weighed against the magnitude of what was achieved in Bomber Command over the four short years 1935 to 1939. The foundations were laid for what became a mighty force. Its creators were sorely pressed men.

Co-operation with the Royal Navy

The flying service was no stranger to the difficult problems of co-operation with the Royal Navy. We have described earlier how these problems were tackled by the Royal Naval Air Service. Twenty years later, in the late Thirties, the problems had from some points of view been eased. The difficult problems of flying on and flying off warships had been solved and by 1939 the Royal Navy had no less than five aircraft carriers, the *Glorious*, the *Courageous*, the *Ark Royal*, the *Furious* and the *Hermes*.* So the Fleet now had its eyes and a modest amount of offensive power through the development of the torpedo bombers. Meanwhile, the problem of optimising our sea/air potential had been complicated by a series of Whitehall battles between the Admiralty and the Air Ministry about the ownership and control of aircraft embarked in warships. It was a dispute in which both sides were right. The Admiralty were right because it was reasonable that they should have total control over aircraft embarked in warships on which their very lives depended. Moreover, the system of divided control was responsible at least in part for the fact that the aircraft of the Fleet Air Arm were inferior in performance to their American and Japanese counterparts. The Air Ministry were right because in the Twenties the severance of the Fleet Air Arm would have been a mortal blow. We have referred earlier to some episodes of the Admiralty/Air Ministry battle, and there is no reason to repeat them now. But in 1937 a large part of the problem was resolved. Inskip, the Minister for Co-ordination of Defence, after an enquiry, awarded the Fleet Air Arm to the Royal Navy and decreed that shore-based squadrons dedicated to naval air work should stay with the Royal Air Force. The decision stuck, at any rate for quite a bit. Thereafter a harmony of purposes developed between the two services in this important area of maritime defence. The Fleet by now had its own air contingent but provision for land-based squadrons including flying boats was pressed on as rapidly as circumstances permitted. Area Combined Headquarters were developed at Plymouth, Chatham and

* There was also a training carrier, HMS *Argus*.

Rosyth where naval and air commanders sat side by side and worked with a combined staff. Coastal Command Headquarters, originally at Lee-on-Solent, was moved to Northwood in the suburbs of London where it was in close touch with the Admiralty War Room in London. Close relationships developed, and when in 1941 an official committee decided that the operational control of the shore-based squadrons of Coastal Command should pass to the Admiralty it was accepted, at any rate by the Air Ministry, that this was already the *de facto* position.

When war broke out in 1939 Coastal Command was organised in three groups. In Scotland there was No 18 Group (headquarters at Rosyth) with stations at Lerwick (in the Shetlands), Invergordon (Cromarty Firth), Leuchars (on the Fifeshire coast), Montrose (Angus), and Thornaby (near Stockton-on-Tees, Yorkshire). No 16 Group (headquarters at Chatham) had stations at Bircham Newton (Norfolk), Thorney Island (near Portsmouth), and Detling (in Kent). No 15 Group (headquarters at Plymouth) had stations at Warmwell (near Dorchester), Mountbatten (on Plymouth Sound), Aldergrove (Northern Ireland), and Pembroke Dock. These three Groups between them disposed of thirteen squadrons of aircraft and six squadrons of flying boats. Twelve of the aircraft squadrons, ten squadrons of Ansons and two of torpedo-carrying Vildebeests, were obsolete. The modern squadron was equipped with Hudsons (converted Lockheed planes bought from the United States). The only modern flying boats were two squadrons of Sunderlands, an aircraft built by Short Brothers as a military version of the civil flying boat which laid the foundations of the Empire Air Mail Scheme.

In 1937 the Admiralty and Air Ministry estimated the requirements for maritime defence at 261 shore-based aircraft (165 for convoy escort and ninety-six for reconnaissance) plus surface and submarine patrols by the Royal Navy. For the protection of convoys the Royal Navy relied on escorts of warships fitted with Asdic and on aircraft. In August 1939 Coastal Command had a front line strength only three short of the planned figure of 261. It might have been supposed from these figures that maritime defence had been well cared for. In fact this was not so. Many of the aircraft in service at the outbreak of war were obsolete and it took time to replace them. No doubt this was inevitable having regard to the general stringency of aircraft production and the priority given to Fighter Command and Bomber Command. Another factor was the Admiralty/Air Ministry dispute about the future of the Fleet Air Arm. Until this was resolved in 1937 the Air Ministry were cautious about committing resources to Coastal Command. Indeed, it was not until

December 1937 that the Air Ministry was ready to agree that the primary role of Coastal Command in war should be 'trade protection, reconnaissance and co-operation with the Royal Navy'. Air/surface radar, known as ASV, which made it possible to detect ships and surfaced submarines was under development, but the equipment had not yet reached the squadrons. Priorities were involved here as well. The Admiralty and Air Ministry gravely underestimated the importance of aircraft for the protection of shipping, especially of convoys against U-boat attack. This was surprising because the importance of aircraft in this role had been fully demonstrated in the First World War. Probably the Admiralty over-emphasised the capabilities of Asdic. Air escort resources had to be rapidly augmented after war broke out. No doubt because of inadequate trials pre-war anti-U-boat bombs proved ineffective. This was convincingly if alarmingly demonstrated when a Coastal Command plane secured a direct hit on the conning tower of a British submarine. The damage amounted to four broken electric light bulbs. Bombs were exchanged as rapidly as possible for depth-charges. The protection of shipping against air attack was also neglected almost until the outbreak of war. Perhaps the requirement fell down the crack between Fighter Command and Coastal Command. Four squadrons were hastily added to the programme. So urgent was the need for these squadrons after the war broke out that they had to be hurriedly improvised in October 1939. Only converted Blenheims were available to start with but they were better than nothing. And of course Fighter Command did what it could to help as well.

Co-operation with the Army

In the First World War the overall task of the Royal Air Force was to co-operate with the Army and the Royal Navy. The so-called Independent Force in France, which was independent only in name, was notionally under the control of Foch and *de facto* under the control of Haig. So far as the Army was concerned, therefore, the system of command and control was crystal clear and it worked well. By 1939 the situation had changed. The Royal Air Force had become a separate service. It had many formidable tasks. First, the defence of Britain from attack by the German Air Force. Second, because it believed in the strategic air offensive, the defence of Britain by the employment of the Bomber Arm. Third—the order is not important—to stand side by side with the Royal Navy in the war at sea. Fourth, to play its part in our overseas defences.

The other great task of the Royal Air Force was to support the Army. This had been clear enough in 1918. What about 1938? Britain had never readily adopted the idea that its destiny was linked with placing large land forces on the continent of Europe. Sometimes it had no alternative but overall it was not in the British style. So in 1914 Britain was dragged reluctantly but magnificently into France and Flanders. The experience was traumatic and with the disillusion of the Twenties and the Thirties, the view emerged that Britain would never again fight a great land battle on the continent of Europe as it did with enormous distinction in the war of 1914–1918. Accordingly, when re-armament began in the middle Thirties, the Army, even when reinforced in due course by the Royal Ordnance Factories (ROF) was last in the queue, as the following figures demonstrate:

Expenditure on Military Equipment per year in £m[5]

Year Ending March	ROF	Army	RN	RAF	Total
1934		6.9	20.9	9.4	37.2
1935		8.5	24.2	9.9	42.6
1936		12.5	29.6	18.6	60.7
1937	1.5	21.4	42.0	39.3	104.2
1938	8.7	44.3	63.2	66.0	182.2
1939	12.7	67.6	82.9	109.9	273.1

Under the impulse of tremendous events leading to the collapse of Czechoslovakia on 15 March, Britain's Army policy was changed in disturbingly short order. The Territorial Army was to be doubled, conscription introduced and the initial contingent of the British Expeditionary Force raised to two Corps each of two regular divisions. These developments were part of a plan which would provide Britain with an Army of thirty-two divisions. The BEF was also to include an Air Component of the Royal Air Force consisting of two bomber reconnaissance squadrons, six Army co-operation squadrons, four fighter squadrons and two flights of an HQ Communications squadron. This was not a completely new commitment for the Royal Air Force. Successive expansion schemes had made provision for a number of Army co-operation squadrons and nine such squadrons were in the expansion scheme current in 1939. The Air Ministry had also sponsored the development of a specialised aircraft for Army co-operation, the Lysander, named no doubt after the Spartan general who knew how to sew the skin of a fox over that of a lion. The Lysander was a single-engined high-wing monoplane with fixed undercarriage. Its wheels were housed in two spats, each of which mounted a machine gun. It was designed for landing and taking off in limited space and it gave a good view for military observation. Alas, when war came the Lysander proved virtually defenceless and so a failure in its original role. It gave good service later in clandestine operations, landing and picking up agents and so on. Further support for the Army in the field was to be afforded by ten squadrons of Battles which were to move to France on the outbreak of war on account of their inferior range. The British Expeditionary Force could also call for assistance from Bomber Command.

Overall these arrangements proved unsatisfactory and were later the cause of acrimonious debate with the Army. The fact is that after the end of the First World War the Royal Air Force abandoned its original role as an ancillary to the Army and had only imperfectly worked out a new one. This is not altogether surprising. The idea that Britain should mount a substantial Army for land operations on the continent of Europe was developed very late in the day. The new role was worked out not in France or Britain but in North Africa, and its authors were General Montgomery and Air Marshal Coningham. This story belongs to a later chapter.

Overseas

To complete this survey of Royal Air Force responsibilities it is necessary to mention its substantial commitments overseas. Until September 1939 the assumption was made that Italy would enter any future war on the side of Germany from the start. In the event this did not happen, a circumstance which added to the burdens of those whose duty it was to handle the vast assembly of War Book telegrams (see p. 104). Still, preparations had to be made on the basis of a possible war with Italy. The Italian Air Force was strongly represented in Libya, Italian East Africa and the Dodecanese and could be reinforced from aircraft based in Southern Italy and Sicily. The Headquarters of the Royal Air Force in the Middle East was at the Villa Victoria in Cairo and from here in 1939 Sir Arthur Longmore, the Air Officer Commanding-in-Chief, controlled some twenty squadrons located variously in Egypt, the Sudan, Kenya, East Africa, Gibraltar, Malta, Palestine, Iraq and Aden. The aircraft types involved were an amazing medley, including as they did Gladiators, Blenheims, Sunderlands, Lysanders, Bombays, Valentias,

Wellesleys, Vincents, Battles, Ju 86's, Hardys, Audaxes, Harts, Harte-beests and Londons. From the spares point of view, an equipment officer's nightmare.

There were six Royal Air Force squadrons in India and nine Royal Air Force squadrons under the Air Officer Commanding-in-Chief, Far East whose headquarters was at Singapore. The Far Eastern Air Forces were part of the provision made against the possibility of war with Japan. They had a controversial history in that in Trenchard's day a bitter battle took place between the Air Ministry and the other two service Departments to decide how the main Fleet base at Singapore should be defended. The melancholy sequel is related in Chapter 17.

In the last expansion programme before the outbreak of war plans were made for forty-nine Royal Air Force squadrons amounting to 636 first line aircraft to be located overseas. In the event thirty-five squadrons were in position in September 1939, little enough in all conscience for the defence of a mighty empire.

Aircraft and engine production

On 20 August 1940 Churchill made his noble and timely tribute to 'The Few'. A few weeks earlier he was in a different mood. In a minute dated 3 June 1940 to Sir Archibald Sinclair, who was to endure many a verbal thrashing in the months to come, Churchill, after complaining of Air Ministry failures in the field of pilot production, continued:

> Lord Beaverbrook has made a surprising improvement in the supply and repair of aeroplanes, and in clearing up the muddle and scandal of the aircraft production branch. I greatly hope that you will be able to do as much on the personnel side for it will indeed be lamentable if we have machines standing idle for want of pilots to fly them.[6]

Churchill had every excuse to be tense. Dunkirk was but a few days past. Still, even in a crisis, there are better ways of encouraging a willing horse than by clouting it over the head. It was not Churchill's practice to publish the replies to his minutes. There was, of course, no scandal about aircraft production and still less about pilot production. In both areas, given the limitations of time and money, vigorous, enlightened and successful policies had been adopted, the fruits of which became apparent as the war proceeded.

In 1934 the British aircraft industry, looked at in the round, was in a state of considerable disarray. Civil production, though capable of the occasional miracle like the production of the prototype De Havilland Comet, was minuscule. The military end was still languishing from the all but fatal mauling it had received from successive British Governments under the successive and occasionally overlapping headings of economy and disarmament. It was surely right that the Treasury and Foreign Office members of the Defence Requirements Committee of 1933/4 should press for a removal of our worst defence deficiencies, and it is to be hoped that they did so with due concern for the main causative factors, namely the policies of the Ministers they represented. Criticism may also be directed against the Air Ministry for supporting too many design teams on a shoe-string budget. This argument, however, needs to be handled with care because if rationalisation had become the order of the day it is a reasonable bet that some of the best teams would have got the chopper. The British Government, whatever may be said, did not take re-armament seriously until at the earliest the spring of 1936.*

Not much could be done in the way of increasing the potential of the aircraft industry until the first substantial programme of air rearmament was approved early in 1936. Henceforward under the vigorous direction of Swinton and Weir the capacity of the industry was steadily developed not only for aircraft and engine production but also for the production of specialised products such as propellers, radio valves and special components like light alloy forgings and extrusions. Some of the additional capacity was developed in the form of shadow factories, ie factories built in peace-time but not to operate until time of war. In fact, in the urgency of the times, these factories were pressed into production from the date of their completion. In June 1938 Ernest Lemon, a highly regarded railway engineer, was appointed Director-General of Production under the Air Member for Development and Production. He pressed forward with a policy of sub-contracting, a policy hitherto eschewed by the aircraft industry, and by these and other means secured a rapid rate of increase in the labour force devoted to aircraft production. 1938 also saw the end of the 'civilian trade' restriction and to some extent of the financial restrictions. By the outbreak of war there existed in effect an embryo Ministry of Aircraft Production, still part of the Air Ministry and under the leadership of one of the ablest and most respected senior air officers, Air Marshal Sir Wilfrid Freeman of whom more will be heard in this story.

One of the many criticisms directed against Air Ministry policy was that they underestimated German air production. In fact the Air Ministry

* It could even be argued that they were not taking it seriously in the summer of 1938. See Chapter 5.

estimates were pretty accurate. Accordingly, their plans for the scale of British air production were well conceived and as financial and economic restraints were removed the plans bore fruit. The following figures illustrate the remarkable success of the British programme:

Aircraft Production[7]

	Germany	Britain
1938	5,235	2,827
1939	8,295	7,940
1940	10,826	15,049
1941	11,424	20,094
1942	15,288	23,672
1943	25,094	26,263
1944	39,275	26,461

In effect Britain equalled German air production in 1939 and surpassed it by a wide margin in 1940, an achievement due almost wholly to the admirable work of Freeman and his Department from 1936 onwards. Why then did Churchill speak of 'the muddle and scandal of the aircraft production branch'? Well, partly perhaps because he was cross, and partly to chastise the Air Minister and so encourage him to greater efforts. More importantly, perhaps because he was disappointed at the flow of aircraft into fighting units and did not fully appreciate the high proportion of production which an air force in process of rapid expansion has to devote to its training organisation. This point can be illustrated by some figures given to an Enquiry conducted by Mr Justice Singleton, at the request of Churchill, into British aircraft deliveries.[8] Churchill could not understand where all the new aircraft deliveries were going to. The Enquiry was told that during the period September 1939 to November 1940 the Royal Air Force received from all sources 13,400 aircraft. Of these, losses accounted for 6,000, 4,850 went into training, 1,200 to increase the reserve and only 900 to increase the front line.

Flying training

Churchill, had he known it, had even less to complain about in regard to pilots. It is of course understandable that a man chosen to lead a great nation in the greatest crisis in its history since the Armada, and, unlike Queen Elizabeth the First, facing immediate disasters, might assume that political associates like Beaverbrook and Sinclair could reverse in weeks the neglect of years. Understandable indeed, but sensible not at all. Waterloo may or may not have been won on the playing fields of Eton, but the Battle of Britain was emphatically not won by the skills of Beaverbrook, Sinclair or for that matter Dowding. These skills played a necessary part but nothing could substitute for four years of intensive and devoted preparation in the Royal Air Force and in the Air Ministry which ensured that when Britain faced her most critical hour she could match the German Air Force in the production of aircraft and pilots. It takes at least two years to achieve production capacity for aircraft and not less to produce pilots. By May 1940 the die was cast. The achievements in the way of personnel were not less remarkable than those in the matter of aircraft production. A few figures will provide an insight into the scale of events. In 1934 the personnel strength of the Royal Air Force amounted to some 30,000. By September 1939 it had grown to 174,000. By May 1945 the strength of the Royal Air Force, including Dominion and Allied officers and airmen, amounted to some 1,080,000 of whom over 190,000 were aircrew. The Royal Air Force was thus some five times greater in manpower than it was at the end of the First World War. The immensity of the training effort which made possible the creation of this gigantic force will readily be perceived. When Britain began to re-arm in real earnest, that is to say in 1938 or thereabouts, the decision was made to achieve the maximum possible production of aircraft. Estimates were made that in time of war aircraft production in Britain could be pushed as high as 2,500 aircraft a month, a figure which was in fact never realised though it was closely approached. To match such an output of material a prodigious expansion of the training machine was necessary. The fulfilment of this requirement was one of the great triumphs of Royal Air Force organisation. It was realised from the start that the necessary training organisation could not be created in Britain. So the conception developed of moving a large proportion of the flying training organisation into the Dominions. The Empire Air Training Scheme as it was called was one of the most brilliant pieces of imaginative organisation ever conceived. In order to give an idea of size it is necessary to anticipate our story a little. For various reasons, including the political sensitivities of Canada (after Britain the major partner) a real start could not be made on the Empire Scheme until after the outbreak of war.* The necessary negotiations were initiated in October 1939 by a powerful team headed

*A scheme to train fifty pilots a year in Canada had, however, been accepted by the Canadian Government in April 1939 and was due to start in September of that year.

by Lord Riverdale. Courses were started in April 1940. By September 1943, when the scheme was at its peak, 333 flying training schools were serving the Royal Air Force located as follows:

United Kingdom	153
Canada	92
Australia	26
New Zealand	6
South Africa	25
Southern Rhodesia	10
Middle East	6
USA	5
Bahamas	1
India	9

Other personnel developments

The vast personnel needs of the expanding Royal Air Force were also helped by the formation of four new organisations: the Royal Air Force Volunteer Reserve, April 1937; the Civil Air Guard, July 1938; the Reserve Command, February 1939; and the Women's Auxiliary Air Force, June 1939. Here again one is impressed with the sweep and power of the planning. The Auxiliary Air Force had of course existed since 1924, being part of the original Trenchard concept. Linked to the County Associations established in connection with the Territorial Army, the Auxiliary Air Force contributed no less than sixteen squadrons to the first line strength of the Royal Air Force in September 1939, plus a vast number of Balloon squadrons. The Auxiliary Air Force was something of a *corps d'élite* and was composed of formed units. It was therefore an unsuitable organisation to handle the vast number of reserve pilots which had to be recruited and trained. The idea of a Volunteer Reserve was developed in 1936. Broadly the aim was to train 800 pilots a year in an organisation based not on the County Associations but on Town Centres situated in industrial areas. The necessary sites were acquired, the necessary contracts with the civil flying firms concluded and the Royal Air Force Volunteer Reserve came into being in April 1937. By the outbreak of war 5,000 men had been trained as pilots or were in course of training. The administration of the Royal Air Force Volunteer Reserve added much to the burdens of Training Command and accordingly in February 1939 Reserve Command was established to take over responsibility for all elementary and reserve flying training and reserve ground training. The Command was organised in four Groups on a regional basis. The Civil Air Guard was formed in July 1938 to create a reserve of civil pilots, men and women. It was organised by subsidising the flying clubs and it provided the basis for the Air Transport Auxiliary (known to the irreverent as the ATA boys and the ATA girls) which came into existence after the outbreak of war for ferry and communication duties. The Women's Auxiliary Air Force numbered 8,000 officers and airwomen by the outbreak of war.

Churchill's minute of 3 June 1940, quoted at the start of this chapter, began:

Prime Minister to Secretary of State for Air
The Cabinet were distressed to hear from you that you were now running short of pilots for fighters, and that they had now become the limiting factor. This is the first time that this particular admission of failure had been made by the Air Ministry ...*

The Prime Minister went on to claim that the Royal Air Force was more extravagant than the German Air Force in training pilots and rubbed salt into the wound by claiming that a few months earlier there was a mass of trained pilots for whom no aircraft could be found. The first proposition was a dubious one and even if true was not a major factor. As for the second point, the balance of pilot production against aircraft production was always a delicate one. Aircraft production as a whole doubled between 1939 and 1940. Under the impulse of Dunkirk, fighter production which had been running at a level of 150 or so a month in the early months of the year shot up to 450–500 over the period June–November. And of course Fighter Command had lost a great many pilots in the land battle in which it had not expected to participate, at any rate on the scale that occurred. The other factor was the steady and vast build up of the world-wide training organisation which was checked only briefly in 1940. It is a hard proposition but a true one that if you are short of pilots you must raid your inadequate store to produce more instructors. Of course if the supply of pilots for Fighter Command really had run out in the summer of 1940 all the other far-reaching plans for building a great air force might well have been unavailing. Risks had to be taken and risks were taken. Like Waterloo it was a damned close run thing. Churchill's comment was neither generous nor well founded.

* The Royal Air Force had lost 400 pilots, killed, wounded and prisoners in the battle of France over the previous three weeks. They had also lost 1,000 aircraft.

Transport aircraft

When war broke out the Royal Air Force possessed for practical purposes no transport aircraft. It had a few communications aircraft—what today would be called executive aircraft—and no doubt a few dilapidated bomber transports rusting away in Egypt or Iraq. This was a serious weakness as a cheap and effective transport like the German Ju 52 would have been immensely valuable to all three services throughout the war, for example in increasing the mobility of fighter squadrons. The reasons for this sad state of affairs were complex. In the past, the Royal Air Force had flirted with the idea of transports in the shape of Vickers Victorias which were used as troop carriers and for other jobs. They received considerable praise at the time of the evacuation of the British community from Kabul in 1929. These aircraft gradually died out and were not replaced. The failure to develop a modern transport was in part a facet of the Trenchard doctrine which required that the Royal Air Force should not be over-anxious to invest in forms of air activity which could be used as an ancillary service by the Army and the Royal Navy. Another factor was of course shortage of funds. Yet again there was the failure to develop a successful civil aviation industry founded on landplanes, a failure also linked with financial stringency. Anyway, the Air Staff put out no specification for a transport aircraft in the Thirties. The consequences of this unfortunate state of affairs was that when war came Britain had to rely on the United States for transports and after the war finished British airlines were similarly dependent until the British aircraft industry could improvise or design British models. The German Air Force made excellent use of their large transport force throughout the war.

Cryptography

One important pre-war achievement of the Royal Air Force can conveniently be mentioned here. This was the development by the Air Ministry of a high speed cypher machine known as Typex. This was an electro-mechanical device which was in effect a typewriter linked to a high grade cypher machine with a vast choice of settings. Many of the cyphers used in the Second World War were compromised. The Allies read a good deal of the 'Enigma' cypher used by the German forces. The Americans read the Japanese diplomatic cypher ('Purple') also related to Enigma. The German Navy read the Royal Navy cyphers over a substantial, and very damaging, period. Typex, though similar in concept to 'Enigma', was more complex and so far as is known was never read by the Germans. The advantages to the Royal Air Force of the possession of a high speed, high grade cypher machine were great. Its existence was due to a remarkable Royal Air Force officer Air Commodore Oswyn Lywood, who had more than a touch of genius in his composition. In his private life Lywood was devoted to boats. They grew bigger and bigger and the last of the line was so vast that Lywood and his family had to live in it.* In the Royal Air Force he was of course a natural for Coastal Command but his great contribution was in the field of signals. Lywood developed the Typex concept with the help of the Royal Air Force workshops. For this work he received modest awards from the Air Ministry and from the Inventions Awards Committee. Another of his achievements was the adoption by the Royal Air Force of VHF radio at a time when it was generally regarded as the plaything of amateurs. Though it was not in time for the Battle of Britain it was in general use soon after, and brought to the service the blessing of high speech quality. Lywood was also interested in portable huts and caravans and was a pioneer in their development. There was a family business in this line of country. When during the bitter winter of 1939–1940 Royal Air Force radar operators and technicians found themselves operating portable radar sets in the open countryside without proper shelter a supply of Lywood's portable accommodation appeared as if by magic. Alas, there was a great commotion when the bills were presented and the normal channels were alerted. Happily, by this time the accommodation was being put to good use.

---

* RAF officers were given a removal allowance to help meet the cost of moving from one station to another. Lywood claimed this in the ordinary way but then the Air Ministry Accounts department had a brilliant idea. Why pay all that money when all Lywood has to do is drive his boat from one port to another? So he was asked to re-submit his claim on the basis of the cost of the voyage. They hastily dropped the idea when they got the bill. Moving 100-ton yachts is not cheap.

7

The Air Ministry in 1939

Structure

When the Air Ministry was formed early in 1918 its structure reflected both Admiralty and War Office organisational ideas. Principally it reflected the organisation of the Admiralty. The Air Council followed pretty closely the pattern of the Board of Admiralty and the Air Ministry took over from the Admiralty the organisational principle called, rather crudely perhaps, the bedded-out secretariat. Under this practice a section of the civilian staff was attached to each of the Service Members of the Air Council just as in the Admiralty a similar practice was followed for the Departments of the various Sea Lords. The Civil Servants in these secretariats drafted the letters, kept the records, provided the continuity, and generally acted as guides, counsellors and friends to their service chiefs. In the First World War service/civilian relations were good in the Admiralty and bad in the War Office. It was in the latter Department after all, that Ministers were known to senior Army officers as 'frocks'. Between the wars relations improved and in no service Department during the Second World War were they other than good.* But the Air Ministry profited from the experience of the senior service Departments and from the earliest days service/civilian relations became and remained excellent. Relations of trust and confidence prevailed to the great advantage of Britain. In his excellent book on Bomber Command Harris writes:

> I can recall one civil servant whose whole hearted devotion to the country and to his work was worth at least a division to the enemy on every day of the war. But for the human limitations of even his devotion to duty and to an eighteen-hour day he would undoubtedly have been worth two divisions.[1]

*Except perhaps for Air Ministry/War Office relations in the very early days.

Well, Harris was an original as well as a very great man and he did not take kindly to bureaucracy, civil or military. But let no-one be deceived. Harris was happy with his civilian allies. Also, he enjoyed a joke.

The structure of the Air Ministry was fairly straightforward. In 1939 the Department of the Chief of the Air Staff possessed all the normal features: Plans, Operations, Intelligence and (less conventionally perhaps) Signals. Attached to it the bedded-out secretariat, Secretariat 6, S6 for short, modelled on 'M' or Military Branch in the Admiralty. S6 was a faithful ally and, as necessary, a well-informed critic of Air Staff ideas from the earliest days when Charles Evans, the first head of that branch, shouldered the exciting but exhausting task of helping Trenchard compose State papers. The office of the Air Member of Personnel, AMP for short, with its infrastructure and its attendant secretariat, S7, looked after personnel matters. Early in 1935 the office of the Air Member for Supply and Research with its accompanying secretariat split into two, namely the Air Member for Supply and Organisation and the Air Member for Research and Development. The latter post became the Air Member for Development and Production in the summer of 1938. The vast civil engineering programme necessitated by the expansion was in the care of the Directorate of Works and Buildings in the Department of the Air Member for Supply and Organisation. Colonel Turner, the Director, was an ex-Indian Army Sapper known to all as 'Conky Bill'. The opportunities for triumph or disaster in a programme of this magnitude and executed under extreme pressure were great in the functional as well as in the aesthetic sense. In fact Turner was immensely successful. The stations were built speedily, they were efficient and they caused minimum damage to the landscape. The organisation of the Air Ministry was completed by the Department of the Permanent Under-Secretary of State which looked after finance, accounts, contracts, records, civil establishments, the Meteorological Office, and, at the time, civil aviation. Broadly, therefore, the structure of the Air Ministry in 1939 looked like this:

Ministers
Departments of: the Chief of the Air Staff,
                 the Air Member for Personnel,
                 the Air Member for Supply and Organisation,
                 the Air Member for Development and Production,
                 the Permanent Under-Secretary of State

Headquarters buildings

The Air Ministry was never fortunate in its headquarters accommodation,
It started inauspiciously in the old Hotel Cecil in the Strand, moved to
Adastral House, an unlovely building at the bottom of Kingsway, early
in the Twenties and spread itself over several equally unlovely buildings
in the Kingsway area as the staff expanded. In the early days the Department also had the use of Gwydyr House in Whitehall, mainly to give
Ministers a convenient access to Parliament and to Downing Street.
Adastral House was some eight storeys high and the top storey housed,
among other elements, a flat occupied by the so-called Resident Clerks.
These were three young or youngish Assistant Principals who made their
home in the flat attended by a resident housekeeper. They dealt with
urgent telegrams and messages which arrived at night, over weekends and
on public holidays. In the early days, before a round-the-clock cypher
department was installed, the Resident Clerks also undertook any necessary cypher work. The Resident Clerks lived eventful lives because in
the Thirties drama seemed to concentrate on weekends and the silent
hours. Also on the top floor of Adastral House was the Central Signals
Office, an arrangement ill adapted to impending hostilities. Among its
other capacities the Air Ministry was an operational headquarters in the
sense that it co-ordinated and inspired the activities of the various air commands. It was a prime target for attack in the event of war. In Swinton's
time as Secretary of State, the Air Ministry made a spirited attempt to
move itself into a new building in the suburbs of London to be so constructed as to be indistinguishable from the air from surrounding com-
muter housing. This idea was coldly received. Judging from the views
of the critics as expressed at this time the Cabinet may well have felt that
the extinction of the Air Ministry headquarters would have been an
important step in the path to victory. After Munich the most sensitive
parts of the Air Ministry were moved to the New Public Offices in
Whitehall, where space was made by evacuating civil department staffs.
Here, key Air Ministry staffs were housed in a solid building for which
protected accommodation was gradually provided. On the outbreak of
war the Department of the Air Member for Development and Production with its associated civilian Departments moved to Harrogate. A substantial slice of the civilian staff moved to Worcester.

Some Air Ministry personalities

Some of the major figures in Royal Air Force history in the Second World War are discussed later in this book. It is convenient to refer here to certain others who played a formative part in the days of preparation and whose work for the Royal Air Force was completed in whole or part by September 1939. Only a few names are mentioned out of many who served their country well. Among all its Secretaries of State the name of Swinton is of course outstanding. He was the political leader of the Royal Air Force over the crucial period June 1935 to May 1938. During this period many of the main vital decisions affecting the destiny of the Royal Air Force were taken: radar, the choice of fighters, the four-engined heavy bombers, shadow factories, the purchase of American aircraft. The list is endless. He applied to the development of the service at this crucial time drive, imagination and skill. He seasoned his observations with a mordant wit which won enemies as well as friends. Swinton was a considerable figure in the Conservative Party and his word carried weight in the Cabinet. The Air Ministry in its short but remarkable history, and despite many successes, never lacked critics and, as we shall discuss later in this chapter, they were especially plentiful during Swinton's reign as Secretary of State. Swinton often defended the Department's record under the serious tactical disadvantage that whereas the critics could lay every fault at his door major achievements were for the most part secret. His problems were not eased by a dispute with Lord Nuffield about shadow factory policy, a difference of opinion in which Swinton was wholly right. They were equally not eased by a brief but unhappy interlude during which he was given a deputy of Cabinet rank in the House of Commons in the shape of Earl Winterton, Chancellor of the Duchy of Lancaster. This development, which was intended to overcome the embarrassment of Swinton's absence from the Commons, lasted just two months. Swinton's name towers above those of all other Ministers who have served the Royal Air Force.

There is little to add to our earlier references to other pre-war Air Ministers. There were, however, two who, in a minor key perhaps, were both so exceptionally colourful as to call for special comment. They were respectively Lord Thomson of Cardington, Secretary of State for Air in two Labour Governments, and Sir Philip Sassoon, who in two administrations occupied the post of Under-Secretary of State for Air over a period of more than a decade. Thomson, soldier, romantic and protagonist of air travel, owed his peerage and his Cabinet appointment to his friendship with Ramsay Macdonald. He became Secretary of State in the brief Labour Government in 1924 and returned with Labour in the same capacity in 1929. In his first appointment he played a vital part in the decision of the British Government to adopt a policy of airship development and to commission two large airships, the *R100* and the *R101*. Through his friendship with the Prime Minister he also played an important role in preserving the Royal Air Force from destruction in times when, as we have seen, its whole future hung by a thread. On his return to office in 1929 the airships were approaching completion. At 18.36 GMT on 4 October 1930 Thomson climbed on board *R101* for her maiden voyage to India via Egypt, on what he was convinced would be a great and historic flight. Seven and a half hours later he and most of his brave companions died. The blood of the martyrs is the seed of the Church. Had men at all times and of all nations not been willing to back their ideas with their lives we should live today in a different and poorer world. Thomson had been Military Attaché in Bucharest in the First World War and formed a deep friendship with Princess Bibesco. The echoes of this romance were still in his ears as he mounted the mooring mast at Cardington on that momentous journey. This is not the place to tell the story of *R101*. Though deeply linked with one of its most remarkable Ministers it has but small connections with the Royal Air Force. Still, this story must be mentioned in paying tribute to one of the most remarkable men who have tried to serve the Royal Air Force.

Philip Sassoon was the grandson of Sir Albert Abdullah David Sassoon, a rich Indian merchant of aristocratic Jewish descent. Born in 1888, Sassoon served as Private Secretary to Haig in the First World War. He entered Parliament as Minister for Hythe in 1912 and remained their representative until the day of his death twenty-seven years later. After the First World War he was for some years Parliamentary Private Secretary to Lloyd George. He had two spells as Under-Secretary of State for Air, the first starting in 1924. In all they amounted to ten years or so. Sassoon combined great riches with great artistic taste. His houses (Park Lane, Trent Park and Port Lympne in Kent) were sensational manifestations of the ability of men and women with such resources to encompass a style of life which possibly had never been seen before and will surely never be seen again. Sassoon was a benefactor of the Royal Air Force. At times when this great service was in dire trouble and when many were planning its downfall he offered comfort, intelligence, support, prestige. He bought his private aircraft, of course.

Everyone flew. He was an accomplished Under-Secretary of State for Air and he delivered his Estimates speech, year by year, without notes of any kind. Of course, he learnt it by heart. But he also possessed an encyclopaedic knowledge of the Royal Air Force based on deep interest and constant contact. This enabled him to supply fluent and accurate answers to points raised in debate, something that cannot be learned by heart. As we recall these momentous years it is a real pleasure to pay tribute to the memory of Philip Sassoon.

Up to 1939 there had been six Chiefs of the Air Staff; Trenchard, Sykes, John Salmond and his brother Geoffrey, Ellington and Newall. Trenchard and Sykes have of course already appeared in our story and John Salmond too in the capacity of Air Officer Commanding in Iraq, where his masterly handling of the Turkish threat to Mosul did much to secure the survival of the Royal Air Force. He became Chief of the Air Staff in 1930 and handed over to his brother Geoffrey in 1933. Geoffrey died within days of his assumption of office. John was indestructible. He did a variety of important jobs until September 1939 when he returned to the service of the Royal Air Force in important posts in the Ministry of Aircraft Production and the Air Ministry. Thereafter he could be counted upon to appear at any major Royal Air Force function. He was and remained a handsome man, tall, erect, slim, dignified, friendly, alert. For many years his appearance, gaunt though distinguished, suggested the close proximity of the Great Reaper. But no. He attended the dinner given by the Royal Air Force in 1958 to celebrate the fortieth anniversary of the formation of the Royal Air Force. He was the most alert as he was undoubtedly the most handsome man present. He died some ten years later, just after the fiftieth anniversary of the force he had served so well. 'So he passed over and all the trumpets sounded for him on the other side.' A great Royal Air Force figure and a most attractive man.

Air Chief Marshal Sir Edward Ellington, Chief of the Air Staff from 1933 to 1937, was one of the small band of senior Army officers who helped to build the Royal Flying Corps. As CAS he had many detractors both inside the service and outside it. He was criticised for not making bigger claims before the Defence Requirements Committee of 1933/4 when it is said he could have had more money for the asking. This may have been so, but more money would have meant more squadrons and at this stage and indeed right up to the outbreak of hostilities the Royal Air Force were strongly opposed to an over-rapid rate of first line expansion. In this important issue they were partly right and partly wrong. They were right in the emphasis they placed on high standards of quality and training, which were to serve them well in the coming struggle. They were wrong in that both the German Air Force and the United States Army Air Force achieved higher rates of expansion without sacrifice of quality. Ministers overruled the Air Staff on this point and on balance were right to do so. Ellington first and Newall later took the blame. Another factor which may have weighed with Ellington is that more money for the Royal Air Force at that stage meant less money for the Army. As a loyal member of the Chiefs of Staff Committee, Ellington would have found it difficult to defend this. The other complaint about Ellington was that he knew little about aviation. This complaint was well founded. Like so many of the early Royal Air Force hierarchy he learned to fly on a trainer of the most unsophisticated kind, did not fly as a combat pilot in the Royal Flying Corps and did not fly at all as a pilot from 1918 onwards. This was equally true of course of most of his contemporaries, Trenchard included. The lack of the practical knowledge was a handicap but it certainly did not mean that Ellington obstructed the ideas of younger men. What is rarely mentioned is Ellington's superb quality as a Staff Officer. He had an acute mind and a remarkable memory. He was quick to embrace new ideas. His faults, if such there were, did not include lack of understanding. Ellington was not an outstanding Chief of Staff but in the generality of such men he was well above average. His manner and appearance were distinguished. He was painfully shy. This did not inhibit good relations with his service contemporaries but was perhaps a handicap in dealing with senior civilian colleagues like Fisher and Vansittart, and with the young.

Air Chief Marshal Sir Cyril Newall gave great service to the Royal Air Force over many years. He joined the Royal Flying Corps from the Indian Army and learned to fly in the usual happy-go-lucky way. He was a successful squadron commander in the Royal Flying Corps and was awarded the Albert Medal for an act of exceptional bravery. By December 1917 he was commanding the 8th Brigade at Nancy set up for bombing operations against German objectives as a counter measure to the air raids on London. This force was to become the so-called Independent Force and in the spring of 1918 Trenchard was appointed to command it in circumstances which have already been discussed. During the pre-war years up to 1935 Newall was fortunate in being given three key appointments, namely Commandant of the School of Technical Training, Halton, Deputy Chief of the Air Staff (his last year in the post carrying Air Council rank) and Air Officer Commanding-in-Chief, Middle East. Newall rejoined the Air Council as Air Member for Supply and Organisation in 1935. He became Chief of the Air Staff in 1937 and remained the leader of the Royal Air Force until the autumn of 1940. So much for the outline. The detail is more interesting. The duties of the Air Member for Supply and Organisation covered every detail of the organisation and provisioning of the Royal Air Force and for the creation of its airfields, buildings, workshops. Re-armament really began when Newall joined the Air Council and so the task of expanding and equipping the Force rested very largely on his shoulders. As Chief of the Air Staff, Newall saw all that he had created put to the test of war, a test far more severe than the greatest pessimist could have foreseen. Few in 1939 would have forecast the total collapse of France a year later. Newall shouldered these vast responsibilities effectively and cheerfully. He was imperturbable in the gravest situations. He retained his courage and cheerfulness even in the darkest hours of 1940. On the afternoon when Chamberlain returned from Munich to wave his worthless piece of paper and to receive the cheers of the multitude, Newall called his staff together and said that what had happened was a great national humiliation and that they must work night and day to prepare for the trials which would surely come. No-one present ever forgot his words. Newall presided over the destinies of the Royal Air Force until the end of the Battle of Britain. He was then retired in accordance with the honourable tradition of the Royal Air Force that you may not stay for ever. He became a much respected Governor of New Zealand over the period 1941–6 which included of course the desperate days when New Zealand was under threat of attack from Japan. All leaders have enemies and Newall was no exception. In the spring of 1940 Hoare, when Secretary of State for a month or so, tried to replace him with Trenchard, who was then sixty-seven years of age.[2] Happily the idea was sunk without a trace. Newall will always be counted as a most respected and successful leader of the Royal Air Force.

We reserve a discussion of the greatest Royal Air Force figures of the Second World War until our final chapter. But before leaving the pre-war Air Ministry a word must surely be said about what *The Times* of the day called 'The case of Sir Christopher Bullock'. Bullock was Secretary and Member of the Air Council for some six years before he was summarily dismissed from the government service by Baldwin. Bullock was a man of outstanding ability who served with distinction in the Royal Flying Corps in the First World War. He joined the civilian staff of the Air Ministry in its earliest days and after a short period with the Air Staff Secretariat was soon employed as Principal Private Secretary to a series of Air Ministers. In 1930, with the full approval of Trenchard and the Permanent Secretary, Sir Walter Nicholson, he was appointed to succeed the latter when he retired early. The promotion was a remarkable though not a unique achievement, in that it involved skipping two intervening civil service ranks, those of principal assistant secretary and deputy secretary. In all these posts Bullock served the Royal Air Force well. His industry, intelligence and ability as a draftsman were invaluable at a time when the Air Ministry needed all the help it could get. But Bullock had an Achilles' heel, as who does not. His took the shape of a high degree of arrogance. He overplayed his hand particularly in dealing direct with Baldwin over the head of Londonderry. Bullock was a doughty fighter, a quality of great service to the Royal Air Force. He was less than skilful in picking opponents of his own size. Inevitably he made enemies. In 1936, in the course of discussions with Geddes, then Chairman of Imperial Airways, he raised the issue of his joining the Board of that company in what may or may not have been an indiscreet way. A Board of Enquiry was appointed and Bullock was fired. This decision was certainly wrong, as Baldwin subsequently admitted. In 1939 after war broke out Bullock was offered re-instatement in the public service, an offer which he declined. The dismissal was a crushing blow which Bullock survived with characteristic courage to make a successful career for himself in industry. It is a pleasure indeed to record that his two sons are pursuing distinguished careers in the public service.

Critics

The expansion of the Royal Air Force, which began effectively in 1935 and had acquired a remarkable momentum when war broke out some four years later, was on balance an undoubted success story. True, there were some failures and mistakes, but by and large and in the round the Air Ministry and the Royal Air Force evolved over those difficult years a blueprint for victory in the fields of matériel and of personnel alike. In 1935 the Royal Air Force was in the doldrums and the British aircraft industry virtually on its knees as the result of years of disarmament. By the end of 1940 the Battle of Britain had been won and, the Blitz notwithstanding, British military aircraft production exceeded that of Germany by some 40 per cent. Meanwhile a vast expansion of aircrew training was in progress throughout the Commonwealth. There will be some no doubt who might suppose that these miracles were accomplished by the advent of Churchill in September 1939 and of Beaverbrook in 1940. This was not so. The roots lay deeper, in the late Thirties and particularly in 1938 and early 1939, by which time sound foundations had been laid and at last re-armament money began to flow in due proportion to the task. The contemporary judgements handed out to the Air Ministry for these remarkable achievements were surely predictable. The Air Ministry itself was branded as grossly incompetent and in 1938 Swinton, incomparably the greatest defence Minister of the Thirties, was fired. The detailed background to all this is complex. But one fairly simple point may be mentioned at the outset. Basically, the British people dislike innovation. Certainly, they dislike new Government Departments. In the Thirties as in the Twenties the Air Ministry was not an admired organisation. Many senior figures in Whitehall considered it an upstart and took little pains to conceal their opinion. And of course any Department running a re-armament programme at a time of crisis is a fair target for criticism. Still, the story is an interesting one and it is worth devoting a moment to define some of the more notorious points of criticism, and to look at them again in the light of the very considerable new information available as the result of the release of papers under the thirty-year rule.

Critics: Parity

A discussion on this theme will inevitably take us into the realm of first line strength. We may say with Dante, *'Lasciate ogni speranza, voi ch'entrate.'* On the record, German and British alike, there are countless figures of first line strength. The trouble is that many of the figures are wrong and many are prepared on bases which make mutual comparison impossible. This point has been made before (Chapter 5) but it bears repetition. First line strength can be defined as the number of aircraft in formed squadrons and provided with crews but excluding:

aircraft reserves in squadrons,
        in store,
        under repair,
        in the training organisation,
        (usually) in transport and communication units.

Refinements are necessary in the case of the Royal Air Force, where for purposes of comparison with the German Air Force it is necessary to exclude the Royal Air Force overseas and, for the period when it was part of the Royal Air Force, the Fleet Air Arm. Some commentators, including Churchill, would also exclude the Auxiliary Air Force as being mere week-end flyers but since, when war came, they took their place in the line of battle their omission from these calculations could surely be deemed an insult.

First line strength is a poor enough measure of fighting strength. Other factors, just as important, include the capacity and vulnerability of the supporting aircraft industry, the adequacy of reserves, repair organisation, and training organisation, and geographical factors. But politically first line strength was a handy measure, even though its use produced much confusion. Thus in 1934 or 1935, the Luftwaffe was fairly strong on aircraft production, but weak, by and large, in formed units. With the Royal Air Force these factors were reversed. So misjudgements were all too easy.

Readers of *The Second World War* and others of Churchill's books can be pardoned for supposing that the author had access to special sources of secret intelligence which were either not available to the British authorities, or if available were misunderstood or even suppressed by them. These beliefs do not bear serious analysis. The evidence suggests that much the same figures for German aircraft production were available to British and French authorities and to Churchill. It was in the translation of these production figures into the accepted measure of first line strength that the opportunities for controversy arose. Full use was made of these opportunities. Further complications arose from the seemingly simple question 'When is an aircraft an aircraft?' Does it, for example, need, in order to qualify, serviceable military equipment, e.g. guns and instruments that work, or an adequate supply of (say) bombs that work (the Luftwaffe ran out of bombs in 1939)?

Another more serious factor was also present in the shape of straightforward military deception. Thus, when Hitler told Eden and Simon in March 1935 that the Luftwaffe had reached equality of strength with the Royal Air Force, it was probably in the light of hindsight a statement *in terrorem*, a stoat produced to hypnotise the rabbit. The detailed figures are not important but the practical consequences were. Britain, very belatedly, and rather languidly, began to be alarmed. Hence a series of rising but mainly inadequate figures for defence expenditure for 1935 onwards. In January 1937 General Erhard Milch, the German Secretary of State for Air, explained in confidence that the Luftwaffe's aims were far more modest than Britain had

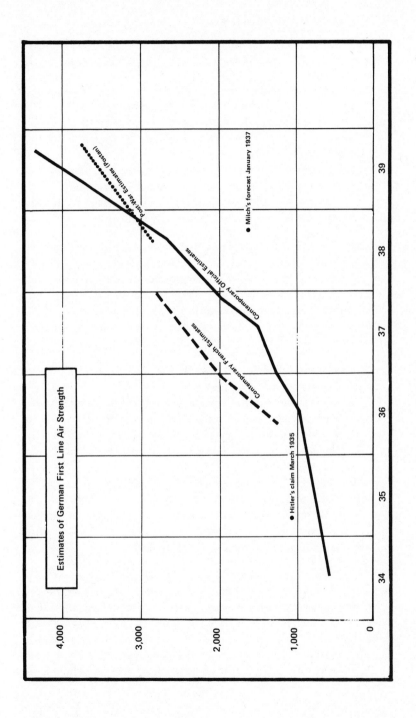

Estimates of German First Line Air Strength

Post-War Estimates (Postan)

Contemporary Official Estimates

Contemporary French Estimates

● Milch's forecast January 1937

● Hitler's claim March 1935

4,000

3,000

2,000

1,000

0

34   35   36   37   38   39

supposed. Britain obligingly dropped her latest air expansion proposals. A glance at the diagram will show in much simplified form what was going on:

Luftwaffe first line strength

1. The curve O.O gives the contemporary British estimates[3]
2. The curve F-F sets out estimates given to Churchill by the French in May 1936[4]
3. 'H' illustrates Hitler's claim to have achieved parity in March 1935[5]
4. 'M' illustrates Milch's re-assurance given in January 1937[6]
5. 'P.P.' illustrates two figures of German first line strength taken post-war from the records of the German Air Ministry[7]

Roskill (p. 664) remarks: 'The broad conclusion reached from study of figures in many sources is that Churchill's figures were unrealistically high ... The Air Staff's figures appear on the whole to be nearer the truth.' This writer's studies would certainly support this conclusion. Churchill often relied on French estimates which were generally too high.

But what was the Air Ministry's part in all this? It can be summed up as follows:

1. In 1934 and 1935 the reaction to Luftwaffe expansion was in general too little and too late.
2. The 1936 expansion plan (Scheme F) was perfectly soundly based. Air Ministry attempts to lever it up in response to increased German momentum (Schemes H, K and L) were frustrated by the unwillingness of the Cabinet to sanction them mainly on financial grounds.
3. After Munich the Chancellor's resistance slowly crumbled and by late 1938 and during 1939 finance was no longer a limitation. By this time the Air Staff (see diagram, p. 93) was probably rather exaggerating the German aims which is no doubt why the Luftwaffe was outbuilt by the Royal Air Force in 1940.

In the detailed debates about Royal Air Force re-armament over the period 1933–1939 Churchill's estimates of German air plans were often wrong but his instinct to which he gave voice so vehemently—that Britain was doing too little to face the threat of the Luftwaffe—was absolutely sound. The question must also be faced as to what weight the Governments of the day gave to his warnings. The answer must surely be—very little. Increasingly until the end of 1938 Churchill found himself politically isolated. The effective spur to British re-armament came not from Churchill but from Hitler.

Critics: Churchill

Churchill's criticisms of British plans was not confined to questions of Luftwaffe strength. Soon he embarked on a broadly based attack on the competence of the Air Ministry's management of the British air programme. In political terms this meant an attack on the competence of Swinton, the responsible Minister from June 1935 to May 1938. Throughout this period Churchill was of course a candidate for office, either as Minister of Defence, First Lord, Minister of Supply (a new post for which he ardently and wisely crusaded) or as Secretary of State for Air. So Churchill's sense of duty, and it was no less, and his political aspirations both pointed in the same direction. In the *Importance of being Earnest* Miss Fairfax remarks that 'on an occasion of this kind it becomes more than a moral duty to speak one's mind. It becomes a pleasure.' Was there a touch of this thought in some of Churchill's criticisms? Perhaps there was. Churchill, though apt to lose his way completely on some political occasions, as for example over India and the Abdication, was nothing if not a political animal.

Churchill, from an early stage, had secret contacts within the Civil Service and the Armed Forces, much to the annoyance of Hankey. And of course by reason of his membership of the Air Defence Sub-Committees of the Committee of Imperial Defence he acquired much secret information through official channels. The overall content of the unofficial communications which Churchill received consisted of a large measure of straight, often secret, information, which tended to put the Churchill *versus* Government debate on Marquess of Queensbury Rules, mixed with usually accurate but sometimes highly idiosyncratic comments on the adequacy of the air re-armament programme. Churchill's Air Force contacts, mainly of middle rank, gave him what can reasonably be called a jeremiad on the air expansion scene. Of course there was plenty of room for criticism of the air expansion programme as it got under way. That would have been true whatever the Minister, whatever the Government, whatever the plan.

In July 1936 a strong Parliamentary deputation led by Sir Austen Chamberlain, Salisbury and Churchill was received by Prime Minister Baldwin.[8] Among its members was Trenchard. A wide variety of topics was touched upon including relative air strengths of course but extending also to questions of air training, numbers of aircraft types, underground hangars, educational standards, numbers of short service officers and the like. Churchill around this time was also doing his best to detach Weir as a main adviser of the Government on re-armament. In a letter dated May 1936 he told Weir plainly that his position was anomalous. In November of the same year, in the course of a debate in Parliament about the Air Ministry dispute with Nuffield, Churchill remarked:

> The revelations for which Lord Nuffield is responsible are important not so much in themselves but because, like a lightning flash, they have illuminated a confused landscape of Air and Army production.[9]

In March 1938, egged on perhaps by his Air Force contacts Churchill addressed a long memorandum to Chamberlain.[10] In this he attacked the re-equipment programme as to rate of delivery of aircraft, shortage of equipment and so on. Strangely, he hurled a brick *en passant* at the eight-gun fighter, saying that the latest developments favoured the turret type. One wonders where he got this idea from. Anyway it was an unfortunate one, for the only turret fighter produced, the Defiant, proved a failure.

Critics: Various

By early 1938 it seems clear that certain members of the Royal Air Force were conveying doubts to the Parliamentary Opposition. No other explanation seems possible for the long memorandum which Attlee, of all people, presented to the Prime Minister in February 1938 and which embraced such matters as the use made of technical officers, flying by senior Air Force officers, slowness in inventing and adopting new devices, size of aircraft hangars, siting of airfields, range of bombers and choice of aircraft manufacturers.[11] This was an attack on the top management of the Royal Air Force by a devious route. The quality of the criticisms was mixed. On balance the criticisms perhaps did good; a slight touch of the whip rarely does management any harm. Still, the re-armament ship was frail and the storm was rising. On 2 April 1938 the Air Ministry's critics were joined, or most likely rejoined by Fisher, the Permanent Secretary of the Treasury. In a minute to Neville Chamberlain complaining of inadequate air re-armament he said: 'For some years we have had from the Air Ministry soothing-syrup and incompetence in equal measure.'[12] He added that the first line strength of the German Air Force at that date was 5,000. As we know this was about double its true strength (see diagram p. 93). In October 1938 Fisher addressed another vitriolic minute to Chamberlain alleging Air

Ministry incompetence. 'There is one—and only one—Crown Servant of first rate ability in high position in the Air Ministry, Sir Arthur Street, a civilian.' He also criticised the air programme as inadequate. One wonders if Fisher cleared his draft with his political master the Chancellor of the Exchequer who two months earlier was addressing Chamberlain in very different terms (see Chapter 5).[13] Soon the Society of British Aircraft Constructors joined the fray.[14] They were angry because Swinton had ordered 400 American aircraft (which proved invaluable eighteen months later). The aircraft were 200 general reconnaissance aircraft (Hudsons) and 200 service trainers (Harvards). Sir Charles Bruce Gardner, executive chairman of the Society, addressed thirty-one pages of criticism to Swinton and also approached Sir Horace Wilson, Chamberlain's special adviser. The Times of 22 April carried a critical leader. Over and above all this there were the deep-seated worries about parity to which we have referred earlier. In political terms the situation was becoming unmanageable and the fall of Swinton imminent. One is thankful that the crisis did not culminate earlier and that it did not result in Churchill entering the Cabinet in the defence field at this or some earlier stage. Such an event would have been a national disaster. No doubt to many, including Churchill, it did not look like that at the time.

The situation finally exploded in the Committee of Supply on the Air Estimates on 12 May 1938.[15] Winterton, Deputy Air Minister, began his speech, a little nervously perhaps, by saying it might take an hour. Rising to a point of order a Member said 'in that case can we have the windows open?' The House dissolved in laughter, as it sometimes does in response to a schoolboy joke. From that moment Winterton was lost. He spoke for some ninety minutes. Turning the pages of Hansard so many interruptions are recorded that it is hard to distinguish the speaker from the critics. Unlike Chamberlain on a later occasion Winterton had no 'friends in this House'. His position was not helped by the fact that until he joined the Government in March 1938 Winterton had been a critic of air re-armament and had been a member of the Parliamentary deputation to the Prime Minister in July 1936. Three days later Swinton and Winterton were fired.[16] Kingsley Wood who succeeded Swinton in 1938 tried with success to do a public relations job for the Air Ministry. He identified the criticisms and sought to deal with them. In particular he healed the breach with Nuffield, by no means an unmixed blessing. Truly, in the words of the Dictionary of National Biography, he laboured indefatigably to increase our fighting strength. The Royal Air Force owe him a deep debt of gratitude. Rather unkindly they rewarded his devotion by doing their best to kill him when in misty weather in July 1939 they flew him and other distinguished passengers into the side of a mountain in the Lake District. Surprisingly, he lived to tell the tale. Ministers were tough in those days.

8

On the Eve of War

General

Our story has now reached the point when the Royal Air Force was about to face its greatest test and it is perhaps a good moment to review what had been accomplished up to this point. At the end of the First World War the Royal Air Force was the greatest air service in the world, victorious on every front. Then, for ten to fifteen years or so, it entered the wilderness amid many who would gladly have broken it up and destroyed it. When a man knows he is to be hanged in a fortnight it concentrates his mind wonderfully. It was a bit like this with the Royal Air Force in the Twenties and early Thirties. A dozen times it had escaped death by a whisker and it had grown wary. The sole reason for the creation of the Royal Air Force had been the need to bring into being a strategic bombing force. Forget this and the Royal Air Force was lost. This was the Trenchard doctrine and it contained much wisdom. But of course it was only part of the truth. Had the Royal Air Force disappeared as a separate service in the Twenties, as it very nearly did, the Battle of Britain would have been the responsibility of the Army. With all respect to that magnificent service the battle would then undoubtedly have been lost. Alternatively the Royal Air Force could have been created in 1936 or thereabouts, with much the same result. But part of the price of the Trenchard doctrine was a decline in the standards of co-operation between the Royal Air Force and the Army and Royal Navy respectively, a decline for which all three services must take roughly equal responsibility. In November 1918 these standards were for practical purposes perfect. In September 1939 they were far from perfect. The lessons had to be learned all over again. The Fleet Air Arm, handed over to the Royal Navy in 1937, was small and its equipment inferior. The shore-based squadrons of Coastal Command were poorly equipped and their armament and tactics were elementary.

The importance of the torpedo had been under-estimated. With the Army the deficiencies were also serious. An Army in the field needs trained and sophisticated air support on a substantial scale. Germany learned this lesson, if indeed she had ever forgotten it, in Spain.

Royal Air Force ideas were far from realistic at this stage. The blame for this rests only in part with the Royal Air Force. The decision to put a sizeable land force on the Continent was a last moment improvisation. Still, a small Expeditionary Force was always part of the plan, though preparations for this were never really adequate either as to size or as to tactical theory. Preparations for the air defence of Britain by day were for practical purposes faultless, though a tribute is appropriate here to the emphasis which Inskip, as Minister for Co-ordination of Defence gave to the fighter force in 1938. There was more to this for sure than the simple thought that fighters were cheaper. As for the strategic bomber force, theory departed from reality. Still, the bomber preparations of the late Thirties in their scale and their imaginative sweep contained much that would prove invaluable later. Overseas, the Royal Air Force got what was left. This was little enough but, in some areas at least, good use was made of it. These comments are of course a counsel of perfection. There were inevitably shortages all round. Had the Royal Air Force been perfectly informed, perfectly wise, perfectly staffed, possessed of unlimited resources and never interfered with, these faults would have been avoided. As it was, the Royal Air Force had to do the best it could. It was a good best. Partly it was a question of spreading limited resources to best advantage. There was also the fact that with crises occurring every few weeks or months the limitation arose that men and women cannot work round the clock and through the week without paying a penalty. Mistakes are made. On balance the Royal Air Force did well.

Money

Re-armament was held back by the consideration that the fourth arm of defence was economic strength. We have seen that in 1937 stern limits were set to expenditure on defence and the decision taken that any excess above an arbitrarily defined limit must either be vetoed or met by borrowing. How sensible was this consideration? The answer must surely be not very sensible, and the fact that the borrowing limits were doubled within a year provides perhaps some support for this. If Britain as a nation was resolved to pursue a peaceful life and in the international sphere was ready to accept what was coming to her, well that was a coherent policy if not an attractive one. But if Britain as a nation was resolved to follow her traditional role as an arbiter of the destinies of Europe that was another matter. There can surely be little doubt that the financial restrictions, imposed on all three services from 1934 onwards and continued a long way into 1938, were a serious mistake. Of course the Royal Air Force fared better than the other two services and its share of the total expenditure on military equipment steadily increased between 1934 and 1939. The following figures for Air Estimates[1] to which have been added the drawings from the Consolidated Fund under the first and second Defence Loans Act are deeply significant:

	£m
1933	16.8
1934	17.7
1935	27.5
1936	50.1
1937	137.6
1938	200.0
1939	314.3

It was the money poured into air defence from late 1938 onward which gave Britain its lead over German air production in 1940.

The central co-ordination of defence

During most of the Twenties and Thirties the central co-ordination of defence policy was effectively in the hands of Hankey, who held the posts of Secretary of the Cabinet, Secretary of the Committee of Imperial Defence, Secretary of the Chiefs of Staff Committee and Clerk of the Privy Council. It was a highly personal arrangement involving a phenomenal work load and it dissolved when Hankey retired in the summer of 1938. Sir Edward Bridges then became Secretary to the Cabinet, and General Ismay became Secretary to the Committee of Imperial Defence and the Chiefs of Staff Committee. Sir Rupert Howarth, the Deputy Secretary to the Cabinet, became also Clerk of the Privy Council. Hankey had of course created the structure of the Committee of Imperial Defence with its elaborate network of supporting committees notably the Chiefs of Staff Committee. Born in 1877 he became Secretary to the Committee of Imperial Defence in 1912 and retained that position for the next twenty-six years. He won great renown as an organiser in the First World War and was among those whose work was recognised by a substantial monetary gift from the Government after the Armistice. Among his many achievements was the recommendation of the Salisbury Committee to create a Chiefs of Staff Committee in 1923, for it is impossible to doubt that his ideas lay behind this development. He remained Secretary of this body for fifteen years. It sounds a small enough matter, this putting together of military ideas. In fact it was a dramatic innovation. The Committee of Imperial Defence had been formed in 1904 on the recommendation of the Esher Committee. Hankey became its Assistant Secretary in 1908 and soon its guiding spirit. In particular he pushed ahead the War Book Sub-Committee which codified all the action needed to convert a country at peace into a country at war, for example in such matters as mobilisation, control of aliens, censorship and the like. One subject with which the Committee of Imperial Defence did not deal was strategy. And so August 1914 found the Cabinet innocent of ideas, except for conflicting ones, about how the war should be waged, even indeed as to where the British Expeditionary Force should take its station. This lacuna was not really filled until the Chiefs of Staff Committee was created. The machinery created by Hankey was splendid. It involved a mixture of soldiers, sailors, airmen and civil servants, including scientists, and it linked civil and military policies within a firm and effective grasp. The theory was that it served the Prime Minister as Chairman of the Committee of Imperial Defence, defence being too vast a subject for any Prime Minister to delegate to another Minister, however exalted. This was Hankey's principle and it meant that in theory the day-to-day supervision of the vast re-armament programme of the late Thirties rested on the shoulders of the Prime Minister. In practice this proved to be out of the question and as the pressures mounted the need for a Minister of Defence became daily more clear. Hankey fought the idea every inch of the way and indeed he continued to fight it, rather unwisely, after Churchill on his appointment as Prime Minister took over the office himself. Hankey had to accept the appointment of Inskip as Minister for the Co-ordination of Defence in March 1936 but, despite loyal service to that office, Hankey continued to regard it as a nullity, which indeed in some ways it was, though there were some useful consequences. The fact is that during the Twenties and Thirties defence policy was run by the Cabinet Office and the Treasury, in effect by Hankey and Fisher. An illustration of this can be found in the fact that when re-armament began to be considered in 1933 the first defence Requirements Committee was composed of Hankey (Chairman), Vansittart (Permanent Under-Secretary of State for the Foreign Office), Fisher for the Treasury and the three Chiefs of Staff. Professor Donald Watt has written an interesting study of this development.[2] Over the period in question Hankey was in effect acting as Minister of Defence and was prepared to fight anyone who would challenge the arrangement. The disadvantage of this set-up was that, short of the Prime Minister, there was no defence authority superior to the Hankey/Fisher axis. This sounds disturbing until one considers the names of possible Ministers of Defence at that time. According to Roskill[3] they included Churchill, Lord Eustace Percy, Sir Robert Horne, Ramsay Macdonald, Trenchard, Hankey, and Neville Chamberlain.* Of this list it is necessary only to comment on Churchill. Had Churchill been appointed Minister of Defence in 1936 the results would have been unfortunate. He would in all probability have made a good Minister from some points of view but come 1940 disaster would have struck just the same and he would have been discredited. His great advantage and the supreme gift he brought to Britain was that he came with clean hands with no responsibility for the errors in pre-war defence preparations. Equally, had a Minister of Defence other than Churchill been appointed it is reasonable to suppose that Churchill would have devoted at least as much loving care to his demolition as he did to Inskip's. And indeed some of the other names in Roskill's list seem, to put it mildly, highly eccentric. It would be invidious to discriminate. So perhaps it may be just as well that Hankey fought off intruders. In conclusion, three shining virtues of the Hankey regime must be recorded. It was impartial. It was superbly efficient and as a pattern of the central machinery of defence was widely copied in the United States and elsewhere. Finally, it suited Churchill, who without it would surely have introduced in major style, as he did only in minor way, his *famille militaire* with results which would surely have been unfortunate.

The night of 2/3 September 1939

As the mighty events of 2 September 1939 developed, tension in the Air Ministry mounted. Of course the key staff there had for some time been equipped to work round the clock, so day merged into night and back again without much notice. There was plenty to be done, not

---

* According to Gilbert (*Winston S. Churchill*, 5), other names considered were those of Hoare, Swinton, Halifax, Weir and Kingsley Wood.

least because the mounting crisis obstinately refused to comply with the rules. In Britain the transition from peace to war was controlled by an immensely complicated set of instructions known as the War Book, a system devised by Hankey before the First World and developed and improved thereafter. According to the War Book, the War Stage should be preceded by a Precautionary Stage. The institution of the Precautionary Stage was a confidential matter which served to trigger off many important defence moves. In fact, the Cabinet never authorised the introduction of the Precautionary Stage for fear that some of its consequences might be deemed provocative. So the various moves had to be made piecemeal thus adding considerably to the complexity of the situation. Other complications arose from the fact that, contrary to earlier expectations, it gradually became clear that Italy would not be at Germany's side when war broke out. So, all the telegrams carefully drafted beforehand had to be done over again. For this and many other reasons there was plenty to do in the Air Ministry on the night of 2 September. The Cabinet's decision to issue the ultimatum was known towards midnight. The ultimatum expired at 11.00 hours on the following Sunday and the Air Ministry's war telegram was issued at around 11.17 hours. The delay was due to political, not administrative, causes. The telephone lines from Berlin were still busy and the Service Departments had to hold their hand for a bit. Within a few moments an unannounced French aircraft entered Fighter Command's territory and Wing Commander Walter Pretty at 11 Group Headquarters pressed the button. So Chamberlain's gloomy broadcast to the nation had a stirring epilogue as the air raid sirens set up what Churchill sometimes called their banshee wail. In King Charles Street, Whitehall, where the central elements of the Air Ministry and Air Staff were installed, some fifty members of the general public rushed through the front door when the sirens blew so the Air Staff and others in their funk hole had for a time some uninvited guests. On the way to the basement at least one member of the Air Ministry staff heard the swish of bombs overhead.

It had been a night to remember. In the small hours the Chief of the Air Staff held a meeting to discuss a proposed assault on German warships on the following day. As the meeting progressed a tremendous thunderstorm swept over Whitehall with vivid lightning and immense rolls of thunder. It was easy at this moment to suppose that the gods were taking a keen interest in our affairs, but whether they were pleased or the reverse was hard to say. And so, on that Sunday morning, Britain was once again at war with Germany. Few of those working in the Air Ministry Headquarters at King Charles Street would have been prepared to hazard a guess at the outcome, but the early arrival of the Luftwaffe was strongly favoured for a place on the agenda.

PART TWO

9

The German Air Force

In the following chapters of this book we shall meet the German Air Force at every turn in all its different roles and in all the different theatres of war. Nevertheless, it is convenient to include at this point in our story a little of the history and a synoptic view of the development and final fate of that force. It holds many lessons.

Military aviation was forbidden to Germany under the Treaty of Versailles but, by an unfortunate aberration, she was allowed to develop a civil aviation organisation and a Defence Ministry. This error allowed Germany to develop a secret air force from a very early date. In 1923 General von Seeckt, Chief of the Army Command in the Defence Ministry, decreed that the future German Air Force should be an independent part of the Armed Force. Former German fliers were distributed discreetly throughout the Ministry. The German aviation industry—Junkers, Heinkel, Dornier, Focke-Wulf, Messerschmitt grew rapidly and by 1926 had developed a rate of production unsurpassed in Europe. In the same year the German airline Deutsche Lufthansa was created as a state monopoly and the steady development of airfields and flying skills followed. Pilots were secretly trained by the Ministry of Transport for the Defence Ministry, and a secret flying training school opened in Russia. The production of military aircraft began in 1934 and the German Air Force was announced officially in March 1935. Goering was Commander-in-Chief and Milch, a former Lufthansa chief, became Secretary of State. Soon the German Military Attaché, General Wenninger was presenting his credentials in London. 'Have you been in Britain before?' said Chief of the Air Staff Ellington, making polite conversation. 'Yes, indeed', replied the General. He had been in prison in Britain during the First World War.

At the outset, the philosophy of the German Air Force was for the most part strategic, that is it expected to perform its primary functions, bombing, fighting and the like, as a principal and not in support of naval and military operations. It was gradually shifted from this concept and in this change one factor was the death of the Luftwaffe's first Chief of Staff, Lieutenant-General Walther Wever, in a crash at Dresden in a Heinkel 70 on 3 June 1936. Wever was a firm believer in a strategic air force on the lines of the Royal Air Force and had instituted a strategic bomber policy with the four-engined Dornier Do 19 and Junkers Ju 89 aircraft. Prototypes were flown and both of them were potentially rather ahead of the Stirling in technical merit. After the death of Wever, however, Goering was prevailed upon by Kesselring and Milch to abandon both the four-engine bombers. Another and greater factor was the German participation in the Spanish Civil War. Germany despatched to Spain a powerful force of fighters and bombers, the Condor Legion, to serve General Franco. It was commanded by General Hugo von Sperrle (later to command one of the *Luftflotten* attacking Britain) and his Chief of Staff, Colonel Wolfram von Richthofen, a cousin of the famous Baron Manfred von Richthofen, worked out a highly successful system of army air support based on fighters, dive bombers and transports. Richthofen rose to command the Condor Legion and after its return to Germany in the spring of 1939 went on to play a powerful part in shaping German Air Force strategy. Thus was engendered a highly significant shift away from strategic air operations in the direction of tactical support of the armies in the field. Other powerful forces were pressing in the same direction. The structure of the German High Command rested on a Supreme Headquarters, the *Oberkommando der Wehrmacht* (OKW), controlling an Army Headquarters, the *Oberkommando des Heeres* (OKH), a Navy Headquarters, the *Oberkommando der Marine* (OKM) and the *Oberkommando der Luftwaffe* (OKL). This structure in itself tended to overshadow the German Air Force. Thus in 1938 Hitler, essentially an infantryman at heart, dismissed General von Blomberg and took over the control of OKW. In the spring of 1942 Hitler took personal command of the Germany Army. At this stage the OKW establishment included no Air Force officer above the rank of colonel, but seven such Army officers and two such Naval officers. A similar pattern obtained in the elements of OKW attached to Hitler's advanced headquarters. Of course, senior officers from OKL were regularly called in but there is no mistaking the fact that the apparatus for presenting air advice to authority at the right level was seriously defective. This weakness was compounded by the character of Goering and his relations with Hitler. Goering commanded the Luftwaffe, often on an absentee basis, and he was determined to have no airman of stature near Hitler. Accordingly he denied to Milch, his Secretary of State, all control of technical matters, which he put in the hands of General Ernst Udet, a famous First World War pilot and a personal friend. This arrangement persisted until Udet's suicide in November 1941.

Fate treated the German Armed Forces badly. Perhaps they deserved no better though on the purely military plane they had a great deal to be very proud of. The secret preparation and swift expansion of the German Air Force over the period 1934–1939 were done very competently indeed. Aircraft production was pressed ahead from a handful in 1933 to 9,000 or so per annum in 1939. Most of the aircraft types selected initially were pretty successful or very successful. There were plenty of brilliant technical ideas. The V1s and V2s were remarkable achievements and the multi-barrel gun to fire on London from Mimoyecques was at least a brilliant idea. And Germany had a jet aircraft flying at least as early as Britain. Yet in the end the German Air Force was destroyed. The principal cause was of course the fact that in the air sense Germany committed herself to a military task vastly beyond her strength. Beyond this, the German Air Force was led or ordered into blunders which made things even worse than they need have been. Witness for example the production rate of fighters being pushed to nearly 3,000 per month in September 1944 at a time when, because of fuel shortage and reduced training standards, the German Air Force was in no position to make good use of them. It is a sad story. The fact is that Germany was committed to a form of government under Hitler which made possible appalling errors of judgement. It started with Hitler overruling his military leaders over the Rhineland and Austria and being proved right. Thereafter, the voice of the professionals was inevitably muted. It continued with Germany developing the idea of the *Blitzkreig* or lightning war in which the German armies were led to speedy victory by an irresistible Air Force. Poland in 1939 and Norway and France in 1940 showed the way. Thereafter, Germany succumbed to dreams of glory. The fateful decision was taken to attack Russia and the parting with reality began. Germany had always dreaded a war on two fronts and here it was brought about by Hitler himself. Many around Hitler at the time knew that a dreadful blunder was being made but they had lost any ability to control events, if indeed they ever possessed it. And after all Hitler had been proved right before. And there were the Russian experiences in Finland to be thought about. So they kept quiet for the most part, and no doubt it would have made little difference had they not.

Much of the history of the German Air Force can be summarised in two tables:

Table A—Aircraft Production[1]

	Britain	Germany
1939	7,940	8,925
1940	15,049	10,826
1941	20,094	11,424
1942	23,672	15,288
1943	26,263	25,094
1944	26,461	39,275

Table B—First Line Strength[2]

	Royal Air Force (United Kingdom plus Middle East)	Luftwaffe (including transport aircraft)
2.9.39	2,451	4,161
1.8.40	3,106	4,393
1.12.41	4,747	5,167
1.6.43	5,474	6,957
1.6.44	7,300	6,358
1.1.45	7,375	6,797

Let us look first at Table A. In 1939 Britain nearly caught up with Germany in the production of military aircraft. In 1940 Britain surpassed Germany by 40 per cent, in 1941 by 75 per cent and in 1942 by 54 per cent. In 1943 production was roughly equal in the two countries. In 1944 Germany had a surplus of some 50 per cent. Clearly, in 1940 Germany felt she had won and proceeded to relax so far as the production of military aircraft was concerned. The German changeover to new types of aircraft which inevitably disrupted production was also a factor. In 1941 Germany was expecting to defeat Russia before the onset of winter. By 1942 and again in 1943 Milch planned a great increase in fighters to cope with the rising threat of the Anglo–American air offensive. Hitler and Goering demurred: German close support bombers were the thing, the idea was not to attack Britain but to support the German Army. By 1944 the Luftwaffe had its way and fighters were produced in very large numbers indeed. By this time, as we have seen, fuel was short and training and morale in the Luftwaffe had suffered. The vast production of German military aircraft was largely wasted.

Let us now look at Table B (the British figures are only approximate but they are near enough). Germany began the war probably twice as strong as Britain in the air (the figures flatter Britain). She proceeded to discard this advantage so that by the end of 1944 Britain was stronger in the air than Germany. Meanwhile, of course, Russia and the United States of America had been added to Germany's enemies. Precise calculations are impossible and are anyway irrelevant. It is the order of magnitude that counts. By 1942 Germany's inferiority in the air compared with her enemies must have been of the order of not less than one to three. This calculation ignores Italy, but this scarcely matters. What did Germany think she was doing?

On the technical side the German record was uneven. They produced some good fighters, the Messerschmitt 109 and the Focke-Wulf 190 for example, but not nearly enough of them until too late. The Me 110, the twin-engine Messerschmitt fighter, was not nearly so successful. They produced the first jet fighter in the Me 262 but its introduction was seriously delayed by Hitler's insistence that it should be developed as a fighter-bomber. On the bomber side they were mesmerised by the early successes of the Ju 87 (Stuka) dive bomber against unsophisticated defence. So all subsequent German bombers had to be capable of dive bombing. This was a serious technical limitation very damaging to the German Air Force. It stopped them for example developing a real four-engine bomber which would have been invaluable in the war against Russia. One of their moves in the direction of a four-engine bomber was the design of the Heinkel He 177. This had four engines for sure, but to make dive bombing possible they were mounted in pairs, each pair driving a single propeller. It was a dismal failure. Its chief fault was overheating of the engines, causing fires, and in addition it was all but impossible to service. Before 1939 Germany had two good four-engine transports the FW 200 and the Ju 90, both used in Lufthansa. The former was used for reconnaissance and as a bomber in the U-boat campaign but neither aircraft was developed as a series production bomber, perhaps because Goering thought that numbers were what mattered. For the most part the German Air Force relied on twin-engine bombers, the Do 17, the He 111 and the Ju 88. The last named was also successful as a night fighter and as a reconnaissance plane. Fairly late in the war the German Air Force received a successful twin-engine jet bomber, the Arado 234, but its contribution was necessarily small. The German Air Force was markedly successful in regard to its transport policy. They attached much importance to squadron mobility which was indeed essential to them in their mainly tactical role. Apart from that old war horse the Ju 52, which served them throughout the war, they made use of the Messerschmitt 323 a six-engined transport and the Blohm und Voss six-engined flying boat.

Apart from the sheer inadequacy of numbers in relation to task, production planning in the German Air Force was often in a state of chaos. In Udet's day there were repeated changes of programme and output failed to rise in a satisfactory way. In February 1941 for example Germany produced 400 fighters and bombers. The corresponding figure in Britain was about 1,000. These failures produced some personal tragedies. Udet, in bad health and torn by technical and production failures, took his life in November 1941. Goering contemplated a posthumous court martial but was dissuaded from this course. A somewhat similar step was taken in Britain many years earlier when Henry VIII tried Thomas à Becket 368 years after his death. The suicide of the German Chief of the Air Staff, General Jeschonnek, in August 1943 after he had held that office since February 1939 reflected the failures of the German Air Force in Russia, and perhaps too Bomber Command's successful attack on Peenemünde which occurred the night before his death. He was succeeded by General Korten who held office until he died from injuries sustained in the attack on Hitler's life.

The Luftwaffe were not helped by the personal interventions of Hitler in air matters. Examples are:

(a) Hitler's ban on the highly successful German Intruder attacks against British airfields. Hitler wanted British bombers shot down over Germany.

(b) His decision to supply Stalingrad from the air, an operation quite beyond the Luftwaffe's capacity and which inflicted grievous wounds on it.

(c) His decision in the crucial days of 1943, as a political gesture, to supply Me 109 fighters to Italy, where they were a total loss to the war effort.

(d) His decision to store large quantities of Luftwaffe material in Norway and Greece before D-Day—again a loss to the war effort.

(e) His refusal to allow a bomber *Gruppe* to be moved to Normandy for D-Day mine-laying operations.

(f) The removal of a large part of the German fighter force to the Eastern Front after the failure of the Ardennes offensive.

(g) His support of the development of composite aircraft at the end of the war, against the views of the Air Staff. They contributed nothing.

One characteristic of the Luftwaffe was its extraordinary toughness and resilience. After shattering defeats in Russia and France it would re-gather its strength and strike hard again. Perhaps the most remarkable example of this was the Luftwaffe's attack on Anglo-American airfields on New Year's Day 1945. After all the blows the Luftwaffe had suffered in the autumn of 1944, it suddenly threw 800 fighters at Allied air-fields, achieving complete surprise. It was a costly operation but a gallant one.

A word must be said about German radar. Radar was developed as a deadly and war-winning secret in Britain. In fact, both Germany and America had the same idea, which is indeed a pretty obvious one, at about the same time. Initial German development of the early warning Freya radar was, however, less impressive than corresponding equipment on the British side. Further, in the highly successful integration of radar information with fighter control Britain was far ahead. Centimetric radar was Britain's special triumph and produced improvements in performance which the Germans did not even suspect for a time. The cavity magnetron which made it all possible was given to the United States without conditions and without consideration in 1940, an imaginative and statesmanlike act which greatly benefited British and American developments later.

Initially the German Air Force was planned for a strategic role. Success in the Spanish Civil War turned it mainly in the direction of a tactical role. German air re-armament went ahead rapidly and there were none of the financial and other restrictions which hampered the expansion of the Royal Air Force. It suited German policy to aggrandise the power and might of the Luftwaffe. Powerful it was but figures put about with some subtlety suggested it was much stronger than it really was. Thus in May 1938 Sir Hugh Seely told the House of Commons that by the end of 1939 Germany would possess a first line strength of 6,000 aircraft rising to 8,000.[3] Churchill's figures too were affected by German propaganda. The British Air Ministry, despite its many critics, got the figures about right. Their figures were only slightly on the high side. This German deception was a double-edged weapon. It scared Europe all right, but it also encouraged Britain to build more boldly in the air than she might have done had British public opinion not been affected by German propaganda.

Table B (p. 112) shows what had happened by September 1939 to Baldwin's pledge of air parity. When war began the Germans became victims of their own propaganda. They were convinced that the Luftwaffe was invincible and they chose to ignore the clear evidence that Britain was determined to overtake them in the air. The easy victories of 1939 and 1940 confirmed them in their error and they entered upon the supreme miscalculation of the Russian campaign, which for quite a time looked like going the same way. When the truth dawned after the terrible winter of 1941/42 on the Eastern Front, the Luftwaffe was still committed to a tactical role and Hitler had parted company from reality. Tanks, guns, always the offensive, no retreat, no surrender were supposedly magic words. As the Allied strategic air offensive gathered momentum it was plain that the Luftwaffe's role was wrong and must be changed. More emphasis must be placed on air defence and Britain must not be allowed to pile up massive resources without interference. Lost in a world of dreams and illusion, Hitler resisted these changes to the last. Britain made serious mistakes too and in a way they were almost as unforgivable. In the late 1930's it was hard to doubt that war with Germany was only a matter of time. This being so it is hard to excuse the continuation of severe financial restraints in Britain until within a few months of war. Also difficult to excuse were the inadequate preparations, notably of the Royal Air Force, for the maritime war, and the fact that the Royal Air Force had no up-to-date and effective techniques for co-operating with the Army. Britain paid dearly for these mistakes but she was sufficiently flexible to learn from them. Foolish ideas of special breeds of bad aircraft for Army air co-operation were resisted and the Royal Air Force, not without a struggle, withstood the temptation to copy the Stukas. Britain never lost sight of the principle of air superiority and slowly effective techniques of Army air support were worked out afresh in the Middle East and applied with immense effect during 'Overlord', the landings in Normandy in June 1944. And by 1943 at any rate the Royal Air Force was very effective indeed in the U-boat war, somewhat late, it is true, but better late than never. By 1943 too Bomber Command was on the road to victory.

After it was all over General Koller, the last German Chief of the Air Staff, had this to say:

We have lost the war. Far-sighted persons had already long seen this coming, but one is always moved by the questions 'Why?' and 'Couldn't it have happened differently?' There are many reasons why Germany lost the war; political, economic and military reasons which were our own fault. None of these reasons were decisive in themselves, nor were they together decisive. Had they been avoided, a more favourable development of the situation might indeed have been possible. Quite apart from them, what was decisive in itself was the loss of air supremacy ...

This is not the whole truth but it expresses an important part of it.

10

The Opening Phases of the War in Europe

Early days

The Luftwaffe did not arrive over Britain on Sunday 3 September, much to the surprise of the Air Ministry and no doubt of many others. Nor indeed did it arrive for many months thereafter, at any rate so far as mainland targets were concerned. Nevertheless, a great deal was happening. The war at sea was in full swing, many U-boats being on their war stations and German commerce raiders passing into the Atlantic and back without serious interference. The U-boats soon gave the Royal Navy some nasty shocks. The aircraft carrier *Ark Royal* had a narrow squeak on 14 September 1939, the *Courageous* was sunk three days later and in mid-October the battleship *Royal Oak* was sunk while at anchor within the innermost defences of Scapa Flow. About this time too the Luftwaffe attacked British warships in the Firth of Forth, giving Fighter Command its first victory in the war. Superimposed on the problems to which these events gave rise was the threat posed by German magnetic mines, which were sown in eastern ports and approaches producing immense disturbance to warships and shipping. An attempt to supplement the surface mining activity by seaplanes proved unfortunate for the Germans as they succeeded in delivering (indirectly of course) a number of German magnetic mines to the Royal Navy Mine Department for dissection. In the ordinary way this highly skilled Department might perhaps have blown itself sky-high finding out how these mines worked. In fact the Admiralty knew quite a bit about magnetic mines from the First World War and, although they had been too busy to put their ideas into practice up this point, they were able to cope. Other problems arose from German air attacks on our coastal shipping. One of the consequences of these developments was that the Royal Navy was temporarily driven away from its bases at Rosyth and Scapa to anchorages on the west coast of Scotland. All things considered there was plenty for the Admiralty to think about. If there were ever any doubts about this, the new First Lord's plans for designing a fleet to fight its way into the Baltic, ideas conceived in the highest vein of Churchillian romanticism, would surely have removed them.

The Army

There were plenty of problems too for the Secretary of State for War. Hore-Belisha was succeeded in December 1939 by Oliver Stanley. By this time a Field Army of thirty-two divisions was the order of the day, six Regular and twenty-six Territorial divisions. The size of the Army was perhaps determined by those lost divisions of the Czech Army. There was some thought that this Field Army of thirty-two divisions was but a step towards a larger Army of fifty-five divisions but this concept was only in the shadows. Ten divisions were to be in France by February 1940 and twenty by September of the same year. The former promise was fulfilled, the latter was overtaken by events. There were of course great discussions with the French Government about strategy and tactics in the event of the German assault on land which was expected to proceed by way of the Dutch/Belgian northern plain in the general direction of Brussels. While Belgium was neutral the British Army was of course confined to the French side of the frontier but plans were made for a swift advance on the outbreak of war to the general line of the River Dyle in front of Brussels and roughly parallel to the Meuse-Albert canal.

The role of Bomber Command

Much thought was also given to deciding what should be the role of Bomber Command from 3 September 1939 onwards. Trenchard wanted an immediate offensive, an idea which had few if any friends. The British and French Governments believed that their interests lay in restricting attacks to purely military objectives. There were of course arguments about what would happen when the armies started to move but until then no attacks were to be allowed save on military targets defined in the narrowest sense. The results of these decisions are discussed in Chapter 19.

Air support for the Army

Another early problem to face the Air Ministry was the revision of its plans for air support for the Army. Before the war, plans had been drawn up for the British Expeditionary Force to be supported by an Air Component under its direct command. In September 1939 this force, which accompanied the British Expeditionary Force to France, consisted of some thirteen squadrons of Lysanders, Hurricanes and Blenheims under the command of Air Vice-Marshal Charles Blount. The British Expeditionary Force also relied in a way then undefined on the support of Bomber Command. As the Battles of No 2 Group Bomber Command were short on range, plans were made for these ten Battle squadrons to move to France on or before the outbreak of war. In fact they flew to their pre-selected bases in the Rheims area on the afternoon of 2 September 1939. The Royal Air Force were not slow to enjoy the attractions of the champagne country, but a back-loading exercise to parent bases in Britain was checked, harshly it might be thought, by His Majesty's Customs and Excise.

Soon the Army had seen the outcome of the Polish campaign and it is sad to relate that they drew all the wrong conclusions. Impressed by the triumphs of the Stukas they wanted specialised aircraft developed and produced quickly and in large numbers for Army support. Further, they wanted the Army to command, train and maintain their own direct support aircraft. Fortunately, the War Cabinet kept its head. Lord Chatfield, then Minister for the Co-ordination of Defence, proposed and it was accepted that the solution should be on Coastal Command lines. In December 1939, a new Royal Air Force command was created in France, called British Air Forces in France. This command, which remained an integral part of the Royal Air Force, included both the Air Component and the Advanced Air Striking Force. The Air Component remained under the operational control of the British Expeditionary Force and the Air Officer Commanding-in-Chief, British Air Forces in France, Air Marshal Barratt, was required to see that the Commander-in-Chief British Expeditionary Force had 'full assurances regarding air support'. This meant that in any particular situation the British Expeditionary Force could determine in consultation with Barratt how many squadrons of the Advanced Air Striking Force should be placed in support of the Army. Thus the more extreme ideas of the Army were rejected, an event little to the taste of their controversial Secretary of State, Hore-Belisha. However, Hore-Belisha seemed to get on little better with his generals and in December 1939 he was unceremoniously fired.

British Air Forces in France had many grave weaknesses. Of course it was too small and its aircraft, at any rate the Battles and the Lysanders, were inferior. Some of its weaknesses arose from failures of the French Government. Foremost among them must be mentioned inadequate air-fields, inferior or non-existent landlines and a banning of R/T, this last in case the Germans should learn the secrets of our cyphers.

How to grasp the initiative

One of the fantasies to which the Second World War gave rise was the suggestion that Britain over the period, say, 3 September 1939 to, say, 9 April 1940 was engaged in a 'phoney war', that is to say in proceedings which amounted to sham or fraud. The essence of the accusation was very roughly that Britain at this stage had no intention of stopping Germany by force of arms but intended simply to go through the motions after the defeat of Poland, and after, say, a few skirmishes in North-West Europe would relapse into a *mariage de convenance* with Germany. The rest of the saga includes the suggestion that Britain was rescued from her trance by the advent of Churchill as Prime Minister and a return to the spirit of Crécy and Agincourt. How much truth is there in these ideas? To answer this question it is surely right to look first to Chamberlain. In November 1939 in one of his regular letters in longhand to his sister Ida he said, 'I have a hunch that the war will be over by the Spring'.[1] What did he mean by this? A reasonable guess at his line of thought might be that he believed that the German state was a fragile structure both politically and economically and that, Poland past, and confronted with the Maginot Line and an iron ring of Allied economic sanctions Germany would realise that she could not win and the occasion would arise for a further political duel. Chamberlain rarely showed his full hand to the Cabinet and it is difficult to assess how many in authority shared his ideas. There were surely some who did. But there was another side to the coin which was at least as important. The fighting services and the civil services of Britain had taken the ultimatum to Germany of 2 September at 100 per cent of its value. The re-armament pro-gramme was pressed on to the limit, though there was inevitably some check to production arising from the introduction of a strict blackout and the advent of an exceptionally severe winter. The remarkable upward surge in aircraft production in the summer of 1940 was mainly the result of the fact that the overall capacity of the industry was in-creasing rapidly because of the vast investment in new production from mid-1938 onwards. (Two years is a fair estimate of the interval between an investment to produce an approved type of aircraft and the appearance of the first resulting production model.) And of course when Britain came under the direct threat of imminent invasion the aircraft industry work force put out a prodigious effort over a period of several months. Such an effort could not in the nature of things continue indefinitely.

On the operational front matters were more difficult. The war at sea began on the morning of 3 September 1939 and continued with un-diminished severity until the end. So far as the Army was concerned the decision to raise some thirty divisions had been taken as recently as the spring of 1939. So clearly at that time there was little scope for action here except to fulfil our promise to send a modest field force to France. And France was in no mood for adventures on the Western Front. In the air, matters were at least as difficult. Government policy was for restricted bombing of military targets, but the traumatic discovery was made that in order to survive Bomber Command had in effect to turn itself into a night bomber force with all the new and difficult problems that such a decision involved. In the background, of course, tremendous progress was being made. Improved brands of air-craft were coming along well, the problems of photographic recon-naissance had been solved in majestic style,* radar was surging ahead. The trouble was that most of these developments were secret and to the vast majority not in the know it was easy to decry the British war effort. Not for the first or the last time, appearance and reality were far apart. So the Government's policy—to which of course Churchill was a party—was bound to attract critics and naturally enough they were only too happy to seize any opportunities that presented themselves for pushing the war along. One such opportunity arose in March 1940 when Bomber Command attacked the German seaplane base at Hornum on the island of Sylt. This attack, the first by the Royal Air Force on a German land target, was welcomed with cheers in the House when it fitted neatly into a Chamberlain speech. Alas, the results seem to have been trifling. The other two ideas for seizing the initiative were both the brain children of Churchill. The first, called 'Royal Marine', was pure comedy. Stimulated by the concept of the German magnetic mine, which was dropped in numbers round our coasts from the outbreak of war onwards and which carried a charge of some hundreds of pounds of high explosive, Churchill embraced the idea of slipping some thousands of 'mini-mines' resembling large pineapples into the Rhine from the French bank above Karlsruhe.[2] Downstream it was hoped that these

* See Chapter 12, p. 168.

mines would deal death and destruction to German barges and bridges. The Royal Air Force were to back up the operation by sowing 'Royal Marine' mines in German canals and rivers. The French would have none of this, deeming it, of all things in wartime, provocative. When the operation was finally launched at the time of the main German offensive everyone was too busy to notice.

Norway

The other idea, which was for interrupting the flow of Swedish iron-ore, was a more serious affair and was in part responsible for the Scandinavian campaign. Swedish iron-ore, an important German import, is mined partly in South Sweden within easy reach of Stockholm and partly at Gallivare in the extreme north. There was nothing the Allies could do about the ore in the south, but the idea was developed that the German ore imports could be stopped in the winter by mining Norwegian territorial waters south of Narvik. This action would not be effective in the summer months when the ore travelled to Germany not down the Norwegian coast but down the Gulf of Bothnia from the Swedish port of Lulea. Churchill was keen on the idea and it gained a great impetus when Russia attacked Finland at the end of November 1939. The poor performance of the Russian forces at the beginning of this campaign gave the Allies a false impression of Russian military prowess. This was unfortunate in minor ways for the Allies, but its effect on Hitler might well have been to encourage him towards the supreme blunder of attacking Russia eighteen months later. The Allies saw in the Finnish campaign the chance to combine business with pleasure so to speak, an operation to bring succour to the gallant Finns and at the same time to get a grip on Narvik. Unfortunately, while all this was being considered, Finnish resistance collapsed and a peace treaty was signed in Moscow on 12 March. The British and French had then to decide whether to go it alone against Narvik. This, without undue alacrity, they decided to do and on 3 April 1940 the British Cabinet agreed that the Norwegian leads should be mined on the 8th and that small land forces should be sent to Narvik, Stavanger, Bergen and Trondheim to deny these bases to the enemy. The Norwegian Government was informed of this plan on 5 April. Even while they pondered their reply units of the German armed forces were moving against their country. In the small hours of 9 April German forces crossed the Danish frontier. Soon German warships and troops were descending upon Oslo, Kristiansand, Stavanger,

Bergen, Trondheim and Narvik. Airborne troops quickly backed them up and that was that. It did not help that on 5 April Chamberlain had informed an influential Conservative Party meeting that Hitler had 'missed the bus'.

And what, it may be asked, were the Royal Navy and the Royal Air Force doing about all this? Both had been on the alert for a possible German attack on Norway and a number of important sightings had been made by Coastal Command. The Home Fleet was at sea. A large part of the German Fleet was also at sea and on the face of it conditions might have seemed to indicate a general engagement on conditions not unfavourable to Britain. But it did not work out like that, for a number of reasons: the ability of German warships to hug the Norwegian coast, thick weather, general confusion, remoteness of British air bases, proximity of German controlled air bases. It does not fall within the scope of this brief history to describe the rest of the Norwegian campaign in detail. The Royal Navy fought as always superbly. Though losses were fairly even, the smaller German Navy lost much of its fighting strength, a matter of real significance in the light of coming events. The Royal Navy, by the way, turned a dangerous corner on their famous sweep in Narvik Fjord where the magnetic pistols of the many German torpedoes fired at British warships, including the *Warspite*, failed to operate. The Army failed to take Trondheim but might have held on to Narvik for a bit had events in France not necessitated a withdrawal. The Royal Air Force did its best under conditions of extreme difficulty, bombing German warships and airfields. Royal Air Force fighters of course had to be carried in carriers of the Royal Navy. They made a great contribution in the unsuccessful Trondheim campaign and their part at Narvik, culminating in the loss of the re-embarked Gladiators and Hurricanes in the ill-fated aircraft carrier *Glorious*, will be long remembered.

In some ways the thinking behind Allied plans for interfering with the flow of Swedish iron-ore to Germany belongs to the world of what Harris in Bomber Command was later to call 'panacea' targets, ie short-cuts to victory. Had the Allied plan succeeded, imports of Swedish iron-ore into Germany would have been affected only in the winter months and Germany would undoubtedly have made good the loss by increased imports from the deposits in South Sweden; or indeed by throwing the Allies out of Norway, which of course is what happened. On the other hand it can fairly be argued that at this stage there was little that Britain could do apart from peripheral strokes of this kind.

The end of Chamberlain

On 7 and 8 May 1940 the House of Commons debated the war situation. The House does not like bad news and when such news comes along its instinct is to look to the Prime Minister and his friends and say '*à la lanterne*'. There was in truth little ground for awarding a monopoly of praise or blame to any section of the House. Baldwin, who had taken the first real measures to re-arm Britain in 1936, was in disgrace at Bewdley. The Conservative Party had preferred a sound economy to sound defence. The Labour Party had fought re-armament tooth and nail and had then played a significant part in bringing an unprepared Britain to war. Churchill had the advantage of having been out of office and so removed from ministerial responsibility for ten years before 1939. On the other hand he had played a leading part in the unfortunate Scandinavian campaign. For the purposes of the debate Chamberlain was clearly in the hot seat. His difficulties were not eased by his reference, goaded on no doubt by raucous Labour taunts, to his 'friends' in the House. Despite a Government majority of eighty-one, the debate demonstrated that the Chamberlain administration had suffered a catastrophic loss of confidence. Fate, which had ordained that our belated descent on Norway should coincide with that of Hitler, now arranged that the British Government should be in a state of total disarray when the German armies invaded Holland and Belgium at first light on 10 May. How Hitler must have laughed.

Sinclair and the Ministry of Aircraft Production

Considering the momentous events proceeding over the Channel and the turmoil surrounding him in Britain, Churchill proceeded with the construction of the new Government with remarkable composure. Two of his appointments were of the greatest consequence to the Royal Air Force. On 11 May Sinclair, the Leader of the Liberal Party, was appointed Secretary of State for Air in succession to Hoare, who had held that office for just thirty-five days. The three Service Minister appointments at this stage were thus given, no doubt for policy reasons, an ecumenical style, the First Lord, A. V. Alexander being a Labour supporter and Eden, the Secretary of State for War, a Conservative. The appointment of Sinclair was a happy one from the Royal Air Force point of view. The creation of a Ministry of Aircraft Production and the consequent partition of the Air Ministry was a bold step at such a cataclysmic time but on balance it was surely a wise and timely one. The appointment of Beaverbrook as the first Minister of Aircraft Production had strong potentialities for good or evil, or both.

The Battle of France

So Hitler turned West to crush British and French resistance. Viewed from OKW it must have seemed a pretty good bet. Looking first at the position of the land forces, France could rely on the so-called Maginot Line, a string of forts and strong points stretching from the Swiss frontier in the south to the Luxembourg frontier in the north. What then? Belgium and Holland having proclaimed their trust in neutrality, Germany was faced by the frontier defences of those countries. When those defences were overcome the matter would pass to whatever defences the British and the French could improvise on the French border north of Luxembourg. In these circumstances it was assumed by all, Germans, French, British, that the German thrust on land would arrive north of the northern terminal of the Maginot Line. This assumption was as sound as a bell. Less than sound, but accepted none the less, was the belief on the part of the French that the German Army would avoid the Ardennes, a hilly and wooded area said to be unsuitable for tanks. They were fortified in this belief by secret documents captured from the occupants of a Luftwaffe aircraft which force-landed in Belgium in January 1940. The forces engaged were something like the following.[3] Germany fielded eighty-nine divisions, ten of them armoured and most of them battle-seasoned. In addition there was an OKH reserve of forty-five divisions. France had in the line some ninety-four divisions and Britain ten, five of them Territorials. There were also twenty-two Belgian divisions, eight Dutch divisions and one Polish division. The air situation was less propitious. The German Army could rely on the tactical support of much of the Luftwaffe, which at this time had a first line strength excluding transport aircraft of some 4,000. The Luftwaffe was of course highly experienced in army support from its operations in Spain and Poland. And of course the Luftwaffe was conceived almost from the start as a tactical force. The French Air Force was in a poor state, 1,000 or so first line aircraft, mostly '*ancien*', and with a poor infra-structure. The Royal Air Force in France, now organised in unitary form under Barratt, had a first line strength of something like 300 aircraft in some twenty-five squadrons, though many of the aircraft were of unsuitable types.

Viewing these opposing forces in the round and in the light of hindsight, the prospects for the Allies for a successful defence of the West could not appear promising. The German Army had the advantage of experience, equipment and to some extent surprise. This was true with even greater emphasis of the German Air Force. And Germany had the best anti-aircraft armament in Europe. But in fact the odds against the Allies were even greater than these facts suggest:

> Whether or not on account of the compromise of German invasion plans in January 1940 the main German thrust which was to have come through Belgium and Holland was moved to the Ardennes. No fewer than forty-four German divisions, seven of them armoured, were concentrated there.
> Dutch and Belgian resistance was undermined by novel paratroop tactics against important forts and river crossings.
> The Dutch were intimidated by the bombing at Rotterdam.
> The fighting quality of parts of the French Army and Air Force was much inferior to what had been supposed.

And so on 10 May the Battle of France began. It ended formally when France received the German Armistice terms in Foch's historic railway carriage on 21 June. On the surface it was a six week rather than a six day war. But in fact the battle was really over much earlier. Three weeks at the very outside were enough to finish for some four years Allied military aspirations on land on the continent of Europe.

Even in the most brief of Royal Air Force histories some account must be given of what happened to the armies of Britain and France, because the fortunes of the Royal Air Force though peripheral to these events were of considerable significance. The main thrust of the German armies came through the Ardennes in the Sedan area and reached the sea at Abbeville on the River Somme some ten days later. By this stroke the German Army divided the French Army into two parts which were never to rejoin. The British Expeditionary Force was cut off from its supply lines, which by and large relied on French ports to the west and south of Abbeville. By 13 May the Dutch Government had been transferred 'elsewhere', to London. By Sunday 19 May General Lord Gort, the Commander-in-Chief of the British Expeditionary Force was left about fifty miles from the sea with a continuous line of German armour to the south and a crumbling Franco-Belgian front to the north.

On this day, at around the time when the German panzers were approaching Abbeville, one of the most remarkable meetings in our history took place in the Upper War Room of the Admiralty* at 19.30 hours. The current military situation was discussed and at the end of the meeting Churchill dictated the following order which was taken down in long-hand by Group Captain William Elliot, a member of the War Cabinet Secretariat:

1. The Cabinet decided that the CIGS was to direct C-in-C BEF, to move southwards upon Amiens attacking all enemy forces encountered and to take station on left of French Army.
2. CIGS will inform General Billotte and the Belgian Command, making it clear to the Belgians that their best chance is to move south between the BEF and the coast.
3. The War Office will inform General Georges in this sense.

This order, which became known as Order A, was remarkable from many points of view. The British Expeditionary Force being under the command of France should scarcely have received an order direct from the British War Cabinet. Many present at the meeting realised that direct tactical interference from the British War Cabinet, out of touch as it necessarily was with battlefield intelligence and scarcely to be regarded as a competent military authority, could only at such a time be pure nonsense, as indeed it was. Nevertheless, not a dog barked. Even General Ironside, who according to the Official History favoured a move to the south-west, must have realised that a firm order to this effect could only be dangerous and inappropriate.

The order was conveyed to Gort by personal envoys headed by Ironside. They arrived at Gort's headquarters at 06.00 hours on the morning of Monday 20 May. As may be supposed the order was received with consternation as bearing little relationship to the current tactical position on land. Had it been acted upon, it would have involved abandoning the Belgian Army and making a flank march across the main lines of the German Army including several German armoured divisions.

The Sunday night Cabinet meeting on 19 May had been sparked off by a telephone call from Gort's Chief of Staff to the War Office, to the effect that in the prevailing situation it might be necessary for the British Expeditionary Force to move north towards the coast. The good effect of this telephone call was that it led to the setting up of 'Operation Dynamo', the evacuation from Dunkirk. The bad consequence was the

* Churchill was still living in Admiralty House.

effect of Order A on Gort and his staff. It was not in Gort's nature to dis-
obey a lawful order and he did what he could to comply with it. The
fact that he could not give effect to the order despite the plain indications
that anyway it would be foolish to do so worried him for months thereafter.
Fortunately, the tactical situation at the time allowed him to do very
little to comply with Order A. On the following day the German War
Diary of Army Group A contained the following entry:

> Now that we have reached the coast at Abbeville, the first stage of
> the Offensive has been achieved ... The possibility of an encircle-
> ment of the Allied Armies' northern group is beginning to take shape.

The melancholy fact must be faced that by 20 May at the latest the
French and British Armies were in a hopeless position. Had Order A
been followed to the letter the whole of the British Expeditionary
Force would undoubtedly have been captured. That it finally escaped
was a miracle in the creation of which the following were the principal
ingredients:

> Separating the British Expeditionary Force from German Army Group
> A was a line of canals stretching roughly south-east from Gravelines
> in the north, through St Omer, Aire and Béthune to La Bassée. Gort
> made early dispositions to defend this line, so leaving an escape route
> open roughly due north to Dunkirk.

On 24 May von Rundstedt halted his armour which had reached
Gravelines, some ten miles from Dunkirk. Roughly speaking the
German armour stopped just short of the Canal Line. It seems
probable, though the evidence is not convincing either way, that this
order which has been attributed to Hitler was in fact merely endorsed
by him.[5] The reason for this decision must have been composed of a
mixture of thoughts. The British Expeditionary Force was surely in the
bag, no hurry; the need for rest and straightening out a little; a desire
to conserve the German armour; apprehensions armour-wise about the
nature of terrain north and east of the Canal Line (rivers and
inundations). And Goering seems to have said that, anyway, the
Luftwaffe by itself could finish the BEF off. The standstill lasted
only two days but it was enough to enable the bridgehead to be
formed at Dunkirk.

On 26 May the Admiralty made the signal 'Dynamo is to
commence'. Owing to the skill and bravery of the British and French

Army units defending the bridgehead and the work of the Royal Navy and the Royal Air Force the position was held until 4 June, when 'Dynamo' ended and one third of a million troops had been evacuated. A miracle indeed!

The Royal Air Force in the Battle of France

Air support for the Allied armies in the Battle of France was afforded in four different forms:

British Air Forces in France under Barratt controlled the Air Component of the British Expeditionary Force and the Advanced Air Striking Force.

Fighter Command provided port and ship protection plus, later, the defence of the beaches.

Bomber Command operated partly tactically and partly strategically, eg through attacks on the Ruhr and on German marshalling yards.

Coastal Command, reinforced by squadrons of the Fleet Air Arm, afforded protection for ships, covering the beachhead at Dunkirk and other evacuation ports.

These various elements enjoyed a very uneven degree of success. All, notably British Air Forces in France, suffered dire casualties. British Air Forces in France was an improvised Force. After all, it was only in the spring of 1939 that Britain agreed to increase her land contribution above two divisions of troops. By 10 May 1940 the Air Component consisted of five squadrons of Lysanders, four squadrons of Blenheim bombers and six squadrons of Hurricanes. The Hurricanes were rapidly and hazardously reinforced from Britain, as we relate later. The Air Component's bases were close behind the British Expeditionary Force. When operations began on 10 May 1940 the Component's fighters gave a good account of themselves. Though all fought bravely, the Lysanders and Blenheims were ill-adapted by training or equipment to a war of movement. By 20 May, when the German Army reached Abbeville, plans for the withdrawal of the Component were well advanced. By 23 May it was back in Britain with a rear headquarters at Hawkinge in Kent. Here for practical purposes it was out of the battle, made impotent by a total lack of communications. It was anyway only a shadow of its former self, there being only sixty-five aircraft left out of an original Component of 261. The withdrawal of the Component was inevitable in tactical terms but the fact that the British Expeditionary

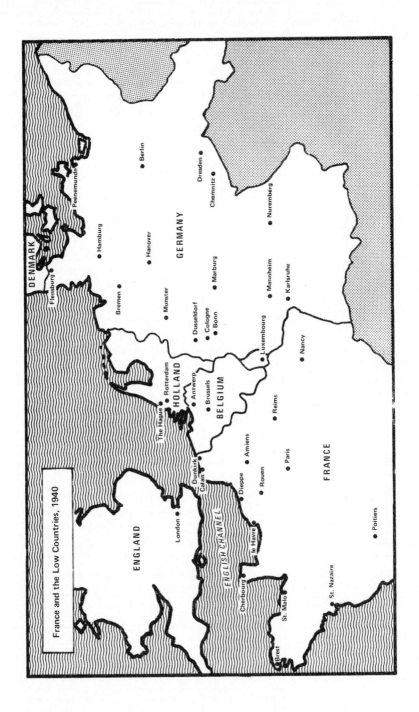

France and the Low Countries, 1940

Force was deprived of it during the critical days from 20 May onwards was a serious loss.

The Advanced Air Striking Force was initially more securely based, mainly to the east and south of Rheims, partly behind the Maginot Line. The main thrust of German Army Group A by-passed them to the north. Their equipment on 10 May consisted of ten squadrons of Battles and Blenheims and two squadrons of Hurricanes. The Hurricanes were reinforced from Britain later. In the early days of the campaign the Battles were employed, as indeed were the Blenheims of Bomber Command and the Air Component, in attacking enemy columns and strongpoints and enemy-controlled bridges. They flew by day at low level and they were met by strong and efficient flak and hordes of Luftwaffe fighters. Casualties were vast. Half the force was lost in the first two days. As an example of this the attack on the Sedan crossing of the Meuse on 14 May may be mentioned. Seventy-one Battles and Blenheims attacked; forty did not return. It is sad to record that in this light bomber attack, as in all the others at this time, very little was done to halt or hinder the German advance, which rolled on regardless. The Battles were driven by these casualties to operate mainly by night. Possessing little navigational equipment this reduced their performance to minuscule proportions. Soon Barratt's bases in the north were threatened and he had to move his squadrons to the Troyes area where spare airfields had most prudently been constructed during the winter. Unfortunately, the Advanced Air Striking Force had been planned as a static force and no transport had been provided. By some species of legerdemain 200 new lorries were wheeled out of the French and the move was accomplished. In the days which followed the Dunkirk evacuation, which ended on 4 June, the Advanced Air Striking Force of Battles and Hurricans, again reinforced from Britain, did everything in their power to support the French and the elements of the British Expeditionary Force left in France. They were driven steadily westward and on 15 June the bombers were flown out. The last act of the Advanced Air Striking Force was a spirited defence of the French ports through which the last of the British forces were being evacuated: La Rochelle, La Pallice, Nantes, St Nazaire, Brest, St Malo and Cherbourg. On 17 June France asked for an Armistice.

Fighters for France

The story of fighters for France is a poignant one. It has to be

considered from three distinct standpoints: the lessons of history as understood in 1940; the problems of the Government in 1940 concerned both
with keeping faith with the French and with the provision for what
was euphemistically called 'a certain eventuality', ie the Fall of France;
and hindsight.

Statesmen and others, Churchill included, who had borne the agonies
of the First World War could only regard the fall of France as the end of
both Britain and France. True there would be speeches. True we should
soldier on and hope that something spectacular would turn up, as
indeed it did in the end. But how could anyone know? And even if
Fighter Command and the Navy could hold off invasion how could
Britain in the long term survive the resources of a German state
stretching from the Russian frontier to the Channel? Hindsight, of course,
shows that the right course was not to squander our fighter resources
in France but to husband them for the coming battle and then to sit tight
and watch Germany add Russia to the ranks of her enemies. The
British Government for its part had to balance as best it could the
problems of the French present against those of the British and French
future. It was not an easy task.

On 10 May 1940 there were six Hurricane squadrons in France.
Four more were sent that day and two more on 13 May. A passionate
appeal for more fighter squadrons for France led to Dowding's appearance at the War Cabinet on 15 May when the decision was taken to
call a halt.[6] The reprieve lasted twenty-four hours. Next day, 16 May,
four more fighter squadrons were ordered to France and later that day,
in the course of which Churchill had met the French Prime Minister,
six more squadrons were committed on his advice. In the event, as the
result of an intervention from Newall stressing the inadequacy of French
airfields, it was decided to employ two pairs of three squadrons working as alternates, based on the United Kingdom but operating from
France. So by this time something like twenty-two squadrons were
committed to France and the balance of thirty-one or so available for
the defence of Britain was down to something like half what was
necessary. It seems probable that had the struggle continued more fighter
reinforcements would have been sent and that in the end Fighter Command would have been brought to its knees. That this did not happen
was the result not of a policy decision but of the implacable unrolling
of events in the field. By the week-end of 19 May it was plain to see
that the French and British Armies were in a position of defeat. Anyway, by this time the decision had been taken to return the Air

Component to Britain and it would surely have been a little strange at this time to start a counterflow to France. From time to time henceforward, the French Government continued to press for the move of further British fighters to France. In consequence, there were further discussions in the Cabinet after 15 May, notably on 3 June when the Chiefs of Staff opposed the transfer of further squadrons. At a meeting of the Supreme War Council at Briare on the Loire on 11 June, a few days from the end, General Weygand pressed that every remaining British Fighter Squadron be sent to France but in fact the issue had lost all reality. All but a handful of the British Expeditionary Force had left and the French Army and Air Force were in a state of manifest defeat. Where could our squadrons have gone? Where would they have found airfields? How were they to be supplied? There were no answers to these questions.

The beaches of Dunkirk

When the bridgehead was formed round Dunkirk it fell to Fighter Command in the shape of No 11 Group to defend it from the air. Most of the Luftwaffe was committed to crush the evacuation so it was a fight at odds. On Newall's orders a supreme effort was made. All but ten Fighter Command squadrons took part and there were over 2,700 fighter sorties. Of course the Royal Force could not provide complete protection. Mere numbers made this impossible. In the later stages the evacuation of troops had to be confined to the hours of darkness, thus enabling fighter protection to be maximised at the most dangerous times, which were dawn and dusk. Without Fighter Command the evacuation would have been a disaster. In fact, according to the Official History, the Luftwaffe only seriously interfered with the evacuation on two days out of nine.[7] So a third of a million men escaped. For this they have to thank first their own efforts nobly backed by elements of the French Army and not least the steadiness and wisdom of Gort. For the rest their escape was due to the magnificent work of the Royal Navy, the Royal Air Force and the civilian skippers who took part in the evacuation.

At the time, not all the Army and Navy saw it that way. The cry went up 'Where was the Air Force?' They expected 'Full air protection'. This they most certainly did not get. No Air Force in the world could have given it. It is impossible not to sympathise with the feelings of troops sitting on the beaches of Dunkirk and being rudely and heavily shot up. Admiral Sir Bertram Ramsay, who was in charge of naval operations at Dover, went so far as to include strictures about the Royal Air Force in his official report. He should have thought better of this for the Royal Air Force was doing its stuff magnificently, though not always within the sight of the troops.

Two further points are worth adding. Army feelings must have been aggravated by the undoubted fact that wherever they met the German Army on anything like level terms they more than held their own. They felt let down and sore. The second point was that neither the Royal Navy nor the Army were reliable judges of what Royal Air Force aircraft looked like. As a result, when the Royal Air Force appeared at reasonable distances they were invariably fired at enthusiastically by the Army or the Navy, or more usually by both. Safety first, no doubt but it seems that more friendly aircraft were around than some people supposed.

The jackals

One sordid page needs to be turned before this chapter can be concluded. It can be compressed into a timetable:

10 June	Italy declared war on the Allies.
14 June	Soviet ultimatum to Lithuania with similar treatment thereafter to Estonia and Latvia.
26 June	Soviet ultimatum to Roumania.
3 August	The Baltic States annexed by the Soviet Union.

The Battle of Britain

Introduction

The story of the battle has been told so often and so well that it is unnecessary to re-tell it in this brief summary of Royal Air Force history. Still, it was a great battle, a great victory and a great story and even in this compressed account a short report is in order.

When France collapsed and the British Army was evicted from that unhappy country, Hitler was in no hurry to take advantage of Britain's humiliation. His motives were no doubt complex but they were certainly not lacking in common sense. Let them look around, said the Reich Chancellor, and see on which side their bread is buttered. A generous peace—indeed a semi-alliance—with Germany, or the full treatment in the now classical Polish/Norwegian/French style. In terms of realism and common sense Britain at that point should perhaps have considered a deal, though for sure the deal would have been dishonoured in the end. But, strangely perhaps in political terms, there was never a chance of this. Britain had found an indomitable leader and under him was ready to fight it out. Hitler was prepared to wait, and of course the German forces had to regroup. So, between 18 June, when the last fighters returned from France, and 10 July, when the battle began, there was a brief pause. The Royal Air Force needed it badly enough, in all conscience. During the Battle of France they had lost nearly 1,000 aircraft including 450 or so Hurricanes and Spitfires. Much more serious, the Royal Air Force had also lost at this time over 400 pilots killed, missing or prisoners. Our problems were compounded by the fact that 400 German aircrew prisoners held in France were permitted to return to the Luftwaffe. So far as aircraft were concerned this was the lowest point in the fortunes of Fighter Command. Hurricanes and Spitfires from the factories rolled out steadily throughout the Battle of Britain at the rate of 100 or so per week. Throughout the four months June to

September 1940 some 1,700 Hurricanes and Spitfires were turned out at a rate greatly exceeding German fighter production—not bad, it might be thought, for an aircraft production organisation tainted, according to Churchill in one of his less felicitous minutes to his Secretary of State for Air, with 'muddle and scandal'.[1] In June 1940, 60 per cent or so of the fighters produced were Hurricanes but the proportion of Spitfires grew as the manufacturing capacity installed under Swinton's leadership became effective. The number of fighters available for operations in Fighter Command rose steadily throughout June, July, August and September. Of course, Fighter Command was too small; not surprising surely after years of financial stringency and the collapse of France but, given this qualification, aircraft were not the most severe problem. This arose partly from a shortage of pilots and partly from the vulnerability of fighter and radar stations to air attack.

Before leaving the question of aircraft production during the battle, it is appropriate to refer to the part played by Lord Beaverbrook in the aircraft production story. Beaverbrook became Minister of Aircraft Production on 14 May 1940. His Department consisted of the aircraft production elements of the Air Ministry located in London, Harrogate and elsewhere which overnight joined his kingdom. The creation of his Department was due to Churchill and it was a development which should have happened earlier. Sophisticated munitions of war cannot be conjured up in days, weeks, months or even in years. It is a slow, complicated and difficult business. Fighters available in the battle were there because of the groundwork done by the Air Ministry over the previous three years or more. Beaverbrook's part must not be over-stated or understated. Had the groundwork not been done Beaverbrook's efforts would have been without avail. Fortunately, the groundwork had been done. Beaverbrook, in his own phrase, provided 'a stimulus'. The presence of a man possessed of such drive with direct access to Churchill at an hour of desperate danger was of incalculable value. Fighters poured out, not because of him, but 'stimulated' by him. Of course a price had to be paid. For example there was the decision, taken within days of the formation of the Ministry of Aircraft Production, to concentrate production on five types of aircraft only: Hurricane, Spitfire, Wellington, Whitley, Blenheim. Fortunately it was abandoned within fourteen days.[2] Spares were used up, corners were cut. All this could be sorted out later. In the long run, of course, Beaverbrook's effect on aircraft production would have been disastrous. He was all for the problems of the hour and for a few months this was the right policy. But if continued, as it would have been under Beaverbrook's regime, it would have stultified the production of new designs of aircraft and denied to Britain the new types which were in the end the agents of victory. We should in fact have fallen into the same blunders that Goering and his staff brought about. But in the long run Beaverbrook was not there. But, for his contribution in the tense and crucial days of the battle, he deserves Britain's gratitude. For a time, short but crucial, he was the right man in the right job.

The odds

How greatly outnumbered was the Royal Air Force in the battle? This is a complex question to which no clear answer can be given. The British defence during the battle depended on an operational force of 600–700 Hurricanes and Spitfires, maintained from day to day throughout the battle fairly comfortably as to aircraft and far from comfortably as to pilots. The German attack was in the hands of *Luftflotten* 2, 3 and 5, giving perhaps an operational strength of 1,000 fighters and say 1,250 bombers. In the air, the German bombers, He 111s, Do 17s, Ju 87s, Ju 88s could not live with the Royal Air Force fighters. All the same they were pretty effective in beating up British fighter and radar bases. At this time German fighters in the battle were mainly Me 109s and Me 110s. In May 1940 an Me 109 was captured and two months later an Me 110. Comparative trials became possible. They showed that the 109 and the Spitfire were pretty evenly matched, the Me 109 having the advantage of climb and the Spitfire that of manoeuvrability. The Hurricane was of course inferior to both in performance but it was a splendid sturdy aircraft and a fine gun platform. Numerically it was of course the major performer in the battle. The Me 110, the German twin-engine fighter, was not in the same class as the others. It is reasonable to say that on balance the quality of British and German fighters was evenly matched. It is also perhaps reasonable to say that the Battle of Britain was really about fighters. If so, on this analysis, we can disregard the German bombers and say that the German advantage in fighters was something like two to one, or perhaps a bit more if account it taken of the fact that the Luftwaffe was better able to concentrate in attack than Fighter Command could concentrate in defence. But the German fighters were attacking a highly sophisticated defence system with fighters being vectored on to German aircraft, a system of which Germany at the outset of the battle had little or no idea. It is impossible to say what weight should be given to all these factors. It is perhaps enough to say that Goering, an amateur in such matters, thought that he was on a knock-out in four rounds. In fact, taking one thing with another, the odds could have been about even.

The miscalculation

When Hitler found his offers to treat with Britain were rejected he invited the German armed forces to apply to Britain the techniques which they had perfected in other campaigns. As Germany had no hope of securing command of the seas through the use of the German Navy this task was entrusted to the Luftwaffe. They were first to destroy the Royal Air Force. This done they would control the Channel and the German forces could roll forward into Britain, if indeed they were not invited in. Goering, the Luftwaffe supremo, had no doubt as to their ability to carry out this task. He thought it could be achieved in a matter of days or weeks. In this view he was supported by the German Air Intelligence. The views of the German pilots who had fought the Hurricanes and Spitfires at Dunkirk would surely have been more cautious. What were the reasons for this gigantic miscalculation? It was certainly not a miscalculation about the strength of Fighter Command. Here the Germans, though they slightly over-estimated, were pretty accurate. The main factor was perhaps a heavy sense of victory, of un-challenged and speedy mastery in other battles. It must be a push-over they thought. There was a delusion about the Me 109. No German dared deny that it was the best fighter in the world, and indeed it was an excellent fighter, though the Spitfire, point for point, was just as good. Then there was the Me 110 on which the Germans relied to escort their bombers. This was a delusion too. The Me 109s found themselves defending the 110s as well as their bombers. Another factor was that the German fighters in battle were at their extreme limit of range. Some of their losses were caused by running out of fuel on the way home. Finally, the German bombers themselves were designed on the theory that they would never have to face sophisticated fighter defence. In con-sequence they had poor defensive armament. Their dive bomber, the dreaded Stuka, proved such a liability that it had to be withdrawn from the front line in the course of the battle. It is much to the credit of the British Air Staff that they resisted stoutly and successfully heavy pressure to make a large investment in dive bombers.

The other miscalculation made by Goering and others about Fighter

Command was in regard to the highly successful way in which the British integrated radar information with fighter control and tactics. This technique added an invaluable bonus to the defences. The Germans did not discover what was going on until the battle was half over.

The battle

It took something like three months to persuade Goering that this time he was not on a push-over. It should have taken less time but Goering's predictions of the hour of victory turned out to be flexible. Derek Wood and Derek Dempster in their excellent and authoritative account of the battle[3] discuss it in five phases:

Phase 1: the concentration on shipping in the Channel, July 7 to August 7

Phases 2 and 3: August 8 to September 6, basically an attempt to destroy Fighter Command on the ground and in the air

Phase 4: September 7 to September 30, the attempt to crush Britain's will to resist by overwhelming assaults on the capital and other major cities

Phase 5: from October 1 onwards, the switch to a night assault on London and other cities, the Blitz in fact, plus roaming German fighter-bombers.

In Phase 1 the idea was clearly that Fighter Command should be brought to battle over the sea so that pilots shot down would be pilots in the sea. Also, of course, an assault on Britain's life-line. Phases 2 and 3 were really the crux of the matter. The maximum strength of the Luftwaffe was hurled against Fighter Command. 'Eagle Day' came in mid-August and there was a second all-out assault a few days later. These phases of the battle drove Fighter Command to the edge of the precipice by reason of loss of pilots, loss of ground facilities and general exhaustion. Miraculously, Goering shifted to Phase 4 on September 7, a Saturday. On a glorious autumn afternoon 300 German bombers and 600 German fighters flew up the Thames Estuary. The Air Staff and others on the roof of the Air Ministry in Whitehall saw the attack coming in, withdrawing at a discreet moment to more prudent quarters. Fighter Command acquitted itself, as always, magnificently. Forty-one German aircraft were destroyed. 300 tons of bombs fell on the East End of London with its oil and paint storage, docks and terraced houses.

London is in flames said Goering, and indeed it was. As the sun set, the flames in the East End could be seen from Central London. It would surely be easy for the Luftwaffe to find London in the dark by the aid of such a beacon, and so it proved. The bombing continued till dawn. To add to the excitement the code word 'Cromwell', meaning 'invasion imminent', was issued at 17.00 that night.

The following night, a Sunday, the fires could still be seen from Central London and the bombers returned. Next day, London, though still conspicuously on fire in parts, was still in business. It must have been a puzzling affair for Goering. Anyway, Operation 'Sealion' (the German invasion code-word) was postponed once, twice. On 15 September 1940, a day now celebrated as 'Battle of Britain Day', Goering tried again. Once again, as on September 7 and on other memorable political occasions, it was a weekend affair. Did Goering really think that Fighter Command was enjoying the traditional English weekend? Anyway, 1,000 sorties were flown against London. The resultant encounter was tense, brave and complex. The outcome can be expressed simply. As the evening of 15 September fell, Britain was told that 185 German aircraft had been lost and a great victory won. It was in truth, a great victory. In fact, only fifty-six German aircraft had been lost. The victory contained two elements. British public opinion thought the Luftwaffe had been defeated and the Luftwaffe had indeed been defeated. So, after various German perpendings, Phase 5, the Blitz, began, an epilogue to the failure of the Luftwaffe to crush the Royal Air Force. Deeper down it was evidence of Britain's ability, suitably aroused, to fight and fight again. It was a great and glorious victory. The German High Command, amid some recriminations, accepted that the attempt to roll Britain out flat from the air had failed. Events such as these which convince one side that it has succeeded and the other that it has failed should not be underrated.

Dowding

So much for the battle. Something must now be said about Hugh Dowding who commanded Fighter Command in those momentous days. By according his *imprimatur* to Robert Wright's book[4] Dowding gave his approval to the propositions that he would have made a natural choice as Chief of the Air Staff in 1937, and that Ellington had led him to expect this appointment; that he won a decisive battle for Britain at a critical hour; that he did so notwithstanding stupid opposition from the Air Ministry; that he was shabbily treated by that Department by being removed from Fighter Command prematurely and without dignified forms. It is also suggested that in the opinion of many officers, particularly in Fighter Command, an error of judgement was made by failing to promote Dowding after the Battle to the rank of Marshal of the Royal Air Force. These views must be put into context. 'Old men forget; yet all shall be forgot but he'll remember with advantages what deeds he did that day!' Dowding was in his eighties when Wright's most interesting book was published. Dowding's claim on history as the victor of one of the decisive battles of Western civilisation is secure. The points recited here are intended simply to form an agenda for a discussion of his career. Dowding possessed great stability of character; he was endowed with *gravitas*; he was the complete professional; he built Fighter Command from its modest beginnings in 1936 and he commanded it successfully in one of the decisive battles of history. But, save in one remarkable quality to which reference is made later, Dowding was by no means exceptional as a Royal Air Force war leader. Some, at least, would place higher the claims of Portal, Harris and Tedder. Nevertheless, he was a man of destiny and in this destiny he proved himself. Dowding may well have supposed that he was the natural heir of Ellington when Ellington retired as Chief of the Air Staff in the summer of 1937, but an apostolic succession in the military sense has never, and fortunately never, been part of our constitutional inheritance. Heads of the armed services are chosen not by their military peers but by civilian Ministers, no doubt after proper consultation with professional opinion. No sensible man takes a major decision without reviewing the facts and the facts certainly extend to contemporary professional opinion. Ellington's successor was chosen by Swinton, the greatest as well as the shrewdest of all the political heads of the Royal Air Force. Ellington could well have suggested Dowding. Had he done so it would certainly have been in character. Ellington was a traditionalist and Dowding was next in seniority. Dowding was highly competent. That was that. So much is surmise; what is not surmise is that the names mainly considered by Swinton as Ellington's successor were those of Air Marshal Sir Christopher Courtney and Newall. Swinton would gladly have appointed Courtney, whose brilliant intellect and attractive personality made a strong appeal, except perhaps to the bluest of true-blue airmen. Swinton's final choice fell on Newall. Taking all the circumstances into account it was almost certainly the right choice. Dowding led Fighter Command to one of the most significant victories in Britain's long and remarkable history. This was immensely creditable to

Dowding in a double sense in that he first created the Command and later led it to victory in action. The suggestion that the obstacles he faced included a grossly inept Air Ministry is of course pure moonshine. Commanders-in-Chief in wartime always regard their claims to available resources as paramount and opposition to such claims acts of stupidity if not of disloyalty. One of the sources of difficulty was Dowding's deep resentment at the fact that his appointment as Commander-in-Chief was subjected to a series of short-term extensions which, looked at in the round, seemed grudging and ungenerous. The Air Ministry was only partly to blame for this; the plan had been that Courtney was to succeed Dowding in the summer of 1939 but this had been frustrated later by the inevitable complications of the war emergency.

On the policy plane, Dowding's greatest complaint about the Air Ministry was that it frittered away the slight and precious resources of Fighter Command in the interests first of the British Army, and later in dark and desperate days of the Battle of France. Of course Dowding had a case. In the years between the wars the Royal Air Force had completely misjudged the air support requirements of the Army and for that matter of trade protection at sea. So a heavy toll was exacted from Fighter Command. During the crisis of the Battle of France, Dowding faced a steady attrition of his squadrons in the interests of land and sea battles. So far as France was concerned he was right to resist this, partly because as we now know it was a lost cause, but also because once Fighter Command squadrons were removed from a highly sophisticated technological environment in Britain to France, where their supporting infra-structure was for practical purposes nil, their effective value was diminished probably to one-tenth. But the matter had to be settled on a wider canvas than this. On all reasonable military argument if France left the war, or worse still sided with Germany which was the likely outcome, Britain was finished. 'Very well: alone' was *Punch*'s cartoon. Magnificent no doubt, but in any practical sense not war. In the light of reason if France in the dark days of 1940 made peace or worse, Britain was finished. These thoughts were not lost on Churchill who had sustained the dreadful days of 1918 when the German armies so nearly reached the Channel. They were not lost on the Air Ministry whose sense of history was fairly alert. Had France not collapsed most of Fighter Command would in the end have been sacrificed, whatever Dowding had to say.

In some ways Dowding ran his Command badly. Operational control was rightly and necessarily delegated to Group Commanders. Facing the main German thrust, the Air Officer Commanding No 11 Group, Air Vice-Marshal Keith Park. On Park's left flank No 12 Group under the Air Officer Commanding Sir Trafford Leigh-Mallory. On Park's right flank Air Vice-Marshal Sir Quintin Brand. During the battle tension developed between 11 Group and 12 Group. This was partly a dispute about tactics, No 11 Group who were closest to the sources of attack, having to scramble what they could as quickly as they could. No 12 Group with more North Sea and more time at their disposal, believed in large formations which naturally enough take more time to marshal. These tensions were bad enough but there was worse to follow. 11 Group claimed that 12 Group failed to protect 11 Group's bases and, further, that they poached. 12 Group felt that 11 Group was hogging the battle, and so on. Either side could have been right. It is a serious criticism that Dowding failed to settle this squabble. Dowding states that he did not know. Commanders-in-Chief have to know. That is what it is all about. Is it conceivable that such a situation would have been tolerated in Bomber Command in the days of Bomber Harris?

In the autumn of 1940, after the battle was over, Dowding was told by the Secretary of State for Air that he was wanted for duties in the United States of America and that he was to be succeeded as Commander-in-Chief Fighter Command by Air Chief Marshal Sholto Douglas. These events have given rise to some controversy.* The facts seem reasonably straightforward. At this stage, despite his great achievements, Dowding was by no means universally admired in the Royal Air Force. Rightly or wrongly his tactics have been criticised by some. He had fallen out very sharply with that most senior figure John Salmond. He was fifty-eight years of age and he had borne the burdens of Fighter Command for four years. In truth, it was time for a change. Around this time, in real and not in contrived circumstances, the need had arisen for a most senior Royal Air Force officer to go to the United States to press upon them the realities of the air war in Europe. Three names were in question: Portal, by this time Chief of the Air Staff; Freeman, then the senior Royal Air Force officer in the Ministry of Aircraft Production; and Dowding. The first two names proving impracticable, Sinclair decided that the post should be filled by Dowding. No doubt other considerations were weighed as well. Dowding temporised, asked to see Churchill. Sinclair, the soul of courtesy, assented to this, though many Ministers would have been less receptive. Churchill ruled that Dowding

*See Appendix I.

should go to the United States, and so it came about. It was in truth a most unhappy appointment. Dowding in the United States, voicing policies gravely at variance with official doctrine, was a serious embarrassment to the Air Ministry. Returning to Britain in the summer of 1941 he was told that he was to retire in the autumn of 1941 and in the meantime he was to write his Despatch. Later he undertook from the autumn of 1941 onwards work connected with manpower management. This too proved an unhappy assignment, and so in June 1942 Dowding's services ended.

This was a sad end to a great career. Dowding had commanded Fighter Command during one of the great battles of history. In the light of hindsight it is clear enough that Dowding should have been given a peerage and made a Marshal. But it is also fair to say that it didn't look like that at the time. The days were dark, Britain's survival looked problematical. At the time, Dowding's promotion would have seemed both irrelevant and, from the Air Ministry point of view, unconstitutional, no Royal Air Force officer up to this time having achieved the highest rank without having held the office of Chief of the Air Staff. Still, the Air Ministry managed all this with some lack of imagination. Clearly they realised this in 1943 when Dowding was given a peerage, the first Royal Air Force ennoblement since Trenchard. But, as it says in the Book of Proverbs, 'Hope deferred maketh the heart sick'.

We have left to last an account of Dowding's greatest service. He was always a modest man. For all his professional skills, his ability to achieve a political judgement was inconspicuous. In fact, despite everything, it fell to him to arrive at such a judgement. In the dark days of 1940 he decided that France would collapse, that our destiny depended on the survival of Fighter Command, and that if Fighter Command survived, Britain would survive. Many arguments could have been adduced against such a view. All the same, it was Dowding's view. Around the time of the fall of France he walked into the office of the Head of the Air Staff Secretariat in Whitehall and said 'Now we cannot lose'. His face was shining. His words and demeanour would have become a major prophet. Marshal of the Royal Air Force or not, that for practical purposes was what he was at that moment.[5]

Other comments

Most of the story of the battle has now been covered in this brief account, but one or two footnotes can usefully be added. The first concerns the Post Office. This organisation is not generally regarded as particularly warlike. During the Second World War and in the years leading up to it the Post Office was superb. Of course high-class communications were vital to the armed forces, and to no one more than Fighter Command. The Post Office was responsible for the vital links between Command, Group and Station headquarters, the Observer Corps and the radar organisation. They were thus in a crucial role. They brought to this task two qualities, among others. They were a vast and powerful organisation and they were immensely competent. Thousands of miles of circuits could be conjured up overnight as if by magic when the need arose. Those who experienced the rigours of the French telephone system as applied to the conduct of warlike operations will recognise how much the competence and skill of the Post Office meant to Fighter Command. During the crisis of the battle, when station operations rooms were being knocked down by German bombs, the Post Office were around to much purpose, fixing up new control points in local grocers' shops or wherever. It was a splendid page in their history. This comment on our first nationalised industry is not made as often as it should be, so it seems right that it should find its place here.

The second footnote concerns the Poles and the Czechs. Bomber Command was always a Commonwealth affair abounding with Canadians, Australians and New Zealanders.* Fighter Command enjoyed the contributions not only of Canadians but also of Poles and Czechs; Poles and Czechs hunted out of Europe and finding their ways, various, back to Britain and mounted on Hurricanes and Spitfires to fight back. How they fought! The bravest of the brave! The trouble was that after the defeat of the Luftwaffe they ran out of enemies. After the war, the political story became sad. Many who fought so superbly for Britain and for the cause had no country to go back to. Still, as the lightning illuminates this page of history the deeds of the Poles and Czechs stand out. Their connection with the history of the Royal Air Force was brief but it was remarkable. For many of us it will not be forgotten.

Next there was General Sir Frederick Pile. Anti-Aircraft Command of the Army was under the operational control of Fighter Command, the situation being a bit like the Admiralty/Coastal Command situation. At Command, Group and Station headquarters there was a soldier longing to loose off his guns, partly no doubt to destroy the enemy but partly too to bring comfort and solace to half frozen anti-aircraft units dotted around the countryside. It was not an easy

* In January 1945, 40 per cent of bomber pilots were from the Dominions.

relationship but it was one which was handled with total success. Much of the credit for this belongs to Pile, who rapidly established a *rapport* with Dowding which lasted. His greatest bonus came when, with the addition of centimetric gun-laying radar and proximity fuses and with units moved by a bold stroke by the Commander-in-Chief Fighter Command right out towards the coastal landfalls of the V1s, the Command had a great bonanza. The Royal Air Force will long remember with respect and affection its happy and fruitful partnership with Anti-Aircraft Command.

The end of the story

And now we come to the end of the story. It is not a difficult one to tell in outline. It can indeed be told in one fairly short sentence. After the fall of France Germany resolved to flatten the Royal Air Force as a precondition to invasion; in the resultant conflict they failed by what has been most aptly called a 'narrow margin'. Still, they failed and one of the great battles in history had been won. Sometimes it is suggested that had the Royal Air Force been defeated the Royal Navy would still have kept the enemy at bay. Had this situation arisen no one need doubt that the Royal Navy would have done all and indeed much more than men can do. Still, the situation did not arise. The Luftwaffe were defeated by the Royal Air Force. That was that.

Nevertheless, a sad appendix has still to be written. In the late Fifties, when some of Central London was being rebuilt, a suggestion was made informally by the Air Ministry to the Greater London Council that some square, road, whatever, should be given the title 'Battle of Britain' to commemorate the victory. No doubt some statue or inscription would have been involved. Details had not at this stage been considered. The Greater London Council having made encouraging noises, the proposal was put to Ministers where it was smartly turned down. That this was a wrong and foolish decision can scarcely be denied. The reasons for it are rather obscure. It could have been a failure of historic sense. It could have been a desire to forget the Second World War and everything connected with it. But a small uncomfortable voice suggests from time to time that it was something different, namely that even after forty years of remarkable service and a great historic victory the Royal Air Force still had not been quite accepted.

12

Coastal Command 1939–1945

Introduction

An earlier chapter of this book carries the history of Coastal Command up to the outbreak of the Second World War. This chapter attempts a brief summary of its fortunes up to May 1945. It is not an easy story to write because the work of Coastal Command interlocked at every point with that of the Royal Navy. It was also related in quite complex ways with the work of other Commands of the Royal Air Force. Because of these factors the great achievements of the Command have been rather overshadowed.

The U-boat war

There was never anything phoney about the war at sea. Before the war began German U-boats were at sea and German warships had been passed into the Atlantic. The liner *Athenia* was sunk on the first day of the war and by the end of September 1939 150,000 tons of Allied shipping had been lost. German ships and aircraft laid magnetic mines in the approaches to British ports and naval bases. The fight was on from the very start.

Hitler was an infantryman. Nothing against this, of course, provided the naval and air arms are not neglected. Where the German Navy was concerned Hitler's eye was on U-boats. He had no great use for big warships and when times were bad for Germany he would suggest from time to time that they should be de-commissioned. Germany had no aircraft carriers. But he was never in doubt about the importance of the U-boat, and when his other strategic ideas fell into disarray he hoped that the U-boat would help to win the war for him. In these ideas he was on to a pretty good thing. Churchill tells us that the Battle of the Atlantic caused him as many sleepless nights as anything. A glance at the relevant figures will show why.

Allied merchant ship losses[1]

(*Tons* × *1,000*)

	U-boat	Other	Total
1939	421	334	755
1940	2,188	1,804	3,992
1941	2,172	2,157	4,329
1942	6,266	1,525	7,791
1943	2,587	633	3,220
1944	773	273	1,046
1945	282	157	439

With the Allies losing tonnage at the rate of 600,000 plus per month by 1942 they were clearly in deep trouble. To get a bird's-eye picture of what happened let us now look at the figures for U-boat sinkings:

German U-boat casualties caused by Allied forces under British operational control

	1939	1940	1941	1942	1943	1944	1945	Total
Ships	6	10½	24	27½	48	57	34½	207½
Shore-based aircraft	–	½	3	25½	84	51	34	198
Ship-borne aircraft	–	1	–	1½	1	10½	1	15
Ships and shore-based aircraft	–	2	1	3½	7	9	1½	24
Ships and ship-borne aircraft	–	–	1	–	2	5	–	8
Submarines	1	2	1	2	5	6	2	19
Bombing raids	–	–	–	–	–	8½	12½	21

(continued over)

	1939	1940	1941	1942	1943	1944	1945	Total
Mines laid by shore-based aircraft	–	–	–	–	1	9	6	16
Mines laid by ships	2	2	–	3	$1\frac{1}{2}$	$2\frac{1}{2}$	$5\frac{1}{2}$	$16\frac{1}{2}$
Other causes	–	4	5	$4\frac{1}{2}$	$16\frac{1}{2}$	$39\frac{1}{2}$	$12\frac{1}{2}$	82
TOTAL	9	22	35	85	237	240	153	607

The following comments suggest themselves:

(1) The foregoing table refers to commissioned U-boats. The figures take no account of the losses by bombing of U-boats not yet commissioned or in course of manufacture, in particular of Speer's planned fleet of prefabricated U-boats. These latter were fabricated in the heart of Germany in sections which, being too large for the railways, had to be sent to the shipyards by canal. Bomber Command breached the Dortmund-Ems and Mittelland canals and left the barges carrying the sections stranded.

(2) Between 1942 and 1943 the figure of tonnage lost fell by nearly 60 per cent and U-boat losses nearly trebled.

(3) Leaving aside 'other causes', the number of U-boat sinkings by ships alone and shore-based aircraft alone are pretty close, 207 and 198 respectively. The number of sinkings for which shore-based aircraft were responsible or in which they co-operated is roughly half the total sinkings.

(4) The great year for shore-based aircraft was 1943. By the end of that year a great victory had been won over the U-boats. It was of course a victory in which the honours were shared between the Royal Navy and the Royal Air Force. Both services acquitted themselves magnificently. Still, this being the story of the Royal Air Force we

shall concentrate on their part, hard as it is to disentangle from the rest.

It is noteworthy that the year 1943, which effectively marked the defeat of the U-boat threat, began inauspiciously. Early in March of that year the U-boats changed their cyphers, thus depriving the Admiralty of a vital intelligence source. Nearly 630,000 tons of shipping were lost in the month and the outlook was grim indeed. Yet by May 1943 the scene had been transformed; sinkings were down, many U-boats had been sunk and by 22 May Doenitz had admitted defeat and withdrawn his U-boats from the northern sector of the Atlantic. Many factors contributed to this: the fruits of the Casablanca meeting in January 1943 which gave first priority to the defeat of the U-boat; more aircraft, especially very long-range aircraft operating in the Greenland Gap; better radar; better tactics, the immense steadiness of the Royal Navy and the Royal Air Force at a difficult time; and last but not least the advent of Air Marshal Slessor at Coastal Command Headquarters.

Aircraft
Between 1918 and 1939 the Royal Air Force forgot how to support the Army, and the Army no doubt was to blame as well. Over the same period the Royal Navy, the Royal Air Force and for that matter the United States Navy forgot how to protect their shipping. The lesson, which had been learned dearly enough in the First World War, was convoy plus aircraft/ship support, with the emphasis perhaps on aircraft. But by 1939 the eyes of the British Admiralty were on the surface raider, the commerce destroyer, the pocket battleship *et al.* Convoy was perhaps deemed a bit defensive and Asdic could look after the U-boats. So there was no great pressure on the Royal Air Force to cope with the U-boat, and when war began Coastal Command was poorly equipped for the purpose. Of course, policy *vis à vis* the U-boat was only one reason. There were plenty of others: shortage of money and resources, preoccupation with the threat of the 'knock-out blow', air defence, and priorities for the strategic air offensive which could provide the answer to all ills. And perhaps, on the Royal Air Force side at least, scars of Admiralty/Air Ministry battles.

So Coastal Command started the war with a bang on 3 September 1939 knowing very little about beating off and sinking U-boats and with a very modest complement of aircraft, weapons and general know-how.

Fortunately there were many bold, brave and intelligent people around, most importantly aircrew. People matter most. So far as aircraft were concerned the trouble was that there were too few of them and for the most part their range was inadequate. When France collapsed, the whole of the Atlantic coast from the North Cape to Bordeaux became available to the U-boats. Britain was denied even the use of the Southern Irish ports conceded to her in the Lloyd George Settlement but surrendered, wrongly it can be argued, in Chamberlain's deal with the Irish Republic in April 1938. The heart of the bravest might surely have quailed. Fortunately, most fortunately, Germany thought the war was over. Her policy was to finish off Russia then deal with Britain. But during this time, Blitz or not, British aircraft production was greatly exceeding that of Germany. So Coastal Command proceeded modestly to increase its strength. Hudsons, bought on the authority of Swinton from the United States in 1938, to the immense disgust of the British aircraft industry, replaced Ansons, and other minor reinforcements arrived. But it was not enough. By 1942 Doenitz had moved his U-boat fleet out to mid-Atlantic. Here they were outside the range of shore-based aircraft and could have a field-day. So it happened, as the statistics quoted earlier in this chapter demonstrate sadly but eloquently. In the Greenland Gap, the area which could not be reached by shore-based aircraft from Britain, Canada, the United States or Iceland, there was a great slaughter. So the call came for the transfer of long-range aircraft, mostly converted bombers, to Coastal Command. This call gave rise to some awkward problems of priorities. Coastal Command was regularly depleted during the war in the interests of the Mediterranean theatre and Bomber Command was regularly raided in the interests of Coastal Command. Two vital policies were in conflict, the building up of the strategic air offensive and the war against the U-boat. The answer was of course a compromise, but the fact that such immensely difficult and painful problems could be solved at all reflected the greatest credit on those concerned and indeed on the defence organisation in which they worked.

Of course the Army were pressing for diversions too. In March 1942 the Admiralty were pressing for 2,000 first line aircraft for naval air co-operation and the Army similarly for 4,000 first line aircraft. The sum of these proposals approximating as it did to the foreseeable future strength of the Royal Air Force, the magnitude of the problem of adjustment can be seen as not an easy one. Still, the problem was overcome. Slowly the strength of the Command especially in Long-Range aircraft developed. With the establishment of an Area Combined Head-quarters in Newfoundland with Very Long-Range (VLR) aircraft operated by the United States Army Air Force and the Royal Air Force, the Greenland Gap was closed. One of the troubles was that the Liberator, the critical aircraft for this work, was also required for the United States Naval build-up in the Pacific. So again awkward questions of priorities arose.

The U-boat fleet

The numbers of U-boats operational in the German Navy tell an eloquent story.

U-boats operational

	1939	1940	1941	1942	1943	1944	1945
January		33	23	89	214	170	155
February		34	22	101	221	167	156
March		31	30	111	231	164	156
April		31	30	119	237	161	150
May		23	40	128	239	157	126
June		26	47	130	218	181	
July		29	60	140	209	180	
August		28	60	152	178	151	
September	42	31	74	169	167	146	
October	49	26	75	192	177	139	
November	38	25	81	205	163	148	
December	38	22	86	203	163	152	

The decline in operational U-boat strength in 1940 is interesting and suggests surely that after the collapse of France, Germany thought she had won. The build-up of strength in 1941 and 1942 illustrates vividly the threat to our survival. The figures for 1943 demonstrate the eclipse of the U-boat at that time. Another chapter, fortunately an incomplete one, had still to come.

Doenitz controlled the U-boat war from Potsdam. He gained a certain amount of intelligence, though a good deal less than he would have liked, from the long-range air/sea reconnaissance of the German Air Force operating their FW 200s, Do 217s and Ju 88s over the Atlantic. For quite a time he read our naval signals about convoys. The U-boats talked volubly to him and to one another. Their very extensive W/T traffic was monitored by Admiralty direction-finding (DF) wireless and was studied in depth and with great skill in the Admiralty U-boat tracking room. The analysis was greatly helped by the fact that British cryptography, code-named 'Ultra', enabled the Admiralty to read, from time to time, at least part of the U-boat W/T traffic. As the U-boats responded to their orders, gathering into their packs, the Admiralty was able to predict with considerable success which convoys were threatened and which were not, and to make their dispositions, naval and air, accordingly. Liaison between the Admiralty and Coastal Command Headquarters was seldom less than good. The success of this intelligence work led Doenitz into some strange aberrations. By the spring of 1942 Germany was aware that Coastal Command aircraft were equipped with radar enabling them to search for surface vessels and U-boats. The Germans had indeed captured a set. By September 1942, the U-boats, to their great advantage, could monitor these *Air to Surface Vessel* (ASV) radiations and take precautions accordingly. Doenitz used this knowledge to dispose his U-boat fleet outside the range of shore-based aircraft. Yet in February 1943, when Allied convoys were eluding his U-boat screens, he was convinced that the explanation was to be found either in treachery or in some crafty 'magic eye' with which Allied aircraft could detect U-boat radiations over vast areas of the Atlantic. He preferred the latter solution. There was indeed a magic eye coming along in the shape of centimetric ASV, but it was not in service at that time, and when it did arrive considerations of its effective range and the numbers of aircraft employing it meant that it made only a small contribution to the picture developed in the Admiralty tracking room. This rested for the most part on a straight intelligence slog.

Radar

For reasons of conflicting priorities Coastal Command was not well up in the queue for ASV. When it first arrived, working on a wavelength of 150 centimetres, it was not and was not regarded by aircrews as an unmixed blessing. So far as U-boats were concerned by day it offered little advantage over the human eye. Thus, between September 1941 and August 1943 there were 1,112 U-boat sightings by day in the Atlantic/ Biscay/Gibraltar area. ASV was responsible for 125 or 11.2 per cent of these. And at night, even though a U-boat could be spotted by ASV, there was not much the aircraft could do about it until the summer of 1942, when the situation was greatly changed by a remarkable invention called the Leigh Light. Squadron Leader Leigh was a Personnel Officer in Coastal Command Headquarters. In October 1940 he proposed to his Commander-in-Chief that Coastal Command aircraft working against U-boats at night should be fitted with a movable searchlight so that they could creep up on U-boats with the help of their ASV and then, just when radar blips were being lost in ground returns, could flip on an intense beam of light and attack accordingly. It was surely no part of the duties of a Personnel Officer to dream up such remarkable ideas. Nevertheless, the Commander-in-Chief was impressed and by the spring of 1941 the idea was being tried out with impressive results. The subsequent history of the Leigh Light is a bit of a cautionary tale. The Air Ministry, mainly in the person of Air Marshal Sir Philip Joubert, then an Assistant Chief of the Air Staff, thought poorly of the idea, deeming it a variant of an idea hatched out by Wing Commander Helmore for a device called Turbinlite designed to illuminate enemy bombers at night. In this matter the Air Ministry and Joubert were in error, two quite different problems and two quite different techniques being involved. In June 1941 Leigh was recalled to his personnel duties. But in the same month, such is the irony of events, Joubert was appointed Commander-in-Chief Coastal Command in succession to Bowhill. In two months a mighty change, and the Leigh Light was in. Alas, the usual production delays ensued and it was not until the summer of 1942 that it was available for service, and then only in trivial numbers. It achieved instant success and by the end of 1942 was the standard night anti-U-boat weapon, being fitted to Wellington, Catalina and Liberator squadrons. It forced U-boats to travel submerged by night, thus exposing themselves to surface attacks by day. During the war Leigh Light aircraft attacked 218 U-boats at night and carried out 206 attacks on enemy shipping. Twenty-seven U-boats were sunk and thirty-one damaged. Not the least factor in these night attacks was the complete surprise, with its psychological effects on U-boat personnel. One of the troubles in the Bay of Biscay at night was that to ASV, fishing boats looked much like U-boats. So there were many abortive attacks warning U-boats in the vicinity to watch their step.

In the spring of 1943 Coastal Command started to be re-equipped with centimetric ASV, a diversion from Bomber Command whose long awaited H2S sets (see p. 258) were available and similar. The great advantage of centimetric ASV was that because of inferior radar techniques the Germans did not learn to monitor it until the end of 1943. This, despite the fact that in the spring of 1943 the Germans had captured an H2S set complete with its cavity magnetron from a crashed British bomber. So, for most of that critical year, 1943, Coastal Command aircraft could observe by radar and not be observed in return. This was of less consequence by day perhaps when that remarkable instrument the human eye was available. But at night allied to the formidable Leigh Light, it was a different story.

Operational Research

Operational Research, that integration of scientific methodology with warlike operations, found its origins in the application of radar to Fighter Command, and in the work of scientists to optimise the consequences of that marriage Coastal Command were perhaps a shade late in the race. But in the early spring of 1941 Joubert, the Commander-in-Chief, appointed Blackett as his scientific adviser. It was the beginning of the Command's long, imaginative and productive alliance with the world of science. It cannot be said that the scientists attached to the work were lacking in prestige. They included five Fellows of the Royal Society (Blackett, Kendrew, Williams, Waddington and Robertson), two of whom became Nobel Laureates (Blackett and Kendrew). An organisation which can attract such scientific support must surely know what it is about. The appointment of Blackett was the key event, and from it the others followed. All the elements required to bring about a successful attack on a U-boat were studied. The standard anti-U-boat weapon was by this time the depth charge. What was the optimum depth setting? Major benefits resulted from reducing it to 25 feet. What was the best spacing of the 'stick' of depth charges? What was the best height and the best angle for an attack? At the Headquarters of Commander-in-Chief, Western Approaches, in Liverpool Blackett looked at the estimated pattern of U-boats in the Atlantic. From his knowledge of Coastal Command sorties he was able to make a rough estimate of the number of U-boat sightings to be expected. It turned out to be four times the actual sightings. Blackett concluded that the U-boats were seeing aircraft before they themselves were seen. 'What colour are Coastal Command aircraft?' he was asked one day. Of course many of them were black—converted bombers which were painted black as a defence against searchlights. Within a few months all Coastal Command anti-U-boat aircraft had been painted white. By these and other means the lethality of the Command's attacks on U-boats rapidly improved. According to Waddington,[2] who worked with the Operational Research Unit at Coastal Command from 1942 to 1945 and was Scientific Adviser to the Commander-in-Chief from 1944 to 1945, lethality per attack on a visible U-boat, which stood at 2–3 per cent in 1941 had risen to 40 per cent by 1944 and reached 60 per cent on the few surfaced U-boats seen in the last months of the war.

Hudson S/269

The Royal Air Force did not secure an undivided victory over a U-boat until the war was nearly two years old. By this time warships alone had sunk some thirty U-boats. However, the first Royal Air Force victory was undoubtedly a spectacular one. On 27 August 1941 Hudson S of 269 Squadron encountered a U-boat north of Iceland and carried out an attack with depth charges. The U-boat surfaced and its crew emerged. The Hudson continued its attack with machine gun fire and soon the U-boat crew were waving an improvised white flag. It was learned later that the surrender was occasioned by chlorine fumes. The Hudson stood by until relieved by a Catalina. An anti-U-boat trawler was summoned but the sea was too rough for boarding. Relays of aircraft plus the trawler stood by the U-boat all night. It had been ordered to burn a riding light. By dawn a destroyer and more trawlers had appeared, but the weather still made a boarding difficult. The U-boat began to settle and orders to blow more fuel and ballast were ignored until reinforced by further judicious recourse to machine guns. Later the U-boat was boarded, the crew disembarked and the U-boat towed to Iceland. Here it was repaired and recommissioned in the Royal Navy as HMSM *Graph*. Naturally the intelligence content of a brand new U-boat captured on its first operational trip was considerable. Had the episode been invented as fiction it would have been laughed off as a piece of nonsense. No doubt for reasons of security, U-boat 570 was recorded as sunk by a Hudson on 27 August 1941. The facts were much more colourful.

Annus Mirabilis

1942 was Doenitz's hey-day. He sank by U-boat nearly 6.3 million tons of Allied shipping for the loss of eighty-five U-boats or nearly 75,000 tons of shipping per U-boat lost. Strangely, he failed completely to upset the landings in North Africa. Huge armadas sailed from Britain and the United States through the Straits of Gibraltar. Hundreds of aircraft were parked on the airfield at the Rock. Something was clearly going to happen and Hitler could scarcely have thought the Allies were about to attack Norway, a favourite preoccupation of his. So German intelligence failed completely to deduce the points of attack and while Doenitz continued his sinkings elsewhere (800,000 tons lost in November 1942) the invasion fleets sailed in more or less unharmed.

1943 was the *annus mirabilis* of the fight against the U-boat. In 1943, 2.6 million tons of Allied shipping were sunk by U-boats, for 237 U-boats lost, roughly 11,000 tons of shipping per U-boat. The loss ratio had improved by a factor of roughly seven over the corresponding figure for 1942. Many factors combined to bring about this great and badly needed victory. So far as the Royal Air Force was concerned, the contribution included more and better aircraft, closing the Greenland Gap, better techniques of attack. But another factor must be mentioned. This was Slessor, Commander-in-Chief Coastal Command for something under a year from February 1943. Coastal Command was lucky with its Commanders-in-Chief. There were four in all: Air Marshal Sir Frederick Bowhill, Joubert, Slessor and Douglas. Bowhill was an ideal Commander-in-Chief for the early days of the war. Ex-Merchant Navy, Royal Naval Reserve, Royal Navy and a former sailor before the mast, he had seawater in his veins. He had an appreciation of naval needs based on a lifetime's experience. In the *Bismarck* action when contact was lost and it was suspected that she was on her way back to a Biscay port it was Bowhill who, for purely instinctive 'sea' reasons, suggested that she would first make for Cape Finisterre rather than direct for Brest. The Catalina search was shifted south and as a result the *Bismarck* was found and later sunk. Joubert was not an ideal Commander-in-Chief for Coastal Command. He was an attractive, intelligent man. He had imagination and understanding and could usually express himself well. And he brought Blackett into Coastal Command. But other qualities are needed in a Commander-in-Chief and Joubert was short on these. Douglas, the fourth Commander, was the complete professional. Shrewd, capable, tough, experienced, intelligent, he served Coastal Command and the Royal Air Force well. But by the time he arrived in Coastal Command the Battle of the Atlantic had been won. It was won while Slessor was in command. This was not, as Slessor has pointed out, cause and effect. 1943 in Coastal Command was the culmination of years of hard slog. But Slessor arrived at the right time and had just the right qualities to make it all gell. He saw the strong points and the weak points and he hammered away at both. He was intelligent, experienced, friendly, receptive of ideas, hard working. Coastal Command and the Royal Air Force owe him much.

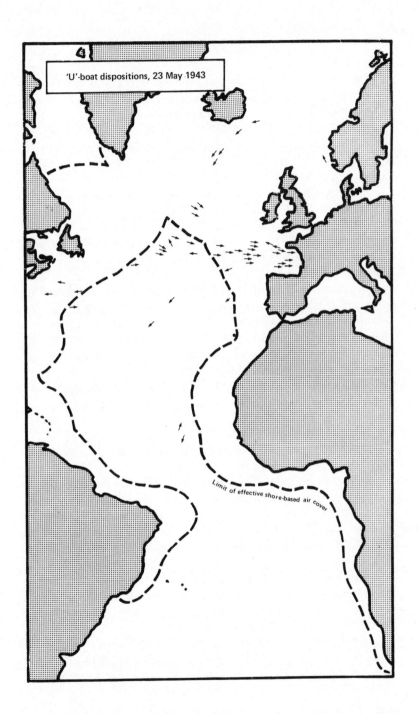

'U'-boat dispositions, 23 May 1943

Limit of effective shore-based air cover

The year included the famous Bay Offensive, roughly from April to August 1943. The broad idea was that as U-boats had to pass through the southern waters of the Bay of Biscay on their way to the Atlantic they should be subjected to intensive attack while in transit. If they surfaced by day, they were attacked after visual or centimetric ASV sightings. If they surfaced by night they faced centimetric ASV and the Leigh Light. U-boats have to surface from time to time to charge their batteries, so Doenitz told his crews to fight it out on the surface and important additions were made to U-boat armour and flak. The Coastal Command crews rose to the occasion. They still went in and delivered their depth charge attacks. From early May to early August the Command sank forty-one U-boats. It was a great victory, but the cost to the Command in crew and aircraft was heavy. By this time Doenitz had had enough. U-boats no longer surfaced by day and for minimum periods by night. The times of U-boats in transit were greatly extended. By October 1943 British forces were established by agreement with Portugal in the Azores. The net was closing on the U-boat fleet and their glory was departing. Not the least important consequence of this great victory was that when D-Day arrived in mid-1944 the U-boats did not fight their way into the 'funnel'—the channels to the beaches from Britain and the United States—till some seven days later. One shudders to think what would have happened to the invasion fleets if the back of the U-boat attack had not been broken by then.

Schnorkels and Advanced U-boats

Germany always had plenty of good technical ideas but was not always clever about using them to the best advantage. One such idea was the schnorkel, a device consisting of tubes sticking out of the water which enabled the U-boat to breathe and to run its diesel engines while submerged. After its introduction it soon had its Coastal Command pursuers in trouble. A conning tower was one thing—a sizeable chunk of metal. A small piece of pipe was quite another. It was difficult to spot and easy to confuse with natural objects such as willywaws (incipient waterspouts), whales and shoals of fish. All of these took a fair pasting with depth charges. But fortunately for us the schnorkel came too late, as the sinkings for 1944 (3,200 tons per U-boat sunk) and 1945 (1,800 tons per U-boat sunk) show so clearly.

Germany had another trick up her sleeve with her new marks of U-boats due to be introduced from early 1945 onwards. The speed of the larger model Type XXI was such that it could overtake a convoy while submerged and with only the schnorkel showing. It was thus a very formidable weapon. The other new model U-boat was smaller, had unorthodox propulsion, but was also very fast. Both models relied on schnorkels, of course. They were designed to be prefabricated but, being too big for the railways, they had to be transported by canal. But by this date German canals, always a favourite of Bomber Command, were in sad disarray. The Mittelland and the Dortmund-Ems canals were drained regularly by heavy bombs at critical points. It was a case of cut and come again. So with all these delays and frustrations the new model U-boats, despite their great potential, made only a small contribution. Once again Britain had been lucky.

The institution of protective controls by the United States in the late summer of 1941

In the summer and autumn of 1941 the United States, a neutral power, took two steps of immense value to Britain. In July 1941 they took over from Britain the defence of Iceland and Greenland, thus making these bases for practical purposes impregnable and relieving hard-pressed Britain of a serious military load. Further, President Roosevelt declared that the sea-routes between North America and Iceland would be held inviolate and that German and Italian warships would enter these waters at their peril. In September 1941 the United States assumed responsibility for the protection of convoys west of a chop-line running east of Iceland and so practically down the middle of the Atlantic. As a piece of non-belligerency these acts possessed some remarkable features. As a piece of President Roosevelt's statesmanship they have an honoured place in history. As an act of enlightened friendship to Britain they will not readily be forgotten by those who served in those dark and dangerous days.

Reconnaissance

On the outbreak of war the Admiralty was more concerned about surface raiders than about U-boats. Some German warships were already at sea but elaborate precautions were taken to detect and, if possible, to attack further raiders making their way to the open sea either south-about through the Straits of Dover or northabout past the coast of Norway. The southern stop relied basically on mine-fields plus surface craft. The northern stop was provided by aircraft most of the way to Norway and then by submarines. At first the northern arrangements were inevitably pretty inefficient, since by night or in bad weather the aircraft could see precisely nothing, and our warships were in scarcely better case. By early 1940 Coastal Command aircraft began to be fitted with ASV, but early marks were unreliable and were distrusted by aircrew. Germany of course took full advantage of these weaknesses and German warships came and went for the most part unobserved. In the early years of the war many of those countless hours that Coastal Command spent over the sea looking for German warships and U-boats were wasted. However, there were some substantial items on the credit side, two of which may be mentioned here. It was, as we have mentioned earlier, a Coastal Command Catalina which found the *Bismarck* when she was lost in the course of the action with the Royal Navy in May 1941. Rather embarrassingly there was an American officer on board the Catalina in question; embarrassingly because, reasonably enough, International Law does not allow officers of a neutral power to take part in warlike activities. The Admiralty considered giving him a silver tray, no doubt suitably inscribed, but thought better of it, whether from motives of prudence or economy is not clear. Perhaps they just lost their nerve. The other episode was the successful interception of the *Lützow* by Coastal Command aircraft on 12 June 1941. Bomb and torpedo attacks followed in the course of which a number of aircraft were lost to flak or fighters. In the early hours of 13 June, however, one Beaufort secured a torpedo hit on the *Lützow* amidships. Severe damage resulted and the German warship only just managed to limp back to Kiel.*

Operations against enemy shipping

The idea that Coastal Command should be employed against enemy shipping was not one to which much weight had been given by the outbreak of war. In September 1939 the Command, it is true, possessed two antiquated Vildebeest torpedo bomber squadrons, but the performance of these aircraft was totally inadequate and they were never used operationally. The subject gained added importance on the opening of the Norwegian campaign. Step by step an anti-shipping role was developed, but with enemy coastal shipping already in convoy with powerful flak

* The *Lützow* was sunk by Bomber Command at Swinemünde on 16 April 1945.

and fighter defence it was a costly business for the Royal Air Force, which suffered severe losses (not least to the Blenheim squadrons of No 2 Group Bomber Command which were temporarily employed in this work throughout 1942) in return for only moderate success against enemy shipping. By 1942 new ideas were coming along. Hampdens, Wellingtons and Beaufighters were equipped with torpedoes and joined the Beauforts already in this role. A rocket projectile was developed. By April 1943 a Strike Wing had been developed at North Coates in Lincolnshire. This consisted of Beaufighters with torpedoes (called Torbeaus) and Beaufighters with cannon, bombs and rockets. The Torbeaus made the strike; bombs, cannon and rockets provided the diversion. A strong escort of, say, four fighter squadrons provided protection against hostile fighters. The whole concept was clearly a great advance on the bleak tactics of 1942. The Strike Wing concept was a success from the time of its introduction in April 1943. The main limitation was the provision of the fighter escort at a time when Fighter Command was heavily engaged in supporting the United States Air Force. However, three Strike Wings were operational by March 1944 and they inflicted mounting damage on enemy shipping till the end of the war.

Air minelaying

Another aspect of naval/air co-operation may be mentioned here namely air minelaying. Preparations for this had been made before the war. In the event the task was shared between Bomber Command, which dealt with the more distant areas, Coastal Command and the Fleet Air Arm. The first air mines were laid by Hampdens of No 5 Group on the night of 13/14 April 1940. These operations were soon followed by Coastal Command Beauforts and Fleet Air Arm Swordfish. So began a massive operation of offensive minelaying by air. By the end of the war it had accounted world-wide for some 940 enemy vessels totalling some 840,000 tons sunk and represented the lion's share of the total results of all British offensive mining in all areas namely some 1,120 enemy vessels totalling about one million tons. The code name for air mining was 'Gardening', derived from the fact that the different mining areas were given the code names of flowers and vegetables. And of course there was a distinct planting connotation.

The Journey of the Scharnhorst, the Gneisenau and Prinz Eugen from Brest to Germany—February 1942

At the end of March 1941 the *Scharnhorst* and the *Gneisenau* were sitting in Brest harbour after a commerce raid into the Atlantic which lasted the best part of two months. In June they were joined by the heavy cruiser *Prinz Eugen* which found refuge there after the sinking of the *Bismarck*. The three warships were immediately subjected to the close attention of Bomber Command and Coastal Command. On 6 April 1941 the *Gneisenau* was severely damaged by torpedo attack while moored in the outer harbour. The successful Coastal Command torpedo bomber was shot down, the pilot, Flying Officer Kenneth Campbell, being awarded a posthumous Victoria Cross. Further severe damage was inflicted on the *Gneisenau* on the night of 10/11 April in a Bomber Command attack which achieved four hits on the warship. One of the bombs did not explode. The *Gneisenau* was out of action for the rest of the year and with the *Scharnhorst* refitting the two warships could do nothing to help the *Bismarck* in the action of May 1941. The *Prinz Eugen* was hit in July and in the same month Bomber Command inflicted five direct hits on the *Scharnhorst* while she was on a training trip to La Pallice. One of the bombs did not explode. Effectively the three warships were out of action for the rest of the year. There were many subsequent attacks on the ships throughout the rest of 1941, none of which did great damage though in one of them, in December 1941, the gates of the dock in which the *Scharnhorst* was sitting were so damaged that she was prevented from leaving for a month. Innumerable bombs flew into Brest harbour, of course. This is a big place and it can be argued that, damage to the warships notwithstanding, the attacks would have been more meaningful if they had been directed against the protected U-boat pens on the Biscay ports, then under construction and especially vulnerable.

German plans

By the end of 1941 the German warships were near to readiness and a decision was necessary as to what should happen to them. In discussion with Hitler four possible courses of action emerged:

1. A return to German bases *via* the Denmark Strait or south of Iceland
2. An attack on a North/South Atlantic convoy

3. A return to German bases *via* the Straits of Dover
4. A decision to decommission the ships.

Hitler was keen that by one route or another the ships should go to Norwegian bases, as he was quite clear that Britain was planning an attack on Norway. Course 4 was often a favourite of Hitler's but in the event he settled for Course 3, much to the concern of the German Naval Staff. As usual their protests were brushed aside, and Vice-Admiral Ciliax was told to get on with it. He proceeded to draw up an immensely skilful plan. The ships were to leave Brest on a moonless night with a good flood tide at such a time as would take them through the Straits of Dover around mid-day, thus facilitating strong fighter cover and suitable light conditions for the flak. The plan was to hug the French coast and in the Straits to keep as close as possible to Cape Gris Nez.

British Plans
The British Admiralty had little doubt that the ships would return *via* the Straits of Dover, probably under the cover of darkness. This is a little surprising in view of German naval hesitations. But in fact in retrospect it does seem the obvious choice—the 27-knot dash in bad weather mainly in the dark in preference to the long journey *via* the Denmark Strait or the hazardous route South of Iceland past the main British naval base. Anyway, what was to stop them—a handful of Coastal Command aircraft, Bomber Command operating under conditions of maximum disadvantage, no heavy ships, a few destroyers and light craft, a few naval aircraft.

The Escape
So the Admiralty, fairly early in 1941, issued their directive and the Royal Navy and the Royal Air Force made their plans. The Royal Navy at this most critical time in their history had little enough to throw in the path of the German warships. In fact, it amounted to six obsolete torpedo Swordfish at Manston in Kent; ten motor torpedo-boats and motor gun-boats at Dover; three MTBs at Ramsgate, and six destroyers at Harwich.

The Royal Air Force was scarcely in better case. Reconnaissance apart, they could offer twenty-nine Beaufort torpedo bombers; a part of Bomber Command; and a part of Fighter Command to help deal with German fighter escorts.

The German warships would surely be surrounded with a strong escort of destroyers, E-boats, R-boats and fighters. Torpedo attacks against warships so escorted and equipped with formidable flak would not be easy.

Bomber Command had no training in attacking German warships making high speeds at sea. With cloud down to sea level and the air full of Me 109s the outlook was unpropitious.

Fighter Command had little practice in escorting bombers, torpedo or otherwise, in attacks on German warships.

Early in February 1942 it became clear to the Admiralty and the Air Ministry that the warships would soon be on their way up-Channel. The main ships at Brest had undocked and a considerable force of destroyers was concentrating. An hour or so before midnight on the night of 11/12 February 1942, held up a bit by a Bomber Command attack on Brest, the *Scharnhorst*, the *Gneisenau* and the *Prinz Eugen* had formed up outside the Rade de Brest and were on their way. They were escorted by a force of destroyers and light craft which gathered in strength as the journey continued. Predictably the weather was bad and there was no moon. To be precise the squadron left Brest at 22.45 hours on 11 February 1942 and it was first identified, by Fighter Command, at 11.09 hours on the following day. So, despite all the preparations, the squadron had a clear run of over twelve hours. How did this come about? Well, clearly enough, there was no intelligence tip-off. Coastal Command had standing patrols at strategic points up Channel. For various reasons, radar troubles among them, they saw nothing. From 08.30 hours onwards, evidence appeared on British radar screens that something was going on. There were hostile aircraft orbiting in the Channel. By 09.30 or so there were attempts to jam our radar screen. What was going on? Spitfires were ordered out, but it was a private venture by Group Captain Beamish and Wing Commander Boyd out looking for trouble which first spotted the ships. Group Captain Beamish landed at 11.09 hours, when the German squadron had been at sea for over twelve hours. Nightfall was some six hours away. There was much to be done and little time to do it in. The Royal Navy attacked with their modest forces with characteristic valour. Little was achieved save the superb attack on the German squadron by Lieutenant-Commander Esmonde RN leading six venerable Swordfish in an indomitable attack. Using second sight he had given instructions that his torpedoes should be set 'deep', i.e. suitable for an attack on capital ships. When he gave these orders intelligence indicating the target was mainly non-existent. All the Swordfish were shot down by German fighters or flak and no hits on the enemy were achieved. Esmonde was awarded a most appropriate Victoria Cross. By his attack he had transformed a desolate scene. In the Straits of Dover the three German capital ships were escorted by about 12 destroyers and an outer ring of E-boats. Strong fighter cover was afforded continuously by the German Air Force. They were thus an exceedingly difficult target to attack and the attacks by destroyers, MTBs and MGBs had little hope of success. Bomber Command played its part well enough, but with clouds down to a few hundred feet it could scarcely hope to provide more than a distraction. The best hope perhaps lay with the Royal Air Force torpedo bombers. When the presence of the enemy warships was first reported these aircraft were widely dispersed: twelve at St Eval (Cornwall), seven at Thorney Island (near Portsmouth), and fourteen at Leuchars (Fife). So a good deal of regrouping had to be carried out in a considerable hurry. Had things worked out perfectly the torpedo bombers had only a small chance of success against such a strongly defended squadron. But in fact things went far from perfectly. The inherent difficulty of the task of the torpedo bombers was compounded by failures of communication within Coastal Command, misunderstandings between Fighter and Coastal Commands, not least as to the meaning of the words 'fighter escort', and finally by serious technical failures. Several most gallant torpedo bomber attacks were made but no hits were secured.

So the German ships proceeded on their way, but their adventures for the day were not yet over. At 14.31 hours east of Walcheren Island the *Scharnhorst* was slightly damaged by a mine. The *Gneisenau* had the same experience at 19.55 hours off Terschelling Island. At 21.34 hours the *Scharnhorst* was mined again, this time suffering severe damage and shipping 1,000 tons of water. And to round off the story, the *Prinz Eugen* was severely damaged by a torpedo from a British submarine on 23 February. On the night of 27/28 February the *Gneisenau*, lying in the floating dock at Kiel, was hit by two heavy bombs from Bomber Command. So the action ended with all three ships out of the line, an episode which the German Naval Staff described as a tactical victory and a strategic defeat.

British Public Opinion

The British people took a poor view of all this, and in many ways they were right to do so. After all, we had been at war for two and a half years.

The Times, rising to the occasion, took out the big stick. 'Vice-Admiral Ciliax has succeeded where the Duke of Medina Sidonia failed', declared 'the Thunderer'. But history has a long memory. There were points of similarity as well as of difference between the fates of the Spanish and German fleets. Both sailed through the Straits intent on victory; neither returned and both fleets in the end were defeated. Of course *The Times* was not to know this and the public relations aspect of the matter was not helped by inability to announce the damage caused by mining. Oddly, for some two months after the defeat of her Armada, Spain believed that she had won a great victory.

Churchill was fond of judicial enquiries and within days of the escape Mr Justice Bucknill and his two assessors, Air Marshal Ludlow Hewitt and Admiral Binney, were sitting as a Board of Enquiry.[3] In fifteen days they produced their report, which gave a lucid account of the events and made some mild comments on operational failures. But they hit the nail on the head when they linked the failure to stop the German Squadron with the inadequacy of the available British naval and air forces to stop them. As a footnote to this comment on the Board of Enquiry, it is perhaps legitimate to add that it was fortunate that no further naval crisis occurred in February 1942 while a high proportion of the high brass of the Royal Navy and the Royal Air Force was sitting in the Admiralty, waiting to give evidence.

The Photographic Reconnaissance Unit

This brief account of the work of Coastal Command during the war must be completed by a reference to three other duties which the Command carried out on behalf of the entire Metropolitan Air Force. These duties were respectively photographic reconnaissance, air/sea rescue and meteorological work.

At the beginning of the Second World War, there were two British units capable of carrying out aerial reconnaissance over Germany. The first was No 2 Group, Bomber Command, well supplied with men and equipment, but which in the opinion of its Commander-in-Chief was unfitted to discharge its photographic reconnaissance role under wartime conditions. There was also a group of civilians at Heston who relied on subterfuge rather than sheer weight of numbers to get through. But once they were started they were expected to stand aside and let the professionals take over.

So Andrew J. Brookes, a PR pilot himself, begins chapter four of his valuable book *Photo Reconnaissance*. It is a true comment. He calls the chapter 'Cotton's Circus', on the whole an appropriate title. No 2 Group, Bomber Command, were equipped with Blenheim bombers. They could defend themselves of course up to a point but by reason of limited speed and ceiling they could not hope to elude German defences. Many were lost. Worse than this, their cameras could not tolerate high altitude as the lenses misted over and froze. Sidney Cotton of 'Sidcot' fame, had a very different background. He had gone into partnership with Fred Winterbotham of the Secret Intelligence Service and for a year or so before the outbreak of war they had roamed around Europe in an ostensibly 'private' Lockheed on ostensibly cultural and social pursuits. But in the belly of the Lockheed were located excellent cameras controlled from the cockpit and heated by air currents from the pilot's cabin, so obviating frozen lenses. Some excellent photographs resulted. So, come September 1939, there was Cotton in this curious civilian set-up at Heston. Clearly, the Royal Air Force needed his help. Blenheims and other military aircraft were made available. Cotton used every trick in the trade and some which he dreamed up himself to improve their performance, smoothing, polishing, refining. He was greatly helped by the work of Flying Officer M. V. Longbottom.

The turning point was reached when Cotton charmed two Spitfires out of Dowding, a remarkable event which reflects immense credit on both men. Soon the Spitfires had been stripped of military equipment, polished, painted duck-egg green* and fitted with wing cameras heated by the engine. The service ceiling had been increased to something like 35,000 feet and the range increased to something like 1,500 miles. Most significantly there had been a change of principle. The first aim of the Spitfire was not to fight but to elude. In a word, its primary aim was to return with its pictures. PR had been born and an enormous debt of gratitude to Cotton incurred. Soon the splendid photographs which resulted were being interpreted illegally but to the immense benefit of Britain by a modest Aircraft Operating Company at Wembley which possessed a massive and highly sophisticated photogrammetric machine purchased in Switzerland and used for civil survey work. The progress of PR from this point was continuous until 1945, and the greatest ally to the Spitfire turned out to be that indomitable aircraft, the Mosquito, which in consequence of its superb performance could offer increased range, a good

* Later changed to light blue for high altitude sorties and to pink for low level sorties ('dicers').

survival rate and, most important of all, could carry a navigator. Of course the control of this priceless PR unit turned out to be a problem. Cotton was made a war-time Wing Commander and was given Wing Commander Geoffrey Tuttle, a former flying instructor and fighter pilot, as his No 2. In the end Cotton was relieved and Tuttle took control, but by this time the road ahead had become clear. The immense services of Cotton were rewarded most inadequately by an OBE and a stuffy letter from the Air Council.

Problems still lay ahead. The PRU was under the direct operational control of the Air Ministry. Tuttle considered that the undoubted achievements of the unit were due to three factors: he could ask for and obtain without hesitation any pilot in the Royal Air Force; he had un- limited purchase powers; the Air Ministry set the tasks but did not interfere with tactics.

Of course covetous barons, not least in Bomber Command and the Royal Navy, were soon seeking to acquire pieces of this precious empire. To avoid this, in June 1941 the unit was put under the operational and administrative control of Coastal Command, where it remained until the end of the war. As a footnote to this remarkable story it seems right to comment that it was lucky that the Royal Air Force was such a young and unconventional service, and included such perceptive characters as Chief of the Air Staff Newall and his assistant, Wing Commander Richard Peck. But for this, the problem of coupling the genius of Cotton and the necessary rigidities of a disciplined service might well have proved unmanageable.

Photographic Reconnaissance soon became a growth industry. Some idea of its scale is given by the fact that in 1942 PRU turned out 204 models, 5,437 reports and nearly $1\frac{1}{2}$ million prints. The Royal Navy were avid customers. 729 sorties were flown over Brest while the *Scharnhorst* and the *Gneisenau* were there, sometimes as many as seven a day. In the end there were four PRU squadrons in Britain, equipped with Spitfires, Mosquitoes and Mustangs.

Air/Sea Rescue

From 1941 onwards, Coastal Command also assumed responsibility for air/sea rescue on behalf of all Allied squadrons operating in Home waters. The problem was tackled from many angles. Crews carried emergency packs containing every imaginable device from food and first aid kits to mini-transmitters which registered on the ASV screens of searching aircraft. Backing them up were some seven squadrons of air/sea rescue aircraft: Lysanders, Walruses, Hudsons, Ansons and Defiants. These aircraft could drop rescue packs, among them the Bircham Barrel, the Thornaby Bag, the Lindholme apparatus and the renowned airborne lifeboat. There was also an armada of high-speed surface craft. Over and above Service support, invaluable aid was given by the Post Office, the Coastguard, the Royal National Lifeboat Institution, the Merchant Navy and amateur radio enthusiasts. In 1943 alone 1,684 Allied aircrew were rescued. Bomber crews flying over the North Sea carried a faithful pigeon in a small wire cage. On ditching, the pigeon was released with a message from the navigator reporting his position. The record of the pigeons was patchy. Sometimes they succeeded, but as often as not the ditched bomber crew sitting in their dinghy had the depressing experience of seeing their pigeon re-alighting on the dinghy after a wide circuit of the heavens. One Bomber Command pigeon, complete with cage, was accommodated in the cloakroom of the Ritz Hotel in London while his shot-down Bomber Command pilot was lunching in the course of his return to his unit from the North Sea. It is to be hoped that the pigeon was well looked after and enjoyed the experience. Peregrine falcons were shot to prevent them preying on the pigeons.* It is said that peregrine falcons were also reared to intercept pigeons used by potential German agents. History is silent as to the degree of co-ordination between the two falcon agencies.

Meteorology

Finally, the Command was responsible for meteorological flying. In the end this absorbed six and a half squadrons in Britain alone (Halifax, Spitfire, Hurricane, Fortress). This was work of critical importance. Bomber Command's operations, for example, were vitally affected, not to speak of the timing of D-Day.

Admiralty/Air Ministry relations during the Second World War

The basic organisation of Coastal Command was sound and stood the test of five and a half years of war. The basic settlement of the Inskip Award also worked well. Under that settlement, it will be remembered, the Fleet Air Arm became an integral part of the Royal

---

* One falcon was delivered alive and in vigorous mood to the Air Ministry in a cage, no doubt to demonstrate the enterprise of his captor.

Navy and the shore-based squadrons of Coastal Command remained with the Royal Air Force. Of course the decision was challenged from time to time but never with quite the same gusto. Thus when in the autumn of 1940 Beaverbrook, then Minister of Aircraft Production (egged on it is said, by First Lord A. V. Alexander and Admiral of the Fleet Sir Roger Keyes), proposed the transfer of Coastal Command to the Royal Navy, the official reaction of the Admiralty was correct but restrained. They had always been in favour they said of having control 'not only of Coastal Command but of all aircraft whose normal function is to fly over the sea'. But while wordy battles took place in the Defence Committee the First Sea Lord and the Chief of the Air Staff were working out agreed plans for increasing the strength of Coastal Command and this was indeed the heart of the problem. These plans were accepted by the Defence Committee and that was that. Thereafter there were plenty of disputes about the allocation of resources and indeed plenty of room for such disputes. But the integrity of Coastal Command as part of the Royal Air Force was never again challenged. A subsequent decision, taken as the result of these discussions, that Coastal Command should come under the operational control of the Admiralty caused scarcely a ripple, as we have already noted. It was agreed that this control should be exercised through the Air Officer Commanding-in-Chief, Coastal Command.

13

Air Transport

Early days

Air Transport had its place, albeit a modest one, in the Trenchard philosophy. Two venerable bomber transport squadrons lurked in the Middle East somewhere between Cairo and Baghdad. They could lift a few tons and with a bit of help from the wind they could often manage all of 90 mph over the ground. They secured surprising publicity. They were active against the Kurds in the early Twenties, they flew soldiers to Cyprus when the locals set fire to Government House. In 1928/9 a remarkable fleet of seven Vickers Victorias, one Hinaidi, twenty-four DH9A's and two Wapitis evacuated the British diplomatic community from Kabul in what must be considered somewhat leisurely style by modern standards. Including King Inayatulla and his household, there were some 600 passengers and 12 tons of luggage. They were flown to Peshawar 200 miles away. The operation took two months.

When the Royal Air Force began to expand in the mid-Thirties there was no money and indeed no industrial capacity for air transport. There was, it was true, No 24 (Communications) Squadron at Northolt equipped with a modest array of light or lightish transport aircraft with minimal air navigation facilities. They were suitable only for strong-minded passengers. One of the many engaging characteristics of the Royal Air Force in the Thirties was that it was usually possible to 'borrow' a military aircraft for a weekend or more extended holiday. Mostly the aircraft turned out to be Gypsy Moths and Avro 504 Ns or Tutors, which could be landed in fields, but later on for the more adventurous week-enders Hurricanes and Spitfires were occasionally enrolled. It was all very gay. No doubt it contributed to air experience and only a few wrapped themselves round trees. But Germany had grasped the point, as Britain had not, that for an air force supporting an army air transport was not so much desirable as essential. The Luftwaffe learned this lesson, and many others, in Spain. The Condor Legion was ferried around Spain in Ju 52s, the Luftwaffe made a great contribution to mobility in the First Battle of France while the unfortunate British Air Forces in France were cadging lorries from the French. In 1939 the production of transport aircraft in Britain was minuscule. There were the Short Empire flying boats, of course, which later did yeoman service in the Royal Air Force as Sunderlands. There were a few Argosies and Hannibals. Britain was too small for internal civil aviation. The empire air routes were flown by flying boats, thus saving money on airfields. But in Europe and in the United States of America it was a different story. Germany and Italy poured out air transports for Europe. The American aircraft production and operating industries covered the United States with a close network of domestic airlines.

Civil aviation in war-time

On the outbreak of war all civil flying in Britain came necessarily under military control. Civil airlines were embodied in an organisation called National Air Communications, which operated under the control of the Air Ministry. Most scheduled air routes to the continent of Europe came to a halt. Elsewhere, much invaluable civil flying continued. Thus Imperial Airways* which moved its headquarters to Bristol controlled most of its main overseas operations. It also gave invaluable support on the various ferry routes.

Tactical applications

In the mid Thirties the Russians had given attention to paratroops, a word which sounded odd or even a little comic to British ears. But on 10 May 1940 there was nothing odd or comic about the German airborne forces which were dropped literally on top of key military positions in Holland. The age of airborne operations had begun and Germany had the drive and the ingenuity to exploit these new possibilities.

The rest of the story can be told quickly enough. Where Germany had shown the way, Britain and the United States quickly followed. American factories poured out a copious supply of admirable and ubiquitous Dakotas. In Britain, Halifaxes, Stirlings and Albemarles were converted into tugs. Furniture manufacturers in Britain turned out gliders

*Imperial Airways merged into BOAC in November 1939.

large and small, to carry jeeps, artillery, bulldozers and countless other items of military equipment. The techniques were tried out in Sicily in 1943 and in France on the grand scale on D-Day, 6 June 1944. In this last operation they played a vital part in securing the flanks of the Allied invading forces. Early in the morning of D-Day three Allied airborne divisions were engaged on the River Orne and on the Cotentin. The same number took part in Montgomery's ill-fated attempt to cut the German armies in two by a northern thrust from Aachen *via* Arnhem to the Zuider Zee. Arnhem was in simple terms a disaster. Everything went wrong. Next year, in crossing the Rhine, the Allies proved that they had learned some hard and bitter lessons in airborne operations. And of course the operations in Burma in the last year of the war transformed the face of jungle warfare.

Air ferries

It is time to say a word about air ferries. 5,000 aircraft, mostly made in Britain, were ferried to the Canal Zone from Takoradi, in what used to be called the Gold Coast, a flight of nearly 4,000 tropical or semi-tropical miles. We discuss this operation in Chapter 15. The aircraft were mostly crated and shipped to Takoradi but some were also flown off from aircraft carriers. Knowledge of the route from Lagos to Khartoum had been acquired from 1934 onwards from some pioneering work by No 216 Squadron from Heliopolis and from experimental operations some two years later by Imperial Airways.

The Atlantic Ferry was a real adventure. In September 1939 the only regular air service across the Atlantic was by Pan American Clipper, a flying boat, which flew from New York to Southampton via Bermuda and Lisbon. In 1937 the Air Ministry had authorised the construction of a major airport at Gander in Newfoundland. In the autumn of 1940 air ferrying across the Atlantic began in earnest. It was a question of speeding up the delivery to Britain of aircraft built in America to British orders. In July 1940 the Ministry of Aircraft Production, then under great pressure, approached the Canadian Pacific Railway Company and invited them to undertake the ferrying of American-built aircraft to Britain. The first aircraft to arrive at Aldergrove in Northern Ireland were seven Hudsons for Coastal Command. The project soon gathered momentum. The Canadian Government built a major airport at Montreal (Dorval) and Britain developed a major airport in Ayrshire (Prestwick). The aim was to create something like a Great

Circle route northabout. Reykjavik in Iceland was soon joined and then there was a chain from Montreal via Gander and Reykjavik to Prestwick. The CPR organisation, known as ATFERO, was established in Montreal and soon a team of pilots was ferrying aircraft across the North Atlantic where a bare year before few had ventured. Of course the wind for the most part was pointing in the right direction. There had to be a return service for ferry pilots and this was established by the British Overseas Airways Corporation flying American-built Liberators with mixed civilian and Royal Air Force crews. The Return Ferry Service was the first all-the-year-round trans-Atlantic passage and freight service. The next development was a remarkable one. In March 1941, at the inspiration of President Roosevelt, the Lease-Lend Act became law in the United States. One of its many consequences was that the United States Government allowed their military personnel to deliver service aircraft, of Lease-Lend origin or otherwise, from United States factories, mostly on the Pacific coast, direct to Montreal. They insisted, however, on dealing with a military command and Royal Air Force Ferry Command with Bowhill as Commander-in-Chief was formed at Dorval in July 1941* to replace ATFERO. The creation of staging posts at Goose Bay in Labrador and at the quaintly named Bluie West in Greenland completed the chain. Ferry Command was in business, which rapidly became big business. Of course the minor staging posts were used only in emergencies or for ferrying the shorter range aircraft, fighters and such. Ferry Command soon introduced a remarkable change of procedure. In the early days, ferrying was done mainly by civilians. By 1942 the 'one-trippers' were taking over. These were graduates of the Canadian flying training schools who, after becoming qualified pilots, were given a brief conversion course and informed that they were now North Atlantic pilots. Instructors and other pilots returning from Canada were also likely to be pressed into the same service. All this when a few years before it was a hazardous and remarkable feat for a landplane to cross the Atlantic. It all sounded pretty dangerous, but in fact the casualty rate was something like 1 per cent, far less indeed than the aircraft would have faced if they had been exposed to the rigours of the Battle of the Atlantic in 1941 and 1942.

A southern route was also opened to ferry aircraft from North America to the Middle East. These proceeded via Nassau, Puerto Rico and Trini-

---

* At this stage the aircrews consisted of: civilians 207, RAF 118, Air Transport Auxiliary 36, BOAC 33, RCAF 18, RNZAF 3. Of the pilots, 59 per cent were American, 28 per cent British, 10 per cent Canadian 3 per cent other.

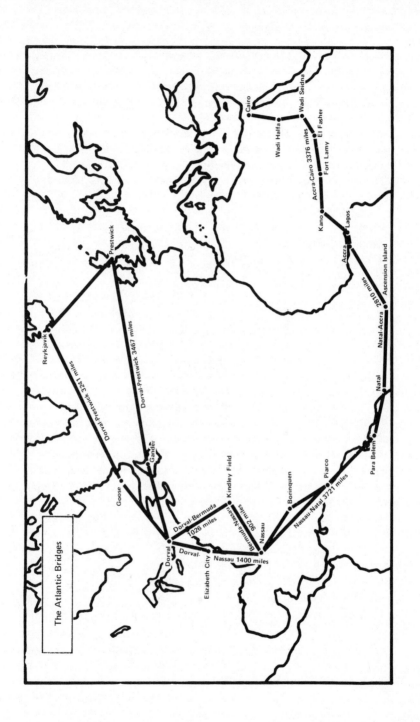

The Atlantic Bridges

Reykjavik

Prestwick

Goose

Gander

Dorval-Prestwick 3241 miles

Dorval-Prestwick 3467 miles

Dorval

Dorval-

Elizabeth City

Dorval-Bermuda 1026 miles

Kindley Field

Bermuda-Nassau 906 miles

Nassau 1400 miles

Nassau

Borinquen

Piarco

Nassau-Natal 3721 miles

Para Belem

Natal

Natal-Accra 2810 miles

Ascension Island

Accra

Lagos

Kano

Accra-Cairo 3376 miles

Fort Lamy

El Fasher

Wadi Halfa

Wadi Seidna

Cairo

dad to Belem and Natal in Brazil, and thence via Ascension Island to Gibraltar and Accra. This was indeed a long way round, but shorter and less hazardous than the double trip from North America to Britain and from there on to the Middle East. This was especially true in the winter months.

Royal Air Force Transport Command was formed in March 1943, to absorb Ferry Command which became No 45 Group in Canada, and No 44 Group which contained the corresponding organisation in Britain. No 231 Squadron was formed as an air communications unit to fly returning ferry pilots and others to and from the United States to the Middle East, India and elsewhere.

It is worth turning aside from the main story for a moment to include a few details of (say) a Liberator flight across the Atlantic in 1942. The Liberator was a big four-engined American bomber fitted with a tricycle undercarriage—a novel feature in those days. When used as a transport it carried no armament, and for good measure it also normally carried no seats. Flying west to Canada or the United States, that is to say against the prevailing wind, it would normally be routed via Reykjavik and Goose Bay or Gander to Dorval. This northerly route would under some weather conditions lead over the southern tip of the Greenland glaciers, a lovely sight in the moonlight. On the eastbound trip via Gander, Reykjavik was often omitted. Take-off was a strenuous affair. To keep the aircraft's tail up passengers huddled together next to the crew cabin. If the passengers were not smartish in moving forward on boarding, the Liberator would display an alarming tendency to sit on its tail. There was no heating. Passengers were fitted with flying clothing plus primitive oxygen gear and lay on the floor head to tail, with blankets over them. Some lay inside the bomb bay, where it was especially cold and the situation encouraged alarming thoughts of what would happen if the pilot pushed the wrong button. Passengers and crew were fitted with parachutes and were instructed in their opera-tion. One waggish sergeant instructor used to tell his passengers that if their parachutes failed to open they should complain to the Air Ministry. And indeed the value of a parachute to a passenger who was unlucky enough to descend in the North Atlantic in winter was obscure. Liberators sometimes dropped their undercarriages in mid-Atlantic, thus reducing flying range and giving rise to awkward problems for the pilot as to whether to continue or turn back. Some disappeared, at least one from metal fatigue. It was all good pioneering stuff and its value to the Allied war effort was immense.

The figures of aircraft despatched from the United States across the Atlantic to the various theatres of war during the period of Royal Air force control, July 1941 to August 1945, are remarkable. For the twelve aircraft types principally concerned the figures were:

	Britain	Middle East	Total
Liberator	847	902	1,749
Dakota	1,174	543	1,717
Baltimore	—	1,000	1,000
Hudson	661	—	661
Mitchell	659	—	659
Mosquito	644	—	644
Ventura	222	306	528
Marauder	70	438	508
Catalina	471	—	471
Boston	318	116	434
Lancaster	393	—	393
Fortress	153	—	153
	5,612	3,305	8,917

In studying these figures we again remind ourselves that in September 1939 a flight across the Atlantic by a landplane was still a notable event. We shall return to the immensely important tactical applications of air transport in Chapters 15, 16 and 20.

14

The Air Ministry in War-time and Some of its Problems

This chapter contains some notes on the Air Ministry in the Second World War, how it was organised, how it worked and how it dealt with some of its problems.

The Air Council

The general structure of the Air Ministry has already been considered in Chapter 7. On the outbreak of the Second World War the Air Council was composed as follows:

Secretary of State	Sir Kingsley Wood
Under-Secretary of State	Captain Harold Balfour
Chief of the Air Staff	Air Chief Marshal Sir Cyril Newall
Air Member for Personnel	Air Vice-Marshal Portal
Air Member for Supply and Organisation	Air Vice-Marshal Welsh
Air Member for Research and Production	Air Marshal Sir Wilfrid Freeman
Director-General of Production	E. J. H. Lemon
Permanent Under-Secretary of State	Sir Arthur Street
Deputy Chief of the Air Staff	Air Vice-Marshal Peirse (Member of Council from November 1939)

On the formation of Churchill's Government Sinclair became Secretary of State for Air, and he held the post until the end of the National Government in May 1945. Sinclair, Leader of the Liberal Party and Member for Parliament for Caithness and Sutherland, was a long-standing friend of Churchill and had served briefly as Secretary of State for Scotland in the early days of Ramsay MacDonald's Government. He had been a stern critic of the Air Ministry in pre-war days. As Secretary of State he served the Royal Air Force well. He fought its battles bravely with Churchill and Beaverbrook, who liked to bully him if given half a chance. Sinclair was not a great Secretary of State but he was thoroughly competent, completely devoted and highly respected. He was also a good speaker and a great gentleman with a total incapacity for departing from the rules of truth and honour. Altogether a most happy and appropriate appointment for a fighting department at a time of grave crisis. Harold Balfour was Parliamentary Under-Secretary of State throughout the Second World War though he was joined by Hugh Seely (later Lord Sherwood of Calverton) as Parliamentary Under-Secretary of State (Lords) in 1941. Balfour had served as an RFC pilot in the First World War and Seely had commanded an Auxiliary Air Force Squadron in the later Thirties. They were both devoted to the Royal Air Force and did much to serve it. The post of Air Member of Personnel was held in succession by five officers during the war, Portal, Air Marshal Leslie Gossage, Air Marshal Philip Babington, Air Marshal Sir Bertine Sutton and, briefly, Slessor. Apart from a short tour of duty by Welsh in the first four months of the war, the post of Air Member for Supply and Organisation was held with distinction by Courtney throughout. He has played his part in our story before (Chapter 11), and it is sufficient to say here that it was much to the advantage of Britain that this responsible and difficult post was held virtually throughout the war by a man of such experience and competence. Finally, Sir Arthur Street was Permanent Under-Secretary of State for Air throughout the war. Permanent Secretaries as a class are divided into those who can work happily with service colleagues and those who cannot. There are few grey areas. It is not a question of ability, which is a necessary quality but not a sufficient one. The Permanent Secretary in a service Department has to win the respect of his service colleagues by competence, by industry and by sympathy. Street, who had no service background when he came to the Air Ministry, had all the necessary qualities. He won a great reputation and it was thoroughly deserved. As the Second World War approached its end it was widely assumed that he would succeed Sir Richard Hopkins as Head of the Treasury. Early in 1945 he was invited to lunch by Churchill and asked if he would like the post. He replied yes he would but could the appointment please be deferred to VE Day which seemed not too far away. Street heard no more and Bridges was appointed instead. This was surely hard. Street was a tiger for work. Being mortal, and who is not, he became more and more tired as the war proceeded. Later and later he worked till his day continued to four or five o'clock in the morning. As an inevitable consequence he rose later and later. And so his working day, which was long enough in all conscience, soon became out of phase with that of his colleagues. Organisationally this was awkward in the Air Ministry and awkward too in his post-war jobs in the Control Office for Germany and Austria and in the National Coal Board. Street died in 1951 while still under sixty years of age, a victim of his labours. It could truly be said of him, as of many other civilians at this time, that he gave his life for his country.

Dispersal

The Air Ministry believed that soon after the outbreak of war its headquarters would be blown sky high by the Luftwaffe. So the Air Ministry took precautions. The central nucleus, Air Staff, Ministers and other essential elements, moved from Kingsway into more robust quarters in the New Public Offices in Whitehall. These quarters were certainly more solid. However, completion of the protected accommodation, which included the floating of a concrete slab many feet thick over the central rotunda of the New Public Offices, overlapped the outbreak of war by many months. So anxious thoughts about air policy by senior officers whose offices abutted on the rotunda were harassed by the noise of concrete mixers. Acting on the hypothesis that the Whitehall headquarters would, notwithstanding the precautions be damaged or destroyed, in the end preparations were made for part of the Air Staff to be evacuated to the Watford area on the outbreak of war. This duly happened and as related in Chapter 7 those parts of the Air Ministry concerned with development and production moved to Harrogate and the Accounts Department to Worcester. The Air Ministry in London was pretty scattered anyway, even without special precautions. Lacking any real home of its own it was spread over some fourteen sites.

Method of working

It is impossible to generalise about methods of working during the war. The machine worked round the clock twenty-four hours a day and 365 days in a year, but pressure was distributed unevenly. The Accounts Department at Worcester, for example, carried an immense load. At its largest the Royal Air Force numbered more than one million men and women. They all had to be paid and the allowances of the married were calculated on regulations of most admired complexity. Here an airman was promoted, here he was killed or wounded, here he had more children, here the children came of age, here his wife ran off, here he was a bigamist. All these matters found reflection in allowances. A small organisational point is worth recording. When the Accounts Department was moved to Worcester on the outbreak of war it inevitably created an organisational vacuum for a week or so. Into this vacuum swept accounting enquiries by the hundred thousand, arising from the call up of the Reserves, moves overseas and the rest. So the Accounts Department when they finally surfaced at Worcester found themselves endowed with unnumbered sacks of anxious letters. Question. Answer the letters? Or get on with the job? They chose the latter course and when calm was restored the sacks were opened, which showed that most of the queries had been dealt with as the result of normal working. The Accounts Department has been mentioned because as a small but vital cog in the machine its activity was vast but measurable. This was far from true of the essential nucleus of the Air Ministry concerned with the policy of managing the war in the air and with relations with central government. Here the load was not only vast but also unpredictable. Hours of work were limited only by the human capacity for endurance. Let us review for example what might have been going on in King Charles Street at (say) 22.00 p.m. on a typical evening in the late winter of 1940/41. Churchill's methods of work have often been described. In general he rose late, took a siesta after lunch and worked late. This technique, which was his personal life style, bore hardly on the staff. So at 22.00 Portal could well have been at No 10. In the next office to his on the central rotunda of the New Public Offices in King Charles Street, and separated from him by a green baize door, the Vice-Chief of the Air Staff, Wilfrid Freeman would be found brooding about problems of Air Force Development or about some more than usually vexatious suggestions from Beaverbrook. That green baize door deserves a second look. Propinquity plays a bigger part in human affairs than is sometimes supposed. On the shoulders of Portal and Freeman most problems of Air Force policy rested. A push on a gently resisting green baize door, a peep, and there they were. It meant much. Further round the rotunda, the Director of Plans putting the final touches to the briefs for the next day's Chiefs of Staff Meeting. Across the corridor, the Secretary of State brooding on Parliamentary business.

Also across the corridor, Street settling down for a final six-hour stint. Throughout the bombing the machine was slogging away, the War Room keeping its constant watch, the sensitive tentacles of Intelligence, receiving their clues and making their judgements, the watch keepers, the late workers, the rest. Normally, at this time an Air Raid Warning Red would be in operation, which meant that all concerned should move to the protected accommodation. In practice this rule was disregarded. People tended to work where most convenient. For many, of course, as for example the War Room, the protected accommodation was a permanent home. There were beds and a canteen. The morning began every day with a nine o'clock situation meeting, the Deputy Chief of the Air Staff in the chair, held in the Air Council Room. The operational directors gave their reports and there was the usual exchange of information. This was usually followed by a smaller executive meeting at which day-to-day operational and administrative questions were settled. The machine had rhythm and momentum. A few domestic details may be added, for instance, the problem of getting home. For many it did not arise and the office bed sufficed. For the Great there were cars. The Underground Railway could only run a restricted service during Red alerts because on the Bakerloo, Northern and East London lines the floodgates had to be closed where the lines crossed the river. A few buses staggered on through the fires and there were surprisingly many taxis. But on the whole public transport was not easy to catch. So for many there were often walks home through the blackout. This could be exciting when the bombs were falling and the path ahead was illuminated by fires. It could also be strangely beautiful when all was quiet and the night sky, sharpened up by the blackout, was there to be studied in all its glory. At least one nightly walker improved his knowledge of the Heavens in this way. No one can work seven days a week for long. The Lord said 'six days shalt thou labour and do all thy work', and as always He knew His business. Attempts at a heavier schedule over a period turned invariably into exercises in self-deception or disaster. The Air Ministry settled for six days a week, often in the form of a Saturday and Sunday off every fortnight. Of course this blessed relief was eroded from time to time, but the rule was there as a standard. Then there was the question of holidays, Leave as it is called in the Services. No one can give of his best without a break. The generous peace-time leave arrangements of the Royal Air Force were restricted to two weeks per annum and the war effort benefited greatly from the fact that leave was not abolished entirely.

Parliament

Parliamentary democracy is a tender plant. As Churchill said in a celebrated speech, it survives only by consent. Over the last thirty years attempts to export it have usually ended in disaster. When Britain comes to the brink of war a high proportion of Parliament's power is dissolved with the advent of Defence Regulations. Thereafter government is largely a matter of decree, *habeas corpus* and the rest being mainly laid aside. This leaves Parliament in an odd position. It can still decide great issues of policy, as when in effect it voted Chamberlain out and later, by massive majorities, it voted Churchill's government in. But short of these large questions, there is not much of substance that Parliament can do in war-time. Of course it could and did make a nuisance of itself from time to time, as when in a critical moment in our country's history it withheld permission for a recording to be taken of a Churchill speech for subsequent broadcast. It could and did insist on debates when the minds of Ministers could have been better occupied. But it could not win the war and realised for the most part that interference in detail could well be fatal. Churchill seldom missed a chance to declare his respect for Parliament and here surely one of his many qualities was displayed. Parliament could not win the war but its ability to cause it to be lost was highly conspicuous. So, there had to be politics.

Fortunately, most fortunately, Churchill's National Government was admirably equipped to deal with such matters. Beside Churchill and his Conservative colleagues stood the redoubtable figures of Attlee, Bevin and Morrison, to name no more. So politics were held in sure hands. Of course, round and about, in twos and threes there could be found the Adullamite camps of the Labour Left, Cripps, Bevan *et al*. The story of Cripps is too complicated for record here. Sent to Russia as Britain's envoy he returned to Britain to become Leader of the House of Commons. Dissatisfied with Britain's performance in a dark hour he proposed privately to Churchill changes in our system of command which would certainly have proved disastrous. Being a gentleman and a patriot as well as a politician he readily agreed to defer the crunch and emerged in the last half of the war as a splendid Minister of Aircraft Production who deserved and received the praise of all. Aneurin Bevan was described by Churchill as a 'squalid nuisance'.[1] It is certainly true that the slightest flirtation with the ideas he promulgated would have plunged Britain into irretrievable disaster. Still, after the war he made an excellent Minister of Health and an excellent Minister of Labour.

Sometimes a storm in the Parliamentary tea-cup wasted much valuable time. One example of this may perhaps be mentioned.[2] Fairly early in the war the Royal Air Force requisitioned a large apartment block facing Regent's Park, which they used as an aircrew receiving centre and which formed part of No 54 Group of Training Command. This Group was commanded by Brigadier-General Critchley until June 1943 when he left to join the Board of BOAC. With typical ingenuity the Royal Air Force proceeded to run a farm in Regent's Park. The swill from the centre was used to feed pigs and the farm also raised vegetables and chickens. The produce supplied the needs of a number of messes including, of course, that in Regent's Park. Later in 1944 Austin Hopkinson, an Independent MP launched a major attack on Critchley in the House of Commons[3] alleging irregularity in running BOAC and irregularities too in the matter of RAF sales of pigmeat which could be linked with Critchley through his connexion with No 54 Group. The Secretary of State for Air had bought some sausages! Hopkinson's speech in December 1944 occupied seventeen columns of Hansard. The Cabinet took it all very seriously. Attlee in particular was strong for a purge. A judicial enquiry was proposed. But then the Cabinet had second thoughts. The Regent's Park affair had already been investigated. The Commander-in-Chief Training Command had made enquiries and dealt with the case summarily and properly, administering admonishments. It would be difficult to re-open. And Queen Mary had had some pigmeat too! The prospect of requiring Her Majesty to give evidence was undoubtedly a daunting one. So Regent's Park was dropped and Swinton investigated the complaints about BOAC, which were found to be without substance. It is difficult to estimate how many hours of Ministers' time were taken up by this episode. The records of the Prime Minister's office devoted to it are three to four inches thick. This was a lot for a land still locked in deadly battles.

Intelligence

The Intelligence organisation at the Air Ministry had to find out all it could about the Luftwaffe and do what it could to prevent the Luftwaffe returning the compliment. Its weapons included the monitoring of Luftwaffe W/T transmissions, the 'Y' Service as it was called, the reports of agents in the Resistance and elsewhere, examination of captured equipment, examination of published material, often most valuable, and a mass of high quality photographic evidence from the PRU. More valuable than all this were the fruits of cryptography, 'Ultra' for short. On the whole, the Air Ministry Intelligence organisation worked well. It had many successes to its credit and it is difficult to point to a serious blunder. In the end it was organised under an Assistant Chief of the Air Staff and several Directors of Intelligence. One of them was concerned with security, ie coping with enemy agents and preventing the inadvertent disclosure of information valuable to the enemy. This last could happen through incautious public statements, careless talk in clubs, pubs or private houses, careless talk on the telephone where a crossed line could lead anywhere. For the most part it was straightforward police work and it was efficiently performed. The Air Ministry Intelligence organisation patiently explored the strength and organisation of the Luftwaffe both before and after the outbreak of war. One of its main points of entry was of course the identification of squadron call signs. By adopting this technique the Air Ministry laid itself open to deception attack. Germany was less skilful than Britain in such techniques and the conclusions of the British Air Staff, though always slightly high of the mark, were on the whole both sound and consistent. It was less successful with the Italian Air Force, where its serious exaggeration of Italian air strength could have had damaging consequences had it been taken seriously, as it was not, by those in authority. In the course of the Second World War Churchill, surely egged on by Lindemann, made several attempts to prove that Air Ministry estimates of German air strength were excessive. Churchill even went so far as to commission Mr Justice Singleton to report on the matter.[4] By this act he displayed a touching but inappropriate faith in the ability of the judiciary to penetrate Intelligence tangles.

Ultra

The story of Ultra is a remarkable one and has been dealt with unofficially in many publications. Though extensive, the literature of the subject is not easy to evaluate and a brief summary may be in order here. To start with some elementary points; a set of cypher books provides only a modest degree of security. Exposed to cryptanalysis, an ancient science, cypher books quickly display soft areas which the strange masters of the art of cryptanalysis—mathematicians, chess players and odd bodies with a strange and subtle extra sense—are quick to spot. There follows the gentle art of re-cyphering in which cyphered messages are submitted to a numerical transformation, that is to say to a set of numerical tables which are changed at regular intervals. If there is plenty of W/T traffic, as happens in times of stress, or if the re-cyphering tables are changed infrequently, the cryptanalysts soon get to grips with this. The final refinement is of course the 'one-time pad', the cypher made up in printed pads which is used once and then destroyed. This should provide 100 per cent security. Still, the essence of the idea is that a one-time pad should be a random selection of numbers, and the thought is bound to occur 'how random is random?' The alternative to a system of cypher tables is the cypher machine. In principle such a machine takes in the text and exposes the letters to vastly extensive transformations by means of electrical circuitry. The pattern of this circuitry can be varied at any time. To exchange messages between two agencies each must have a machine and the receiver must be aware of the exact machine setting used by the sender. It follows that in any cypher machine network there must be top secret documents fairly widely distributed containing cypher machine settings for particular dates.

The most famous cypher machine in history is the German Enigma. This was developed for military purposes from a commercial cypher machine which was patented and could be bought over the counter in Germany as early as 1919. As originally developed for military purposes, Enigma resembled a typewriter attached to a set of three rotating drums. The order of the drums could be changed and each drum had twenty-six different starting positions. The circuitry could also be varied by the use of ten pairs of changeable connecting plugs. Incredibly, Poland, which had a deep interest in German and Russian military moves, succeeded in reading Enigma. This remarkable result came from a long-term research effort which involved buying a commercial Enigma and employing a team of especially trained cryptographers and a specially developed device (in effect a primitive computer, though not an electronic one) to eat away at the secrets of the drums and plugs. It is clear from Gustave Bertrand's fascinating book[5] that the Poles received much help from the French Deuxième Bureau who, through their secret intelligence, contributed a great deal, in particular: the fact that Enigma was a machine, including some valuable information on how it worked; and details of German cypher operating procedures.

The Poles knew that Germany planned to increase the complexity of Enigma, and in 1938 this duly happened. Nothing was learned of the German plans to invade Austria in March 1938 because W/T silence was preserved. Later that year Germany added extra drums to Enigma.

Instead of three there were five drums though only three were in the machine at any one time. This increased the complexity of the machine by a factor of ten. The brave, far-seeing and highly enterprising Poles were cut off.

One of the less conspicuous consequences of the Anglo/French guarantee to Poland in 1939 was that when the Poles felt that the axe was about to descend on their neck they summoned a memorable meeting in Warsaw. At this meeting Poland gave to Britain and France one copy each of their Polish-made Enigma plus an equally invaluable account of their primitive computing device, and of their mathematical theory and techniques. It is difficult to imagine a more noble act. After Poland was crushed her cryptographic team moved to Paris, though she would have preferred a tripartite team. So from October 1939 onwards, separate cryptographic teams were at work near Paris and at Bletchley Park in Buckinghamshire with an agreement to exchange break-throughs, of which there were a modest number. At this stage the Polish/French team was small—perhaps thirty to forty people all told—while powerful forces were moving towards Bletchley Park. After the fall of France the Poles carried on for a time in the unoccupied area at Uzès near Nîmes, later retreating to Spain whither they were pursued by the Gestapo. Bravely and miraculously the secret of Enigma breaking was kept intact at this dangerous stage. One can but admire the bravery and skill by which Poland and France defended the vital secrets.

Let us now look at the value of Enigma-derived intelligence over the period from the summer of 1940 until 1945. Some authors have suggested that over this period we could know and forestall every German move. It was not so, as the following elementary points will make clear:

1. No message could be decrypted unless it was put out on W/T. Many vital messages were not so broadcast eg any relating to the German offensive in the Ardennes over New Year 1944/45.
2. Possession of the German Enigma machine meant in straight intelligence terms, nothing at all. At least one such machine was captured by Britain during the war. This fact, or the suspicion of the fact, of course, must have worried Germany. But after careful thought they continued to use Enigma. Why? Surely because, as their mathematicians could tell you, Enigma was useless without the key. A W/T message in Enigma is received. Here is the message. Here is the machine. What chances of decrypting?

Nothing can be done without knowing the setting for the day. The chances of getting this right have been put at 1 in 6×10^{21}. But even so what chance was there of decrypting Enigma, with a daily change of key, at those odds, given all the computers in the world? German crytographers concluded that there was no risk. They had a case, but they were wrong.

3. Enigma was not tied to a standard procedure used for all secret operational messages. The German Navy, for example, used no less than thirteen cyphers on Enigma and some of them were never decrypted at all. The chance of a break-through was much affected by the volume of traffic and by the incidence of procedural indiscretions.

4. Decrypts are of small value if they are out of date. In the early days they were sometimes months out of date. Admittedly, as Bletchley Park's skills increased and their apparatus grew more and more sophisticated they could be very speedy indeed, even with the cypher key being changed daily.

5. Too obvious a response to decrypted material could easily blow the gaff. So much restraint was necessary. Risks were taken from time to time but on the whole the material was used with discretion.

Despite these inevitable limitations the decrypted material was of immense value to the Allies. The intelligence resulting from this work was named 'Ultra' and an immensely efficient system controlling the security and distribution of the information was devised and implemented. The impression is sometimes given that Ultra 'won the war' for the Allies. This of course is not so, valuable though this intelligence proved to be. Wars are won by soldiers, sailors, airmen, and perhaps most conspicuously of all, by merchant seamen. The point can be illustrated by a reference to the situation at El Alamein in July 1942. Here Ultra could tell you a lot of things you just did not want to know, like how Rommel would be in Cairo in two to three days' time. If Auchinleck or Montgomery on the Alamein Line had had no help from Ultra it would not have been decisive. Of course it was an immense help to know in advance about Rommel's plans about air and sea sources of supply and more often than not to destroy them *en route*. But this was not the decisive reason why Britain won at El Alamein. The reason was more fundamental. At this point in the North African campaign the Imperial forces were in an immensely strong defensive position and they were sustained by more men, tanks and aircraft supplies than their enemies.

Not the least important service rendered by Ultra was its contribution to deception operations. Of this Professor Michael Howard has said:[6]

> To put it very briefly our reading of German traffic gave us some idea of what they feared we might do, which enabled our deception staff to play on their fears. Even more important, it enabled them to see how the enemy was swallowing our deception measures.

Enigma was also used as a basis for Japanese cyphers, and some of the secrets of the Japanese diplomatic code were penetrated by American cryptanalysts in a system called 'Magic'. So it happened that on 7 December 1941, a Sunday for sure, the telegram telling the Japanese Ambassador in Washington that the United States and Japan were at crisis point was presented in decrypted form on an American desk before it reached that of the Japanese Ambassador.

So much for our penetration of German cyphers; what about their penetration of ours? Until June 1943 the German naval cryptanalysis service read the Royal Navy's convoy routing instructions and even their daily U-boat situation reports. The consequences of this may be left to the imagination. In the Middle East from September 1941 until August 1942, Rommel and OKW were fully informed about most British plans and moves as the result of the Germans having obtained a copy of the cypher used by the American Military Attaché in Cairo in his almost daily reports to Washington.[7] This was the period of Rommel's greatest triumphs. One is bound to wonder what other Allied secrets were penetrated in circumstances of which we are still unaware.

Night air defence

When Germany was defeated in her attempt to crush the Royal Air Force in the summer of 1940 and went over to bombing by night, the air defences of Britain in the hours of darkness were largely non-effective. It is true that no less than eleven German night bombers fell victims to a pretty primitive Fighter Command defence in June 1940, but there may well have been special operational reasons for this on the German side. In November 1940 Fighter Command possessed eleven night-fighter squadrons: four of Hurricanes, four of Blenheims, two of Defiants and one squadron of Beaufighters. Six of these squadrons, the

Hurricanes and the Defiants, lacking AI equipment, could see nothing in the dark. The four squadrons of Blenheims, with virtually non-functional AI could see for practical purposes nothing and anyway were not fast enough to catch what little they saw. The Beaufighters were a different story; newly arrived and with a great future before them the main problem at this stage was to make them work. In other words they suffered all the disabilities which inevitably attach to bringing a new type of aircraft into service. What else was there with which to attack the German night bombers at this stage, ie during the winter of 1940/41? The answer was—precious little. There were AA guns of course, but without adequate radar gun-laying equipment these had little chance of hitting an enemy bomber. Indeed, research would probably show that at this stage their activities killed more Britons than Germans. Still, they made a comforting noise. There were the balloons, trailing their steel cables, always liable to break loose in capricious style. There are statistics around, mostly unreliable, which suggest that a few German bombers over the winter of 1940/41 may have been brought down over Britain for other natural (mechanical or meteorological) causes. But for practical purposes it may be taken that resistance to night air attack over the winter of 1940/41 was on the moral rather than the physical plane. Of course many great developments were in the pipeline. For the guns and searchlights there was radar gun-laying gear. This was to improve very greatly during the war, and came to a spectacular climax when in operation against the flying bombs in 1944. Aircraft could look ahead to improved forms of AI, the greatest of which of course depended upon the installation of the cavity magnetron to which reference was made in Chapter 6. The AI of 1940/41 vintage could see its enemy at a range of three miles if all went well. A night-fighter pilot under normal conditions needs more than this to put him on the tail of a bomber. This need was met by two important developments, namely the Ground Controlled Interception set (GCI) and the PPI tube. A GCI station was in effect a caravan sited in a convenient field away from Sector Headquarters, and equipped with GCI radar and R/T from which a Controller could direct a night air interception. There were many advantages in controlling night interceptions away from Sector Headquarters, where there were a multitude of distractions. The heart of the GCI set was the PPI (Plan Position Indicator) tube. In simple terms, the Controller looked at a cathode ray tube on which he would see, among other things, two phosphorescent dots. One represented the German raider, the other the pursuing Beaufighter. Information about heights was available separately. The cathode ray tube was always orientated north and south so it was comparatively simple for the Controller to guide the Beaufighter pilot by R/T towards his enemy. The PPI tube was a great radar achievement. It came not from scientists working in ivory towers but from scientists working with engineers and rubbing shoulders daily with the pilots, controllers and the rest who had to make it all work. This was the mix organised by the Telecommunications Research Establishment (TRE), first at Bawdsey on the east coast, then at Swanage and later (scared out of seaside Swanage by the Bruneval raid) at Malvern in Worcestershire. It is deeply significant that Germany never produced a PPI tube or anything like it. Remarkably, Britain in this field was dominant in practical engineering and military application.

The end of the night-fighter is rather an anti-climax. No sooner had Britain put her night air defences in order than for practical purposes she ran out of bandits. With the opening of the attack on Russia in mid-1941 Germany virtually abandoned the night air assault on Britain in order to point the Luftwaffe eastwards. Of course there was the occasional raid and even the 'Little Blitz' of the winter of 1943/44. But on the whole the Royal Air Force felt that they had been put to much unnecessary trouble. The orchestra was ready but the audience stayed away.

German beams

In June 1940 Dr R. V. Jones, a distinguished physicist and head of the scientific intelligence unit in the Air Ministry, came to the conclusion that the Germans had developed a radio beam system called *Knickebein* for bombing blind targets. His conclusion was controversial, because there were good technical and theoretical reasons for doubting whether a radio beam good for night landings over ten miles or so would work at a range of a hundred miles or more. With the help of Churchill tests were made, and there sure enough over the Midlands were the two beams. The director beam gave the incoming bomber a line to steer on. The pilot's earphones gave him Morse dots on one side of the line, dashes on the other and a continuous note when plumb on the beam. The second beam from a different station informed the pilot when he was over the target. This was the ingenious *Knickebein*, which the Luft-waffe protected by making part of the necessary black boxes look like blind landing gear. But *Knickebein* was soon in trouble. Medical diathermy sets bought up by the Air Ministry and quickly modified soon supplied the Luftwaffe with so many dots that they scarcely knew whether they were coming or going. Worse, the Luftwaffe, realising that we understood *Knickebein*, believed that we would put night-fighters in the beam. The Luftwaffe acquired most of its early operational experience of *Knickebein* in the summer of 1940. This proved unfortunate for them. The device was detected, counter-measures initiated and the Luftwaffe suffered what may well have been avoidable casualties in flving, often at modest altitudes, on what were in fact proving flights. The Luftwaffe had two successor systems up its sleeve, the intriguingly named *X-gerät* and *Y-gerät* (ie 'X-apparatus'). *X-gerät*, an improved *Knickebein*, was designed only to be carried by a handful of pathfinder bombers. *Y-gerät* (of which we were pre-warned by Ultra) was a single beam affair which indicated arrival over the target by measuring distance from the point of origin of the beam by a highly accurate electronic device. Counter-measures to both *X-gerät* and *Y-gerät* were soon devised thanks to the skill of scientific intelligence and the enthusiasm and drive of all concerned.

The Coventry raid

On the night of 14/15 November 1940 the Luftwaffe made a heavy attack on Coventry. It was led by the celebrated *Kampfgeschwader* 100 using the *X-gerät* on a night of bright moonlight. Fires were started, visible at great distances, and heavy damage was caused, not least to the aero engine industry. 600 civilians were killed. The raid illustrates very vividly the kind of problems which confronted the Air Ministry almost daily, if indeed not more frequently in war-time. It also provided examples of the variety of problems which beset historians thirty years or so later. Most of the story is now available in the Public Record Office and it has been admirably written up in an article by Norman Evans of that Department in the *Journal of the Royal United Service Institution* for September 1976.

In essence:

1. In October 1940 information was obtained from Ultra that the Luftwaffe was planning a major night bombing attack on Britain, code name 'Moonlight Sonata'.
2. Indications of the point or points of attack were vague: Greater London, or Harwich, or the Home Counties, or the Farnborough area, or the Rochester area.

3. On 11 November 1940 a captured Luftwaffe pilot revealed that 'Moonlight Sonata' would be directed against Birmingham or Coventry. Also that riots had broken out in London and that Buckingham Palace had been stormed. So much for that.

4. The Air Ministry prepared a counter plan based, as best as it could be, on this elusive evidence—Operation 'Cold Water'. Its elements included alerting the night-fighter forces, intruder activities, bombing German airfields and radio beam stations. There was a bit of a muddle about dates. The code name 'Moonlight Sonata' hinted at an attack at full moon, due at 03.23 hours on 15 November. But 'Cold Water' was planned for any day between 15 and 20 November. In fact 'Moonlight Sonata' was launched on the night of 14/15 November 1940.

5. On 14 November Churchill was informed of these events and advised that the target would probably prove to be in the London area but that if it turned out to be Coventry or Birmingham appropriate action would be taken.

6. It is clear from Sir David Hunt's letter in *The Times* of 28 August 1976 that Churchill received this memorandum on his way to Ditchley Park. He returned to London smartly, intending to be there to face the music in whatever shape it arrived.

7. At 15.00 hours on the day of the Coventry raid the Air Ministry Radio Counter-Measures organisation reported that *X-gerät* beams were intersecting over Coventry. The 'Cold Water' executive was at once issued plus the necessary correcting orders.

So much for the facts. Now for the historians.

1. It has been stated that Coventry was sacrificed to save the deadly secrets of Ultra. Clearly, there is no foundation for this.

2. R. V. Jones in his contribution to *The Secret War* on BBC Television early in 1977 has stated that though the *X-gerät* was well and truly jammed, it was jammed on the wrong modulation frequency.* So KG 100 were allowed to proceed unhindered to Coventry.

The only point of substance arises from Jones' contribution. The essence

---

* It is impossible to avoid technicalities. A beam goes out on a radio or TV frequency and so is received. As such it is inaudible to the human ear and so has to be converted in such a way as to be audible. There is then the choice of what musical note in the scale should be chosen. On this occasion we got it wrong.

of the matter is this. Coventry suffered a deadly attack and the impression has been created that this could in one way or another have been avoided. In this writer's opinion this impression is mainly without foundation. Let us assume that Ultra had revealed (as it did not) that Coventry was the target and that the RCM had worked (as they did not). What would have happened? Suppose that when *Kampfgeschwader* 100 set off they had run into such a muddle of dots that they could make no sense of the beams. It was a bright moonlit night. Collier remarks that beams 'were laid over the city but seem scarcely to have been needed, for bright moonlight clearly revealed its main features'. The features included the spire of Coventry Cathedral, nearly 300 feet high. There is surely every presumption that in the situation hypothecated, the Luftwaffe bombers, led by the crack *Kampfgeschwader* 100 pathfinders, would have set a course for Coventry and in all probability found it. Failing Coventry, they would scarcely have failed to find some other large Midlands city, perhaps Birmingham with its population of roughly one million, most of them devoted to production for the armed forces. In fact, as we know, enough warning was received in Britain to alert the air defences. These defences, guns and night-fighters various, were quite incapable of destroying Luftwaffe night-bombers even in bright moonlight, just as the Luftwaffe night-fighters were incapable of destroying British night-bombers in similar circumstances. The dawn of night air defence was still quite a way off. Given the weather, Coventry or some larger West Midlands city was a dead duck from the start.

The attack from long-range weapons

The start of this story is so well described in Collier's book that it would be foolish to alter it:

Soon after the outbreak of war in 1939 the British Naval Attaché in Oslo received an anonymous letter. His correspondent asked whether the British Government were interested in receiving a report on German technical developments. If they were they should, he suggested, signify their interest by causing a small change to be made in the preamble to our German news broadcast on a certain evening. The offer was accepted; the change was made; and early in November the report arrived. It contained a wealth of information about German technical and scientific projects. Amongst other things, it told us that the Germans had two kinds of radar, that they were experimenting with gyroscopically stabilised rockets, and that they had an important experimental station at a place called Peenemünde, on the island of Usedom off the Baltic coast. The information covered so wide a field, and implied such an intimate knowledge of so many subjects, as to cast doubt on the good faith of our correspondent. It was argued that one man could not know so much unless he had been briefed to hoax us. The outcome showed, however, that much, at any rate, of the report was accurate. The existence of two kinds of German radar—known respectively as Freya and Würzburg—was confirmed by testimony not to be denied. In due course the sets were photographed, and in 1942 a Würzburg set was inspected and dismantled by a British radio mechanic in the course of a daring raid on the coast of Normandy. Again, the Oslo report said that the enemy was experimenting with remote-controlled glider bombs. After nearly four years the Henschel 293, a weapon conforming with that description, was used against our shipping. And these were not the sole examples of a prescience which caused a leading member of the Intelligence Branch of the Air Ministry to say later that 'in the few dull moments of the war' he used to turn to the Oslo report 'to see what should be coming along next'.[8]

The Oslo report must be regarded as one of the most significant documents in military history. It all came true but acceptance of the reality of the rocket threat was slow in arriving, as our story will make plain.

Germany as a military nation is undoubtedly ingenious. Take, for example, Big Bertha in the First World War, a railway-borne gun that threw a shell into Paris at a range of 75 miles. The range calculations had to allow for the rotation of the Earth during the passage of the shell. It thus furnished ideal pabulum for problems in dynamics for aspirant Cambridge wranglers. The technical problems were no less formidable. In the Second World War German ideas about artillery and rocketry were ingenious to a degree. In the conventional field there was the magnificent 88mm weapon equally at home for anti-aircraft and anti-tank work. In the unconventional field Germany produced at least three brilliant innovations: the multi-barrelled long-range gun, the V1 and the V2. The first idea never came to fruition, which was certainly just as well for London. It consisted of an underground installation at Mimoyecques, near Calais, housing two twenty-five-barrelled long-range guns firing 6-inch shells and lined up on London. Had the idea been fulfilled that would certainly have been the end of London. The reason why it failed can be found in a mixture of technology and timing. Technically, the idea was capable of being made to work, though there were plenty of difficult problems to be overcome. The main problem was timing. The project began late and by the time it was nearing completion D-Day was not far away. So from the start it ran the risk of its site being overrun. More serious than this, the necessary excavations produced mounds of spoil which the Allies assumed arose from V1 or V2 storage sites. The spoil was conspicuous and the Allies were plastering anything in this line. So Mimoyecques received the full treatment from the Allied air forces, and that for practical purposes was that.

The other threats were from the German 'Revenge' weapons the so-called V1s and V2s. It is interesting to look at this story first in the round and then in a little more detail. First the V2s, the long-range rockets. One thousand or so of them fell on Britain and each of them had a warhead weighing 1 ton. So the total V2 assault throughout 1944/5 amounted to less than Bomber Command could deliver with much greater accuracy in one night. But this of course is hindsight. At the time no one knew how many rockets were coming or how large their warhead would turn out to be. Warheads of up to 10 tons were mentioned. The possibility that hundreds of these would be lobbed into London daily was not reassuring. The V1, the flying bomb, was a different story. No less than 10,000 of these were thrown at us. Only one-third arrived. The rest were shot down, hit balloons or fell by the wayside for reasons various. So, once again, viewed in hindsight this was not a great matter. But in fact, if Germany had been more fortunate, the results could have been very different. The V1 was a simple weapon, unlike the V2 which was far from simple. A modest monoplane, a ram-jet motor of the simplest kind, a simple magnetic/gyroscopic guidance system. Point it off; tell the engine to stop after X miles and that was that. The first V1 fell in Britain on 12 June 1944. It was aimed at London. But if the V1 attack had been, say, one month earlier, if production had been improved by, say, ten times (which was perfectly possible) and if the attack had been pointed not at London, where the scale of assault could be absorbed, but rather at the invasion assembly ports while the D-Day forces were assembling, what then? And suppose the German organisation had been capable of turning the V1 force on the invasion beaches on the night of D-Day plus one? The danger from the V1 was very real.

Despite the Oslo report, Britain was late in waking up to the V1 and V2. In April 1943 evidence of German long-range rockets was received in Britain. Though scanty, this evidence was deemed sufficiently serious to warrant the appointment of a Minister to concentrate on the problem. The task was given to Duncan Sandys, Joint Parliamentary Secretary to the Ministry of Supply. In May 1943 he circulated a paper postulating a multi-stage rocket, weighing 70 tons, a warhead weighing up to 10 tons and a range of up to 150 miles. In June 1943 two large rockets were photographed at the German rocket research station at Peenemünde on the Baltic. The technology required to send rockets of this size over long distances was unknown in Britain and there was in consequence much scepticism, particularly on the part of Cherwell who thought the V2 might be a hoax to conceal the development of a flying bomb. He was right enough about the development of a flying bomb but wrong about the V2 rocket. And as R. V. Jones, the Air Ministry scientist who was at the heart of investigating these matters, remarked the Germans would scarcely parade a bogus V2 rocket at Peenemünde, so encouraging an air attack on what was by any test an extremely important German research establishment. On the night of 17/18 August 1943 Bomber Command carried out a heavy and successful raid on Peenemünde. The target was some 600 miles from Bomber Command bases and the tactical requirements called for the destruction of specified buildings. The attack, which was carried out in clear moonlight and was attended by heavy casualties, was supervised by a Master Bomber, Group Captain Searby, who remained in the vicinity and controlled the oncoming bombers by R/T. Great destruction was caused resulting in a serious delay to the rocket and flying bomb programme. Early reports in Germany exaggerated the damage caused and this may have been one of the culminating causes of the death of Jeschonnek, the Luftwaffe Chief of Staff who killed himself shortly after the raid. Supporting attacks were made on sites in France thought to be connected with the V2, for instance at Watten near Calais, and factories thought (wrongly) to be producing rocket fuel were also attacked. Not much more was heard of the V2 until the summer of 1944, when the Polish Resistance captured parts of a fallen V2 near Blizna and in circumstances of the greatest gallantry arranged for them to be flown by Dakota to Britain. In June 1944 a V2 landed intact in Sweden and was removed after suitable bargaining to Britain, where it was re-assembled and tested. This cleared up the mystery of the propellant (alcohol plus liquid oxygen) but misled the scientists by containing an a-typical collection of radio aids.

Nevertheless, with the help of this data, Jones was able to write a paper giving a pretty accurate description of the V2. Time was now growing short and the first V2 fell on Britain twelve days later. Technical delays, premature detonation and such were largely responsible for the delay in introducing this weapon, which had been under development for some eight years and had received the personal backing of Hitler in July 1943.

By the summer of 1943, evidence of the existence of the V1 was reaching London. By October 1943 a possible V1 had been identified in a PRU shot of Peenemünde; by November it had been photographed on a launching site and by the beginning of December 1943 no less than seventy-two launching sites had been identified in France. They were a trifle too conspicuous for the keen-eyed PRU, and in December 1943 they were well and truly blitzed by the Anglo-American Air Forces. Germany responded with modified launching sites which were more difficult to detect. The first V1 was the forerunner of some 3,500 more, not counting those that were shot down or went astray. The V1s and the V2s between them delivered some 4,500 tons of warheads on Britain. The Anglo-American response was to drop 35,000 tons of bombs on V1 and V2 sites over the period August 1943 to 12 June 1944 and no less than 118,000 tons of bombs on similar targets from 12 June to the end of August 1944.[9] By early September 1944 the V1 sites were overrun. That was virtually the end of the V1, except for weapons launched from the air of which there were still more to come. The V2 was just getting into its stride and continued in its modest way until the spring of 1945. On 7 September 1944 Sandys stated, no doubt on the strength of an official brief, that the Battle of London was over except for 'the last few shots'. The first V2 arrived next day and there were a thousand or more to follow, plus some hundreds of V1s. London was not amused.

There was little enough that the defences could do about the V2 attack. After the attack on Peenemünde the assembly of the V2 and the manufacture of many components was removed to an underground factory in the Harz Mountains. No launcher was needed. The V2 could be shot off from any place on any road. Factories suspected of contributing to the V2 set-up could be and were bombed, but it is hard to believe that much was achieved along this line. Defence against the flying bomb was a very different matter. 10,000 or so were launched and roughly 7,500 were observed by the British defences. No less than half the V1s observed were destroyed in the air, a superb achievement. There were three forms of overt defences: balloons, fighters and guns. Our old favourite the balloon came into its own in a modest way, claiming 6 per cent of the victories. When the V1s cut the balloon cables Fighter Command had the cables fitted with separable linkages with attached parachutes, which caused the V1s to stall. It can have been no fun for citizens living near such installations. Fighters claimed 47 per cent and AA guns about the same. The success of the fighters was due in part to the fact that the V1 was slower than its design speed. So the fastest fighters, the Mosquitos, Mustangs, Spitfire XIVs and Tempests, could just catch it.* Why design an unmanned terror weapon that enemy fighters could catch? The success of the AA guns was due to three factors: the brilliant performance of the American gun-laying radar set (a heritage of Tizard's trip to the US in 1940 and to admirable achievements at the Radiation Laboratory at the Massachusetts Institute of Technology), an American-designed proximity fuse in the AA shells which ensured detonation on a near miss, and finally a bold decision to redeploy the gun defences on the coast taken by Air Marshal Sir Roderick Hill of Fighter Command, to the dismay of the Air Staff who were fortunately not consulted. On the coast, firing seawards the AA gunners had no cause to worry about where their shells would end up, and of course their radar, looking out to sea had an ideal environment. So a great success came our way. We have spoken of overt defences. There was also a covert defence. The V1 was essentially a cheap and crude weapon, though none the less valuable for that. Its navigational facilities were simple; it was pointed off, allowance was made for wind, and when the fuel ran out it fell. So it was vital for Germany to learn what sort of range errors were resulting. Press censorship was useful up to a point, but until Britain got the message much valuable information reached Germany from obituary columns in local newspapers, for instance in the Croydon area which achieved the dubious distinction of heading the League Table for 'incidents'. But the German *Abwehr* also came to our aid. Their agents in Britain, controlled, strange as it may seem, by British MI5, were provided with range information thought up by clever men and women in Whitehall and elsewhere. Of course, deflecting flying bombs involves some tricky problems. We deflect the bomb from point A to point B. This is fine for point A if it works, as it may not. But what about the citizens at B if it works, as it might? These are

---

* Of 1,771 V1s destroyed by aircraft, 638 fell to Tempests, 428 to Mosquitos, 303 to Spitfire XIVs, and 232 to Mustangs. The remaining 170 were destroyed by Spitfire XIIs, IXs and Vs, Typhoons and Meteors.

difficult areas. Home Security Minister Morrison was troubled, as well he might have been. Those who take upon themselves such responsibilities surely take much upon themselves.

So we reach the end of our brief account of the V1 and V2. 5,000 tons or so of German explosives descending on Britain, mostly on London, and aimed with great inaccuracy. In reply 150,000 tons aimed by the Allies at the sources of this assault, including, it must be mentioned, the great attack by Bomber Command on the V1 storage site at Saint-Leu-d'Esserent where, using the Wallis 'earthquake bombs', the Command entombed countless V1s and all their keepers. In retrospect the revenge assault sounds trivial. But in fact it was not so. The V2 did not matter. As things turned out the scale of attack was trifling. As a personal experience facing the V2 presented no problem. If you heard the bang everything was all right. You were safe. The V1 was a very different matter. One heard the approach of the V1. The ram-jet stopped. Who was to get the chop? Most affected were men and women working in offices with glass windows which the V1 turned into arrow-heads. Seasoned surgeons who had to deal with the end product of such attacks were appalled. One V1 fell near the Air Ministry, Kingsway, in the summer of 1944; many were killed and injured. These attacks fell on London after five years of war and it is hard to overstate the moral achievement of London in resisting them. Strange as it may seem, London in 1944 was braver and tougher than London in 1917. These events were serious enough but matters could have ended very differently. Had PRU been less skilful, had Peenemünde not been attacked, had Germany pursued a more consistent policy about revenge weapons, had the delays been reduced and the attack directed to the points of departure of the 'Overlord' forces, most of all, had the Allies not commanded the air over France and the Low Countries—what then? Once again Britain, and for that matter the United States, were lucky.

15

The Air War in the Mediterranean and Middle East

Introduction

In this chapter the term Middle East is used in its special Royal Air Force sense to cover areas which in 1940 included Palestine, Transjordan, Iraq, Malta, Cyprus, Egypt, Aden, the Sudan and East Africa. The historical origin of this rag-bag of territories is mixed, partly colonial of course, but it also bears the impress of the early ideas of Churchill and Trenchard about the role of the Royal Air Force.

The story is an exciting one. In June 1940 such limited units of the Army and the Royal Air Force as existed in these areas should have been cold meat for Germany, Italy and France and their stray allies like Syria and Iraq. But it did not work out that way. There were of course ups and downs, but in the end Britain and her allies swept the Mediterranean clean. The story begins on 10 June 1940. On this day Italy decided that her moment of destiny had arrived and that she should link her fortunes with those of Hitler. She had left the decision late enough in all conscience, as hostilities in France ended only a fortnight later. So the die was cast. A disastrous decision for Italy in the military sense and a cowardly one in the moral sense. 'On this tenth day of June 1940', said President Roosevelt in a remarkable address, 'the hand that held the dagger has struck it into the back of its neighbour.' Still, that was the way it was. There followed some minor and rather ineffective Bomber Command attacks on Northern Italy, attacks which were impeded by the French, who were far from keen to see their great cities of the south exposed to retaliatory bombing at this stage of the game, but more seriously by the weather. It was no fun flying heavily loaded Whitleys and Wellingtons over the Alps in 1940 with minimal navigation resources. But the main scene of activity was of course in the Middle East. Here the set-up was roughly as follows. The Royal Air Force was established in Egypt, Palestine, Transjordan, Iraq, Aden, East Africa, the Sudan and Malta, some twenty squadrons in all numbering perhaps 250 first line aircraft. It was always a firmly held logistic rule of the Royal Air Force that the further the squadron was away from home the older must be its aircraft. So to many Royal Air Force aircraft in the Middle East in mid-1940 the expressive term '*ancien*' would have been appropriate. Nevertheless our story will show that much life remained in those old dogs. On the Italian side aircraft quality was little better but there were many more aircraft, nearly 500 in Libya, East Africa and the Dodecanese alone which could be reinforced at will from Italy and Sicily. Italy was for the most part on interior lines but after the French defeat Britain had to rely on the Takoradi reinforcement route for supplies of short-range aircraft. Such aircraft were crated and shipped to Takoradi on the Gold Coast, re-erected and flown to Cairo via Accra, Lagos, Kano, Maiduguri, Fort Lamy, El Geneina, El Fasher, El Obeid, Khartoum, Wadi Halfa and Luxor. This was a journey of 4,000 miles in conditions for the most part both tropical and primitive. It was suitable only for the hardy. Sturdy Hurricanes thrashed along it mile after mile but never a Spitfire. Reinforcement requirements were high. To maintain a Hurricane squadron in Egypt 50 per cent of new aircraft were needed monthly.

The Royal Air Force was fortunate in its Air Officer Commanding-in-Chief in the Middle East. When Italy joined the war this was Longmore. Longmore was a sailor by origin who before taking over Middle East Command in May 1940 had filled with distinction a wide variety of senior commands in the Royal Air Force. He was intelligent, polished, highly competent and imperturbable, just the man for stormy days in 1940. His naval background was a help in the complex inter-service background of the Middle East at the time. He had held the command for about a year when he handed over to Air Marshal Arthur Tedder. Longmore returned to give other years of invaluable service to the Royal Air Force.

One further comment must be made on the Royal Air Force in the Middle East at that time. Ever since 1918 a high proportion of the Royal Air Force had been stationed abroad. They had been much exposed to deserts whether in Egypt, Transjordan, Iraq, India or Aden. They understood how to handle aircraft under such conditions. Further, though the Middle East presented navigational problems of its own, these problems were on the whole less severe than those which applied in North-West Europe. A pilot flying a Hurricane over the Western Desert in 1940 was more at home than one in charge of a Wellington over the

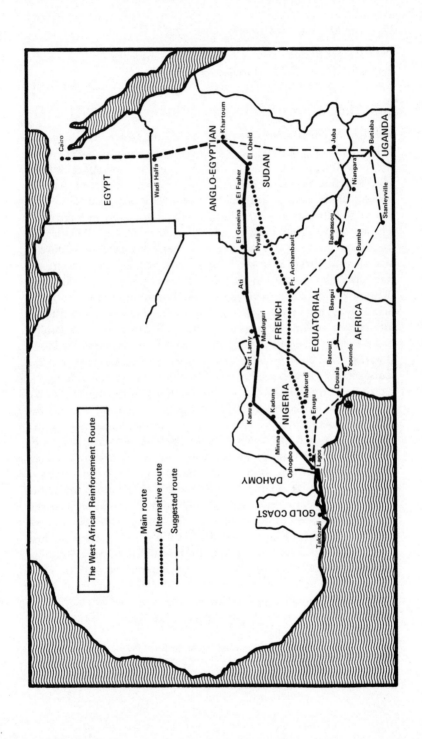

The West African Reinforcement Route

— Main route
····· Alternative route
– – – Suggested route

Ruhr at night during the same period. All this made the Royal Air Force especially effective in this theatre.

The Middle East war, 10 June 1940 to 6 April 1941

This part of our story of the war in the Middle East covers the period from the entry of Italy into the war until the German invasion of Greece and Yugoslavia in April 1941. In the Air Ministry, as in other Defence Ministries, the War Book still sat in the safe with part of its contents unused. As the political and military scene darkened it was dusted off and studied afresh. Once again history refused to comply with the rules. The impending involvement of Italy was clear enough for all to see. But the declaration of war by Mussolini in the course of a speech was a novelty in diplomatic practice. In the military sense it was also a novelty for Italy. As Philip Guedalla in his excellent book remarks,[1] the war in the Western Desert came as a surprise to the Italian forces stationed there. British forces had been on a war footing for nine months so they listened with interest to Mussolini's speech broadcast live from Rome. Mussolini said that Italy would be at war with Britain and France from midnight onwards. What could be more natural therefore than that that splendid Canadian, Air Commodore Raymond Collishaw,* then commanding the Royal Air Force units on the western boundary of Egypt, should take him at his word and move swiftly into action. After all, that is what war is all about. The *Regia Aeronautica* was surprised, painfully and expensively surprised, the following morning. The next nine months of the Second World War saw a procession of British victories over Italian forces in North Africa and the Mediterranean. As Britain did not throw up the sponge in the summer of 1940 Marshal Graziani was denied his triumphal entry into Cairo. Instead, and no doubt to his surprise, he found himself unceremoniously bundled out of Egypt. By February 1941 the British Army, superbly supported by the Royal Air Force, had reached Benghazi in Tripoli and by early April 1941 the Italian forces in Abyssinia and East Africa had been overcome, and that colourful and much travelled Emperor Haile Selassie was on his way back to his capital city of Addis Ababa. The Navy of course added to their glory at Taranto and at Matapan. It was in truth a glorious page in the history of British arms. Denis Richards put it like this:

* Later Air Vice-Marshal Collishaw, he had joined the Royal Naval Air Service in 1915 and from 1916 to 1918 had commanded a number of scout squadrons in France. He finished the First World War as the second highest scoring British Empire pilot, with sixty enemy aircraft destroyed.

A force never exceeding two divisions, helped by an average of 200 aircraft, had within two months utterly routed nine Italian divisions and 400 aircraft. It had captured 130,000 prisoners, 1,290 guns and 400 tanks at a cost to itself of less than 3,000 casualties. It had advanced 600 miles over territory aptly described as 'the tactician's paradise and the quartermaster's hell'. In this almost unprecedented feat of arms the Royal Air Force had borne a full share, the measure of which may perhaps be gauged from the fact that on no single occasion were our troops seriously held up by enemy aircraft.[2]

In surveying these activities it is a pleasure to recall that in July 1940 Collishaw was rebuked by Longmore for excessive zeal. Commenting on a particularly thrustful episode by some of Collishaw's pilots, the Commander-in-Chief said 'I consider such operations unjustified having regard to our limited resources.' Collishaw may perhaps have thought this an honourable wound. In an age when it seems fashionable or profitable or both to send up the British armed forces for acts of incompetence or worse, events such as these, which are more common than is supposed, should be remembered. And what a lift it gave to the great British public. For the British public can produce qualities of greatness if great men like Churchill appear to evoke them. In the autumn of 1940 the great cities of Britain, notably London, were submitted to destruction, fire and death. They did not flinch and their behaviour compared very well indeed with that of their predecessors in the First World War. And then a series of victories! On small scale perhaps, but victories. 'It's all going much better,' they said. It was indeed, but war, as Churchill has remarked, is full of unpleasant surprises. The harbingers of the future had arrived already. In October 1940 Mussolini invaded Greece. In January 1941 Hitler ordered German troops to North Africa. In February 1941 General Rommel started his offensive. On 6 April 1941 Germany invaded Greece and Yugoslavia. The Indian summer was over and a grimmer situation faced British arms.

The Middle East war, 6 April to 21 June 1941

This section carries our story forward to 21 June 1941, a date which marked the firing of Wavell and the arrival of Auchinleck. The public announcement came a few days later. And on the following day, a Sunday for sure, Germany invaded Russia. In April 1939 Britain and France had guaranteed the integrity of Roumania and Greece. However, when Italy invaded Greece in October 1940 British aid was restricted, with the approval of the Greek Government, to the move of a few Royal Air Force squadrons. The situation changed on 6 April 1941 when Germany invaded Greece and Yugoslavia. What should Britain do? Rommel had already begun his swift advance which was to take him, a month later, to the frontier of Egypt. The fateful decision was taken to go to the assistance of Greece. In some ways, as an act of integrity and comradeship between allies, it is difficult to criticise this decision. As a practical matter the decision was almost certainly wrong. In the event the Imperial forces were thrown out of Greece and later out of Crete, to which they retired with considerable speed and with a great lack of ceremony. It was all over by the end of May 1941. There was a vast loss of equipment and the Royal Navy suffered severely. Considered from the air point of view the move into Greece made little sense. Armies and navies cannot operate without air support. That lesson was clear enough from Poland, Norway, France ... The German Air Force was on interior lines. But where was the air support for the Imperial troops in Greece to come from? Of course there were a few Royal Air Force squadrons in Greece but their main logistic support was 400–500 miles away. Airfields in Greece or Crete were few or non-existent. Communications by road, by landline, by radio or wireless were minimal. Viewed coldly the operation was just not on. So a sad page was turned. Before leaving it a few points must be made:

1. Crete was conquered by German airborne forces. This statement is a condensation of facts which probably contains a small margin of truth. By a concentration of air power at Maleme airstrip in Crete the way was cleared for the arrival of the German paras. They suffered desperate casualties. The OKW never attempted these tactics again. Desperate casualties both in ships and men were suffered by the Royal Navy, doing as always more than all that was possible to sustain British arms.

2. In these events, in distinction to events a few months earlier, the British Army felt that the Royal Air Force had let them down. So soon had the honeymoon days of Army/Royal Air Force co-operation during General O'Connor's advance to Benghazi been laid aside. This view, wrong but understandable, was dealt with. The controversy that ensued laid the foundations of a strong and enduring partnership which lasted to the end of the Second World War.

3. Churchill was of course the greatest statesman of our time. Without his transcendent qualities Britain and perhaps the Western world

would scarcely have survived. But his greatness did not rest on isolated tactical judgements. After Crete all he had to say to his devoted Secretary of State for Air, Archie Sinclair, was to urge him to make every airfield 'a stronghold of fighting air-groundsmen, and not the abode of uniformed civilians in the prime of life protected by detachments of soldiers.'³ These comments did not reach the defenders of Maleme under their torrent of bombs. Considered coldly, they tell us that Churchill's tactical ideas were those of Flanders, if not Omdurman. Fortunately, being right in detail has little part in real greatness. Still, Churchill was carrying a crushing burden. The German attack on Russia, which added a brave nation of 200 millions to the ranks of Hitler's enemies, was a mere month away. The entry of the United States of America was little more than six months away. After that we could not lose. In the early summer of 1941 these events lay in the future; Britain was alone and outnumbered and Churchill was the man bearing the main responsibility.

4. Three other dramatic developments must be recorded. Two ended well for Britain. The third was something of a disaster. The first event concerned Iraq. Early in April 1941 Rashid Ali, backed by four Iraqi generals known, 'not without reason' as Denis Richards remarks, as the 'Golden Square', seized power in Baghdad. Taking a keen look at British misfortunes in the Mediterranean, they decided that the moment had come to crack down on British forces in Iraq, notably at the Habbaniya cantonment fifty miles west of Baghdad, where the main British forces in the shape of the Royal Air Force were concentrated. Rashid started by forbidding the British to reinforce and when this request was disregarded he moved the Iraqi Army to a desert plateau looking over Habbaniya. The Iraqi forces included 9,000 troops, aircraft and twenty-eight guns and were soon reinforced. Inside Habbaniya there were an aircraft depot and a flying training school commanding between them some seventy non-operational aircraft, mostly *ancien*. There were also six companies of native levies, a company of Royal Air Force armoured cars and 400 men of the King's Own Royal Regiment flown in from Karachi. In this menacing situation Wavell proposed treating with Rashid, though what kind of a deal could have been fixed up other than a humiliating one was hard to see. Unsurprisingly, this advice was little to the taste of Churchill. On 1 May 1941, encouraged by Churchill and our Ambassador in Baghdad,

Habbaniya went into the attack. It was in some sense a *levée en masse*. There were the Habbaniya aircraft, hastily fitted with improvised armament, the Levies, the Army, the ground forces, Wellingtons flown in from Shaibah, Swordfish from HMS *Hermes*. It did not help that our airfield was under direct fire from Iraqi cannon. Against all the odds it was too much for the Iraqi forces. On the fourth night the siege was over. This was not the end of the Iraqi rebellion, which lasted in all four weeks, but it was emphatically the beginning of the end. It was good news for Britain at a time when such news was scarce. These events partly overlapped with those in Crete so Tedder, who by this time was in charge, Longmore having been recalled to London on 3 May 1941, had plenty to think about. More was to follow.

5. The second event concerned Syria. In mid-May 1941 the, reasonably, reluctant Wavell was ordered to move into Syria to forestall a pre-emptive descent by Germany. There were few enough resources to spare for this adventure but fortune smiled and, though the Vichy French fought fiercely, by mid-July 1941 it was all over. A glance at any map will show that the next step for Britain would be to deal with Persia and its oilfields, and this was accomplished without undue difficulty in August.

6. The third event, the resumption of the offensive against Rommel, was less fortunate. Rommel had begun his offensive in February 1941 and while Britain was preoccupied with Greece he had reached the frontier of Egypt, leaving Tobruk as a sally-port in British hands. Wavell, reinforced by some hundreds of tanks convoyed through the Mediterranean, and prodded on by Churchill, launched Operation 'Battleaxe' to relieve Tobruk. Our tanks suffered gravely both from mechanical breakdown and from the German 88mm anti-tank guns. Rommel had his troubles too. On 18 June 1941, says Denis Richards, air reconnaissance disclosed 'the curious spectacle of both armies in retreat'. It was all over in a few days. Churchill was angry. On 21 June 1941 Wavell was fired, and about the same time Longmore too for good measure. There was little logic in this. Both men had done all and more than can be expected of brave and experienced commanders. Still, Churchill could well have been right. History has little use for logic. Graver events were impending. On the following day, 22 June 1941, at 04.00 hours, Ribbentrop delivered a formal declaration of war to the Russian Ambassador in Berlin.

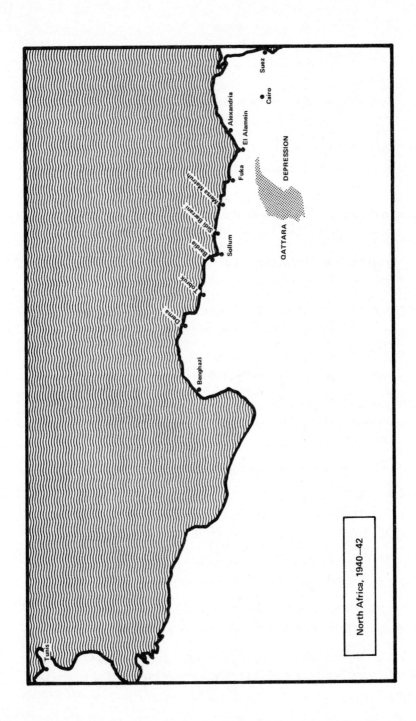

North Africa, 1940—42

The Middle East war, 22 June 1941 to 1 July 1942

In war, as in peace, it is necessary to preserve a sense of proportion. Never was this more necessary than on Sunday 22 June 1941. Germany, looking for a quick kill, invaded Russia. By this act, though many missed the point at the time, Germany increased the ranks of her enemies by a factor of, say, times four. Six months later, with the Japanese attack on the United States, the odds on a German victory were divided by, say, 100.

In the Middle East the number of armed men engaged was measured in hundreds of thousands. In the Russian campaign they were numbered in millions. Still, for Britain the Middle East campaign was of deep significance. It was our only outlet at that time for fighting the enemy on land. It ended in a notable victory. And in the course of the campaign the Army and the Royal Air Force rediscovered how to work together.

Wavell was succeeded by General Sir Claude Auchinleck, at this time Commander-in-Chief, India. Auchinleck was undoubtedly one of the greatest soldiers of the Second World War. Competent, fit, calm, courageous, he was just the man for dangerous days in the Middle East. He made an immediate partnership with Tedder, who had succeeded Longmore as Air Officer Commanding-in-Chief, and from that moment Army/Royal Air Force misunderstandings in the theatre were for practical purposes at an end, though a few ill-informed and mainly unjustified complaints continued. The events of the year June 1941 to July 1942 look something like this:

1. It was agreed that Auchinleck should mount an offensive against Rommel in the autumn ('Crusader'). Churchill of course was strong for an earlier date than Auchinleck and Tedder thought possible. The interval was devoted to reinforcement and training. Special emphasis was put by Auchinleck and Tedder on improving the techniques of tactical air support for the Army, particularly in the direction of communications and combined staffs.
2. 'Crusader' was launched on 18 November 1941, Tobruk was relieved later that month and Benghazi was again in British hands by Christmas Eve 1941. The success was shortlived. Early in 1942 Rommel turned east, and he was soon engaged in a triumphant advance.
3. Early in 1942 Germany resolved belatedly to eliminate Malta, where the Royal Air Force had played a most effective part in attacking

Rommel's lines of sea communication between Tripoli and Sicily. It was easy enough to plaster Malta with bombs from nearby bases. It was hard to defend Malta, because only Malta-based fighters plus AA guns could be used in defence. The figures speak for themselves. The island of Malta is roughly sixteen miles long and nine miles across at its widest point. In the first four months of 1942, 11,000 tons of bombs descended on Malta. 19,000 tons of bombs fell on Greater London, a vastly larger area, during the whole period of the Second World War. The survival of Malta in these circumstances was a miracle made possible by the gallantry of all the island, population and garrison alike. In particular, the part played by the Royal Air Force Commander Air Vice-Marshal Hugh Lloyd was beyond all praise.

4. Malta could only be supplied from the sea. With Crete and Sicily in enemy hands the eastern and western approaches to Malta soon became all but severed. Many gallant convoys were attempted. Some succeeded. Many failed and the loss of merchantmen and warships was most grave. By the spring of 1942 Malta was still operating as a fighter, bomber and transit base. But gliders were beginning to arrive in Sicily, the island was beginning to starve and the writing was on the wall. The island was saved by Rommel who, dazzled by his astounding advance to Alamein in the summer of 1942, decided to postpone Operation 'Hercules', as it was called, and deal with Egypt first.

5. The virtual neutralisation of Malta allowed a number of convoys to reach Rommel who was entirely dependent on such supplies. With their help and vast supplies of stores, especially petrol, captured from the British he continued the series of offensives which brought him to Alamein at the end of June 1942. Rommel thought he would be in Cairo in a few days and so too did Mussolini, who is said to have ordered out his handsome but probably fabulous white charger to ride through the streets of that city. The same view seems to have been held by British staffs in Cairo, for soon the sky over the city was darkened by smoke from burning confidential documents. Combustion proved imperfect, paper being notoriously difficult to burn, and the fall-out is said to have included sizeable chunks of secret papers which were used, tradition says to wrap purchases in the Mousqee. The day became known as Ash Wednesday. Actually, the position of the British forces was far stronger than it seemed. The Alamein Line, thirty-eight miles wide,

was flanked to the north by the sea and to the south by the impenetrable Qattara Depression.

6. The fact that the Eighth Army could reach the Alamein Line without being Stuka-ed, was a triumph for the Allied Air Forces. This term includes with pride South African, American, Australian, Greek and Yugoslav squadrons. And of course many of the aircrews in the Royal Air Force squadrons came from the Dominions. The narrow coastal road could so easily have been a disaster area. Of course not everything could be protected. Tobruk was Stuka-ed and there was not much that the Royal Air Force could do about it. Still the Eighth Army (less many stores) arrived back at this strong defensive line more or less intact. The Desert Air Force was also intact and had lost none of its possessions.

7. The darkest hour precedes the dawn. While the Eighth Army was re-forming on the Alamein Line in the summer of 1942, and the skies of Cairo were dark with the ash of partly consumed secret documents, inconspicuously but profoundly the pattern of the Mediterranean war was changing. At one moment Rommel saw himself as a conqueror in Cairo. A few months later he was chased with considerable lack of dignity out of Egypt. So the fortunes of war changed. What happened? The answer is to be found in many things. We can place first the fact that on the Alamein Line Rommel faced a strong, united and highly professional Allied Air Force. Tedder, its Commander, had more than a touch of genius. Germany had demonstrated clearly enough the power of air forces to control the battlefield. And now the Allied Air Forces had learned their lesson. Strange to say, and tough as the path had been, they were better at it than the Luftwaffe. Tedder had been driven back nearly to Cairo, with the Allied Air Forces displaying immaculate discipline. In this journey he had been driven closer and closer to his basic sources of strength, the supplies, reinforcements and maintenance facilities of the Delta. What of the Army? Under Auchinleck they had chosen a defence line of immense strength. In Washington, Churchill, faced with the dire news of the fall of Tobruk, had been sustained by a characteristically generous act of President Roosevelt. In the 'Crusader' battles the British tanks had faced German 88mm anti-tank (and also anti-aircraft) guns which could outrange and destroy them. The 300 American tanks (Shermans) sent to the Middle East by Roosevelt had a profound effect in the last battle of Alamein. And, finally, Malta had been

let off the hook. Quickly reinforced, it was soon to exact a heavy toll on Rommel's lines of communication with Sicily. Soon he was short of petrol, his supply ships sunk by the Allied Air Forces and no abandoned petrol around for the taking. So, in the twinkling of an eye, triumph into disaster. Rommel at Alamein had reached, all unknowing no doubt, his moment of destiny.

The Middle East war, 1 July to 7 November 1942

This section of our story stretches from the arrival of Rommel on the Alamein Line to the 'Torch' landings in North Africa on 7 November 1942.

During the summer of 1942 attempts to break out by Auchinleck, at this time commanding the Eighth Army as well as acting as Commander-in-Chief, were unsuccessful and many tanks were lost. Equally, Rommel failed in his renewed assault on the Alamein Line. Another German assault on Malta in October 1942, somewhat half-hearted, also failed. Early in August, Auchinleck was replaced by General Sir Harold Alexander from Burma and General Sir Bernard Montgomery was brought from Britain to lead the Eighth Army. A. J. P. Taylor[4] calls Montgomery 'the best British field commander since Wellington'. It is certainly doubtful if Montgomery was a better general than Auchinleck, who possessed every military virtue. Auchinleck was also a great gentleman which was not always helpful, war being often a dirty if brave business. But perhaps it was time for a change. One great benefit which resulted was that from this moment onwards the Commander of the Eighth Army and the Commander of the Desert Air Force, Air Marshal Sir Arthur ('Mary')* Coningham, could work side by side as could Alexander and Tedder. Auchinleck was a great co-operator and a great friend of the Royal Air Force. Montgomery, strangely perhaps, was not less so. The technique of army/air co-operation had been perfected during these testing years in the desert. Three vital elements were involved. The first was tactics and principles, the second communications, and the third joint staff co-operation.

In the last few years of peace there was still something called 'Army Co-operation', a specialist art carried on, figuratively speaking, in dark corners and, to be plain, not taken very seriously. Venerable Audaxes had been seen picking up messages (in the notional battlefield) with sticks attached to their undercarriages. It was of course all undiluted

* 'Mary' is a corruption of 'Maori', Coningham being a New Zealander.

nonsense, the tactics involved belonging to the world of fantasy. The fault must be shared between the Army and the Royal Air Force. In the Battle of France the Royal Air Force learned its lesson the hard way. The Battle of the Desert gave a positive impulse. The Royal Air Force learned its lesson well. There was no special art. There was no question of air forces acting as long-range artillery in fancy and unsuitable aircraft, or as purveyors of fighter cover. It was a question of three services fighting as one, with the air forces exploiting to the full their remarkable capacity for flexibility. Here they intervened in the land battle, but with aircraft that could stand on their own in the air battle. Here they assaulted enemy airfields. Here they attacked enemy convoys. Maximum power could be switched with minimum delay to the point of maximum need. It is immensely to the credit of Tedder that he understood all this. And it is immensely to the credit of Auchinleck and Montgomery that they understood too.

Next, communications. The Royal Air Force, not least because of Lywood's contribution as a signaller, were good communicators. The Army, less so. During many battles before mid-1942 the air forces could do less than they might have done to help because the whereabouts of Army units were unknown. In the summer of 1942 all this was changed. To put it mildly, communications improved.

Lastly, staff work. To conduct a land battle the three services must sit together. In those days there was trouble about the Navy, whose Commanders-in-Chief rarely thought they could contribute unless they could see the sea out of their office windows. There is another matter. During 1941 and 1942 the system of servicing and supplying the Allied Air Forces in the Middle East was transformed. It is no good having 1,000 fighters if three-quarters of them are unserviceable and grounded. In May 1941 Air Vice-Marshal Dawson (from Australia, with which land the destinies of the Royal Air Force have always been so happily associated) was sent from the Ministry of Aircraft Production by Beaverbrook to tidy up maintenance and supply in the Middle East. It was one of Beaverbrook's more successful ideas. There is no space in this brief narrative to describe in detail what he did. Suffice to say that this Engineer officer, strongly supported by Tedder and such able staff officers as Air Vice-Marshal George Pirie, transformed the maintenance situation. The point can be simply expressed. If there are N first line aircraft and their supporting services double in efficiency we have effectively 2N first line aircraft. This is more or less what happened. For this and other reasons, when the last Battle of Alamein began Tedder disposed of around 100 squadrons with a first line strength of (say) 1,200. The Luftwaffe (in this theatre and at that time) could manage perhaps one third of this. On land, Germany was greatly outnumbered in guns, tanks and fighting men. Of course, no sensible man takes statistics too seriously. Still, for what they are worth the figures suggest that the Allies were not badly placed. There was more to it than this. By the autumn of 1942 the Allies had regained the control of sea communications in the Mediterranean. In consequence Rommel was cut off from his supplies. All these advantages could have been thrown away by foolish commanders. Tedder, Alexander and Admiral Sir Andrew Cunningham were not foolish. By November 1942 Rommel had been chased back to Benghazi. Victory fell to the big battalions, operated with high professional skills at all levels.

'Torch'

When the United States joined the war at the end of 1941 one of the first problems to be faced was whether priority should be given by the Allies to the defeat of Japan or to victory in Europe, or whether there should be some kind of compromise. The decision taken by the Allies after a Washington conference in which Churchill participated was to deal with Germany first. In practice, of course, a compromise resulted but on paper Germany was to come first. Stalin's call for an immediate Second Front supported as it was by vehement elements of the British Left, found an echo strangely enough in the mind of General Marshall. In the early months of 1942 there were endless discussions regarding an operation called 'Sledgehammer', involving a 1942 descent on the coast of France. The British Chiefs of Staff successfully resisted this proposal which could only have ended in disaster. Instead, a plan was devised for an allied descent on North-West Africa, an operation ultimately christened (by Churchill) 'Torch'. For a time it was discussed as a possible alternative to a 1943 Allied descent on the coast of France called 'Roundup' with plans to be prepared for both operations. However, by mid-1942 a firm decision had been taken in favour of 'Torch' and the necessary preparations began. The objects of 'Torch' were clear enough; control of the Mediterranean and of the whole North African shore, a springboard to attack the famous soft underbelly of Europe, a chance to exploit our sea and air power under favourable conditions. The difficulties were also clear. The year 1942 was the heyday of the U-boat. What about the safety of the convoys? Then, what of Spain? The landings could only occur more or less under her nose. Franco might not like this and, more seriously perhaps, Franco might fear that Germany would move into Spain. Finally, intelligence. 'Torch' could not be sustained without a massive build-up in Gibraltar. Here, in the late Thirties, the Royal Air Force had constructed, rather daringly in view of ambiguities of the Treaty of Utrecht, a modest air strip stretching our from the north face of the Rock towards the sea. Many hundreds of aircraft must necessarily be parked there before the operation. German agents who were thick on the ground in the area must surely have wondered where they were bound for. Geography scarcely supported Hitler's pet theme of a descent on Norway. And if not Norway what then? Finally, the attitude of France. Her North African colonies were mainly pro-Vichy. What would happen when the Allies descended on Casablanca, Algiers and Oran? These difficulties were clear enough, but Britain and the United States decided to face them. As it turned out all went well. The U-boats were eluded by a combination of good luck and good management. Franco held his hand. Germany did not invade Spain. German intelligence, surprisingly, did not get the message. And Vichy, though it put on a show, did not in the end drastically interfere with events. The problems which arose and which were considerable came from other causes.

The landings took place as planned on 8 November 1942. Slow as Germany had been to appreciate the Allies' plan their reaction was apt and immediate. It is only 100 miles across the Sicilian Narrows and within twenty-four hours German units were pouring across, ferried for the most part by air, and being welcomed at the municipal airport of Tunis by representatives of the French Resident General. France, which fought to keep the Allies out of Morocco and Algeria, welcomed the Germans into Tunis. So the tactical situation was this. Rommel was being chased rapidly westwards towards Tunis by the Eighth Army. The Allied forces landed at Casablanca, Oran and Algiers were moving rapidly eastwards towards Tunis. Considering the relative strengths of the forces involved, which must have been at least three to one against Rommel even if no account is taken of the Allied advantages over Rommel's sea and air communications, there could only have been one end to this, namely that the Axis forces should be put in a box in the north-eastern tip of Tunisia at Cape Bon and forced to surrender. And this indeed is what happened. One quarter of a million Axis personnel, mainly army, were captured. Their aircraft flew back to Sicily. By 12 May 1943 all the Axis forces in North Africa including General von Arnim were taken prisoner, Rommel, by now a sick man, having handed over his command two months earlier. This was the only end to the tactical situation, but in war as in peace logic often does not prevail. And, indeed, the Allies encountered, and survived, many problems, mentioned here without regard to order of importance. First, the weather. Those who contemplate winter holidays in North-West Africa can reflect that in November 1942, twelve inches of rain fell on Gibraltar. This helped roads, airstrips and the rest scarcely at all. Second, basic contacts and communications. Casablanca, the most westerly point of the Allied invasion, is separated from Algiers, the easterly point, by a distance of perhaps 700 miles. This factor presented serious problems of communication and liaison. Next, the command structure. To the east, Alexander and Tedder commanding, with great success, our forces in the Mediterranean. There descend on North-West Africa a splendid Supreme Commander in the shape of General Dwight D. Eisenhower, two armies, one British, one American, plus air and other forces various. How was it all to work together? Thanks to Eisenhower and Tedder, this cat's-cradle of problems was sorted out. Next, inter-nation rows. There was surely plenty of room for these. The countries involved: Britain, the United States of America, the British Dominions and, not least, France. Here was surely a chance to stop fighting Germany and give suitable time to sorting out these (clearly important) quarrels among friends. That this was avoided is due perhaps to three people. Roosevelt and Churchill, of course, but most of all to Eisenhower, the man on the spot who knew, from whatever star, how best to handle angry commanders, diplomats, countries. The solution in detail was due mainly to Portal and Tedder and involved the creation of an Air Command under Tedder to control all Allied air forces in the Mediterranean. Under Tedder, who was directly responsible to Eisenhower, were grouped three main air formations: Royal Air Force Middle East (Sholto Douglas), Royal Air Force Malta (Park), and North-West Africa Air Forces (General Spaatz). This last command also split down into three formations, namely the Strategic Air Forces under General Doolittle, the Tactical Forces under Coningham and the Maritime Forces under Lloyd. As regards land forces Eisenhower appointed Alexander to be his deputy for land operations. So it became possible for Tedder to locate himself with Eisenhower in Algiers, and for Coningham to locate his headquarters next to Alexander's, wherever that might happen to be. American commanders were given British deputies and vice versa, an arrangement which looked extravagant on paper but which worked well. There was a unified Air Service Command. Importantly, the Allies were learning the organisational style which was to serve them well for 'Overlord' a year and a half later.

Sicily

With the North African shore in Allied hands the decision was taken to attack Sicily. This decision, which seems an obvious one, was in fact the subject of much debate, the alternative plan being an assault on Sardinia. The objection to Sicily was that, being the next obvious objective, the enemy would be waiting for the Allies to arrive. On the other hand Sicily was clearly the gateway to Italy, the Straits of Messina being a mere three miles across. Better air cover could be given from Tunisia and Malta if Sicily was chosen. So the decision was made. Elaborate deception arrangements were put in hand to suggest that the next Allied stroke would fall elsewhere, including, in the shape of the somewhat macabre Operation 'Mincement',* the planting of bogus documents pointing to an assault in the Eastern Mediterranean. These deceptions earned a modest dividend but there was never any doubt that the assault on Sicily would be an extremely tough proposition.

Sicily is a remarkable island, not least because of its natural beauty. In shape like an isosceles triangle with its apex pointing towards the west, its base, roughly north and south 100 miles or so wide and its length nearly 200 miles. It is the largest island in the Mediterranean. The Western Desert has been described as a tactician's paradise. The same could be said of Sicily, provided always that one's task is only to defend it. Sicily is a mountainous island with a northern spine stretching from the west at 3,000 feet or so and culminating in the glories of Mount Etna, an active volcano nearly 11,000 feet high, in the east. Land communications were, and in many cases still are, primitive, for the most part narrow mountain roads; a great place to defend. Airfields, surprisingly numerous at the time we discuss, were concentrated in the Catania plain, in the south-east corner and in the extreme west. The first step towards the reduction of Sicily took the form of the capture of the islands of Pantelleria and Lampedusa, a pair of Italian fortresses lying in the Sicilian Narrows. Both fortresses were strong only on paper, being completely vulnerable to air attack. Both were deluged with bombs and Lampedusa also received the attention of Allied warships. Pantelleria lasted four days; Lampedusa only two. Pantelleria yielded no less than

---

*The body of a British officer, ostensibly drowned, carrying a chained briefcase full of misleading letters invented for the purpose was planted on Spain, who passed copies of the documents to the Germans.

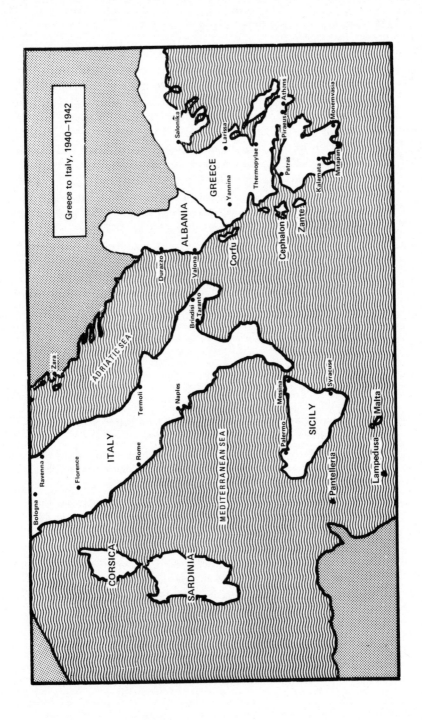

Greece to Italy, 1940—1942

11,000 Italian prisoners. All this took place in June, a month before the invasion of Sicily. The attack on these islands was much influenced by the work of Professor Solly Zuckerman, a member of the Combined Operations Staff in London. Zuckerman, an anatomist by trade, had begun his war work as a member of staff of the Ministry of Home Security. He carried out some vital and most original research into the physiological effects of bomb blast, appreciations of the effects of which had been magnified out of all reality by scientists who should have known better, from fairy tales emerging from the Spanish Civil War. This work led to a study in detail of the effects of bombing both as regards lethality and also as to overall effects on man-made structures. In 1943 he carried his studies to North Africa, where they aroused a degree of interest which resulted in his playing an important role in the attacks on Pantelleria and Lampedusa. The attacks were an undoubted success and many conclusions, some of them mistaken, were drawn. One aspect of the work was that it attempted to evaluate, and so to optimise, the separate elements in the operational chain, thus:

the Air Plan
its execution
pilots reports
actual results.

Much improved efficiency resulted from a careful comparison of plans and actual achievements.

The assault on Sicily never looked like being a picnic. The Italian and German forces included some 1,850 aircraft operating from Sicily, Italy, Sardinia or Southern France. Eisenhower could call on some 250 squadrons, roughly half and half British and American. Sicily has four main ports, none really large, Palermo near the apex of the triangle and Messina, Catania and Syracuse on the base. The airfield question being crucial and the south-east corner of the island being the best endowed in this sense, the Allied assault was delivered in this area by the British Eighth Army on the Gulf of Noto and by the United States Seventh Army just round the corner to the west in the Gulf of Gela. Airborne assaults with gliders went mostly astray. The date was 10 July 1943. As those who have visited Sicily in the summer will realise it was pretty hot. The assault lasted just over one month. By 17 August it was over. For the loss of 400 aircraft, 1,850 enemy aircraft had been destroyed or captured. On land, the Axis lost 200,000 men; 30,000 killed, and the rest, mostly Italian, prisoners. Most of the German forces engaged, and who fought magnificently, escaped across the Straits of Messina, a Dunkirk in reverse. Why was this? The reasons can be found in the mountainous character of the island which impeded R/T and W/T communications and made identification of targets most difficult. The defence of Messina on the ground and with highly effective AA guns by the Germans was resolute and skilful in the extreme and the escape route from that port very short and highly organised. So, most of the German forces escaped. Still the Allies had tackled and succeeded in their first frontal assault on the European continent.

The Balkan Air Force

It is suitable to include here a note on the Balkan Air Force. Germany attacked Yugoslavia in April 1941, and Italy, Bulgaria and Hungary soon followed suit. It was all over in ten days and the young King Peter was installed with a government in exile in London. Two resistance groups arose in Yugoslavia, the first under General Mihailović who was made Minister of War by King Peter's government. The second followed the German attack on Russia which automatically made Russia the enemy of the Axis regime in Yugoslavia. It was led by a Moscow-trained communist of shadowy origin named Josip Broz, code-name Tito. During the next two years a number of British or Allied missions were infiltrated into Yugoslavia mostly by parachute or clandestine sea landing. The intelligence picture was of course immensely confused in this complex territory of the Serbs, Croats and Slovenes. But in the summer of 1943 a mission led by Captain William Deakin, earlier a literary and historical aide to Churchill and later Warden of St Antony's College Oxford, was parachuted into Yugoslavia. From its work, followed up as it was by other missions, notably that under Brigadier Fitzroy Maclean, the pattern became clear. Mihailović was collaborating with the Germans in order to frustrate Russian aims in Yugoslavia. Tito was collaborating with Russia and fighting Germans, Italians and the rest in order to make Yugoslavia safe for communism. British military and political policy reorientated itself in somewhat leisurely style, but by late 1943 aid had been switched from Mihailović to Tito. In May 1944 the Germans made a final attempt to polish off Tito. Accompanied by his dog Tiger, he was briefly evacuated to Bari. The Allied air forces in the Mediterranean inflicted a severe defeat on the Germans in Yugoslavia and from the talks between Slessor and Tito in Bari there arose the Balkan Air Force a sub-command of the Royal Air Force in the Mediterranean and Middle East.* This force, under Air-Vice Marshal Elliot, commanded the Allied air forces operating in and over Yugoslavia and co-ordinated all other trans-Adriatic operations. Among these operations it is a pleasure to record the evacuation of some 10,000 partisan wounded to Royal Air Force hospitals in Italy. The German Army at this time was killing all captured partisans whether wounded or not. Belgrade was liberated amid great jollifications in October 1944.

The Dodecanese

Italy surrendered to the Allies, after some dickering between Eisenhower and Marshal Badoglio, on 8 September 1943. Clearly, Italy was now ripe for the *coup de grâce*. But in the meantime what about picking up a few quick Greek islands occupied by a mixture of Germans and Italians such as Rhodes, possessed of useful airfields, the gateway to Greece and the close neighbour of Turkey? The origin of this idea is difficult to state but in the light of subsequent events it is difficult to believe it was not British, perhaps Churchillian. It was certainly ill conceived. A few swift calculations rapidly disposed of the idea that we had the resources necessary to capture Rhodes. So what about Leros, Kos and Samos? No sooner said than done. By mid-September 1943 they were all in British hands. And a few weeks later they were back in German hands with nothing to show for the effort on the British side save unnecessary casualties. It is difficult to see how this blunder could have been permitted. No Allied air base lay closer to (say) Leros than 400 miles. The newly acquired bases in Sicily were over 600 miles away. Yet here was Rhodes, with its German air bases, less than 100 miles away. The capture of these islands was no doubt a possible military operation, though perhaps unwise, if only the necessary resources could have been spared from the assault in the mainland of Italy which was just about to start. They could not be spared and were not spared. American suspicions, wholly unjustified, about British motives in Greece and the Balkans ruled out the possibility of their assistance in this operation. This did not help, but was scarcely a deciding factor.

* Slessor had succeeded Tedder in command of the RAF in the Mediterranean and Middle East in January 1944.

Italy

And so, Italy. A promising plum to fall into Allied hands if ever there was one. The Italian armistice meant that the Germans were now in a hostile land. Germany now faced an air situation which veered between vast superiority and supremacy for the Allied forces. Yet the German forces were still fighting, admittedly without much hope in May 1945 just before VE Day; scarcely what Eisenhower could have expected when the British Eighth Army crossed the Straits of Messina on 4 September 1943 followed a few days later by the descent of the United States Fifth Army on the Gulf of Salerno just south of Naples. Why did this great prize elude the Allies? There were many reasons; to start with, the terrain. Italy was in those days a splendid country to defend. The central spine of the Appenines runs from the Straits of Messina in the south to the French frontier in the north where it joins the Maritime Alps. Next, the rivers. Italy abounds from north to south and from east to west in rivers. Again, splendid defensive positions. Next, the strength of the forces engaged. Alexander, who succeeded Eisenhower in January 1944, never had much superiority in land forces. For whatever reason Germany decided to reinforce the Italian front very strongly indeed with troops that cannot easily have been spared from the defence of the homeland. Next, diversions. In August 1944 the Allies assaulted the south of France. It was a push-over, and a month later a union was effected with General Patton and a continuous Allied front established from Holland to Monaco. Whether the consequent sacrifice of our hopes in Italy was justifiable may be debated. Two other points of somewhat different weight must be mentioned. The first concerns air policy. There was certainly a considerable dispute between the Zuckerman school, which believed in attacking railway repair and servicing facilities, and the tactical school which favoured attacking communications targets: bridges, viaducts and road junctions near the battlefield. This dispute was resolved in the end by Slessor, who decided in effect to do both.

Finally, the weather. It is always easy to blame the weather but two winters, 1943/4 and 1944/5 with rivers turned into torrents, flooded airfields and clouds down on the mountains did not help.

The Italian campaign brought some vastly important strategic dividends. Our occupation of air bases in central Italy made possible an air assault on aircraft factories and oil installations in Germany, Austria, Roumania and Hungary. Best of all, the Royal Air Force was able to revert to its old love, air mining, 'Gardening', as it was called. By August 1944 traffic on the Danube was down by 60–70 per cent with crucial consequences to the German war economy.

16

'Overlord' and the Battle for Europe

The approach to 'Overlord'

The United States of America had entered the Second World War in December 1941. For Britain and surely for other nations as well, after many dreadful nights, it was the dawn. Earlier, Roosevelt's policies, aimed at saving Britain from disaster, had been brave and original. The most sensational was perhaps the decision that the United States Navy would protect Lease-Lend supplies to Britain half way across the Atlantic Ocean even if this meant sinking U-boats. A brave decision indeed. Strangely, as 1941 wore on, the United States' interest in Britain seemed to wane. No doubt there were political aspects. Still, those in Whitehall whose duty it was to deal with United States representatives found the temperature falling. But on 7 December 1941 Japan, pursuing one of the greatest political, military and economic blunders in world history, attacked the United States of America, Britain and the Netherlands. Four days later Germany and Italy, following their treaty obligations, declared war on America, an event surely little to Hitler's taste. The United States accepted the challenge in somewhat leisurely style, the right to make war being reserved under the United States Constitution to the Congress. News that the United States had declared war on Germany did not lead the headlines in the *Evening Standard* of the day. Still, that great nation had been treacherously and wickedly attacked, without warning, without reason, without justice, without humanity. It is difficult to imagine a more sordid and stupid crime. Those who assault great nations in such circumstances must pay a heavy price, and indeed in due course such a price was paid.

In parenthesis, it is interesting to reflect upon the respective positions of Hitler and Churchill so far as the fortunes of war are concerned. First, Hitler. Early in 1941; master of the world, or thereabouts. Two gigantic miscalculations—Russia and Japan—and he is doomed. Churchill early in 1941; still in control but facing desperate problems. Two gigantic miscalculations—Russia and Japan—and for practical purposes he is home and dry. So much happened between June and December 1941.

In the dark days of 1940 and 1941, when Britain was alone facing the combined resources of Germany, Italy, France, Belgium, Holland, Poland and Czechoslavakia, the idea that Britain could win the war by invading Europe was in no-one's mind. The entry into the war of Russia and the United States changed all that. By early 1942 there was a firm commitment among the Allies to invade Europe. The question was when. Stalin, of course, was strong for 1942, which would have meant certain disaster. The Americans flirted with this idea and with 1943, which would also have been disastrous, perhaps indeed more so as we had more to lose. Gradually mid-1944 was accepted and gradually too the concept of 'Overlord', the suggestive code name of the operation, became clothed in reality. There were plenty of grounds for apprehension. Wherever the assault might fall troops would have to approach the Atlantic Wall across open beaches equipped with every defensive device available. The Dieppe raid of August 1942 showed clearly enough what could happen. Germany had devoted many months and countless hands to the Wall and in November 1943 Rommel was appointed, nominally under von Rundstedt, to perfect the defences.

Initial planning for 'Overlord' was started in London in May 1943 by an Anglo-American team under General F. E. Morgan, Chief of Staff to Supreme Allied Command (COSSAC) as he was called. His office was located in Norfolk House, St James's Square where a wall plaque commemorates the event. This book attempts no more than a brief look at the history of the Royal Air Force from its earliest beginnings until the close of the Second World War, and any attempt therefore at a description of 'Overlord' would be out of place. Nevertheless, the contribution of the Royal Air Force to this remarkable operation was not the least of its many achievements. We shall therefore attempt to summarise the operations on land and then describe the part played by the Royal Air Force which was both crucial and remarkable.

Where to invade Fortress Europe? Hitler's eyes of course were never far removed from Norway but, once the construction of the Atlantic Wall had begun, OKW expected the blow to fall on the Pas de Calais. Here maximum air cover could be provided, and ports were available for capture. All this was a little too obvious for COSSAC, who chose instead a stretch of French coastline some fifty miles long, stretching from the mouth of the River Orne (near Caen) in the east to the mouth of the River Vire (near Carentan on the south-east base of the Cotentin peninsula) in the west. The attack was to be made by three seaborne divisions with two more such divisions to follow and two airborne brigades. The modest proportions of this force, which would certainly have led to its destruction were dictated by the supplies of landing craft and transport aircraft from the United States, where the needs of the war in Europe were in competition with those of the Pacific, and the key to the store was controlled by the formidable and Pacific Ocean-minded Admiral King. The seaport to be captured was of course Cherbourg.

The Quebec Conference between Churchill and Roosevelt in August 1943, followed in November 1943 by the meeting with Stalin in Teheran, resulted in some unfortunate new decisions. France was to be invaded not only on the Normandy beaches but also on the Riviera (Operation 'Anvil'), a questionable decision of strategy. In Italy, Britain was not to progress from the valley of the River Po to Austria or through Greece into the Balkans. This decision pleased not only Uncle Joe, who thus became sole executor of South-East Europe, but also Roosevelt, who saw as part of his American heritage a duty to clip the claws of supposed British imperialism. A sad page of history.

On Christmas Eve, 1943, a bare five months before D-Day, Eisenhower was announced as Supreme Commander for 'Overlord'. In the history of warfare there can have been few more felicitous decisions. The alternative was the United States General George Marshall, who in truth could not be spared from Washington and who would certainly have been less effective than Eisenhower in Europe. Eisenhower, with General Bedell Smith as his Chief of Staff, chose Tedder as his deputy and Leigh-Mallory to command the Allied Air Forces. To command the Allied Naval Forces, Admiral Sir Bertram Ramsay. No comment here except of praise, as the naval aspects of 'Overlord' were carried through with remarkable efficiency. To command the land forces in the assault phase, Montgomery. After all, he had done it before successfully on the beaches of Sicily and of the Italian mainland. This appointment must be viewed in retrospect as a less than open-and-shut one. The alternatives were General Sir Alan Brooke (CIGS) who, like Marshall, could not be spared from the centre, or Alexander who had at least as many military qualities as Montgomery and added to them the ability to communicate with his military associates and, specifically, an ability to subsist on harmonious terms with American generals. No doubt it was hard to spare him at that time from Italy. Still, the question must persist, what would have happened at Caen and on the Rhine if Alexander, not Montgomery, had been the man?

Montgomery, once in charge, rapidly reached some decisions so good that his faults, which no doubt were many, must surely be forgiven. The assault forces were too small; and indeed they were. The beachhead was too narrow; and indeed it was. The airborne assault was too meagre; three airborne divisions, not two airborne brigades, were necessary: one such division to protect the left Allied flank east of the mouth of the River Orne, north of Caen; two airborne divisions to protect the right Allied flank in the flooded areas of the Cotentin, north of Carentan. So, the plan developed. On the left, the British 6th Airborne Division under Major-General Richard Gale landed east of the River Orne to secure the bridges over the Orne and its parallel canal, and over the River Dives some six miles further east. These operations started soon after midnight, so in the next six hours or so before troops began to land on the beaches the airborne forces had plenty to think about. Stretching westwards from Caen there were three British beaches: Sword, Juno and Gold. On the American front, two beaches: Omaha and Utah (stretching half way up the eastern side of the Cotentin) with their western flank protected by two American airborne divisions landed in advance of the beach assault.

The Allied landings achieved almost total surprise. Nevertheless, their fortunes were gravely endangered by the fact that German forces in Normandy were strongly reinforced in May 1944, seemingly at the insistence of Hitler. For a month or more before D-Day an Allied deception plan ('Fortitude', later called 'Bodyguard') aimed to convince the Germans before D-Day that the assault would fall on the Pas de Calais and after D-Day that the operations were only a diversion. The deception prevailed well into July. By then the Allied forces were firmly established and there was no question of their being driven into the sea.

The battle for the beaches was won, but only just. On the American Omaha Beach a critical situation prevailed for a time. The battle of the build-up followed. In this, German efforts were harassed by the immensely successful Allied Transportation plan (see below, p. 236), general Allied air supremacy and the OKW insistence on being ready for an assault in the Calais area. The Allied build-up was harassed by stormy weather, the effects of which included the destruction of one of the two Mulberry harbours.

Rommel's plan, and it was a good plan, was to annihilate the invaders on the beaches. The annihilation was to be achieved by underwater

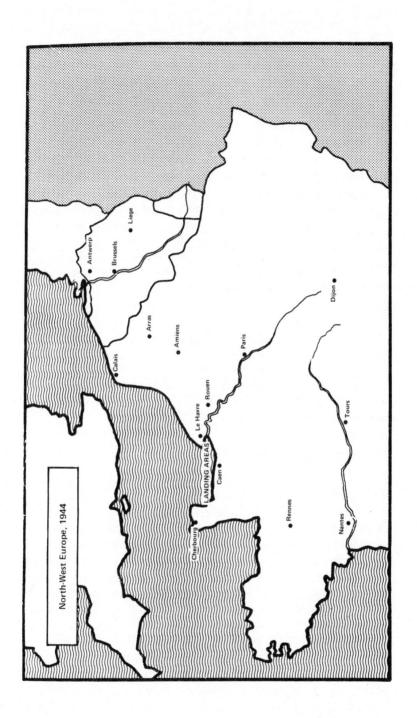

North-West Europe, 1944

Antwerp
Brussels
Liege
Arras
Amiens
Calais
Paris
Dijon
Le Havre
Rouen
Tours
LANDING AREAS
Caen
Cherbourg
Rennes
Nantes

obstacles, beach defences and alerted garrisons. In the crucial few hundred metres between disembarkation in a metre or so of water and reaching the sea-wall or whatever, every known device was used by the German forces. The secret of success was found by the British Army. The part of Major-General Sir Percy Hobart deserves honoured mention for the ingenuity and variety of the armoured weapons he produced for D-Day. To quote Chester Wilmot

> Before D-Day, British inventiveness and industry were to produce bull-dozer tanks to clear away beach obstacles; flail tanks to beat pathways through minefields; tanks which would hurl explosive charges against concrete fortifications; turretless tanks which were in effect self-propelled ramps over which other tanks could scale sea walls; tanks carrying bridges to span craters and ditches; flame-throwing tanks to deal with pill-boxes and, most important of all, amphibious or D-D (Duplex-Drive) tanks which could swim ashore under their own power.[1]

Next, the plan provided that the invading armadas should come ashore with all their guns blazing. And overhead, not unchallenged Stukas, but the immense and unchallenged supremacy of the Allied Air Forces, the reward of deep and bitter experiences in London, Coventry, the Ardennes (1940 style) and Pearl Harbour. Germany, which had sown the wind, was now to reap the whirlwind.

The Battle for Europe

The break-out from the bridgehead was a slow and bitterly contested affair. It was not until some two months after D-Day that Brittany was in Allied hands. Montgomery was much criticised for over-caution, not least by Tedder. In fact, by drawing the main weight of the German attack on to the British front at Caen he made it possible for the American armies to break through in the west and to capture first Cherbourg and then the whole of Brittany. When the German position in Normandy became hopeless, tactical interference by Hitler in forbidding retreat led to an encirclement of the German forces at Falaise where 50,000 German soldiers were captured and 10,000 slain. From this moment there could be no respite for the German armies short of the River Seine. Paris fell to the Americans on 24 August. On 4 September the British Army entered Brussels and a day later captured Antwerp intact. Alas, the key to the port of Antwerp was held at the coast in the Island of Walcheren,* so that although the port was intact it did not become operational until later.

The German armies were falling apart. A string of catastrophic defeats plus an Army attempt to assassinate their Fuehrer did little to restore confidence. The war must surely be over by Christmas. And, indeed, perhaps it might have been. But, in fact, by New Year's Day 1945 the outlook for the Allies seemed somewhat desolate. What happened, then, to Allied hopes in the last quarter of 1944? The explanation must be complex and that now attempted surely most inadequate. Three elements can be mentioned. First, luck. Napoleon said he preferred lucky generals. Since 'Overlord' began the Allies had had their fair share of luck. There were bound to be bad patches. Next, strategy. With the Allies poised as they were in early September 1944, the British and Canadian armies to the north and the American armies to the south, Montgomery produced the concept that all available resources should be concentrated for an enveloping thrust round the Ruhr valley and on through the North German plain to Berlin. With the German forces in disarray, as indeed they were, this idea looked like a winner. But it was never really a starter. Although he conceded that Montgomery should have priority, Eisenhower was never ready to depart very far from the concept of a uniform advance to the Rhine. Had Alexander not Montgomery been chosen to command the land forces, a northern strategy might perhaps have been possible though the political difficulties facing Eisenhower could well have ruled this out. Supplies were still reaching the Allied armies along supply lines which stretched back to Normandy. More petrol for Montgomery meant stopping General George Patton in the south, which would surely have caused trouble.

The northern strategy proving unattainable, Montgomery obtained approval for the Arnhem airborne operation. This was a bold plan to outflank the Siegfried Line to the north by dropping two American and one British airborne divisions over the Maas at Grave, the Waal at Nijmegen and the Lower Rhine at Arnhem. Once the bridges were secured the British XXX Corps was to strike north along the corridor

---

* The failure to clear the islands in the mouth of the Scheldt of their German Army occupants was to have disastrous consequences for the Arnhem operation later in September. German troops pulled back from these islands were regrouped near Arnhem, and thus formed a reserve of reinforcements—of which Allied Intelligence was virtually unaware until too late—when the airborne landings took place.

thus opened towards the Zuider Zee 100 miles away, dividing Holland and the German Army in those parts into two and outflanking the Siegfried Line. Montgomery claimed that the operation was 90 per cent successful.[2] As Churchill might have said, the opposite of the facts could scarcely be stated with greater precision. Operation 'Market Garden', as it was called, designed to over-leap the river obstacles in Holland and then strike east towards the heart of Germany, was in simple terms a disaster. The Americans secured their bridges, but the Lower Rhine bridge at Arnhem proved too tough a nut to crack, and the British 1st Airborne Division was thrown away in the attempt. Badly delayed, XXX Corps could not break through, and all that was left was a salient into the German line. And several wasted weeks. What went wrong? First, the plan was too ambitious. It depended on good weather to put the airborne formations down in the right places at the right times. The weather was bad. The weather is always bad if depended on. In this operation, timing was crucial. Second, communications. Everything seems to have gone wrong. Third, caution. The survival of the British Airborne Division at Arnhem depended upon the success of the thrust of British XXX Corps towards Arnhem. For reasons too complicated to explain in this brief account they arrived too late. Arnhem and the 1st British Airborne Division were lost and the German forces poured south over the Arnhem bridge over the Lower Rhine to stabilise the German Front.

So the war did not end in 1944. A great opportunity had been lost. The German Army, whose valour seems seldom to be less than admirable, was enabled to consolidate. On the Allied side, mopping-up operations went on, and ports were cleared. But Germany was still intact and by the late autumn of 1944 she had consolidated behind the Siegfried Line and the River Maas. From the high opportunities open in the summer of 1944 this was a steep and grave descent. Worse was to follow. By the end of 1944 the Allied line, now joined to the strategically unfortunate thrust from the Riviera, was strung out over 600 miles. In the centre, in the forest of the Ardennes, where four and a half years before the German armoured divisions had leapt through to the Atlantic coast, Hitler prepared in deadly secrecy a final throw. The German armies, on their knees it might be thought, would break through this weak centre and push on to Antwerp, thus dividing the Allied armies in two and threatening death and destruction to their hopes. And so to some considerable extent it happened. The Allies were taken by surprise and considerable consternation prevailed, not least at the highest levels. In the end, the line was stabilised and by the spring of 1945 the Allies rolled forward by-passing the Ruhr, where 250,000 prisoners were taken, towards Berlin. In this advance their only enemies were politicians. In the north, Eisenhower stopped on the Elbe to meet Stalin's wishes. In the south, George Patton stopped short of Leipzig for the same reason. The battle of soldiers was over and the battle of politicians was about to begin.

The contribution of the Allied Air Forces

The purpose of this brief account is to provide a structure on which to base a description of the part that the Allied Air Forces played in these remarkable events. This part is often forgotten or overlooked so a brief account is perhaps in order. The matter can be considered under five heads:

Deception plans for 'Overlord'
If Hitler had known that the Allies would descend on the Normandy beaches and there alone, the Allied forces would have been hurled back into the sea. If, in addition, Hitler had known *when* the assault would fall the matter would have been put beyond doubt. But, as it happened, Hitler was deceived on both points by a combination of luck and good management on the part of the Allies. First, good management. The whole apparatus of Allied Intelligence was deployed to suggest that the cross-Channel thrust, so long foreseen, would for sure descend on Calais. That was what OKW had in the book, so why disappoint them? So, Montgomery's signals, signed in Portsmouth, hit the ether in Kent. So bogus gliders and equipment appeared on Kentish airfields. So, seaside towns in these parts were denied to summer visitors. Vastly more important than this, the air interdiction plan, designed with immense skill to isolate the point of assault from German reinforcements, had as its essence the suggestion that the Allied assault would be north of the River Seine. This suggestion was based on the formula that tactical interdiction should be twice as heavy north of the Seine as south of it. The majority of German radar stations were destroyed, but enough were suffered to remain to allow the Germans to see on their radar screens the approach of the bogus invasion fleet towards Calais, a fleet fabricated by Bomber Command by methods described in Chapter 18. All this was a part only of the full deception plan. When the first Allied blow fell on the Normandy beaches, the whole apparatus of the intelligence deception through the

use of double agents (as described in Sir John Masterman's classic book *The Double Cross System*) was devoted with astounding success to persuading the German High Command that the Normandy assault was a mere side show to the impending descent on the Pas de Calais, and further that an Allied army was assembling in Scotland in preparation for the invasion of Norway. These deception operations, which proved durable beyond any reasonable expectation, were brought about by W/T transmissions between phantom armies backed by double agents' reports of phantom units arriving at phantom camps. These remarkable operations were greatly assisted by the fact that, at this stage of the war, the ability of the Luftwaffe to make a physical inspection of what was going on in the west, the south-east and the north of Britain was minimal. Mention must also be made of good luck. The timing of D-Day was of course crucial. The moon had to be right, the tide had to be right, the weather had to be right. The weather was so nearly wrong that a couple of points worse on the Beaufort Scale—and this could easily have happened—and all could have ended in disaster. This is how Germany read the weather on the week-end of 4 June 1944. So the defences were stood down and Rommel departed for a week-end at home. Even after the landing of the paratroops soon after midnight on 5 June, the German High Command could still not take it seriously. So Hitler, woken at 04.00 hours on D-Day, forbade the strategic employment of the German armour. It was not released until 16.00 hours at Hitler's regular afternoon staff conference. A small point perhaps in absolute terms, but when the balance is so delicately poised trifles light as air can turn the scale.

The Transportation Plan

This plan was largely due to Portal and Tedder, but it owed much to Zuckerman, whose operational research work has been discussed in Chapter 15. For the Normandy operation a committee on which Zuckerman served produced, largely at his instance, a transportation plan designed to isolate the road and rail links leading to Normandy, thus slowing up the arrival of German reinforcements. This was done in three ways, first by attacking locomotive servicing facilities and so upsetting the supply of trains, secondly by cutting road and rail bridges over rivers (and linking this skilfully with the deception plan) and thirdly, when the battle was joined, by shooting up actual trains. Bomber Command made a notable contribution to all this. Of course many of the transportation targets were in France and there was much concern at the possible loss of many French lives. However, the attacks were delivered with great accuracy and in practice French civilian casualties from this cause were slight.

Tactical Air Forces for 'Overlord'

The Allied Expeditionary Air Force for Overlord was commanded by Leigh-Mallory and consisted of the Second Tactical Air Force, the United States Ninth Air Force, Air Defence of Great Britain, and two Royal Air Force Transport Groups. Fighter Command, by some strange Air Ministry aberration had been rechristened Air Defence of Great Britain in November 1943 only to revert to its earlier and honoured name of Fighter Command months later. The Second Tactical Air Force consisted of a Photographic Reconnaissance Wing of three squadrons, an Air Spotting Wing of six squadrons, twelve squadrons of light bombers in No 2 Group, twenty-nine squadrons of fighter bombers in No 83 Group, and a similar force in No 84 Group. The United States Ninth Air Force was constituted on the same lines. Leaving ADGB aside, Leigh-Mallory had under his direct control some 3,200 tactical aircraft and (say) 1,100 transport aircraft. Over the period April–September 1944 the Supreme Commander also had operational control of the Strategic Air Forces— Bomber Command and the United States Eighth Air Force. The total front line strength of the German Air Force in mid-1944 was in theory about 6,000. The proportion of these concentrated on the Western Front varied with the tactical situation and with Hitler's whims. But in fact the figure of 6,000 greatly exaggerates the strength of the German Air Force at this time. With the hammering it had been given at the hands of the Royal Air Force and the United States Army Air Force it was now poorly trained, short of fuel and partly demoralised. When Hitler felt that the German fighters had failed him he used to threaten to phase them out in favour of flak. So, whatever the figures may say, the Allies possessed something between immense air superiority and air supremacy. The contribution of this factor to the saving of human lives, especially soldiers' lives, is beyond computation, but it was without question immense. In the First World War, 750,000 members of the Armed Forces from Britain were killed. In the Second World War this grievous total was divided by three.[3]

On D-Day the Allied armies would have faced disaster but for the Allied Air Forces. This sounds a facile comment, for indeed what we are discussing was a combined operation. The armies, the navies, the air forces all played their parts and they played them splendidly. The emphasis put on the contribution of the air forces does no more than call attention to facts which are often forgotten or overlooked. On D-Day the German Air Force flew 300 sorties, the Allied Air Forces 14,000. It is fearful to contemplate what would have happened to the Allied armies if these figures had been reversed. The Strategic Air Forces, having made their immense contribution to the transportation plan, switched on the dawn of D-Day to the coastal batteries. Here, as far as we can see, they were often wide of the mark, but the moral effect made itself felt none the less. Faced with a torrent of destruction the gun crews, reasonably enough, had removed themselves elsewhere.

The Strategic Air Forces

Although operational control of the Strategic Air Forces passed out of the hands of the Supreme Allied Commander in September 1944, this by no means brought to an end either the strategic or the tactical use of these formidable commands in the land battle. Once the armies were ashore the Allied Air Forces gained two resplendent advantages. To put it in crude and no doubt inaccurate terms, the depth of the German air defences was halved; the efficacy of the Allied offensive aids, Oboe and such, was doubled—a factor of shall we say times four. All this meant that Bomber Command could drop thousand of tons of bombs in half an hour or so with an error measured in terms of yards. So Bomber Command was employed tactically both before and after September 1944 to support the Allied armies. This remarkable fact has given rise to stupid criticism. For example, it has been stated by some who should know better that the German army would have been crushed at Caen if Bomber Command had not made the roads and streets impassable. A different message comes from those responsible, from Eisenhower over the operations at Bastogne; from Montgomery on the crossing of the Lower Rhine. 'We shall do everything except the impossible' said Bomber Harris. Eisenhower, with characteristic generosity, said, 'they have already done the impossible'. We return to this subject in Chapter 19.

Difficulties

Of course, things did not always go well for the Allied Air Forces. The 1940 situation in the air had been reversed and Germany was now on the receiving end of air superiority. When it didn't work there were complaints. Usually, the culprit was the weather. This was partly the cause of the disaster at Arnhem, when shortage of transports and fog at bases delayed the airborne build-up. Weather also played its part in the German offensive at Christmas 1944 in the Ardennes; bad weather, so no fighters or fighter-bombers. Occasionally the situation on land was so confused—as in the closing phases at Arnhem—that air intervention was deemed unwise.

VE Day

And so on to VE Day, with Hitler planning phantom victories with non-existent divisions to the very last. As the curtain falls on this remarkable page of world history one can but remark in wonder on the strength and valour of Germany, which could challenge for so long the combined resources of the British Empire, the United States and the Soviet Union. One must reflect, too, on disastrous personal interventions by Hitler in land battles, as at Stalingrad and Falaise. We remember the bravery and competence of the Luftwaffe wasted away by technical blunders and a false sense of strategy. How would the history of the Third Reich have been written if Germany had not made so many disastrous mistakes? Perhaps victory goes to the side which makes the fewer mistakes. But as we leave VE Day our final thought must be to recall with pride the stupendous contribution of the Allied Air Forces, and not least of the Royal Air Force, to the final victory. They too made mistakes, but they were quick to learn and to try again.

17

The War in South-East Asia

The beginning

When the Defence Requirements Committee met for the first time towards the end of 1933 under the distinguished chairmanship of Hankey, their eyes concentrated for the most part on Japan rather than on Germany. This was logical. The shadows of Nazi Germany were there for sure, but they had not yet lengthened. On the other hand the menace of Japan to British interests in the Far East had grown steadily ever since the end of the Anglo-Japanese Alliance in 1922. The occupation of Manchuria by Japan in 1931 did nothing to allay the growing fears.

The Imperial Conference of 1923 agreed that in the new strategic situation the main naval base should be moved from Hong Kong to the island of Singapore. Singapore is some 2,000 miles distant from the nearest point of Japanese territory. Over the next sixteen years the British naval base was constructed, with some pauses occasioned by Labour Government hesitations. The construction of the base gave rise to a celebrated, but in the event disastrous, dispute between the Admiralty and the Air Ministry as to how the base was to be defended. The general belief was that the Japanese attack, if it came, would come from the sea around Singapore Island itself. After all, with Japan 2,000 miles away how else could it come? The Admiralty wanted to rely on sea power, coastal artillery of 15-inch calibre and downwards, plus some fighter and AA defences. The Air Ministry put their faith in aircraft of all kinds, partly located near the spot and partly in the shape of reinforcements to be flown down the chain of airfields stretching from Britain to the Far East. The controversy was settled mainly on Admiralty lines, but in the event the arguments of both parties turned out to be faulty. By 1940, the base had been built and its defences installed but owing to the collapse of France and the desperate problems besetting Britain at that time there was no adequate fleet to send out and the aircraft component was defective

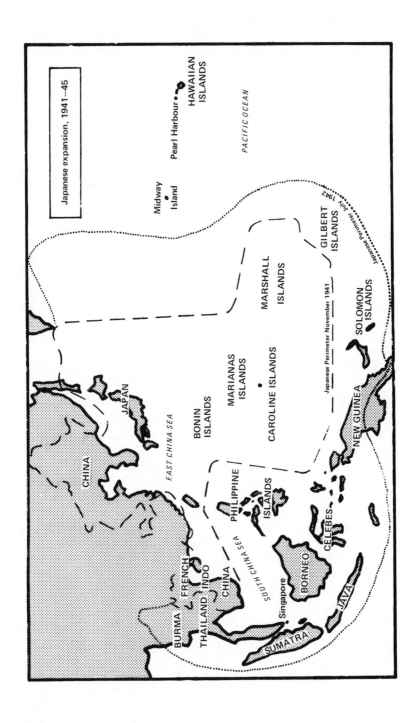

Japanese expansion, 1941–45

in concept, in numbers and in quality. The future tragedy was taking shape.

It is now appropriate to review briefly the circumstances in which Japan entered the Second World War. These circumstances were remarkable to say the least. Japan is a country which possesses few natural resources. In particular it is largely dependent on imported coal, oil and iron. Furthermore, it had imperial ambitions. The occupation of Manchuria in 1931 was one attempt to gain living space on the mainland, and indeed the attack on China in 1937 was another. By 1938 Japan had captured most of the great cities and ports of China and the Chinese National Government had fled to Chungking far away in the mountains, 900 miles to the south-west of Peking. The political consequences of Japanese aggression were in the long run at least as significant as the military consequences. From that moment forward there could be little trust or liking of Japan on the part of Britain and more particularly on the part of the United States, whose emotional links with China were close. The outbreak of the Second World War was seen by Japan as a promising development and after the fall of France Japan threw in her lot with the Axis powers through the Tripartite Pact of September 1940.

Another consequence which was to have profound effects was the Japanese occupation of French bases in Southern Indo-China undertaken with the approval of the Vichy Government in July 1941. The distance of Japanese bases to Singapore had now shrunk to 600 miles. Thus a deadly blow was dealt by Vichy France to Britain and more obliquely to the United States. This was really the moment of destiny for South-East Asia and the Pacific. As a result of the occupation of Indo-China, the United States, Britain and the Netherlands placed an embargo on financial and commercial relations with Japan. Thus Japan was isolated so far as vital supplies were concerned and it is clear she believed she had to fight an aggressive war or forego for ever her dreams of empire. With an eye no doubt to Britain's difficulties as well as those of Russia, then in full flight from the German invasion, the decision to attack was taken at a meeting of the Japanese War Lords in the presence of the Emperor held in July 1941. The decision was confirmed at later meetings and became irrevocable after an Imperial Conference in Tokyo on 1 December 1941. The plan was to attack Malaya, Singapore and the Netherlands East Indies through a southward assault, and there was to be a parallel assault on the Philippines and Borneo. These decisions involved an unprovoked assault not only on British and Dutch sovereignty but also on the sovereignty of the United States of America. Thus Japan committed herself to combat with the greatest power in the world whose economic and potential military strength far exceeded her own. What did she think she was doing? Well, she might well have banked on Britain and Russia being defeated with Burma and the Netherlands East Indies remaining as a soft touch. So a vast empire would become possible, all contained within a circle roughly 4,000 miles in diameter and stretching from the Kurile Islands in the north through Japan, Formosa, Burma, Malaya, the Dutch East Indies, New Guinea and northward to the Marshall Islands and Midway. True, the United States would smart from the casualties to her Fleet at Pearl Harbour, but a vast area of the Pacific would still lie between the eastern limit of the Japanese Empire and the western coast of the United States, and when Japan had con-solidated, the United States might well weary of trying to subdue such a vast area. Anyway, the Japanese War Lords argued, it was all or nothing. Wrapped in this supreme miscalculation on the part of Japan there lay another, equally great. The American people are brave and proud. After the attack on the American Fleet at Pearl Harbour there was never the remotest chance that they would rest until Japan was utterly defeated. There was never the remotest chance of a negotiation with Japan on any other basis. 'Remember Pearl Harbour' said the American posters in those dark days of December 1941, and remember they did.

The Japanese assault began on 7 December 1941 (a Sunday of course), when air attacks were launched on targets in Hawaii, Manila, Shanghai, Malaya, Thailand, Hong Kong and Singapore. Seventy days later all resistance in Malaya and Singapore was at an end, the Japanese held vast quantities of British equipment of all kinds, oil, air bases and a multi-tude of prisoners, British, Australian, Indian, Malayan. Britain had suffered the greatest and most humiliating defeat in her long history with effects which are deeply felt even today. This is not the place to discuss this campaign in detail. The Official History devotes a massive volume to the subject where we must confine ourselves to a few sentences. It is, however, appropriate to consider briefly the main causes which led to this most crushing defeat to British and Imperial arms in South-East Asia, and indeed the share of the air forces in the defeat.

Before starting this review, however, a brief reference should perhaps be made to the working of the official and governmental machine on the night of Sunday, 7 December 1941. We have referred earlier in this narrative to the War Book, this being the secret official handbook which details the various things that have to be done when war is declared.

There was of course much action of this kind in the weeks leading up to the outbreak of war with Germany. Similar action was necessary when Italy declared war. The first Japanese landing in Malaya took place at roughly 17.00 hours Greenwich Time on 7 December, and Pearl Harbour was attacked an hour and a half later. News of these attacks reached London very soon afterwards and a meeting of the Defence Transition Committee was hastily called. This was the official committee which supervised the details of the action to declare a Precautionary Stage or a Declaration of War. The meeting was not a satisfactory one. Information was fragmentary and the meeting was brief. For officials the problem remained whether to send off the war telegram. This would be dispatched in clear and read simply 'Commence hostilities against Japan'. According to the book the despatch of this telegram should await a Cabinet decision and a final declaration of war. Still it was hideously clear that British territory had been attacked. There was nobody much to consult and it seemed silly not to send it, so off it went. Next day the War Cabinet authorised the immediate declaration of war upon Japan and a formal communication was sent to the Japanese Ambassador. So the war telegram beat the gun by many hours. It could not have mattered less of course. The defenders of Kota Bharu and Hong Kong, for example, might well have regarded the telegram as superfluous or even eccentric. Still, the incident shows what a difference there is between what is written in books, even official books, and what happens in practice, especially when it happens on a Sunday.

The fall of Singapore

Churchill considered that the fall of Singapore should be made the subject of a formal enquiry after the fighting was over.[1] No such enquiry was held but in the light of hindsight it does not seem too difficult to set down in pretty simple terms the basic reasons for our defeat in Malaya and Singapore.

1. The basic idea of a naval base in Singapore island was to provide for the defence of Australia, New Zealand and British possessions in the Far East by the exercise of sea power. The idea dated from the early Twenties and it became rapidly obsolete. The concept that sea power can only be exercised with appropriate land-based air power and protection was far too slow in establishing itself.

2. In the event, the Japanese attack was launched at a time when the Commonwealth was engaged in a life and death struggle in

Europe. In consequence, the available sea and air forces in the theatre were grossly inadequate. A misconceived decision to reinforce our naval strength in Far East waters by the dispatch of the *Prince of Wales* and the *Repulse*, for which Churchill must shoulder much responsibility, met with disaster as the result of bad luck, bad intelligence and bad judgement.

3. Even as late as January 1942 Churchill was referring to Singapore as a 'fortress'. Singapore was no more a fortress than Portsmouth or the Firth of Clyde. Singapore was a smallish island separated from the mainland of Malaya by a narrow strip of water a mile or so across. On its northern shore stood the great naval base with its stores and workshops, and ten miles further south, on the southern face of the island, the city of Singapore with over a million multi-racial inhabitants. There was no fortress. For good measure there was no civil defence, primitive military communications and practically no radar. There were a few airfields and only a few obsolete military aircraft. Curiously, for an island richly if not over-richly supplied with rain, Singapore was critically dependent on its water supplies. Destroy the reservoirs, which wasn't difficult, and Singapore was in dire trouble. The existence of the city of Singapore made the concept of defending the island an illusion. One could scarcely see the military fighting to the death in their non-fortress while the million or so inhabitants of Singapore city were starved or murdered.

4. It is difficult to say at precisely what date the idea of an attack on Singapore from the north began to be taken seriously. Certainly, by 1940 a substantial number of airfields were under construction in Malaya and plans for modest air reinforcements* had been authorised by the Chiefs of Staff. But airfields without adequate troops to defend them are useless or worse, and some Royal Air Force airfields in Malaya were sited without adequate regard to what the Army could do to protect them. And of course once the enemy got to Johore Singapore was finished, as the naval base, the airfields and the rest could be brought under direct attack from aircraft and artillery. Although most of the naval artillery could fire northabout, it was ineffective against land targets largely invisible in the jungle. Armour-piercing shells are no good for such operations and none other were available.

* In 1941, however, the bulk of the aircraft reinforcements earmarked for Malaya—over 300 aircraft—was diverted to help Britain's newly found and hard pressed ally, Russia.

5. In the event there was a remarkable mismatch between the forces of Britain and Japan in Malaya and Singapore. Even before the loss of the *Prince of Wales* and the *Repulse* the Royal Navy was far the weaker force. After the loss, the Japanese had complete control at sea. In the air, Britain was not in the same class as Japan. Her air force was far inferior in numbers, in quality and in technique. On land, the numbers available to General Yamashita were trifling in relation to those available to the defenders. But numbers did not matter.

6. There was a gross misappreciation on the part of the Air Ministry and the Admiralty as to the quality of Japanese aircraft and crews. The performance of Japanese Zero fighters was far superior to any British fighter except the Spitfire. The Japanese bombers and torpedo-bombers had performances far in advance of British intelligence appreciations, particularly in regard to range. Japanese torpedoes were better than their British counterparts. Japanese torpedo-bomber tactics were better than ours and in particular they allowed the torpedo to be released at a greater height than British practice could manage. Finally, the Japanese forces in the air, on land and at sea were impelled by a demoniac will to carry their native land to swift and total victory, regardless of loss.

7. The resistance of the Imperial forces to the southward advance of the Japanese forces was not very effective. The Japanese were better trained and better equipped, and they had the initiative. Strong points were by-passed, spies abounded and the Imperial forces, numerous as they were, were forced into a long series of demoralising retreats. Morale suffered. By the time Johore was lost, the loss of Singapore was certain.

8. Finally, for one must not rub it in, the Imperial High Command was in a state of disarray. There was an Imperial Commander-in-Chief for sure, but he had to have regard to the wishes of the Australian, Dutch and United States Governments. Considerable authority was still vested in the civil power both in Singapore and Malaya. The situation was compounded by a significant degree of bad relations between the services and obstruction from local governments, who to a very late date were told that their first priority was the production of rubber. Finally, the quality of the Imperial troops was poor.

It is pointless to continue. No enquiry was or is necessary. Britain was at no time capable of taking on Germany and Japan simultaneously.

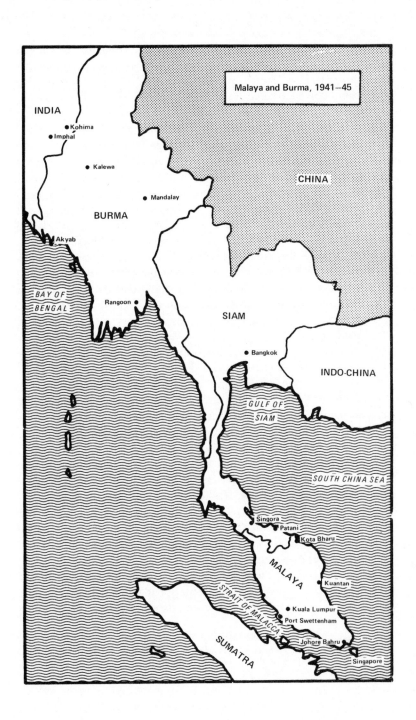

Malaya and Burma, 1941—45

True that when war came to the Far East the United States was brought in as well but for quite a time her hands were completely filled by her own problems. But Britain in December 1942 found herself fighting Germany, Italy and Japan at one and the same time, and there was for sure no future in that. In one sense Britain was unlucky. Viewed dispassionately, the odds on Japan taking on Britain and the United States together must surely have been much less than even. Such an event could only result from a gigantic miscalculation and could only end in disaster for Japan. Was Japan likely to take such a risk? It was surely against the odds. But what if Japan had contrived to attack Britain but avoid a conflict with the United States? On paper it was a possibility. But could the United States afford to see Japan devour all the British and Dutch possessions in the Far East, and perhaps Australia and New Zealand as well, without lifting a hand even on the narrowest grounds of self-interest? So perhaps it was a reasonable guess that Japan would stay out. But no-one can have had any doubt that if the bet did not come off the penalty would include the loss of South-East Asia.

The handling of the Allied forces in the seventy days to the fall of Singapore was poor. The *Prince of Wales* and the *Repulse* should not have been lost. The errors in intelligence were catastrophic. Allied soldiers had to face Japanese tanks not only without tanks of their own but without adequate instruction in how to defend themselves against tanks.* Many Allied soldiers had never seen a tank. Airfields were sited in indefensible positions and were nevertheless defended by the Army for air forces which lacked suitable aircraft to attack the Japanese. Vast quantities of petrol, oil and stores of all kinds were abandoned to the Japanese. In Penang, an armada of coastal boats was left behind which were used by the Japanese to mount seaborne attacks on Malaya from the west. Penang Radio, which was left intact, was used to saturate the entire peninsula and beyond with propaganda. There were no air raid precautions. And finally, the haste with which General Yamashita concluded the armistice with General Percival was influenced by the consideration that the Japanese forces in Singapore Island were greatly outnumbered.

This book is about the Royal Air Force and in this brief account of the fall of Singapore we have said little about it. This, however, must be said. The men of the Royal Air Force, the Royal Australian Air Force

---

* The Commander, Royal Engineers, Brigadier Ivan Simson, had been sent from England specifically to advise on construction and siting of anti-tank defences, even having pamphlets on anti-tank defence printed and issued. His proposals, however, were not entertained by his superiors.

and the Royal Netherlands Air Force fought bravely and did all that could be expected of them. But it must also be said that the effect of these air forces on the events leading to the fall of Singapore was negligible by reason of inadequate numbers and grossly inadequate quality of equipment. An elaboration of these melancholy events can serve no useful purpose.

Before the end in Singapore the air forces were withdrawn to Sumatra where, later in 1942, they were forced to surrender to the Japanese. The story of the cruelty and the hardships they endured and of the many who succumbed needs no repetition. No-one who survived was ever the same again. It is a story illuminated by many flashes of selfless and occasionally of saintly behaviour. Air Vice-Marshal Paul Maltby, the Air Officer Commanding, was responsible for the prisoners. He fought their battles with the Japanese prison camp commandants to the end with exemplary dedication.

The campaign in Burma

The fall of Singapore, unparalleled catastrophe as it was, was not the last Allied disaster in South-East Asia. 'When sorrows come, they come not single spies, but in battalions'. Sumatra and Java were soon in Japanese hands and the toll included heavy naval losses in the Battle of the Java Sea in which five Allied cruisers and six Allied destroyers were sunk. In April 1942 the British Far Eastern Fleet was driven from Indian waters after a Japanese descent on Ceylon which inflicted on the British Navy the loss of one aircraft carrier (the *Hermes*), two cruisers (the *Dorsetshire* and the *Cornwall*), and on the part of the Royal Australian Navy the loss of the destroyer *Vampire*. Meanwhile a crisis was approaching Burma, the gateway to India. Rangoon and Mandalay soon fell and the Japanese Army stood poised for the assault on the plains of India and the welcoming arms of that aspiring quisling, Subhas Chandra Bose. Salvation from this further disaster was largely due to the south-west monsoon, which blows from the early summer to the autumn and is responsible for most of Burma's heavy rainfall, which in places approaches 200 inches a year. India was defended by the jungle, the mountains and by torrential rains as well as by the Imperial forces. Japan could ill afford this substantial pause in the campaign against Burma and India. The military strength of the United States was growing apace and in May and June 1942 two great victories won by the United States Navy in the Coral Sea and at Midway destroyed much of the Japanese

Navy. British air strength in South-East Asia was in the early stages of rapid expansion, as the following figures clearly show.

	British operational squadrons
June 1942	26
July 1943	38
October 1943	49
April 1944	64

Over the same period, substantial measures of re-equipment enhanced performance. Particular red-letter days occurred in October 1943 with the arrival of the first Spitfires and again in February 1944 with the first Spitfire VIII. By the autumn of 1943 the Japanese were outnumbered in the air in Burma and there had been a big reinforcement of American transport squadrons.

We shall now describe the main features of the Burma campaign 1942–1945 and attempt some comments on the lessons it provided.

The first Arakan operation, December 1942 to May 1943
This was an over-ambitious attempt by Wavell to recapture the island of Akyab in the Arakan Peninsula, 200 miles south-east of the Ganges delta. It failed, but by the time the monsoon moved in in May 1943 there had been no disastrous consequences.

The first Chindit operation, February to June 1943
This was an event of a different order. In February 1943 seven columns trained to operate behind the Japanese lines left Imphal on a four months operation. They moved through jungle and mountains, and like Elijah they were fed with bread and meat brought by ravens. The ravens, which in this story consisted mostly of Dakotas, also brought ammunition, mail and other supplies. This operation, master-minded by that eccentric genius Major-General Orde Charles Wingate, pioneered a new form of army/air strategy in which the Army disappeared into the blue (in this case the jungle) without lines of surface communication of any kind and was supplied entirely from the air. Two conditions needed to be satisfied if this kind of hazardous operation was to succeed. First, the Allies needed at least a reasonable degree of air superiority over the Japanese. Second, the air transport force had to be big enough for its task. Both conditions were satisfied in the event and the first Chindit operation was a success. Not long before, in the winter of 1942–43, the Luftwaffe's attempts to

supply the besieged German Sixth Army at Stalingrad ended in a disaster from which the Luftwaffe never really recovered. In that campaign neither of the necessary conditions was satisfied. Russia enjoyed air superiority over the skies of Stalingrad and all the transports that Germany could muster could not supply the needs of General von Paulus and his army. The first Chindit operation was well judged and its seminal effect transformed army operations in the rest of the Burma campaign.

Supreme Headquarters South-East Asia

The establishment of this headquarters in Ceylon did much to consolidate and to galvanise operations in this theatre. Founded in the autumn of 1943 at the Quebec Conference with the strong support of the United States, it took over control of all forces land, sea and air, British, Allied and American in the theatre. Admiral Mountbatten (substantive rank at this stage Captain, RN) was the Supreme Commander. General ('Vinegar Joe') Stilwell, who commanded all American and Chinese forces in the theatre, was his deputy. Richard Peirse was given command of the Allied Air Forces with General Stratemeyer as his second-in-command. The Allied Air Forces were organised with a Tactical Force under Air Marshal Sir John Baldwin, a strategic force under Brigadier-General Davidson (USAAF), a Troop Carrier Command under Brigadier W. D. Old (USAAF), and a combined PRU outfit. The consequences of the establishment of South-East Asia Command, and indeed of putting it into the hands of a youthful and charismatic Supreme Commander, were most fruitful. True, Mountbatten came at a good moment when things were going better all round. But then luck is a necessary quality in the equipment of all successful commanders.

The turning point

Late in 1943 Mountbatten decided upon an offensive with four distinct elements. There was to be a renewed assault on the Arakan with the idea once again of capturing Akyab. Stilwell was to strike south from Ledo. The Chindits were to have a repeat operation across the Japanese lines of communication. Finally, there was to be an advance across the Chindwin River. Each of these separate operations, of course, was totally dependent upon air support. A few weeks later, Japanese General Hanaya decided, very belatedly it might be thought, to throw his entire stake into opening the path to India. His plan, known as Operation C, was made up of two parts. The first a descent on Chittagong (200 miles east of Calcutta); the second an attempt to sweep away the Allied positions in Imphal and Kohima. It was inevitable that the Allied and the Japanese plans should collide head on in what was to be the turning point of the war in Burma. The Japanese relied on the tactics which had served them so well in Malaya, by-passing Allied strong points and so encouraging Allied retreats which soon became disorganised routs. These tactics no longer worked. The Imperial forces had learned from their misfortunes in Malaya and their earlier experiences in Burma. Garrisons stood fast and were supplied and supported from the air. The newly arrived Spitfire VIIIs did deadly work in happy comradeship with American long-range Mustangs and Lightnings. So the second Arakan expedition held firm despite everything the Japanese could throw against it. So too, in due course, Imphal and Kohima, the objects of Phase 2 of the Japanese Operation C, managed to survive despite desperate dangers. Here matters swung in the balance until Mountbatten, in a major crisis, turned a Nelsonian blind eye to the categorical orders of the Combined Chiefs of Staff and diverted substantial additional air transport resources to the threatened front. Massive reinforcements, including the 5th Indian Division, were flown in. Imphal and Kohima were saved and the Japanese sun in South-East Asia had begun to set. Mountbatten's action was one of great personal courage; in itself it provided a total justification for the creation of Allied Supreme Headquarters in November 1943. By now the south-west monsoon was starting but air operations continued. The meteorological and other hazards of this monsoon are not easily appreciated unless one has seen the terrain. The heaviest rains in the world; the menace of cumulo-nimbus clouds capable of breaking the strongest aircraft and of throwing a Spitfire in an uncontrolled lift of 10,000 feet, smashing it to pieces. All this among mountains of alpine dimensions. It was in such circumstances as these that, by mid-1944, Japan lost control of Burma. Their air forces had no reply to the Allied air strength. The Imperial forces, 350,000 strong were now supplied by a modest air transport force in circumstances of virtual Allied air supremacy. Now the Japanese Army was in disarray. It faced a crushing assault from the tactical air forces operating in the battlefield, the Chindits operating against the Japanese lines of communications and the Allied strategic air forces striking against railways, dumps, bridges, bases and even (falling back on an old skill) mining the Burmese rivers. Akyab fell in January 1945, Mandalay in March and Rangoon in May. The Burma campaign was over. Hopes that South-East Asia Command could take part in the liberation of Malaya were frustrated by lack of sea transport resources, priority being given to the Pacific. A plan to divert part of Bomber

Command towards the final flattening of Japan fell through, partly on the time factor, but more perhaps on account of major political considerations *vis à vis* the United States.

Medical

Before concluding our brief account of the campaign in Burma a reference must be made to aero-medical matters. It is in a way an exhilarating story. In the Malayan campaign, and indeed the early part of the Burma campaign, the way of the sick and wounded was a nightmare—a brutal terrain, a brutal foe and a more or less complete lack of facilities for evacuation and tending the wounded. The later stages of the Burmese campaign brought a miracle. It resulted from plenty of air transport including 'puddle-jumpers'—light aircraft with stretchers—in circumstances of virtually total air supremacy. A soldier could be injured in battle and be on the operating table in a field hospital within the hour. Nowadays such ideas are perhaps commonplace; in 1944 they seemed miraculous.

Reflections

The Burma campaign marked a new epoch in military history. Large land forces operated successfully without communications on land, supplied from the air and supported strategically, tactically and medically from the air. It was a great achievement and it was realised by soldiers and airmen operating in the most exacting circumstances. If names must be mentioned in regard to what was, in the truest sense, a combined operation two seem outstanding; Mountbatten who, as Supreme Commander, saved Kohima and Imphal in a critical hour, and General Slim who, as a man and as commander of the victorious Fourteenth Army, has a claim to be regarded as the greatest British soldier of the Second World War.

18

Bomber Command: Plans, Diversions and Devices

Plans

When France collapsed and Britain faced the might of a German domain which stretched from the Russian frontier to the North Sea, two problems stood out among many others. First, how was Britain to avoid invasion and defeat? Second, a somewhat hypothetical question, how to defeat Germany, whose military potential was greater than that of the British Commonwealth by a factor of perhaps times three? The answer to the first question was provided by the Battle of Britain. In this battle, as we have seen, the German Air Force faced a sophisticated air defence for the first time. Britain was victorious and Hitler experienced his first defeat. Amazingly, he decided to turn aside from Britain to crush Russia. This staggering misjudgement was of course the turning point of the Second World War. Had Hitler been content to consolidate his victories, the end of Britain could only have been a matter of months. But no, dazzled by cheap victories in Czechoslovakia, Poland and France, the unheralded pounce, the Stukas and the rest, Hitler took Russia for a dead chicken. As Churchill said on a different occasion referring to the belief that Britain in 1940 could be dealt with like a chicken: 'Some chicken, some neck'. No doubt Hitler felt that with Russia under his belt Britain would present few problems. He could well have been right. Anyway, as the result of all this, Britain had the opportunity to consider how she would win the war. The answer was that Britain would win the war by bombing Germany into submission. The writing on the wall said Britain was exceptional in the air. The Navy was supreme at sea. Germany was unsound politically, morally and economically, and in the end she would crack. There were weaknesses in all these arguments of course, as was to appear later. Fighter Command won a great victory, but only just. Bomber Command won a great victory, but only just. The Royal Navy and the Royal Air Force won the war at sea, but only just.

And finally Germany was tougher, braver, better organised and much stronger than anyone supposed. Most of this comment is hindsight of course. Had Britain been endowed with a deeper and clearer appreciation of the problems she faced in the autumn of 1940 the outlook would surely have appeared daunting if not unmanageable. Fortunately, Britain had found a leader who had a perspective of history and was prepared to soldier on till better times appeared. In truth, the basic problem at this stage was not how to win the war but how to avoid losing it. Fortune favours the brave, and Churchill was both brave and fortunate. In consequence of two astounding miscalculations, Hitler in the course of little more than a year added to his enemies the might of Russia and the power and determination of the United States, the greatest industrial state in the world. From this moment Hitler's fate was sealed. In the autumn of 1940 these astonishing events were of course veiled. On balance it was lucky that it was so. So Britain, once again in a tight corner, had to do the best she could. Her eyes fell on Bomber Command.

In September 1939 the first line strength of Bomber Command was in the region of say 500. By the end of the war first line strength had increased by a factor of four but the hitting power of the Command had increased beyond measure. More ambitious plans of expansion were considered at various times during the war. For example, plans were drawn up for a first line of 4,000 heavy bombers. For various reasons, including diversions to the war at sea and to the Middle East, this target had to be abandoned and the first line strength of Bomber Command in heavy bombers never exceeded 2,000. The light and medium bombers of 1939, Battles, Blenheims, Whitleys, Wellingtons, Hampdens, gave way from 1941 onwards to Stirlings, Halifaxes and Lancasters built in conformity with the notion of the 'ideal heavy bomber', a notion developed in the Air Ministry in 1936.* It is interesting to reflect that one of the many criticisms levelled at the Air Ministry in pre-war days was that they ordered too many types of aircraft. Had concentration on one type been decided upon at the outset it is likely that the Stirling would have been chosen. A little later it would have been the Halifax. At no stage would it have been the Lancaster, the ultimate winner which, in its earlier twin-engine version as the Manchester, was a failure.

Diversions

Throughout the war Bomber Command was the target of many who

* Though the original concept was to develop one type of 'ideal' heavy bomber only.

would have diverted its resources elsewhere. The claimants included the Army, the Navy, the Middle East, the Far East, the needs of transport and the Special Operations Executive. Some of the claims were wrong-headed, as for example were the proposals of the Army based on a mis-reading of the lessons of the Polish campaign for specially adapted or designed aeroplanes for army/air co-operation. The other demands were reasonable enough and were met in whole or in part. Still, it was exasperating for the Air Ministry, for the Royal Air Force, and for Bomber Command to see the growing strength of the bomber force attenuated in this way. It was however a tribute to the inner harmony of the three services and the experience and leadership of Churchill that these hard and divisive problems were solved as they arose.

Equipment

As we have discussed in Chapter 6, Bomber Command in September 1939 was not well equipped for war. Aircraft were deficient in range, bomb load, crew facilities, defensive characteristics, navigational equip-ment and bombsights. As the war moved on some of these defects were removed. The arrival of the new generation of heavy bombers removed the problems of range and load. The problem of keeping the crew warm and mobile was solved, bit by bit. The problem of defensive characteristics in a bomber was, sad to relate, never really solved in Bomber Command. Throughout most of the war Bomber Command could never oppose the cannon and rockets of the Luftwaffe with anything better than guns of 0.303-inch calibre, basically weapons of the First World War. It was not enough, as Harris in his lucid and well-documented Despatch makes clear. No doubt considerations of added weight played an important part in deciding policy.

The Mosquito

The early types of light bombers were phased out of Bomber Command early in the war, but by its close one light bomber had achieved a place of honour in the first line. This was the redoubtable de Havilland Mosquito, lineal descendant of the Comet which won the MacRobertson race to Australia in 1934. The company had proposed a military version of this aircraft to the Air Ministry but the idea was coldly received, partly because they had outgrown the idea of wooden aeroplanes and partly perhaps because the Air Ministry had no recent tradition of working with de Havillands except over the production of light aircraft. In the end an order for fifty Mosquitoes was placed, amid considerable uncertainty as to what its role should be. It was triumphant in many roles. As a fighter it outpaced all German fighters until German jet fighters arrived on the scene. As a fighter-bomber it was a tremendous asset to the Tactical Air Force. As a photographic reconnaissance aircraft possessed of extreme altitude capability it could fly over Germany with almost total immunity. As an unarmed bomber it could fly regularly to Berlin with a 4,000-pound bomb and with an exceptionally low casualty rate. It could be fitted with a six-pounder gun and, remarkable as it may sound, the idea was considered of fitting it with a 3.7-inch AA gun for use in an anti-tank role. The Mosquito has claims to be considered the outstanding aircraft of the Royal Air Force. In 1940, when the Ministry of Aircraft Production under Beaverbrook was concentrating on the production of five in-service types at the expense of other production and development, it escaped the chopper by a whisker and its successful emergence as the only unarmed bomber in any air force in the Second World War was due to the brilliance of the conception and design backed by the wisdom and courage of Wilfrid Freeman.

Navigational devices

In September 1939 the navigational facilities of Bomber Command were primitive in the extreme and there was inevitably no experience of using them at night under black-out conditions. There was dead reckoning, of course, a little wireless direction-finding gear, and some facilities for astronomical navigation. When conditions were very favourable, targets could be found and bombed but otherwise errors of fifty miles or more could easily be made. Electronic devices to overcome this weakness were under development before September 1939, but the work was given a tremendous impetus when a report on bombing accuracy, or rather the lack of it, reached Churchill on the initiative of Lindemann. This report, which was based on the evidence of cameras fitted to bomber aircraft, is discussed in the next chapter.

There were in effect four electronic navigational devices:

Gee (short for grid) pin-pointed the position of an aircraft by measuring its distance by electronic means from three ground stations in Britain. This enabled the position of the aircraft to be plotted on a specially prepared grid printed on a chart. Gee (range 300–400 miles) became less effective the greater the range, and it could be jammed. Nevertheless it was a great comfort to crews, not least in helping them to navigate back to their home bases, and when introduced in 1942 it brought an important increase in bombing accuracy.

Oboe (so named for the supposed resemblance of the sound it made to that of the musical instrument of that name) was a device which enabled a bomber to fly on a course and attack the target under conditions of zero visibility, and to bomb on a command signal from base in a way which made appropriate allowance for height, wind, heading and airspeed. Properly used, Oboe was capable of great accuracy—to within 500 yards or so. It had several weaknesses. Each aircraft had to be separately controlled from base and this of course limited the number of Oboe aircraft that could be operated. It would only operate on an optical line of sight, ie a straight line drawn from base to aircraft must not intersect the earth. Finally it could be jammed. Despite these limitations Oboe was an aid of immense value which played an invaluable part in the final victory.

H2S (origin obscure) was a radar scanner which afforded on a cathode ray tube display a rough picture of the terrain over which the bomber was flying. H2S had several defects. Over large built-up areas the tube became swamped with returns and the picture became unreadable. Moreover H2S signals could be monitored in Germany while aircraft were tuning up over Britain. It would also be monitored by a German airborne device called Naxos. H2S thus conceded valuable intelligence.

G-H was a development of Gee which, like Oboe, gave a blind bombing facility. Its main defects were limited range, liability to jamming and the strain it put upon aircrew. Many aircraft were lost while the crew were concentrating on the G-H dials.

Techniques of bombing

The bombs available to Bomber Command at the outbreak of war were unsuitable (see Chapter 6). As the war proceeded, improvements came along. Thanks to lessons dearly learned, partly from the Luftwaffe, better and larger bombs and improved incendiaries were developed. Later still, the genius of Barnes Wallis produced the skipping bomb of the Dambusters, the 12,000-pound Tallboy and the 22,000-pound Grand Slam, the Earthquake Bomb, all carried by the magnificent and long-suffering Lancaster.

Once navigational devices enabled bombers to navigate to the vicinity of the target the question arose of how to marshal the final attack. The answer developed was to use high-flying Oboe Mosquitoes to mark the target with coloured pyrotechnics called markers. The main force then bombed visually on the markers. If the target was invisible because of cloud or (as happened so often in attacks on industrial plants in the Ruhr) because of industrial haze, the Oboe Mosquitoes dropped sky markers and the main force bombed on them. Bombing by sky-marker was inherently less accurate. Late in 1942, against the judgement of the Commander-in-Chief who wished to develop these techniques in a different way, a Pathfinder Force was developed to undertake the marking of targets. Later still the post of Master Bomber (plus deputies on suitable occasions) was developed. The Master Bomber took no part in the main attack but monitored the position of marker bomb bursts and issued correcting orders by radio telephone. New markers of different colour were then dropped and crews were told to disregard markers wrongly sited.

Bombsights

Until the problem of navigating to the target had been solved the role of the bombsight was to some extent academic. On the outbreak of war the Command was equipped with a Course-Setting Bombsight which suffered the severe disability under operational conditions that the bomber was required to fly on a straight and level course to the target. The Course-Setting Bombsight was replaced from the summer of 1942 onwards by the Stabilised Vector Sight, the so-called Mark XIV bombsight.* This bombsight used a computer to simplify the bomb-aimer's task and allowed mild evasive action to be taken up to the moment of bomb release—a great advance. An even more sophisticated bombsight, the Stabilised Automatic Bombsight, was introduced in 1943 but only on a limited scale, for instance in the famous No 617 squadron (the 'Dambusters') as it demanded an exceptional standard of skill on the part of the bomb-aimer. It was, however, invaluable when the very highest order of precision was demanded.

---

* Its development owed much to the ideas of Harris, Tizard and Blackett.

The electronic war

When Britain and Germany started to bomb each other's cities by night in 1940, night air defence was for practical purposes quite ineffective. In both countries the techniques of night air defence came under intense development. In Germany, ack-ack and searchlights were a function of the Luftwaffe. Soon, under radar control, they were effective up to 20,000 feet or so. So far as nightfighters were concerned Bomber Command soon had to face a line of fighter 'boxes' with GCI equipment, the famous Kammhüber Line. The construction of this line began in 1940 and by September 1942 it extended from the north of Denmark to Paris. In each 'box', German night-fighters were free to hunt with AI radar and ground controller assistance, free from the embarrassment of flak. Bomber Command's answer was to pass large numbers of bombers through the screen in a short time. The German response to this tactic was to divide their night air defence into 'Tame Boars' and 'Wild Boars'. Tame Boars were German night-fighters equipped with AI and directed by a ground controller. Wild Boars were German fighters, often single-engine day-fighters, that swarmed over the target freelance aided by radar-guided searchlights, and pounced on unwary or even wary bombers. As Bomber Command stepped up its attack a second Kammhüber Line was developed and the Tame Boars were directed by Ground Control into the outward and returning bomber streams. Most British bombers were equipped with a tail device called 'Monica' which gave warning of tail attacks by German fighters. Unfortunately Monica could be and was monitored by the German Air Force. For this and other reasons the electronic war was on.

For night air defence the German Air Force relied on:

A listening service which monitored the transmissions of Bomber Command and its aircraft.
Freya radars, the German early warning system.
Würzburg radars, two per box, the German GCI which controlled the night-fighters.
The German ground controllers, broadcasting to the Tame Boars.
Lichtenstein, the German airborne radar.
Radar-controlled flak.

Listening to Bomber Command traffic alerted the German Air Force of the imminence of a raid and Freya observations were used at an early stage to deduce the targets chosen, often successfully. Instructions went to the air defence organisation and the system carried on from there.

Many and ingenious were the techniques used by the Royal Air Force to combat this system:

> The 'Y' Service. All the transmissions of the German air defence system were monitored by a Royal Air Force listening system known as the 'Y' Service.

> Freya was submitted to both ground and airborne jamming, a transmission known as 'Mandrel'.

> R/T traffic between the German ground controllers and the German night-fighters was jammed by an airborne device called 'Tinsel'. When this traffic shifted to the VHF band the Royal Air Force responded with 'Ground' and 'Airborne Cigar'. Airborne Cigar, or ABC as it was usually called, carried a German-speaking crew member who monitored and jammed the R/T traffic between the German ground controllers and their fighters.

The German running commentary giving general directions to the Wild Boars was attacked by a powerful system of ground transmitters known as 'Corona', which issued false instructions about bases, landings, and so on. Its greatest hour was when the entire German nightfighter force was grounded by a bogus order. The use by the Germans of women controllers was also replied to in kind. Part of the aim of Corona was to distract hard-pressed controllers and pilots. Extracts from Hitler's speeches were occasionally used for this purpose. In the main, straightforward jamming proved the most effective, though bogus test messages and irrelevant technical instructions also proved valuable.

The most effective weapon against the German night fighter was 'Window'. This device consisted of strips of aluminium foil cut to correspond to the wave-length of the German radars. When scattered in large numbers Window confused the German radars in a masterly way. Britain and Germany both thought up Window and both delayed its introduction, fearing that on balance it might work out to their disadvantage. Britain was the first to start its use. This was at the beginning of the great attack on Hamburg on 24–25 July 1943 when the use of Window was a triumphant success. There were various ways in which Window could be circumvented, at any rate in part, but on balance it was immensely valuable to Britain and, as Harris remarks in his Despatch, German fears about it were well founded.

The German AI was attacked by 'Grocer', a powerful ground station operating in Suffolk on the German AI frequency. A device called 'Serrate' was also developed to enable fighters accompanying our bombers to home on the German AI. The Germans in turn could home on 'Serrate'. After July 1943 of course Window was also available. When the effectiveness of Window against German AI began to decline in October 1943 it was suspected that the Germans had changed their AI frequency. This was indeed so, but the new frequency was not discovered until July 1944 when a Ju 88 equipped with the new German AI set landed undamaged in Britain. The device was then jammed by a new type of Window.

Radio counter-measures for D-Day

Bomber Command played a vital part in RCM for D-Day. New types of Window dropped by aircraft were used to simulate the approach of heavy ships at seven knots or so towards the French coast, between Cap Griz Nez and Le Havre. A Mandrel screen carried by Royal Air Force Stirlings and USAAF Fortresses covered the actual assault by jamming all the German coastal radar in the Channel area. Finally, Bomber Command dropped dummy parachutists in chosen areas as a diversion to the real airborne landings. The size of the (dummy) paratroop force was magnified by a judicious use of Window. The contribution of these highly sophisticated devices to the tactical surprise achieved on D-Day was profound.

Tactics. Bomber Command made skilful and effective use of tactical routeing and deception. As the German defences increased in strength, extent and complexity the Command constantly and elaborately varied its routeing plans in order to minimise casualties. In this matter, the use of Window, particularly in combination with the high-flying Mosquito, conferred an immense advantage because it enabled the Command to simulate a heavy attack by the use of a handful of aeroplanes. German fighters were diverted to meet bogus attacks while the main force came in elsewhere. One German tactic was developed which was responsible for a high proportion of Bomber Command casualties. In the main our heavy bombers were defenceless from below. German fighters learned how to approach our bombers from below and to fly beneath them without being seen. Using upward-firing cannons they would then fire at the fuel tanks in the wings of their opponent with devastating effect.

The tactic is believed to have been discovered by accident. The German night-fighters had been shooting down their own Me 110s, which resemble Lancasters when viewed from behind. So they came close and underneath their target in order to identify. They found that they could do so unobserved. The upward-tilted cannon firing through the roof of the Me 110 cockpit was also a sudden inspiration. This tactic, which the Germans called '*Schräge Musik*' ('Slanting Music') was responsible for many casualties. No whisper of it reached Britain either through the Resistance, which had many members working on airfields in occupied countries, or through the decyphering of enemy messages. It is said that Bomber Command had a suspicion of what was happening and tried to persuade the Air Ministry to provide a downward view facility or a dustbin turret. No 6 (Canadian) Group had an inkling at least of what was going on and were fitting ventral gun positions to their aircraft as a lash-up as fast as they could.

19

Bomber Command: The Battles

The strategic air offensive against Germany can be studied in five distinct phases:

Phase 1: The period of restricted bombing, September 1939 to May 1940.

Phase 2: The period of inadequate navigational facilities, May 1940 to March 1942.

Phase 3: The beginnings of the major assault on Germany, March 1942 to April 1944.

Phase 4: The period of control by the Supreme Commander, April to September 1944.

Phase 5: The final assault, September 1944 to May 1945.

Bombing restricted: September 1939 to May 1940

After the defeat of Poland in September 1939 it suited Britain, France and Germany to confine their attacks to strictly military objectives. None of the three countries was ready for full-scale war. Germany had been taken rather by surprise by the Anglo/French declaration. France was apprehensive of the consequences of a German attack. British aircraft production was increasing fast and she was anxious to complete her preparations. So it came about that until 15 May 1940, a few days after the massive air attack on Rotterdam when the British Cabinet approved attacks east of the Rhine, only attacks on naval and military targets were permitted. Few bombs were used during this phase, perhaps fifty tons out of the Command's war total of some 900,000 tons. Nevertheless, these eight months brought a total revolution in tactics. One of the great tactical lessons of the war was that, as between reasonably matched and sophisticated air forces, bombers without fighter support are at a grave disadvantage in dealing with an unbroken enemy fighter force, whether by day or by night. The only exception to this rule was the Mosquito. Britain learned this lesson by day in the autumn and winter of 1939; the Germans learned their lesson in the Battle of Britain; the United States learned it in Europe in 1943. In the autumn of 1939, only naval and military targets being available, Bomber Command took on the German fleet. Little more than twenty-four hours after Britain declared war on Germany, Wellingtons and Blenheims of Bomber Command attacked German warships at Wilhelmshaven and Brunsbüttel. It was a gallant start which did much honour to the Royal Air Force, but little damage was caused and casualties, mainly from flak, were heavy. In December 1939 a number of armed reconnaissances of German coastal waters were undertaken. The Wellingtons were attacked by German fighters alerted by the German early warning radar and severe casualties were suffered. Painfully, Bomber Command realised that unescorted bombers could not take on German fighters by day. Meanwhile, however, Whitleys and Wellingtons were flying over Germany by night on leaflet raids virtually without opposition, the German night-fighter defences, like their British counterparts, being at this stage virtually non-existent. The value of the leaflets as an aid to our war effort was perhaps questionable and the accuracy with which they were delivered at this stage of Bomber Command's development was no doubt poor. The Command's principal enemy at this stage was the weather. The winter of 1939/40 was hard and the available bombers were poorly equipped to cope with it. There were serious problems of icing, navigation and crew comfort. The operations of the Command in this phase were mainly valuable for the experience they afforded to crews and technical men of the problems to be faced in operating over enemy territory, in blackout conditions and in bad weather.* The sea-mining operations of No 5 Group referred to in Chapter 12 were also useful and led to greater things later.

Phase 2: May 1940 to March 1942

When at last Germany made her long-predicted assault on the West in May 1940 by the long-predicted strategic route north of the Maginot Line there was little that Bomber Command could do. The air forces attached to the British Expeditionary Force, their counter-parts in the Advanced Air Striking Force and the Blenheims in No 2 Group Bomber Command sacrificed themselves with the greatest gallantry and in the highest traditions of their Service. Bomber Command could at first do

* They were also valuable to Germany in giving night-fighter experience.

nothing by day and little by night. But on 15 May 1940 the Royal Air Force was authorised to attack targets east of the Rhine. That night ninety-nine aircraft of Bomber Command set out to attack oil and railway targets in the Ruhr. In the words of Webster and Frankland:

> Thus began the Bomber Command strategic air offensive against Germany. For many years it was the sole means at Britain's disposal for attacking the heart of the enemy, and, more than any other form of armed attack upon the enemy, it never ceased until almost exactly five years later Germany, with many of her cities in ruins, her communications cut, her oil supplies drained dry and her industry reduced to chaos, capitulated to the invading armies of the Grand Alliance. It was probably the most continuous and gruelling operation of war ever carried out.

This is a true comment and it is appropriate to reflect on what would have happened to Britain if there had been no Bomber Command in 1940, 1941, 1942 and 1943. In fact, as we know now, Bomber Command did little damage to Germany in the early days. The bombers which set out from Britain in May 1940 and for many months thereafter scarcely scratched German oil and communications. And the same was true of countless other brave attacks over the next two years. Navigational and other facilities were just not up to it. But to discuss history in these terms is to mistake the shadow for the substance. Even in this phase Bomber Command achieved victories great and small.

Small: Bomber Command's attacks, modest as they were, achieved some significant successes.

Examples: The bombing of the German invasion barges in 1940[1] and the raid on Berlin in the summer of that year, which led Hitler in a fury to divert the Luftwaffe from attacking Fighter Command bases, which could take little more, to attacking London, which could and did take plenty. The damage inflicted by Bomber Command on German warships in French harbours in 1941.

Great: In 1940 and in most of 1941 Britain was in a siege position. The fact that in 1940 Bomber Command could bomb the German capital, and that throughout 1940 and 1941 Britain could hear her bombers setting out, night after night, to attack Germany, was a matter of immense psychological significance for Germany as well as for Britain. Most important of all,

Bomber Command was gaining experience over the whole spectrum of strategic bombing which would prove of immense value in future years.

Precision Bombing

In September 1939 Bomber Command believed that it could bomb precise targets. This belief was based on peace-time exercises in daylight against zero opposition in good weather. The transition from such exercises to the realities of war and bad weather was, as Churchill might have said, a hard and heavy experience. The fact that the Royal Air Force pressed on through these difficult and dangerous days and did not lose heart was of great service to Britain. In the beginning, things went about as badly as they could. The Wellingtons and Blenheims that set off on 4 September 1939 to attack the German Fleet found little comfort. One-third became lost and returned to base. Those that attacked, using unsuitable bombs dropped from low altitudes, did little damage, and of these over one-third were shot down. One aircraft bombed the Danish town of Esbjerg, a navigational error of 110 miles. Photographs of the resulting damage to the town gave rise to doubts, in some minds at least, as to the efficiency of our bombs.

Between September 1939 and February 1942 some twenty directives were issued from the Air Ministry to Bomber Command as to the targets they should attack. At various times they were told to attack oil plants, aircraft factories, marshalling yards, German warships, German forests, submarine building yards and pens, invasion ports, German ball-bearing plants, and other industrial and military targets. Much of this, though by no means all, was far removed from reality. When conditions were favourable, as for example in the attacks on the invasion barges in the summer of 1940, precise or semi-precise targets could be and were attacked successfully. But when conditions were poor, errors of many miles were possible or even probable. So matters went on into 1940. Portal replaced Air Chief Marshall Sir Edgar Ludlow-Hewitt as Commander-in-Chief in April 1940 and was in turn replaced by Air Marshal Sir Richard Peirse in October 1940, Portal at this stage succeeding Newall as Chief of the Air Staff. Ludlow-Hewitt had given great service to Bomber Command and was indeed a most distinguished officer. Those who seek a professional evaluation of Ludlow-Hewitt should turn to Harris' account in *Bomber Offensive*. Ludlow-Hewitt was a man of total integrity, total dedication and immense professional skills. He was not an ideal leader for Bomber Command, knowing perhaps too much about the detail. On leaving Bomber Command he became Inspector-General of the Royal Air Force, in which post he was an immense success and gave service of great value to Britain.

Peirse held the post of Commander-in-Chief, Bomber Command for some sixteen months from October 1940 to February 1942. It was a difficult time for the Command. A trickle of heavy bombers had come forward, but as always the early days of the introduction of a new generation of aircraft were not easy. The new electronic aid, Gee, was not to be used on a large scale until March 1942. In the summer of 1941 there occurred one of the great turning points in Bomber Command history. Lord Cherwell,* Churchill's scientific adviser, sent a member of his staff to Bomber Command Headquarters to examine some 600 photographs taken by night-bombers over the period June to July 1941. The result was sensational. To quote from Webster and Frankland:

> Mr Butt concluded that of all the aircraft recorded as having attacked their targets, only one-third had got within five miles of them. The percentage of success, however, varied greatly with the geographical position of the target, the state of the weather and the intensity of the anti-aircraft defences. Over the French ports, for example, he calculated that two-thirds of the aircraft reported to have attacked the target had actually been within five miles. Over the Ruhr the proportion was reduced to one-tenth. A French port, he estimated, was more than twice as easy to find as a target in the interior of Germany, but a target in the Ruhr was four times as difficult to locate as one elsewhere in Germany. In full moon, two-fifths of the aircraft reported to have attacked their targets had, according to Mr Butt's calculations, got within five miles of them. Without a moon the proportion fell to one-fifteenth.

Bomber Command Headquarters found this hard to take, and who shall blame them. But it was a true bill and the reaction of authority was a war-winner. The decision was taken not to throw Bomber Command away but to improve it. Advised by Cherwell and Portal, Churchill re-doubled the emphasis on improving our navigational methods. In consequence of these decisions Gee was ready by the spring of 1942 and its introduction inaugurated a new chapter in the history of the Command. For his part in these events Lindemann deserves the

---

* Professor Lindemann entered the House of Lords as Baron Cherwell, and became Viscount Cherwell in 1956.

gratitude of Bomber Command, the Royal Air Force and of Britain. He was a useful and wise critic, and indeed a friend. So, by the summer of 1941, the idea that Bomber Command was in the ordinary course capable of precise bombing was finished. From then until, say, February 1944, from which date onwards they began to develop precision capacity, Bomber Command recognised that it was an area bombing force. This does not mean that during this period Bomber Command was wholly incapable of precise attacks. Far from it. Precise and successful attacks could be and were accomplished, but they were the exception. For three years or so from mid-1941, area bombing was the rule save for magnificent exceptions. All this put Peirse, the new leader of Bomber Command, in something of a dilemma. For the rest of his tour of duty he had a force of extreme dedication raring to go, but alas lacking the navigational facilities even for area bombing. Various unsuccessful attacks resulted, notably the operations against Mannheim, Berlin and the Ruhr on the night of 7 November 1941, when thirty-seven bombers were lost out of 400. The Commander-in-Chief was criticised for this and a few days later was instructed to conserve his force. He replied that this was not too easy. It is difficult to create a force like Bomber Command, feed it on optimistic press reports and then say that, current results being ineffective, it must pipe down till better days appear.

Bomber Command was now (autumn 1941 to spring 1942) approaching one of its great climacterics. The story is immensely complex, but its main elements included the following:

The realisation that the bombing of precise targets was impracticable for quite a time ahead.

A degree of disillusionment with the results of bombing Germany.

On June 22, 1941, Germany invaded Russia. By this act Hitler turned aside from his dominant position in Europe to undertake a hazardous adventure in Russia adding in the process some 200 million men and women to the ranks of Germany's enemies.

Six months later Japan attacked the United States which was soon at war with Germany, a development which Germany can scarcely have relished. Thus in the space of six months the military and political situation had been transformed. These developments inevitably reacted on the standing of Bomber Command which no longer looked so indispensable.

The Battle of the Atlantic was still a cause of great anxiety to Britain and a major diversion of effort to the war at sea was inevitable.

So Bomber Command had to fight hard to survive. When Portal pressed his plan for a first line of 4,000 heavy bombers Churchill was cool. He thought that the most Bomber Command could achieve was to cause Germany 'a heavy and seriously increasing annoyance'. Of course Portal resisted this and the bombing offensive was never at any stage ousted from its formal position as one of the mainstays of British strategy. Nevertheless the situation was not easy.

It is convenient at this stage to refer to the controversy between Tizard and Cherwell about bombing policy. The quarrel between those men is admirably described in the biographies of Ronald Clark and Lord Birkenhead and it is unnecessary to this story to consider it in detail. The trouble had its origins, or at any rate increased, when Tizard was in the ascendant as Chairman of the Committee for the Scientific Survey of Air Defence in pre-war days. We have already described how Lindemann used Churchill to secure his addition to the committee. At this stage Tizard was in a key position and Lindemann was routed and, in the opinion of most authorities, rightly routed. The position was altered completely when Churchill entered the Government and Lindemann joined his personal staff. Now Lindemann was in the key position and Tizard less happily situated. It has been suggested by some that the Lindemann–Tizard controversy really determined the shape of bombing policy throughout the war, but this was certainly not so. British bombing policy flowed from Government decisions taken on the advice of the Chiefs of Staff Committee. Germany was bombed because the Chiefs of Staff, as they said in countless appreciations, wanted it that way. And Churchill seldom if ever overruled the Chiefs of Staff. Churchill was usually a supporter of the bombing offensive, and Lindemann also. But though Lindemann undoubtedly helped Bomber Command in many vital ways (eg in regard to speeding up special bombing aids like Gee and H2S) his help was not in any sense the decisive factor. Without Lindemann, bombing policy would have been much the same though it would have been the poorer without his help. Turning over the files in the Public Record Office it is impossible not to be impressed with the immense services that Lindemann gave to Churchill. Churchill used him to condense, to analyse and to illuminate technical ideas. This he did with immense competence and lucidity. Some of his notes gave rise to serious misunderstandings both during and after the war. In the spring of 1942, although the bombing of Germany was still the official policy, the doubters were growing more outspoken. In February 1942 their doubts slopped over into a speech by a Minister of the Crown. Cripps, then Lord Privy Seal, winding up a debate in the House of Commons said of our bombing policy:

> ... this policy was initiated at a time when we were fighting alone against the combined forces of Germany and Italy and it then seemed that it was the most effective way in which we, acting alone, could take the initiative against the enemy. Since that time we have had an enormous access of support from the Russian armies, who, according to the latest news, have had yet another victory over the Germans, and also from the great potential strength of the United States of America. Naturally, in such circumstances, the original policy has come under review. I can assure the House that the Government are fully aware of the other uses to which our resources could be put and the moment they arrive at a decision that the circumstances warrant a change, a change in policy will be made.[2]

This speech caused dismay not only in London but also in Washington, where preparations for the United States Army Air Force's operations against Germany were being made. Nevertheless, criticisms of bombing policy continued to be made in public and it was against this background that Cherwell, in March 1942, addressed a short minute* to Churchill in which he calculated that a continuation of the bomber offensive until mid-1943 would de-house a third of the German people and would have a decisive effect on the war. This minute was not a happy one. As was quickly pointed out by Tizard and others it contained a number of serious errors. It overstated the number of bombers available, overestimated the accuracy of the bombing, and assumed a linear connexion between bombs dropped and houses destroyed. Lindemann scarcely attempted to rebut these criticisms but pointed out, quite fairly, that his minute was only intended to be illustrative. But the episode was important because it was used both during and after the war to suggest that the aim of Bomber Command was to win the war by knocking down German houses, and that this policy was adhered to because Cherwell sold it to the Prime Minister on the basis of faulty calculations. Nothing could be further from the truth. Bombing policy was determined initially by the fact that, when Britain was alone, Bomber Command represented the only hope of winning the war. When Britain secured allies the situation changed, and all the various claimants for diverting heavy bombers away from Bomber Command redoubled their efforts. It was a 'pull devil, pull baker' situation in which none of the parties got what they wanted. In the end,

* Later circulated by Churchill to the Defence Committee.

Bomber Command's decisive and essential contribution to the German defeat came not from destroying houses but from forcing the German Air Force on the defensive, diverting it on a massive scale from the Eastern Front, and finally helping to shatter it completely through the destruction of German oil and communications, from the overwhelming measure of support for the Allied armies, and in the end from the destruction of the German will to win. All this would have crumbled if the critics of Bomber Command had had their way in 1941 and 1942. The collapse would also have involved the United States Army Air Force, which at the time was facing difficulties of its own including the serious risk of diversion to the Far East war. It is fearful to contemplate what would have happened to the Allied armies in 1944 and 1945 if Bomber Command and the United States Army Air Force had been destroyed or gravely weakened. So, great issues lay behind the attempts to weaken or destroy Bomber Command in 1941 and 1942. The upshot was a compromise, but in the event it was a compromise which worked. It was brought about by many hands, principally the Chiefs of Staff, the Prime Minister and Harris himself. Cherwell played a useful and prominent part but the suggestion that he was the dominant factor cannot be sustained.

It is also suggested on occasions that Tizard opposed the bombing policy. Certainly in his address to the Royal United Service Institution in August 1946 he said, 'The actual effort in manpower and resources that was expended in bombing Germany was greater than the value in manpower of the damage caused . . .' This comment, which most certainly cannot be sustained, was scarcely a characteristic one and perhaps reflected, at any rate in part, the Lindemann controversy. Tizard's usual attitude, and one that was reflected in his minutes to the Secretary of State, was to say that he believed in giving more heavy bombers to the war at sea and doubted perhaps whether Bomber Command would get enough to be really effective. The differences between Tizard and Cherwell were unfortunate and something of a tragedy for Tizard. Both were excellent scientists possessed of immense ability and devoted to their country. One unhelpful factor was that Lindemann could not bear to be proved wrong. When defeated in a straight battle of fact and reason he had a way of saying 'very convenient', which did little to endear him to his associates. Tizard had a masterful way too. Anyway, the personalities just did not fit. Tizard's problems were aggravated by the fact that for one reason or another he never found the right slot either in the Air Ministry or in the Ministry of Aircraft Production.

Phase 3: March 1942 to April 1944

According to Webster and Frankland, March 1942 'marks the time from which Bomber Command began decisively to advance towards an ultimate operational efficiency which was astonishing.' It is a true verdict. There were three principal reasons, among many others, for the change. The first factor was the introduction of Gee, followed nine months later by Oboe. Gee was demonstrated to Bomber Command in October 1940, underwent service trials in 1941 and came into operational use on the night of 8 March 1942. The second factor was the rapid improvement in the production rate of heavy bombers which nearly trebled throughout 1942. The third factor was the appointment of Harris as Commander-in-Chief on 23 February 1942, one of the really great commanders in the Second World War and indeed in British history. Within two weeks of his arrival Bomber Command had carried out an immensely successful attack on the Renault factory at Billancourt just south of the Bois de Boulogne and about six miles from the centre of Paris. This attack, planned some time before, had no assistance from Gee but the extraordinary S-bends of the River Seine near Paris must surely have helped. Nearly 500 tons of bombs were dropped, a high proportion of them within the factory then in full production for the German war economy. Conditions were favourable, good weather, full moon and only light defences. The history of Bomber Command from that date until the end of 1943 is of a rising crescendo of assault on Germany matched by a massive development in the German air defences. By the spring of 1944 the strength of the German night-fighter force was such that Harris had to press the Air Ministry to provide ten squadrons of escort fighters, a request which was met only in part. Checks of this kind had occurred before and Harris was certainly in no mood to modify the offensive. In fact two vastly important developments at this stage changed the picture. Bomber Command turned to attack targets connected with the preparations for 'Overlord', different targets in different areas which led to an immediate drop in the casualty rate. The other major development at this stage was that the United States Army Air Force, which had sustained terrible losses when it attempted deep penetration of Germany by day, recovered the initiative with the adoption of long-range escort fighters and inflicted a series of crushing blows on the German Air Force. A detailed study of the operations of Bomber Command over the period March 1942 to April 1944 would be beyond the scope of this book, but the highlights can be summarised as follows:

The Pathfinders

The advent of Gee was a great benefit to Bomber Command's navigation even after August 1942 when it was jammed by the Germans.* However it did not solve the problem of finding the target, especially if obscured by cloud, industrial haze or massive searchlight defences. After much discussion Bomber Command turned over to the Pathfinder system. With the advent of Oboe in December 1942 and the belated arrival of effective marker bombs the technique of bombing rapidly improved.

Famous Attacks

Even before the advent of Oboe, Bomber Command achieved a number of spectacular victories including for example the attacks on Rostock and Lubeck and, most astonishing of all, the Thousand Bomber attack on Cologne. Apart from its material effects this last attack profoundly raised the prestige of the Command and was a morale-raiser on the great scale. Two other Thousand Bomber raids, on Essen and Bremen respectively, were less successful.

Daylight Operations

Several attempts were made using ingenious tactics to carry out daylight attacks with heavy bombers. They included the attack on the MAN† works at Augsburg in April 1942, on the submarine yards at Danzig in July 1942 and on the Schneider armaments factory at Le Creusot in October 1942. None of these attacks was really successful. The first incurred heavy casualties; the second, owing to navigational difficulties, took place mainly in darkness; and the third achieved only disappointing results. The time was to come when Bomber Command would resume daylight operations with immense success, but this was not to be in 1942 and 1943.

The Great Battles

By the spring of 1943, with Gee, Oboe, H2S and the Pathfinder Force all geared for action, Bomber Command began a series of major assaults on the German economy. Webster and Frankland describe them as battles, which is indeed what they were; successively, the Battle of the Ruhr (March to July 1943), the Battle of Hamburg and subsequent operations (July to November 1943), and the Battle of Berlin (November 1943

---

* Gee was jammed only over enemy territory. It never lost its value as a navigation aid for returning to base.

† Maschinenfabrik Augsburg–Nürnberg Aktiengesellschaft.

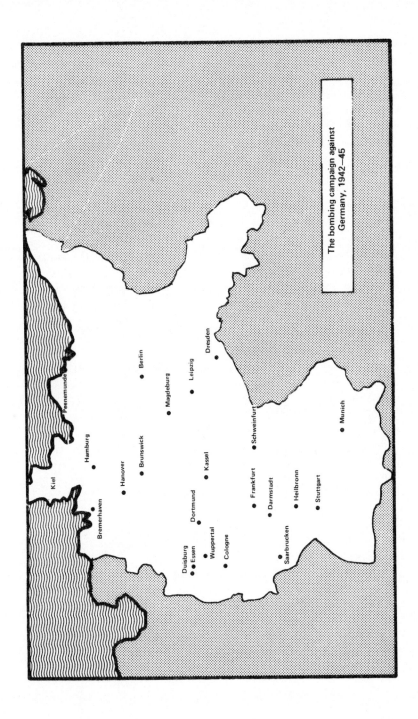

The bombing campaign against Germany, 1942—45

to March 1944). The scale of the attacks may be gauged from the fact that over the year April 1943 to March 1944 nearly 200,000 tons of bombs were dropped on Germany. Immense damage was done to German cities and industries and, particularly in the case of Hamburg, large numbers of civilian casualties resulted. Strangely, German armament production did not decline as the result of this torrent of bombs. It increased during the first half of 1943, remained fairly stable in the second half of 1943 and rose sharply in the first half of 1944. It would be easy to conclude from these statistics that the Anglo/American bombing offensive was a failure. It would be easy, and some have fallen into the trap, but it would be quite wrong as such a conclusion would ignore the following considerations, among others. The labour in Germany diverted to deal with bomb damage ran into millions of men and women. They were diverted from the munitions industry, from the armed forces and from the work on the Atlantic Wall. The vast German investment in guns, radar and electronics of all kinds was at the direct cost of other German forces. The consequence of keeping Germany in a defensive posture had the result that, amazing to relate, she developed no strategic air offensive against Britain. Although German aircraft production greatly increased in 1944 and exceeded that of Britain, in numbers if not in total weight, German air attacks on Britain in 1943 and 1944 were trivial. How many civilian casualties might the German bombers have inflicted on Britain while they were still in occupation of France and within 100 miles of London? By D-Day, for all the massive production of fighters, the German Air Force was on the way to defeat. Finally, the German Admiralty complained that they could not train U-boat crews or test U-boats because the Baltic Sea, their natural training and testing ground, had been mined by Bomber Command.

Berlin

Berlin proved a tough nut to crack, and in the first quarter of 1944 Bomber Command sustained a casualty rate to their heavy bombers which could scarcely continue indefinitely. Fortunately, the casualty rate improved in April 1944, and anyway at around this time the pattern of the air war was about to change. By the spring of 1944 Bomber Command was about to turn its attention to the needs of 'Overlord'. An exception to the high casualty rate in Bomber Command was of course the Mosquito, which continued to operate over Germany in comparative safety.

The United States Army Air Force

At a conference in Washington attended by Churchill and Roosevelt soon after America entered the war it was agreed, though not without a struggle, that the defeat of Germany should be given priority over the defeat of Japan. The United States Army Air Force, at that time part of the United States Army, immediately began preparations to join in the strategic air assault on Germany. Their tactics were different from those which Bomber Command had developed in the light of experience, namely to rely for the most part on area attack by night. They proposed instead to attack precise targets by day flying in formation and mainly without fighter escort. Their aircraft, Boeing B17s (Fortresses) and Consolidated B24s (Liberators), were heavily armed with 0·50-inch calibre machine guns and their crews were highly trained in tight formation flying. The Royal Air Force regarded these plans with some misgiving as hard experience had taught them that—Mosquitoes apart—unescorted bombers could not escape destruction by German fighters in daylight operations. Nevertheless, there was little to be done as General Arnold, the Chief of the United States Army Air Force, was determined to put his plans to the test. British opposition or criticism would simply have played into the hands of the powerful forces in Washington, which would happily have seen the Fortresses and Liberators diverted to the Far East. Throughout most of 1942 the United States Army Air Force was building up in Britain under its Commander, General Eaker, in close and cordial partnership with the Royal Air Force. By the summer of 1942 attacks on fringe targets began and encountered no serious trouble but when in the following year deep penetration of Germany was attempted the United States Army Air Force suffered a serious defeat. The climax was reached in an attack on Schweinfurt on 14 October 1943, when 198 American bombers were destroyed or damaged out of a total force of 291. It was time for a new look at policy. The answer came in a surprising and dramatic way. The American bombers became vulnerable when their escorting fighters, Lightnings and Thunderbolts, ran out of range and had to return, ie about 200 miles out. What was needed was an aircraft with the characteristics of a day-fighter and the range of a heavy bomber. Portal thought it could not be done and he had much logic on his side. The most that could be squeezed out of the Spitfire with drop tanks was a radius of 195 miles. But way back early in the war and before America entered it the British ordered some fighters from the famous North American company. At that company's suggestion a new design was developed and, incredible as it may sound, the prototype was flying in little over 100 days. It was named the P51 Mustang. The Mustang with its Allison engine was rather a disappointment, particularly at altitude, but then the idea was put forward of changing the engine to a Packard Rolls-Royce Merlin. The effect was phenomenal. The performance equalled that of the best day-fighters and the range with tanks was gradually extended to equal that of the heavy bombers. A miracle had been accomplished. With characteristic competence and drive the United States turned out the new-style Mustang in thousands in a matter of months. Speedily, the Fortresses and Liberators were setting out with their attendant Mustangs. The Mustangs did not so much escort the bombers as clear the skies and so achieve air superiority. The effect was dramatic. In the early months of 1944 the United States Army Air Force inflicted heavy damage on the German economy and a severe defeat on the German day fighter force. So well had American courage, persistence and enterprise prevailed. The Merlin/Mustang concept was valiantly supported by Wilfrid Freeman.

The Selection of Targets
Targets for Bomber Command, for the United States Army Air Force and for the joint force were suggested by organisations which in their complexity almost defy analysis. On the British side, those whose views were heard included the Air Ministry, the Ministry of Economic Warfare, the Joint Intelligence Committee of the Chiefs of Staff Committee, the Research and Experiments Department of the Ministry of Home Security, Bomber Command, Cherwell and his staff. In addition, of course, there were crackpots various. On the American side the apparatus was scarcely simpler. Targets proposed for Bomber Command at various times included the following:

> Strategic and tactical targets connected with 'Overlord'
> U-boat manufacture and U-boat pens
> Peenemünde and rocket sites and depots
> German oil
> Ball bearings
> Communications
> The German aircraft industry
> Molybdenum
> Heavy water

Some of these targets were chosen on the basis of military considerations, others for economic reasons. It was on the economic front that the recommendations inspired the least confidence. At the beginning of the war the economic authorities on which the British Government relied came out with predictions about the German economy which were almost totally wrong. They described the German economy as precarious when for practical purposes it was relaxed. This is hard to explain because, as Webster and Frankland point out, at this time only single shifts were being worked in practically all industries. The economists were also wildly wrong about the resources of German industry in machine tools. Of course the calculations and estimates were intensely difficult, a point which can be eloquently demonstrated by war-time predictions about German resources in ball-bearings. Half Germany's need for ball-bearings was met from factories in Schweinfurt, a small town of some 60,000 inhabitants about eighty miles east of Frankfurt. An important part of the balance was imported from Sweden. So here was a possible plan for bringing German industry and German arms to a standstill—pre-empt the Swedish supplies and blow up Schweinfurt. But things did not work out that way. After the great but disastrous American attack on Schweinfurt in October 1943 the Germans became convinced, reasonably enough, that a concerted attack was to be made on their ball-bearing industry. They at once took three important steps. They ordered new machinery, they arranged for the industry to be dispersed, and they also arranged for a census of existing stocks, with severe penalties for false returns. The result of the census astonished them. There were 8 million bearings in stock, enough with appropriate redistribution to keep the armaments industry going for months. The Germans had had no idea of this. Other attacks on the factories followed, notably those by Bomber Command and the United States Army Air Force in February 1944, but so far as military needs were concerned the outcome was nugatory— not a truck suffered from lack of bearings. A number of important reflections arise from this episode:

1. The basic reasoning was wrong. Had Schweinfurt been a real Heel of Achilles for Germany, and had it been destroyed *in toto*, Germany would not on this account have been gravely or even seriously embarrassed. As Webster and Frankland comment, the resources of a brave, determined and resourceful state would have been concentrated on the problem. Buffer stocks or not, Germany would soon have had bearings running out of her ears. The truth, as Oscar Wilde so wisely remarked, is seldom pure and never simple.

2. The limits of knowledge. If Germany in 1943 was ignorant of the basic statistics of her own ballbearing industry it was scarcely likely that British intelligence authorities, including the Ministry of Economic Warfare, could do better.

3. The effect on Bomber Command. The Commander-in-Chief put no trust in economic predictions about ballbearings. They were professionals, he was not. Nevertheless in the event, history shows that in this matter they were wrong and he was right. Anyway from this, as from other experiences such as with molybdenum, he was led to a deep distrust of what he called 'panacea' policies, that is short-cuts to victory. In this view he was partly wrong and partly right; no-one possesses a monopoly of the truth. But this too must be said: if Bomber Command had followed rigorously all the instructions given to them at various stages of the war much confusion would have resulted, 'For if the trumpet give an uncertain sound, who shall prepare himself to the battle?' From first to last the trumpet that sounded from High Wycombe sent a message which, if not always right, was of an ear-splitting clarity. Not for nothing had the Commander-in-Chief started his military career as an Army bugler.

Precision Bombing at Night

The impression is sometimes given that one of the important differences between Bomber Command and the United States Army Air Force was that the former went in for area bombing by night and the latter for precision bombing by day. Although there is an element of truth in this, the distinction is not really a realiable one. Even before the advent of Gee, Bomber Command was capable of precise attacks at night in certain rather specialised circumstances, as witness for example the attack on the Renault works at Billancourt in March 1942. And with the advent of Oboe in December 1942 markers could be put down within a few hundred yards of a specific target. Many of the conditions which confronted bombing by night—cloud, industrial haze, fighter attack—applied equally by day. From 1942 onwards it is doubtful if there was much to choose between the two Forces in the matter of accuracy. In 1943, No 5 Group Bomber Command, and especially its famous No 617 Squadron, began to develop techniques of high-precision bombing by night. The attack on the Mohne and Eder dams in the Ruhr is the supreme example of precision bombing by night, but there were many other accurate attacks, for example those on the aero-engine works at Limoges and on the rubber factory at Clermont-Ferrand. And of course precision bombing by a small force could on occasion be coupled with an associated area attack by a larger force. These factors must be borne in mind when an attempt is made to distinguish in any arbitrary way between precision and area attacks.

Peenemünde
Another example of precision bombing by night is afforded by Bomber Command's attack on Peenemünde in August 1943. Peenemünde was a small town on the Baltic coast about as far from Bomber Command bases as Berlin. It was the research station for the German development of the V1s and V2s. Reconnaissance aircraft had photographed the station and for the attack to succeed it was necessary that particular buildings should be destroyed. The attack, by some 600 heavy bombers, was a masterpiece of tactics. The nature and position of the target called for bright moonlight, good visibility and deep penetration, conditions ideal for the German night-fighters. The target was marked by the first 'red spot fire' markers and the attack was controlled by a Master Bomber who remained in the vicinity and issued directions. Good use was made of 'Window' and tactical routeing and the German controller described the target successively as Kiel, Berlin, Rostock, Swinemünde and Stettin. Even so, forty aircraft were lost and thirty-two damaged. It is estimated that the attack on Peenemünde delayed the opening of the V2 offensive by two months, but it may well have been more. The V1 programme was almost certainly also affected. These delays were of crucial importance. Had the V1s and V2s come into production earlier they could have been used against the invasion beaches with deadly consequences. As it was, they were just too late.

Phase 4: April to September 1944

In mid-April 1944 the control of Bomber Command was placed under the direction of the Supreme Allied Commander, General Eisenhower, the main object being that the Command should contribute to the invasion plan by the dislocation of railways in North-Western Europe. Opposed landings across beaches had been regarded with disfavour in Britain since Gallipoli and, more recently, since Dieppe. Even as late as 1943 there were those who thought that Europe would only be re-entered on a route march after Germany had been subdued by other means. At Bomber Command, plans for a land assault on Fortress Europe were in general regarded without enthusiasm, not least by the Commander-in-Chief. He feared that the operation might fail or, almost as bad, that the Allies might be committed to a small and costly bridgehead resulting in an expensive stalemate and, of course, extensive diversions from the main strategic assault on Germany. There was substance in these fears. Bomber Command believed that they could make their greatest contribution to victory by continuing with their strategic air offensive against Germany. Nevertheless, once the die was cast and 'Overlord' became a matter of settled Government policy, Bomber Command played their part with a will. Harris was never a man to do things by halves. The results surpassed all expectations, not only in a strategic but also in a tactical role. In fact, Bomber Command's contribution began in March, well before the formal commencement of Phase 4. Up to and including D-Day its contribution to 'Overlord' included:

The shattering of the rail communications in France which could have been used by Germany to reinforce the invasion beaches. In these attacks a degree of accuracy and effect was achieved which surprised the Commander-in-Chief himself. This was due to the skills developed by the Command in the strategic assault on Germany. The number of Allied soldiers and sailors who owe their lives to these operations is beyond computation, but it was without question vast.

The destruction of the coastal radar stations which would have enabled the Germans to observe the approach of the invasion vessels and aircraft. These operations were part of the Allied plan to put out of action at the critical stage the German radar system looking westwards from the French coast. The plan was highly successful. The Allied armada arrived off the Normandy coast without detection. Three airborne divisions proceeded to their dropping points without Luftwaffe opposition. Much of the work of attacking German radar stations was undertaken by the Second Tactical Air Force. It called for great precision and determination. The results were splendid but casualties were high.

On D-Day a massive assault on German coastal batteries in the invasion area.

The use of Bomber Command jamming and spoofing techniques to conceal the actual area of assault and to simulate a non-existent assault on the Pas de Calais.

Bomber Command's contribution to 'Overlord' produced a remarkable change in the bombing pattern. According to Webster and Frankland[3] the proportion of bombs dropped on Germany fell from 40 per cent in April to 8 per cent in June. Over the three months April to June as a whole, the proportion was about 17 per cent. After D-Day Bomber Command could be and was used as a tactical force in support of the Allied armies, and it began to operate by day with fighter support. In both day and night operations it was now capable of great accuracy. So there were now four sources of tactical air support for the Allied armies, Bomber Command, the Eighth Air Force and the British and American Tactical Air Forces. Soon it was clear that the armies had vastly more support than on any rational basis they needed. After all, it was not just a question of helping the armies on their way but rather of ending the war as quickly as possible. These thoughts were pressed by Portal at the Quebec Conference in the summer of 1944, with the result that as of September 1944 the Supreme Commander relinquished the direction of the two strategic bomber forces. The consequences of this decision were complex in the extreme.

Phase 5: The final triumph, September 1944 to May 1945

So, from September 1944 onwards, the two strategic bombing forces returned to the control of the Combined Chiefs of Staff, exercised effectively through Air Marshal Bottomley for Portal and through Spaatz for General Arnold. A new directive was issued which, as conveyed to Harris from Bottomley on 25 September 1944, required Bomber Command to attack the following objectives:

First Priority
(1) Petroleum industry with special emphasis on petrol (gasoline) including storage.

Second Priority

(2) The German rail and waterborne transportation system.
(3) Tank production plants and depots, ordnance depots.
(4) MT production plants and depots.

The directive went on to mention the need for policing action against the German Air Force, direct support for the Allied armies in the field, and concluded by saying that when weather and tactical conditions were unsuitable for operations against specific primary objectives attacks might be delivered on important industrial areas. This directive was the cause of a highly charged correspondence between Portal and Harris over the period November 1944 to January 1945. In the course of this correspondence Portal in effect said that Harris was paying too little regard to the most recent directive, and in particular too little regard to the requirement that he should give special priority to the attack on German oil. Harris vigorously rejected this complaint, saying that his operations were necessarily conditioned by weather and tactical considerations and that, subject to these considerations, he was doing his best to carry out the directive. In the course of the debate, however, he hurled many a brick at his old enemies the 'panacea' mongers, and it is clear that at all times he was seized with a profound distrust of economic prophecy and short-cuts to victory. In the end, Harris demanded in effect to be left to carry out the directive in his own way or to be removed from the Command. As this latter course was clearly out of the question, Harris being accepted by all as a very great commander indeed, Portal dropped the argument. Webster and Frankland characterise this dispute as tragic and imply that, had it been settled as desired by Portal, the war would have ended earlier by reason of lack of oil and without Germany being overrun by the Allied armies; thus, the contribution of the strategic air forces would have been seen in due proportion. The Official History may be right, but it is difficult to be sure. No-one had the monopoly of truth in this argument. It was a question of degree. The following points must be made, among others:

Between D-Day and the end of the war, Bomber Command dropped 90,000 tons of bombs on oil targets. Because of the high accuracy of Bomber Command attacks at this stage in all conditions of weather these attacks were especially effective. Coupled with those of the United States Army Air Force, they crippled German oil production and in the end virtually grounded the German Air Force and immobilised much of the German land forces. In the same period Bomber Command also dropped 190,000 tons of bombs on industrial targets, that is on cities. For reasons of tactics and of technical equipment it was clearly wasteful if not impossible for the whole of this effort to be directed to oil. Had a larger proportion been so directed it is a matter of judgement what difference it would have made. As it was, enough bombs were dropped on oil targets to bring oil supplies to a standstill. A heavy burden still rested on Bomber Command to support the Allied armies in the land battle. Examples of this can be found in the Command's decisive interventions in the Ardennes offensive and in the Battle of the Rhine in March 1945. The latter enabled Montgomery's armies to cross the river with trifling casualties. The Ardennes offensive was undertaken by Germany, no doubt deliberately, at a time of widespread fog and low cloud. But by this time Bomber Command's navigational aids had moved deep into France and the Command could undertake precise attacks in conditions in which the Tactical Air Forces were grounded.

Between D-Day and the end of the war in Europe Bomber Command's efforts were divided roughly as follows:

Area bombing	32 per cent
Military targets	28 per cent
Oil	17 per cent
Transportation	15 per cent
Naval targets	3 per cent
Airfields and aircraft industry	2 per cent
Other	3 per cent

The figure for military targets covers military installations as well as direct support to the land forces. Bearing in mind that a substantial proportion of the bombs directed at area targets would necessarily have hit war production directly or indirectly, we have a pattern not much out of accord with the directive. Webster and Frankland may be right in saying that if part of the 32 per cent devoted to area bombing had been diverted elsewhere, the course of the war from say September 1944 onwards might have been dramatically altered. It is a doubtful point. What is not in doubt is that the actual bombing pattern made a contribution to the running of the war which Webster and Frankland rightly characterise as 'decisive'. Harris carried a greater burden of responsibility than any British commander. Other commanders committed their forces at intervals. He sent out the whole of his Command night after night. On his shoulders rested the responsibility for Bomber Command's casualties. He felt a burning compulsion to operate the force he had built up in the way most effective and least expensive.

So much for the Portal-Harris dispute. To round it off it is appropriate to record the letter Portal wrote to Harris on the day after VE-Day:

My dear Bert,
    All *official* congratulations are going out in the name of the Air

Council, but I would like to send you a personal note to tell you how deeply and sincerely grateful to you I feel for all you and your command have done. It has been truly magnificent.

I also want to thank you for never letting the inevitable differences of opinion in a long war affect our personal relationships, and I would like also to say how tremendously I admired the way you refused to let ill health affect your grip and mastery of your great three year battle.

For the support you have always given me, and for your tremendous personal contribution to the achievement of the RAF in this war I can never adequately thank you, but I do want to send you this short note with all best wishes for the future,

Yours ever
Peter Portal

As a final footnote to a contest of will and intelligence conducted under the pressures of a great war by two strong characters, this letter surely reflects the greatest credit on both.

As 1944 wore on, the power of Bomber Command increased day by day. The German day-fighter force having been subdued by the United States Army Air Force, Bomber Command returned to daylight operations escorted by Spitfires, Mustangs and Tempests. Later, the German night-fighter force which had posed such a threat to Bomber Command early in 1944 began to crumble. As the Allied armies advanced, the German night air defences lost their early warning areas. Night-fighter stations had to be moved, fuel was short, training suffered. These events took an accumulating toll. Bomber Command now had numbers, range, accuracy, powerful weapons and a high degree of immunity from attack. As Webster and Frankland point out, the question was not whether the Command could deliver accurate and devastating attacks but which targets to go for. The actual targets selected covered a wide spectrum. The German Navy suffered severely. The *Tirpitz* and the *Scheer* were sunk and the pre-fabricated U-boat plan was defeated by the attack on communications and the assembly yards. Even the massively protected U-boat pens were shattered by earthquake bombs designed by Barnes Wallis. German tanks were immobilised from lack of fuel. Obstacles to the advance of the Allied armies were blasted away by precision attacks, often in conditions of zero visibility. Germany could not and did not survive such an assault.

Finally, a word must be said about the attack on Dresden, since this has attracted so much comment and so much controversy. Early in 1945, it seemed to the Allies that Germany was far from beaten. The Ardennes offensive had a profound impact. There was the threat of other new weapons; there was even the risk of nuclear attack. Unless the war could be ended quickly, countless more Allied lives must surely be lost. With the Allied armies halted in the west and the Russian armies advancing in the east, what could be done to advance the end of the war? The idea emerged from discussion among all concerned that Bomber Command and the United States Eighth Air Force should mount a massive attack on selected East German cities (as yet relatively undamaged) with the aim of harassing the German retreat on the Eastern Front and discouraging the transfer of German troops from the west. This concept received strong support from, and was in part inspired by, Churchill. The idea of area bombing attacks on targets behind the German armies was of course not new. What was new was the proposal to apply these tactics in support of the Russian offensive on the Eastern Front. After full discussion with the United States authorities these ideas were put into effect in February 1945. The cities chosen for assault were Berlin, Dresden, Chemnitz and Leipzig, these being cities fifty to a hundred miles or so behind the Eastern Front. The United States Eighth Air Force opened the attack on 3 February with a massive daylight raid on Berlin. On the night of 13 February 1945 Bomber Command despatched over 800 aircraft to Dresden. This attack was followed up in daylight on the following day by more than 400 bombers of the Eighth Air Force, which also attacked Dresden again on 15 February and 2 March. On the night of 14 February Bomber Command carried out a major attack on Chemnitz and on the 26 February the Eighth Air Force made a further large-scale assault on Berlin. The Bomber Command attack on Dresden made the greatest impact. The city was largely untouched at this stage of the war and the German night-fighter force was for whatever reason grounded during the attack, which produced scenes of total devastation. One unfortunate development occurred a few days after the first attack on Dresden when a war correspondent attached to Supreme Headquarters Allied Expeditionary Force put out a despatch which spoke of the 'Allied Air Chiefs' as having adopted a policy of deliberate terror bombing of German population centres. This despatch, which received wide publicity, created a false impression prevailing in part even today, to the effect that the attack on Dresden, apart from its fearful intensity, involved some change of policy. This it certainly did not. The attacks on Berlin, Dresden and Chemnitz were a part of the Combined Bomber Offensive conducted with the approval of the British and American Governments. What was a little unusual on the British side was the fact that these particular attacks were made only after a full discussion with the Prime Minister and the Chiefs of Staff.

20

Bomber Command: The Reckoning

The verdict of Webster and Frankland's history on Bomber Command's achievements is unambiguous. At the end of a scholarly analysis it says:

> In the final phase of the war, when air superiority had been achieved, the potential of the strategic air offensive was greater than its achievement. This was primarily due to the difficulty of obtaining a unified and concentrated policy through the channels of divided command and in the conditions of divided opinion. The striking force was stronger and more precise than the organisation which directed it. Even so, both cumulatively in largely indirect ways and eventually in a more immediate and direct manner, strategic bombing and, also in other roles strategic bombers, made a contribution to victory which was decisive. Those who claim that the Bomber Command contribution to the war was less than this are factually in error. Those who claim that its contribution under different circumstances might have been yet more effective disagree with one another and often overlook basic facts.

It would be difficult for any serious student to challenge this verdict. Nevertheless, it is melancholy to recall that from the early days of 1943, when Bomber Command first began to achieve its triumphs, many in high places as well as low began to avert their faces from bombing. And in 1965 A. J. P. Taylor wrote:

> [By early 1945] . . . the strategic air offensive belatedly achieved decisive results. This was mainly the work of the Americans.[1]

Today, many regard the strategic bombing programme in the Second World War as a costly failure. This conclusion is in plain contradiction of the facts and it is a matter of interest to consider the arguments by which it is arrived at.

The war-time history of Bomber Command can be summarised as follows:

In September 1939, Bomber Command, though developed on good principles and with many a good idea in the pipeline, was poorly equipped to carry out the strategic plans which the Air Staff had prepared.

In the Battle of France, Bomber Command attacked industrial and other targets in Germany. The damage it inflicted was minimal. Air Ministry claims made in good faith were baseless. Throughout 1941 Bomber Command lacked the equipment to find targets let alone to hit them. The Air Ministry continued to claim major hits against precise industrial targets. In the course of this year the Air Ministry realised, thanks to Lindemann, that Bomber Command was not in general hitting its targets. Drastic measures were taken to improve accuracy.

In 1941, Germany enlisted Russia and the United States of America among the ranks of her enemies. The outlook for beleaguered Britain changed dramatically. With the United States as an ally Britain could scarcely lose. Superficially, the importance of Bomber Command declined.

In 1942, Bomber Command acquired the means of hitting hard at area targets in Germany. Precision attacks were possible only in special circumstances. The Thousand Bomber raid on Cologne had a tremendous moral effect.

In 1943, with the advent of new navigational aids, Bomber Command developed the capacity to hit with tremendous effect and with increasing accuracy at area targets. In special circumstances, it could hit precise targets. Vast damage was inflicted on Germany. Vast resources were diverted by Germany to defence against air attack. The German Air Force was driven on to the defensive.

By the end of 1943, the United States Army Air Force, roughly handled in its attempts to bomb Germany by day, got the measure of the German day-fighter force which suffered a major defeat.

By early 1944 the German night-fighter force had become extremely formidable. Like the United States Army Air Force, Bomber Command called for escort fighters and heavier armament. Unlike the United States Army Air Force it did not get them.

In the spring of 1944 Bomber Command was diverted from the assault on Germany to preparations for 'Overlord'. Skills developed over the previous four years paid off. The Command demonstrated its ability to hit precise targets in Occupied France with dramatic accuracy and effect. The prospects for 'Overlord' were transformed.

After D-Day Bomber Command carried out with precision every tactical or strategic task. Oil, communications, naval targets, military targets, area targets. Inevitably, there was a controversy about whether the optimum mix of targets had been realised.

In the final phase, the German Air Force was crushed and Germany was wide open to Bomber Command. Even before the end of the war, the attack was called off. So much had happened since Rotterdam. Bomber Command turned to the agreeable tasks of repatriating its brothers from German prison camps and dropping food on starving Holland.

Without the harsh lessons learned between 1939 and 1942 the final triumphs of Bomber Command could never have been attained.

So much for the military record. We must now turn to the treatment which Bomber Command received at the hands of the Government and of various commentators after the end of the war. This turned out to be chilly. The Labour Party won the post-VE Day election of 1945. This was unfortunate for military leaders in several ways. To start with, the traditional practice of paying substantial sums as honoraria to leading commanders and staff officers (and to the Secretary of the Cabinet) was abandoned. There were at this stage and earlier a number of peerages. The Chiefs of Staff, of course, and beyond this on the Army side Wavell,* Alexander, Wilson and Montgomery; on the naval side Fraser, Mountbatten, Mountevans and Tovey; on the Royal Air Force side Dowding (at an earlier stage) and Tedder for his services as Deputy Supreme Commander. The peerage awarded later to Sholto Douglas was partly on political grounds and that to Newall in part at least to his successful tour of duty as Governor-General of New Zealand.

The absence of a peerage for Harris was conspicuous at the time and since, and was widely regarded as a slight on Bomber Command. Harris was one of the greatest commanders in the war. His command had struck at Britain's enemies from the first day of the war until the last; it had exercised a profound effect on the outcome of the war. The absence of

---

* No doubt Wavell's earldom was connected with his service as Viceroy of India. Gort was an Irish viscount by birth. In February 1946 he was made an English viscount for his services in the Second World War and in Palestine. As he was then suffering from a mortal illness from which he died in the following month and had no son to succeed him this must have been a sad occasion.

a peerage for its leader was bound to attract attention. No doubt the mind of the new Labour Government was directed to other thoughts. Still, in retrospect this decision by Attlee must be regarded as a mistake. The mistake was rectified when Churchill again became Prime Minister. Harris was immediately offered a peerage which at that date and for family reasons he declined, accepting instead a baronetcy. On 1 January 1946, Harris and Sholto Douglas were made Marshals of the Royal Air Force. This is worth comment because up to this point no Royal Air Force officer, apart from Tedder as Deputy Supreme Commander, had achieved the highest rank unless he had held the post of Chief of the Air Staff. However, in the Army, Montgomery, Alexander and Wilson became Field-Marshals without previously holding office as Chief of the Imperial General Staff.

More serious than the question of peerages was Churchill's victory broadcast on the conclusion of the war in Europe. In this, apart from the Battle of Britain, references to the air forces are of a subdued character. The construction of such messages is of course a difficult exercise. So much has to be mentioned. Names must be put in. Names must be left out. Still, giving due weight to these thoughts, it is difficult on reading the broadcast thirty years later not to share the dismay which Harris and Eaker experienced when they listened to it at the latter's headquarters on the afternoon of 13 May 1945.

Finally, there was the question of the Bomber Command campaign medal or rather the absence of it. The award of campaign medals is determined by inter-service regulations which defy the comprehension of most men. It could well be that Bomber Command's claims were non-suited as the result of some venerable, obscure and nonsensical technicality. Be this as it may, there was no medal. Once again the fact was conspicuous not least when considered in relation to the heavy casualties involved. During the war Bomber Command lost over 55,000 killed, mostly aircrew, a rate heavier than that suffered by any other element of Britain's armed forces.

But there was worse to come. The impression gained ground that Bomber Command's battles had been failures. The impression was widespread, grossly mistaken and should be analysed. It can well be crystallised in a comment by Patrick Blackett, an outstanding man of science well versed in military and especially in naval matters. In an article in the *Scientific American* for April 1961 he wrote:

No part of the war effort has been so well documented as the (bombing)

campaign, which had as its official objective 'the destruction and dislocation of the German military, industrial and economic system and
the undermining of the morale of the German people to the point
where their capacity for armed resistance is fatally weakened.' Immediately after the war the US Bombing Survey was sent to Germany
to find out what had been achieved. A very strong team (which included
two men who are now advisers to President Kennedy, J. K. Galbraith
and Paul Nitze) produced a brilliant report which was published in
September 1945. Without any doubt the area bombing offensive was
an expensive failure. About 500,000 German men, women and children
were killed but in the whole bombing offensive 160,000 US and British
airmen, the best young men of both countries, were lost. German war
production went on rising steadily until it reached its peak in August
1944. At this time the Allies were already in Paris and the Russian
armies were well into Poland. German civilian morale did not crack.

Well, one could scarcely speak more plainly than that. 500,000 German
civilians and 160,000 Allied aircrew dead, German military production
rising and the Allied armies moving in triumph towards the frontiers
of Germany. To start with a technicality, the statement of the objective
of the strategic air forces is a quotation, and a rather inadequate one,
from the celebrated Casablanca Directive of 21 January 1943. It was
neither the first nor the last bombing directive. Indeed, so far as Bomber
Command was concerned it was Number 28 in the series and it was
followed by twenty more. Next there is the reference to area bombing.
Blackett is clearly speaking about the Anglo-American bombing offensive,
not just about its Bomber Command component. American bombing
is not normally considered area bombing because the bombs were aimed
at precise targets. In fact of course there was little to choose in the matter
of accuracy between the British and the United States bomber forces.
In reality it is impossible to distinguish between area and other kinds
of bombing. For the first three years of the war Bomber Command was
capable only of area bombing. Had there been no area bombing the
techniques of precision bombing would never have been developed. So
it is necessary to consider what weight Blackett gave to the following
aspects of the Anglo-American bombing programme:

1. The diversion of immense resources of labour to deal with bomb
   damage.
2. The diversion from German offensive strength of the vast resources
   in weaponry, electronics and engineering for German air defence.

Albert Speer[2] stresses the contribution made to the German defeat by the necessity to deploy huge resources for the air defence of the German homeland. He rates the resulting losses as greater than those involved by the Stalingrad débâcle and the retreat from Russia. The 20,000 AA guns deployed in Germany could have doubled the anti-tank defences on the Eastern Front. The celebrated 88 mm AA gun also became the prime anti-tank weapon. Something like a million German soldiers were required to man the AA defences and so removed from the fighting lines.

3. The surprise achieved at D-Day, the softening of the German defences and the isolation of the battlefield by the cutting of German military communications.

4. The paralysis of the German armed forces through the loss of oil production.

5. The virtual destruction of the German Air Force.

6. The absence of any air offensive against Britain, and especially against British ports when the invasion fleets were being collected.

7. The massive contribution of the bombing forces to the land battle through the reduction of fortresses (eg Walcheren), the elimination of strong points on the battlefield, and the fact that the Rhine crossing and reduction of port defences from Le Havre to Boulogne were achieved with minimal British casualties.

8. The contribution to the war at sea through the destruction of a large part of the German Navy and merchant fleet and the attack on U-boat manufacture. 30,000 tons of mines were laid resulting in the loss of some 500 German ships.

9. The successful assault on German non-conventional weapons, V1s, V2s, long-range guns and multiple-barrel guns.

Perhaps Blackett would have accepted these points but argued that the attack on cities was useless. There are two comments on this. Had Bomber Command not attacked cities there would have been no Bomber Command, since before 1944 there was little other than cities that they could attack. The second point is that the attack on German cities hit their war production very hard indeed. The argument that German war production increased until August 1944 takes no account of the levels it would have achieved if free from air attack. And there is a distinction between arms produced and arms put to effective military use. Thus, in 1944, Germany produced over 20,000 fighters but by the end of that year the German fighter force was on the road to destruction.

Blackett's thesis cannot be sustained. The question must therefore be asked why such a brilliant man could make so gross a misjudgement. The answer must lie in the fact that few men, however talented, make no mistakes. Often, the greatest men make the greatest mistakes. Blackett was at heart a naval officer. He had been present as a midshipman at the Battle of the Falkland Islands and at Jutland. He certainly felt passionately that greater air resources should have been devoted to the battle against the U-boats—a highly tenable point of view, though inevitably a controversial one. This may have coloured his views. More importantly, Blackett seemed to show an emotional or political aversion to Bomber Command. Whatever the reasons, in his attitude to Bomber Command, as on so few other matters, he was just wrong.

We have dealt with Blackett's views in detail because coming from such a distinguished man they are necessarily of special interest. But what of the man in the street? Many of course had no connection with the Second World War and know little and care little about it. But it is sad to note that many who do think about these matters feel in retrospect that the strategic bombing offensive was partly pointless, partly ineffective and partly immoral. The suggestion that the offensive was pointless or ineffective can readily be disposed of by examining the facts. So far as morality is concerned a passage in Lord Snow's pamphlet *A Postscript to Science and Government* can perhaps be taken as a text. After quoting a minute dated 15 February 1942 by the Chief of the Air Staff emphasising that aiming points should be defined as areas and not (for example) as factories, Snow continues:

> As a piece of information, what percentage of Americans and English realised that this was their countries' intention? It is a very interesting example of collective moral responsibility. In the long future, perhaps the history of our times, and our methods of making war, will be written by some Asian Gibbon: if so, 'The Strategic Air Offensive' will provide him with a good many of his most sardonic laughs.

From this passage and from passages in *Science and Government* (see, for instance, p. 49 in that work), it may be deduced that Snow believed that the attack on area targets was barbarous and immoral, and that had the people of Britain known that such was the policy, they would have forced the Government to change its strategy.

At the date of the minute by the Chief of the Air Staff, Bomber Command could either hit German area targets, or for practical purposes Bomber Command could hit nothing at all. Let us suppose that the decision had been taken that, since Bomber Command could not hit precise targets and since the bombing of area targets was immoral, the Command should be divided between the Navy for the war at sea and the Army for air support. In February 1942 the United States Army Air Force had started to build up forces to join in the strategic air offensive. With the disappearance of Bomber Command the plans of the United States Army Air Force would inevitably have been prejudiced as there were powerful forces in Washington only too anxious to divert it to the war against Japan. So the whole development of strategic bombing would have faltered and the immense contribution it made to the defeat of Germany would have been forfeited. Area bombing is barbarous. Precision bombing is barbarous. War itself is barbarous and as the years go on there is little to suggest that it will lose this quality. Cities have always been bombarded when they got in the way of the land battle and the fact that a new dimension, the air, was involved in the Second World War simply brought them into the front line, with Warsaw, Rotterdam, London and Coventry as openers. The suggestion that public opinion would have caused area bombing to be brought to an end is untenable. As Dr Noble Frankland pointed out in his Lees Knowles lectures in November 1963 the average Briton can get very ruthless indeed when he feels that his life is in danger. His instinct is to hit his enemies with every weapon he can lay his hands on. Long may he feel this way. It is interesting but sad to note that with the rise of anti-bombing sentiment from say 1943 onwards this section of public opinion had turned full circle. In the First World War, British soldiers died in France and Flanders in distressing numbers in direct confrontation with enemy armies on land. It was precisely to avoid this senseless slaughter that the strategic air force developed. The idea proved itself. In the war against Germany from 1939–1945 the British Army lost about 150,000 men killed or missing. It is shattering to consider what that figure would have been had the British Army attempted with its allies to invade Fortress Europe without the strategic air forces.

The strange and depressing history of anti-bombing sentiment is brilliantly analysed in Frankland's lectures. He suggests as part of the explanation the traditional British pre-occupation with 'defence' rather than with 'fighting services', and the instinctive hatred of the bomb as the weapon of the assassin. Certainly, the Archbishop of Canterbury, the Moderator of the Church of Scotland and the other significant religious leaders who expressed concern about the morality of bombing Germany seemed to believe that wars should be won by the bayonet or by the torpedo rather than by the bomb. They never objected to the devastation of the French Atlantic ports where, after the bombing, Admiral Doenitz said that no dog or cat remained. One event which did not help the establishment of the truth was the reception given by the British Press to the publication in 1961 of Webster and Frankland's history. The history is an exhaustive and scholarly account of Bomber Command's defeats and triumphs, and of the final and decisive contribution to the defeat of Germany. Press comment suggested, by selective quotation, that much of the Command's efforts had been wasted. It is difficult to believe that the reviewers read the history, which indeed contains nearly a million words. Like the Thirty-Nine Articles of the Anglican Church, it remains more often quoted than read and more often read than understood. This is sad because in that book the troubles and the triumphs of Bomber Command are plainly and honestly recorded.

PART THREE

21

The Summing Up

The development of the Royal Air Force

We have reached the end of our brief story and it is time to sum up. We have followed the history of the Royal Air Force from its modest ancestry in the Royal Engineers to the triumphs of 1945. On Armistice Day 1918 the Royal Air Force was beyond question the greatest air force in the world. In 1945 it was beyond question one of the two greatest air forces in the world. This was a superb achievement for Britain. Let us pause for a moment and try to assess some of the triumphs and some of the failures on that momentous journey from the formation of the Royal Flying Corps in 1912 to VJ Day, a span of thirty-three years.

As we have seen, the initial attitude of the Army and Navy to nascent military aviation was absurdly myopic. They wanted none of it. As the First World War drew near attitudes changed and Britain, which had been such a laggard, became a front-runner. Remarkably, Britain became the first nation to invent the idea of a 'third service'. This was an ideological rather than a practical advance. The third service was formed, to be sure, but this had small effect on day-to-day events. Perhaps the most remarkable aspect of the change was the quality and character of the men attracted to the new service. Of course in describing this most important aspect of Royal Air Force history one has to over-simplify. This said, one can add that many of those who came over to the Royal Flying Corps, the Royal Naval Air Service and later the Royal Air Force were one-off originals or rebels. Originals came because they loved flying, though often they flew badly, or because they loved flying-machines which could be nursed or taken to bits or borrowed. Rebels, because they disliked the strict (and admirable) discipline of the older services or because they loved flexibility and hated rigidity. Rebels too because they would rather die on a dangerous sortie from a comfortable Royal Air Force base in France than survive (or not) amid the squalor of trench warfare. The greatness of Britain came from its mixture of races: the westward move of Continental tribes, traders from the Mediterranean, Romans and their camp followers from Europe, Asia and Africa, the Armada and the rest. The Royal Air Force from its outset was a mix of tribes, disciplines, interests and services. Later, of course, it became a truly international force with brave Czech, Polish and French additions. Royal Air Force victories in the Second World War were in truth victories of an international partnership, a remarkable fact that is stated less often than it should be.

At the end of the First World War the state of the Royal Air Force can be simply described. It was the greatest and indeed the only independent air force in history and it had won a great and resplendent victory. What was to follow? It is a sad story. The minds of politicians were directed elsewhere. Churchill appointed Secretary of State for War and Secretary of State for Air clearly expected to give the new service its *quietus*. This did not happen for reasons discussed earlier, and the remarkable figure of Trenchard with all his faults, which were considerable, must be cited again as the man who made it possible for the Royal Air Force to endure. We must pause at this point to mention the attitude of the Royal Navy and of the Army to the survival of this ludicrous *tertium quid*, the Royal Air Force. Stated in plain but not unfriendly terms this attitude was understandable but deplorable. Royal Air Force officers were barred from military clubs* and partial social ostracism was the order of the day. These wounds took time to heal, but healed they were in the end. Forty years or so later, Field-Marshal Sir Gerald Templer, at the end of his tour of duty as Chief of the Imperial General Staff, was dined out by the Air Council, whose regard for him was a mixture of respect and affection. In his thank-you speech he said that the Royal Air Force of 1918 vintage had much to endure. Indeed they had, but how lucky it was that thirty or forty years later there were men like Templer who understood.

Britain, emerging victorious from the First World War and with a much enlarged empire, proceeded to disarm in the most perilous fashion. Britain always liked to run its empire on the cheap. So fifteen years after the 1918 Armistice the Royal Air Force, while still intact thanks to the inspired hand of Trenchard, lacked every element save one necessary

---

* This deprivation disappeared in 1919 when the generosity of Lord Cowdray made available to the Royal Air Force the magnificent site in Piccadilly now occupied by the Royal Air Force Club. Cowdray should have been the first Secretary of State for Air but the post was denied him by an unworthy act on the part of Lloyd George.

to sustain a modern fighting service. The saving grace was the quality and training of Royal Air Force personnel. It was customary in those days for the Royal Air Force to be referred to in Parliament as 'small but highly efficient'. It was small all right, but efficient it was not save in the quality of its people. Realisation that in technical terms Britain was outclassed in the air arrived around 1934. Five short years remained before Britain had to fight for its life. During this time it had to modernise, to expand and to prepare the foundations of a force which by 1945 would contain more than a million men and women. The elements of all this have been recounted earlier. Despite all the faults, and putting aside all ignorant or malicious criticism, the build-up was in truth a great triumph. In the end and in the round the Royal Air Force proved itself better equipped for war than either the Army or Royal Navy. 'As between the different Services', said Churchill in September 1943 'while avoiding invidious comparisons I should certainly say that the outlook of the Royal Air Force upon this war was more closely attuned to the circumstances and conditions as they emerged by painful experience than those of either of the other two Services.'[1] In the end, Britain, with her allies, was victorious and Germany collapsed in defeat and disaster. Today Germany is prosperous and Britain skids on the edge of disaster. It might seem perhaps that the better idea would have been for Britain to lose the war, not to win it. But what would have happened if Britain had collapsed in 1940? What if Hitler had driven down the Mall as well as down the Champs Elysées? Who can doubt that in that event surely Britain and her splendid race would have disappeared, perhaps for ever. So it was fortunate that Britain was victorious, though it seems sad that the courage and enterprise displayed in the Second World War should have been followed by some thirty years of such sad decline.

Looking back on the years of expansion before the Second World War a number of comments must be made. First, the political plane. It was astonishing surely that a few weeks before Munich British statesmen, notably Chamberlain and Simon, were telling each other that the major problems facing Britain were economic. And is it not astounding that when war finally arrived Baldwin, who had done so much to re-arm Britain, should have been disgraced and the legend put about that, had Churchill or Attlee been in charge in the late Thirties, a strong and resolute Britain would have rallied a united Europe in successful resistance to Hitler? This legend was supported by Churchill, who should have known better. One of the ironies of the situation is that the pace of British air re-armament would have been much slower had Germany not spread exaggerated estimates of German strength in the air in the hope of scaring Britain. The German figures were swallowed whole by Churchill but resisted for the most part by the Air Ministry.

One final comment on politics. The foremost critic of Britain's performance in resisting aggression in the late Thirties was the extreme Left of the Labour Party. They launched the mainly fictitious assaults on so-called 'Appeasers' and 'Guilty Men'. We may be sure that had a Labour Government been in power in the late Thirties the rearmament programme, if any, adopted by the Government would have been fought tooth and nail by the extreme Left. The air would have been filled with cries of 'Collective Security', of 'the Popular Front' and of 'Shoulder to shoulder with our Soviet Brothers'. And looking back it is impossible to forget either the changes pressed upon Churchill by Cripps in the darkest days of the North African campaign (which would have been disastrous) or the severe distractions caused to deeply burdened Ministers by the activities of Aneurin Bevan. As a Minister in the Attlee Government Bevan was admirable. As a politician in the Second World War he was a potential disaster area. A question perhaps of increasing maturity and, on the political plane, of the different views engendered among politicians by sitting in the chair and taking responsibility for decisions, as opposed to trying to saw off the legs.

Air policy

In the field of air policy the level of Royal Air Force achievement was mixed. The idea of the strategic air offensive which dates back at least to the Smuts report was sound enough but there was certainly a marked tendency in the early stages to overestimate the material and moral results of bombing and to underestimate the weight and sophistication of the weapons necessary to give effect to a modern bombing policy. The difficulties which arose here were certainly linked with the fact that practically all the bombing carried out by the Royal Air Force between the wars was amid deserts with good visibility and little or no opposition. The Royal Air Force treatment of the problems of air defence was in the main brilliant. By 1935 the problems of intercepting and attacking a German bomber force had been fully appreciated, and the structure and equipment of Fighter Command were developed with admirable efficiency. But in the matter of supporting the Army and the Royal Navy, the Royal Air Force ideas were at the outset lamentably deficient. The lessons of the First World War had been forgotten, the techniques had to be studied all over again and the period of adjustment was costly and painful. It must not be supposed that the responsibility for this state of affairs rests on the shoulders of the Royal Air Force alone. The Army had little care for the help that the Royal Air Force could bring them. 'Believe me', wrote a most responsible Royal Air Force officer much concerned with army co-operation matters around the outbreak of the Second World War, 'it was quite impossible to make the Army believe we could have contributed anything worthwhile to the land battle.' The Royal Navy believed that they could cope without major air assistance with U-boats and, even more dangerously, that warships could protect themselves by their own efforts in a hostile air environment. These notions were rapidly and tragically dispersed in the Atlantic, the Mediterranean and the Pacific. The Royal Air Force for its part suffered its views about the vulnerability of warships to be overridden, and no doubt it would have made little difference had they pursued these views more strongly. A fair apportionment of blame would be to award black marks to all three services. Of course it is easy to be wise after the event. It is important, however, to remark on how quick all three services, particularly the Royal Air Force, were to learn from their mistakes. The fact that they were given time to re-equip, to relearn and to retrain and that they were not crushed by their initial mistakes was due in the main to the transcendent blunders of their German and Japanese enemies. In the end, the achievements of the Royal Air Force, which we remind ourselves again was an international force, were resplendent in every field. These achievements shine the more brightly because of the earlier mistakes and disappointments.

Harsh things have been said in Webster and Frankland's history of the strategic air offensive against Germany, and by other commentators, as to the quality of the military aircraft ordered before the war. The finger of scorn has been pointed at the Fairey Battle, put into the front line in large numbers and grossly inadequate for the role ascribed to it; at the Bristol Blenheim, an improvised military version of an executive aircraft ordered by Rothermere, and at the Handley Page Hampden which, to say no more, lacked armament, navigational aides and adequate facilities for aircrew. These criticisms undoubtedly have substance. The British aircraft industry of the mid-Thirties was a child of its time. Civil aviation, condemned by Churchill 'to fly by itself' was in its infancy: no help there for an impoverished industry. Military aviation was kept in penury. One effect of financial starvation was that the time-table for a new design was stretched out unduly in the hope of ensuring that all the snags were eliminated before a production order was placed. Thus the first production model of a so-called 'large' military aircraft at this stage could be expected (hopefully) some eight years after the Air Staff had notified its requirements.[2] By this time, in all reasonable probability, the aircraft was obsolescent. All this in the main was the consequence of a harsh and unrealistic view of the economic climate. The difficulties were compounded by the extraordinary fact that the Air Ministry was trying to support on a tightly restricted budget no less than sixteen design teams. It was in these circumstances that the Air Ministry, some three years before the outbreak of war, had to order aircraft on an unprecedented scale. Of course by this time the climate had changed, corners were cut, and many aircraft were ordered 'off the drawing board'. But while all this was going on, the industry had to have orders so that it could build up capacity, create a skilled labour force and come to grips with large-scale production. And the Royal Air Force itself had to have aircraft, however inadequate, with modern features to cut its teeth on. Hence the Battles, Blenheims, et al.

One fact less easy to explain or excuse was the performance of the bombs used by the Royal Air Force. This was inadequate in the First World War and at least as bad at the start of the next. The bomb, after all, is what bombing is all about. If the final link in the chain fails all the others are meaningless. There is plenty of room for argument about comparative tactics, designs and so on, but in judging the performance of a bomb one is on firmer ground. It is dropped. Leaving aside the question of accuracy of aim, a vastly important point but a different one, it either detonates or it does not. Further, if it detonates, it either achieves its tactical purpose or it does not. These points are capable of empirical test. Of course, there were difficulties about ranges. By and large, the British landowner does not like bombing ranges or, if he does, he feels that they should be located in the next county. Often, the local population welcomes ranges as providing employment. Wildlife certainly welcomes bombing and never fails to display in most marked ways its preference for bombs as against tourists. So, it was hard work for the Royal Air Force to site bombing ranges. Nevertheless, what about all those deserts to which the Royal Air Force of those days had almost unlimited access? One hopes that the lesson has been learned, though perhaps it has not. There were some alarming rumours about the performance of our bombs at Suez.

In the field of training the achievements of the Royal Air Force were seldom less than magnificent. They included the improved methods of pilot training involving the devolution of elementary training to civilian schools; the far-reaching concept of dispersing service training of pilots throughout the world under the Empire Air Training Scheme, and the massive and highly successful plans for training vast numbers of technicians. Above all, when war began, there was a readiness to learn from mistakes, to persevere and to make rapid and drastic changes. The quality of aircrew throughout was never less than superb. The Air Staff were wrong in the late Thirties to resist rapid expansion. They were overruled, and rightly overruled, on this point, but in so far as their views were based on the belief that rapid growth might lead to inferior aircrew standards they were right to be cautious. Fortunately, all turned out well, but only just.

The great leaders in the Second World War

The Royal Air Force was exceptionally fortunate during the Second World War in the quality of its leaders both in Whitehall and in the field. There were a few failures, though not many, and on the whole the Royal Air Force was splendidly served. On the side of administration and organisation one must mention again the masterly performance of Street, Permanent Secretary from the first day of war to the last, and of Christopher Courtney, responsible for Royal Air Force supply and organisation from January 1940 until the end. Looking at the Royal Air Force leaders in the Second World War, four stand out as surely the greatest. Of course, all such judgements must be subjective but in this writer's opinion the names which stand out from the rest are those of Portal, Harris, Freeman and Tedder. The greatest of course was Portal.

Portal was Chief of the Air Staff from October 1940 until December 1945. A product of Winchester and Christ Church, his military career included driving his Army motorcycle down the platform at a London railway terminus on his way to France as a dispatch rider in 1914. The addiction to motorcycles is of course significant. Soon in the Royal Flying Corps, he was noticed almost at once by Trenchard and in due course annotated in the latter's famous personal Air Force List as a future leader. This fact surely does great credit to both men. They could scarcely have been less alike. Portal, soft spoken, a withdrawn and introspective Wykehamist. Trenchard, booming away, with qualities which, however great, did not lie in the field of abstract intellect. The bond can perhaps be found in the facts that they were both great men, they were both men of action, and they were both excellent judges of character. We may be sure that they judged each other accurately as well. Dr Johnson said of Oliver Goldsmith that in his various styles of writing he touched nothing which he did not adorn. With the usual limitations the same could be said of Portal. Everything he did, he did well. He went to Aden, took up dinghy sailing and beat the locals at their own sport. He was a keen falconer a fact which for practical purposes defies comment. As Wodehouse has wisely remarked, 'Golf and the world golfs with you. Hawk and you hawk alone.' Transcending these details, Portal was in Royal Air Force terms, and indeed in national terms, the complete professional. Let us look at his qualities. First, he was a leader. After all, without this quality in military affairs, nothing much matters. He was of course personally brave in physical and more significantly in moral terms. He was calm. He was detached. He was cool. In the Travellers' Club, whither he walked for his austere war-time lunch, he sat alone and in silence reading the journals various. In this matter his behaviour conformed with the highest traditions of the older London clubs. However, in Portal's case the chance of an agreeable chatty dialogue was perhaps subnormal even in this frosty area. History has so far recorded no serious breach of Portal's post-luncheon retreats. Portal had an excellent brain and the ability to express himself with total clarity. He never shirked the facts, however ugly. Above all, he was a positive person: he formed decided views on the matters put before him. His 'no' meant no and his 'yes' meant yes. All this would have taken Portal a very long way, but he had two other qualities which enormously enhanced his contribution to winning the war. First, he was in point of courage a match for Churchill. Churchill liked to steam-roller his military Chiefs if he had a chance. He never tried it on with Portal and indeed the chances of succeeding with such tactics were unpromising. Finally, Portal was immensely successful with the Americans. On the whole the Royal Air Force and the United States Army Air Force got on splendidly during the Second World War. There was great mutual confidence, trust, comradeship and indeed plain liking at all levels, and a remarkable ability to cut the formalities and get on with each other and with the war. Nevertheless, at the highest levels of the United States Army Air Force there was a degree of suspicion about British motives—'Watch out for these crafty Limeys and don't trust them an inch.' Perhaps the words were never used but the thought was sometimes, though by no means always, there at the highest level. This is where Portal made one of his greatest contributions. The High Command of the United States Army Air Force and the United States Administration trusted and admired him. When it came to planning and organising at every level, the significance of this fact was incalculable.

Portal was beyond dispute one of the greatest if not the greatest of all the British war leaders and it is most appropriate that his statue should flank that of Trenchard on the Victoria Embankment, though some of us regret that the sculptor provided him with such a bizarre attire.

In *Bomber Offensive*, one of the best war memoirs, Harris tells us that 'I was, and I still am a Rhodesian'. Harris served in the 1st Rhodesian Regiment in the First World War in the campaign against German West Africa, so this statement may well be legally correct. Less difficult to establish are the facts that Harris's father was an Indian Civil Servant, that his son, Arthur, was born in Cheltenham (of all places) and went to school in Honiton. When he was sixteen years of age he told his father that he would like to seek his fortune in Rhodesia. Somewhat to Arthur's surprise his father took him at his word, and soon he was earning his living mainly through providing transport (animal and otherwise) in a country which was then (1909–1914) in a most primitive state. This is not the place to discuss Harris's career in detail, but rather to evaluate the qualities which took him to the top. These basic elements included immense practical experience, great shrewdness and commonsense, an excellent brain, a subtle instinct for separating the true from the false, complete personal integrity, and finally courage and the power to command on the level of greatness. Harris came to Bomber Command at the right moment, just as Montgomery came to the Eighth Army at the right moment. This was good luck for both of them, but luck is necessary for greatness. When Harris arrived, Bomber Command was beginning to acquire the techniques necessary to navigate and to carry out accurate attacks in the dark. Harris became Commander-in-Chief in February 1942 and he carried this momentous responsibility until Germany was defeated. Over and above the qualities mentioned already, the Commander-in-Chief, Bomber Command needed something more. Indeed, a lot more. In the First World War the British Fleet used to take its fortunes in its hands very seldom indeed. No fault of theirs: there was very rarely any enemy to fight, at any rate on the surface. But when the Grand Fleet went out Jellicoe, as Churchill has pointed out, was the only man on either side who could lose the war in an afternoon. Throughout the span of Harris's leadership of Bomber Command he put the lives of his squadrons and the future of the Command at risk many times every month. It was not a question of the Commander-in-Chief taking the final responsibility for an operation organised by the staff. It was in fact a decision taken by the Commander-in-Chief in person. There is a picture, of which a few reproductions exist, which records with accuracy the physical circumstances in which such decisions were taken. It was painted in the headquarters of Bomber Command by a relative of one of Harris's staff officers. In the centre Harris, seated at a typical Ministry of Works desk of the quality usually considered appropriate to minor civil servants, cheap and nasty. Around him a tight circle of five. On Harris's left General Frederick Anderson, commanding the American Eighth Air Force, the chief meteorological officer (in plain clothes), Harris's deputy, Air Marshal Saundby, and the Royal Navy liaison officer Captain De Mowbray. Beyond this tight circle, a wider circle consisting of the staff officers who had to translate into operational and administrative orders the decisions taken as to weather, targets, diversions, routes, bases and electronic counter-measures. This exchange of views rarely lasted more than twenty to thirty minutes. The decision was taken. That was it. All that remained was to watch and wait. Of course, this kind of situation is common enough in war; before D-Day, of course; in the great carrier battles in the Pacific, when squadrons of aircraft took off not knowing whether their parent carrier would still be afloat when they returned; and before the great assaults at Alamein, Sicily, Anzio. What was exceptional in regard to Bomber Command was that this situation happened night after night. Bomber Command's casualties were grievous both as to numbers and as to quality, for of course the Bomber Command aircrews were the élite. Harris's hold on the Command was never less than total even in the darkest hours. As Webster and Frankland point out, it was a hold achieved without a personal presence among pilots and squadrons. Harris rarely if ever visited his units. Harris was widely known throughout his Command as 'Butch', short for 'Butcher Harris'. It would be easy for outsiders to suppose that this title was used to suggest insensitivity to his men or indeed to his enemy. It would be easy, but it would be wrong. As Martin Middlebrook has rightly remarked,[3] the nickname was inspired partly by black humour, and for the rest by the recognition that here was a man who would spare no-one, inside or outside his Command, who did not commit himself totally to victory.

His men recognised Harris as a hard driving commander who would not hesitate to send men to their deaths for as long as the war lasted. But they recognised also that all this was necessary for final victory.

Harris was indeed a most sensitive and humane man. He made an admirable partner with the Americans. His robust, forthright and intensely practical approach removed all risk of doubt or hesitation, as the United States found in the strategic air offensive against Germany. When D-Day was joined, the contribution made by Bomber Command to the land battles was so remarkable and evoked such tributes from American partners that in view of the gross misrepresentation that the work of the Command has received some of the tributes are printed as an Appendix to this book. It is an interesting sidelight on Harris that he chose as his Personal Staff Officer at Bomber Command Headquarters Thomas Dewar ('Harry') Weldon, Fellow and Tutor of Magdalen College, Oxford. Harris met Weldon in Washington when Harris was Head of the Royal Air Force delegation there. Harris invited Weldon to join him at High Wycombe. Here, apart from his normal duties, Weldon took part in countless official and semi-official meetings in the Commander-in-Chief's house. This cohesion between the man of action and the distinguished authority on Kant was not a relationship which could have been predicted with confidence. Nevertheless, a firm friendship resulted. Although Harris has an excellent literary style there are certainly passages in his writings where the Magdalen connection is not to be missed.

Bomber Command's respect for their wartime leader was demonstrated in a most remarkable way thirty-two years after the end of the war. To celebrate Harris's eighty-fifth birthday which occurred on 13 April 1977 two former members of the Command organised a dinner in his honour. The dinner, which was attended by no less than 750 Bomber Command veterans and wives, was a huge success. The Marshal gave a stirring address which brought the audience to their feet again and again.

Next Tedder. Tedder was a university graduate of great intelligence and with great powers of leadership. He was an intellectual with military leanings. Though the two men were not really alike and, or so it is said, did not like each other, he was in some ways another Wavell. After great services as Director of Training and Director-General of Research and Development, Tedder found himself appointed as successor to Longmore in the Middle East Air Command, after Boyd, the Air Marshal first chosen for this appointment, was captured when an aircraft in which he was travelling flew down the Italian radio beam into hostile Sicily and not down the British beam into friendly Malta. In handling the immensely complex problems of air forces in the Middle East both before and after the entry of the United States, Tedder proved himself a master. It must be realised that Tedder's forces at all times comprised tactical, strategic and specialised air forces, a situation quite unknown in the United Kingdom. Tedder quickly won the confidence of the Americans in general and of Eisenhower in particular. Soon he was commanding all the Allied Air Forces in the Mediterranean, and when Eisenhower became Supreme Commander for 'Overlord' he chose Tedder as his deputy. The Americans saw in Tedder a man on the British side with whom they could work. There were several men, Montgomery in particular, of whom this was not true. This was a help, but Tedder won his commands by his professional skills. Among Tedder's many credits is the fact that he attracted Zuckerman to his orbit both in the Middle East and in Europe, thus bringing into his tactical and strategic ambience one of the best minds in operational research. The range of problems successfully handled by Tedder as Eisenhower's deputy calls for no elaboration. But Tedder's admirers did not include Churchill, who tried to supplant him in the Middle East in October 1941, and to replace him as Deputy Supreme Commander with Alexander late in 1944, at a time when the Italian campaign had run into the doldrums. Both attempts were defeated by Portal.

Tedder's place among the greatest Air Marshals is secure, despite a degree of arrogance and a sharp though puckish sense of humour which some found distasteful.

So, finally, to Wilfrid Freeman. Freeman's claim to greatness rests on three massive foundations, namely his work as the member of Air Council responsible for research, development and production before and for a period after the outbreak of war; his work as Vice-Chief of the Air Staff (separated from Portal by the celebrated green baize door); and his final term as Chief Executive in the Ministry of Aircraft Production. Freeman's contribution was thus more in the technical than in the operational sphere. Freeman's supreme accomplishment was to harmonise the Royal Air Force's need for technical equipment of the highest quality with the maximum capabilities of the aircraft and associated industries. This achievement would have been impossible without the confidence and trust of the Royal Air Force on one side, and of the industries concerned on the other. It called for subtle intelligence and great qualities of judgement. Among the achievements of Freeman's reign must be mentioned the Lancaster, the Mustang, the Mosquito, the Tempest and the Typhoon. When one considers the technical disasters which beset the German Air Force despite immense German technical ability one realises the depth and scope of Freeman's achievement. Freeman was a most attractive man. He was a bit of a rebel. His Air Marshal's cap was never adorned with the statutory golden oak leaves. The top button of his tunic was normally undone. He displayed (if the phrase may be used, which is doubtful) a woman's taste for liking and disliking. In his mental spectrum there were no greys. There were rogues and heroes, cops and robbers. Fortunately, he was on the whole a good picker. Britain and the Royal Air Force owe him an immense debt.

These then were the four men selected in this brief account as the greatest. It is interesting to remark on the diverse and complementary nature of their qualities. First Portal, differing by a quantum from the rest, superb in intellect, in resolution, in calm and in stability. No nation could expect a greater military leader. Harris with his massive intelligence, his experience and his ability to sustain incalculable responsibility over long periods, one of the great commanders in our long history. Tedder, the cleverest of all perhaps, and possessing great professional qualities as a politician and as a commander. Finally, Freeman, another intellectual, whose gifts optimised operational and technical possibilities. Happy is the land that finds such men in adversity.

Many no doubt will criticise this choice of four men. Some will regret the omission of Dowding who carried the supreme responsibility in the Battle of Britain. Dowding's place in history as the victor of the twentieth century Trafalgar is secure, but in the opinion of many his achievements do not equal those of Portal, Harris, Tedder and Freeman. The closest contender is perhaps Slessor, much junior to the other names discussed but who by his warmth, knowledge, experience and adaptability made a massive contribution as a man and a planner and as an admired and successful Commander in Coastal Command and in the Mediterranean. There was also Newall, whose great contribution to Britain's achievement is discussed earlier. Then there were the backers-up to the great leaders, men whose quality would have been outstanding in any sphere of action. Again, the choice must be subjective. The names that occur to this writer are those he happened to know well but there are many more. They are Air Chief Marshal Lord Bandon, Air Chief Marshal Sir Leslie Hollinghurst, Air Chief Marshal Sir Ralph Cochrane, Air Chief Marshal Sir Harry Broadhurst, Air Vice-Marshal Musgrave Whitham, Marshal of the Royal Air Force Sir William Dickson and Air Marshal Sir Francis Linnell. Considerations of space inhibit other examples. Above all this, and in some, but not all, ways more important, the quality of the great fighting leaders, Gibson, Cheshire and Embry to name only three. Warren Fisher said in 1938 'there is only one crown servant of first rate ability in the Air Ministry . . .' Well, the words 'crown servant' and 'Air Ministry' are capable of various interpretations. If the definition includes, as perhaps it should, those capable of fighting the King's enemies either in personal combat or in the battle of minds, this writer could suggest many more.

A final look

The defence preparations of the British Government over the period 1935–1939 would not in themselves have saved Britain from defeat. Salvation was brought about by Hitler's blunders in attacking Russia and making an enemy of the United States as a consequence of his alliance with Japan. Even with those disastrous decisions behind him Hitler, as we have seen, could have come much closer to staving off defeat had he only refrained from personal intervention in the fields of strategy, tactics and military equipment. The fact is that Britain, by her policies before 1939, accepted military risks which on the facts as now known should in all reasonable probability have destroyed her. Hitler's blunders saved the day and Britain had the courage, the leadership and the skills needed to avoid destruction and to win a most honourable place in the final victory. Should those risks have been run? Was it right in 1939 for Britain and France to challenge Germany to fight? Perhaps it was. Still it can rarely be right to resort to war if the probable outcome is a humiliating defeat. Our ignorance at that time of such vital points as French military competence and the real strengths of the German economy made a disturbing background for decision making.

These points are mentioned here because they seem to be relevant to the politico-military scene today. The Western world which was so signally victorious in 1945 found itself again on the edge of the abyss three years later, at the time of the Berlin confrontation. Miraculously, the dangers passed and out of them the West created the NATO alliance which has already some twenty-five years of invaluable service to its credit. The Western world stood on the verge of the abyss again two years later when the United Nations forces in Korea so narrowly avoided being driven into the sea by the North Koreans and Chinese. All this has passed, but it is surely the case that the military dangers to the West are increasing fast. If we have learnt anything from the past, and perhaps we have not, it would surely be that in dangerous times we should keep our military forces, upon which our future as a race depends, in a high state of efficiency, accepting without hesitation the social and economic consequences of that policy. It is a matter of deepest concern that Britain, despite her experiences, seems set to ignore this devastatingly simple point.

Appendix I

Dowding's posting from Fighter Command[1]

The circumstances of Dowding's posting from Fighter Command in November 1940 gave rise to controversy. The relevant facts are therefore set out in a little more detail. Dowding, through Robert Wright's biography, is on record as saying that he was dismissed as Commander-in-Chief Fighter Command in the second week of November 1940 by a sudden telephone call from Sinclair, saying that he was to relinquish his Command 'immediately'. This account, though supported by Dowding in a letter published in *The Times* of 19 January 1970, is plainly wrong. On 22 January 1970 A. J. P. Taylor sent to *The Times* from the Beaverbrook Archives the minutes of a meeting between Sinclair and Dowding on 13 November 1940, in which Sinclair stated that the Government wished Dowding to go to the United States as adviser on the production of military aircraft. The context made it clear that Sinclair had already consulted Churchill. Dowding asked to see Churchill. A meeting took place at which Churchill confirmed Sinclair's decision, and in consequence Dowding was in the United States from December 1940 to May 1941. This appointment was not a success. There was in truth a great job to be done, that of galvanising plans for American war production especially of aircraft, plans which were and remained, at least until the end of 1941, quite inadequate. Dowding was no man for this job. His comments were highly personal and they had the effect of throwing doubts on the British air programme. Complaints reached the British Ambassador and were forwarded to Beaverbrook. After reference to Churchill, the Dowding mission was brought to a close, despite the support of Beaverbrook. Churchill pressed for Dowding to be given another command, but the Air Ministry was opposed to this. Instead, in June 1941, Dowding was asked to write a Despatch on the Battle of Britain and this was submitted on 20 August 1941. Dowding was then told officially that he was to be retired in October 1941 and the retirement was notified in the *London Gazette*. Although Dowding's previous appointment had been cleared with Churchill, his retirement was not so cleared and in a matter of micro-seconds a large rocket was directed on the devoted head of Sinclair. The retirement was to be cancelled and a further job found. The Air Ministry then proposed that Dowding should undertake a survey of manpower economies in the Royal Air Force. All this was tricky, as Dowding was in no accommodating mood and wanted to devote himself to getting his book, *Twelve Legions of Angels*, through the publishers. Dowding therefore resisted the proposed appointment and again had a meeting with Churchill, who decided that the appointment must stand. Manpower usage was a vital subject for the Royal Air Force, but Dowding was quite unsuited for the job on temperamental and other grounds. So the sad story wound on. The end came by mutual consent in June 1942. This time Sinclair made no mistake about consulting Churchill. Dowding's book, slim and odd, was held up by Churchill for a bit and then was caught by the general ban on memoirs. It was finally published in 1946.

Appendix II

Letters from Eisenhower
to Harris and Marshall

SUPREME HEADQUARTERS
ALLIED EXPEDITIONARY FORCE
Office of the Supreme Commander

13 July, 1944

Dear Harris:

Your recent performance in the Caen area was an eye opener to me, and emphasizes in my mind, again, the magnitude of the debt that this Allied Command owes to you and your officers and men. Your long record of pounding vital targets in Germany, of interrupting enemy communications, of preparing the way for our invasion forces and now, literally, becoming an agent in proper circumstances, of close battle support is one to excite praise and admiration.

I am truly proud to have you and your command in this Allied Team. We could not possibly get along without you.

Good luck!

Sincerely
DWIGHT EISENHOWER

Air Chief Marshal Sir Arthur T. Harris
KCB, OBE, AFC,
Air Officer Commanding-in-Chief,
Bomber Command

At the Quebec Conference (19 September 1944) it was decided that as the invasion of Europe had progressed so well the control of the strategic Bomber Forces should revert from General Eisenhower's Supreme Command to the control of their own service chiefs—ie General Arnold, head of the United States Army Air Force and Marshal of the Royal Air Force Sir Charles Portal, head of the Royal Air Force. The following is an extract from a letter dated 25 September 1944 to General George C. Marshall, Chief of Staff United States of America War Department, from General Eisenhower:

> ... you might be interested to know, in view of earlier expressed fears that Air Chief Marshal Harris would not willingly devote his command to the support of ground operations, that he actually proved to be one of the most effective and cooperative members of this team. Not only did he meet every request I ever made upon him, but he actually took the lead in discovering new ways and means for his particular types of planes to be of use in the battlefield. I am quite sure he was genuinely disappointed to lose his status as an integral part of this organisation. However, he keeps his representative right here at my Headquarters and it is because of the perfection of our past association that I have no real fears for the future. When the great battle occurs for the real entry into Germany he will be on the job ...

Gettysburg
Pennsylvania

June 5, 1964

Dear Bert

On this Sixth of June I suspect that your memory goes back, as mine does, to live over again the gnawing anxieties, the realization of unavoidable sacrifices, and the bright hopes that filled us on D-Day, 1944.

Never, during the two decades that have since passed, have I ceased to render daily and devout thanks to a kindly Providence for permitting us to achieve in eleven months the complete victory that so many believed would require years.

In the same way, I have always felt a deep sense of appreciation and gratitude to all who took part in, or who served in a supporting role for, that great Allied venture.

To you, one of my close associates in OVERLORD, I am impelled to send, once more, a special word of thanks. Your professional skill and selfless dedication to the cause in which we all served will be noted by the histories of those dramatic months, but no historian could possibly be aware of the depth of my obligation to you.

With warm regard,

As ever
IKE E
President Eisenhower

Sir Arthur T. Harris

References

Chapter 2
1 W. J. Reader, *Architect of Air Power. The Life of the First Viscount Weir* (1968), p. 63.
2 Royal Society biographical memoir on Lindemann; articles in *Aeronautics*, July, December 1960, February, September, November 1961.
3 H. A. Jones and Sir Walter Raleigh, *The War in the Air 1914–1918* (Vol. 1 Raleigh, Vols. 2–7 Jones; 1922–1937), 2, pp. 345–6.
4 *Ibid.*, 7, Appendix 45. The estimate of damage is given to seven significant figures.
5 *'Per Ardua'. The Rise of British Air Power 1911–1935* (1944), p. 207.
6 Jones, *op. cit.*, 3, p. 270.

Chapter 3
1 Jones, *op. cit.*, 6, p. 19.
2 Andrew Boyle, *Trenchard* (1962), p. 250.
3 *Men and Power 1917–1918* (1956), p. 220.
4 See *The Aeroplane*, 18 February 1955.
5 Boyle, *op. cit.*, p. 278.

Chapter 4
1 Boyle, *op. cit.*, p. 325.
2 See Sir John Slessor, *These Remain* (1969), p. 80.
3 Cmd 2029, 21 July 1923.
4 Cmd 467, 1919.
5 Cmd 4189.
6 Cmd 4279.

Chapter 5
1 A. J. P. Taylor, *English History 1914–1945* (1965), p. 297.
2 Leo Amery, *My Political Life* (1955), 3, p. 324.

3   Hugh Dalton, *The Fateful Years. Memoirs 1931–1945* (1957), p. 133.

4   Winston S. Churchill, *The Second World War* (1948–1954), I, *The Gathering Storm*, p. 201.

5   For Churchill's opinion of Eden see Martin Gilbert, *Winston S. Churchill*, 5, p. 696. See also Ian Colvin, *The Chamberlain Cabinet*, p. 97.

6   Harold Nicolson (*Diaries and Letters 1939–1945*, p. 355) reports Jan Masaryk (Czechoslovak Minister to Britain 1925–1938) as saying that after Munich Lord Brownlow, Personal Lord-in-Waiting to King Edward VIII, gave Chamberlain a cigarette case on which was engraved a map of Europe, with sapphires marking Berchtesgaden, Godesberg and Munich. It sound implausible but, as we have seen, fiction was hard put to it to keep up with the truth. See also Lord Winterton's Christmas card (S. W. Roskill, *Hankey, Man of Secrets*, 3, p. 33) which, when referring to Chamberlain, whose portrait with Mrs Chamberlain the card embodies, remarks with Horace Walpole 'Who gives a nation peace gives tranquillity to all'.

7   Hansard, 26 June 1923, col. 2142.

8   PRO PREM 1/236.

9   Churchill, *op. cit.*, I, p. 93.

10 *Ibid*.

11 Hansard, 28 November 1934.

12 Cmd 5107.

13 These figures are taken from Basil Collier, *The Defence of the United Kingdom* (1957), p. 78, and should be treated only as a guide to orders of magnitude. On paper, the French first line strength was greater than the British, but their total had no reality as a measure of fighting strength.

14 Taylor, *op. cit.*, p. 378.

15 It seems clear that in the background there were also growing personal/political tensions between Chamberlain and Swinton. In *Sixty Years of Power* (1968), p. 114, Swinton remarks that after he became Prime Minister, Chamberlain became increasingly intolerant of criticism. Around May 1938 Swinton fought for the needs of air re-armament at the price of his personal relations with Chamberlain (see Keith Middlemas, *The Diplomacy of Illusion*, p. 249). A strong case could be made for the proposition that Chamberlain was never whole-hearted about the need for re-armament.

16 M. M. Postan, *British War Production* (1952), pp. 471, 484.

Chapter 6
1 P. M. S. Blackett, *Studies of War* (1962), p. 103.
2 *Ibid.*
3 Sir Arthur Harris, *Bomber Offensive* (1947), p. 59.
4 Collier, *op. cit.*, p. 74.
5 Postan, *op. cit.*, p. 12.
6 Churchill, *op. cit.*, II, *Their Finest Hour*, p. 561.
7 Postan, *op. cit.*, pp. 471, 484.
8 PRO AIR 20/2500.

Chapter 7
1 Harris, *op. cit.*, p. 164.
2 Viscount Templewood (Sir Samuel Hoare), *Empire of the Air* (1957), p. 279.
3 Roskill, *op. cit.*, 3, p. 664.
4 Gilbert, *op. cit.*, 5, p. 738.
5 *Ibid.*, p. 630.
6 *Ibid.*, p. 843n.
7 Postan, *op. cit.*, p. 471.
8 PRO CAB 21 437/8.
9 Hansard, 12 November 1936, col. 1108.
10 PRO PREM 1/237.
11 PRO CAB 21/518.
12 PRO PREM 1/252.
13 For Kingsley Wood's reaction see Colvin, *op. cit.*, pp. 119–20.
14 PRO PREM 1/236.
15 Hansard, 12 May 1938, cols. 1758–1790.
16 For an account of the dismissal see Colvin, *op. cit.*, p. 126.

Chapter 8
1 Roskill, *op. cit.*, 3, Appendix A. Figures given by Norman Gibbs (*Grand Strategy*, I, p. 532), which refer to expenditure and not to estimates, show £82.3m for 1937 and £133.8m for 1938.
2 D. C. Watt, *Personalities and Policies. Essay on Sir Warren Fisher and British Re-armament against Germany* (1965). See also P. J. Grigg, *Prejudice and Judgment* (1948), p. 53.
3 Roskill, *op. cit.*, 3, p. 206.

Chapter 9
1 Postan, *op. cit.*, pp. 471, 484.

2 *Ibid.*
3 Hansard, 12 May 1938, col. 1758.

Chapter 10
1 Colvin, *op. cit.*, p. 255. And of course, as late as 5 April, Chamberlain was to say that Hitler had missed the bus.
2 Slessor in *The Central Blue* (1956), p. 257, gives an amusing account of post-prandial trials of this device in fire-buckets at Admiralty House.
3 J. R. M. Butler, *Grand Strategy*, II, p. 177.
4 *Ibid.*, pp. 187–8.
5 L. F. Ellis, *The War in France and Flanders* (1953), p. 350.
6 Butler, *op. cit.*, p. 184.
7 Ellis, *op. cit.*, p. 312.

Chapter 11
1 Churchill, *op. cit.*, II, p. 561.
2 Denis Richards and Hilary St George Saunders, *The Royal Air Force 1939–1945* (Vol. 1 Richards, Vol. 2 Richards and Saunders, Vol. 3 Saunders; 1953–1954), 1, p. 154.
3 *The Narrow Margin* (1961).
4 *Dowding and the Battle of Britain* (1969).
5 See also David Dilks (ed.), *The Diaries of Sir Alexander Cadogan*, p. 299. 'I don't mind telling you', Dowding said to Halifax with deep emotion, 'that when I heard of the French collapse I went on my knees and thanked God.'

Chapter 12
1 Roskill, *The War at Sea* (1954–1961).
2 *Operational Research in World War 2. Operational Research against the U-boat* (1973), p. 168.
3 Published as Cmd 6775, March 1946.

Chapter 14
1 See Michael Foot, *Aneurin Bevan*, 2 (1973), p. 61, and Hansard, Vol. 416, col. 2544.
2 PRO PREM 4 4/1, 4/2.
3 Hansard, 19 December 1944, cols. 1723–40.
4 PRO AIR 19/493.
5 Gustave Bertrand, *Enigma* (1973).

6 In his *Times Literary Supplement* review of Anthony Cave Brown's *Bodyguard of Lies* (1976).
7 See David Kahn, *The Codebreakers* (1965), pp. 472–6.
8 Collier, *op. cit.*, p. 331.
9 *Ibid.*, Appendix XLVI.

Chapter 15
1 *Middle East 1940–1942. A Study in Air Power* (1944).
2 Richards and Saunders, *op. cit.*, 1, p. 280.
3 *Ibid.*, p. 335.
4 Taylor, *op. cit.*, p. 557.

Chapter 16
1 *The Struggle for Europe* (1952), p. 182.
2 *Ibid.*, p. 523.
3 Taylor, *op. cit.*, p. 120; Cmd 6832, June 1946. *Chambers's Encyclopaedia*, Vol. 14, p. 404, gives a figure nearer to one million for members of the Commonwealth Armed Forces killed in the First World War.

Chapter 17
1 Churchill, *op. cit.*, IV, *The Hinge of Fate*, p. 81.

Chapter 19
1 This was extremely effective. See Ronald Wheatley, *Operation Sea Lion* (1958), pp. 88–9.
2 Hansard, 25 February 1942, cols. 316–17.
3 Sir Charles Webster and Noble Frankland, *The Strategic Air Offensive against Germany* (1961), 3, p. 141.

Chapter 20
1 Taylor, *op. cit.*, p. 591.
2 *Spandau, The Secret Diaries* (tr. R. and C. Winston; 1976).

Chapter 21
1 Hansard, 2 September 1943.
2 Postan, *op. cit.*, p. 333.
3 In *The Nuremberg Raid* (1973).

Appendix I
1 PREM 3/4 66; PREM 4 68/9. Letters in *The Times* of 14, 19, 20, 22 and 24 January 1970.

Bibliography

The Air Ministry: *The Rise and Fall of the German Air Force, 1933–1945*, Air Ministry Pamphlet No 248.

Allen, H. R.: *Who Won the Battle of Britain?*, London, Arthur Barker, 1974.

Andrews, Allen: *The Air Marshals*, London, Macdonald, 1970.

—— *Exemplary Justice*, London, Harrap, 1976.

Babington Smith, Constance: *Evidence in Camera*, London, Chatto & Windus, 1958.

—— *Testing Time*, London, Cassell, 1961.

Balfour, Harold: *Wings over Westminster*, London, Hutchinson, 1973.

Barker, Ralph: *Aviator Extraordinary. The Story of Sidney Cotton*, London, Chatto & Windus, 1969.

—— *The Schneider Trophy Races*, London, Chatto & Windus, 1971.

Barnett, Corelli: *The Collapse of British Power*, London, Eyre Methuen, 1972.

Beaverbrook, Lord: *Men and Power, 1917–1918*, London, Hutchinson, 1958.

Bekker, Cajus: *The Luftwaffe Diaries*, London, Macdonald, 1966.

Bertrand, Colonel Gustave: *Enigma*, Paris, Plon, 1973.

Birkenhead, Earl of: *The Prof in Two Worlds. The Official Life of Professor F. A. Lindemann, Viscount Cherwell*, London, Collins, 1971.

Blackett, Professor P. M. S.: *Studies of War*, Edinburgh, Oliver & Boyd, 1962.

Bond, Brian (ed.): *Chief of Staff. The Diaries of Lieutenant-General Sir Henry Pownall*, Volume I, London, Leo Cooper, 1972.

Boyle, Andrew: *Trenchard*, London, Collins, 1962.

Butler, Professor J. R. M. (ed.): *History of the Second World War. Grand Strategy*, Vol. I. Norman H. Gibbs; Vol. II, J. R. M. Butler; Vol. III Pt. 1, J. M. A. Gwyer, Pt. 2, J. R. M. Butler; Vol. IV, Michael Howard;

Vol. V, J. R. M. Butler; Vol. VI, John Ehrman; London, HMSO, 1956–1976.

Calvocoressi, Peter: 'Enigma', BBC Radio 3 talks printed in *The Listener*, 22 and 27 January, 3 February 1977.

Cave Brown, Anthony: *Bodyguard of Lies*, London, W. H. Allen, 1976.

Clark, Allen: *The Donkeys*, London, Hutchinson, 1961.

Clark, Ronald W.: *The Man Who Broke Purple. The life of the world's greatest cryptologist Colonel William F. Friedman*, London, Weidenfeld & Nicolson, 1977.

—— *The Rise of the Boffins*, London, Phoenix House, 1962.

—— *Tizard*, London, Methuen, 1965.

Collier, Basil: *The Defence of the United Kingdom*, London, HMSO, 1957.

—— *Leader of the Few*, London, Jarrolds, 1957.

—— *A History of Air Power*, London, Weidenfeld & Nicolson, 1974.

Collishaw, Air Vice-Marshal Raymond: *Air Command*, London, William Kimber, 1975.

Colville, Sir John: *Gort, Man of Valour*, London, Collins, 1972.

Colvin, Ian: *The Chamberlain Cabinet*, London, Gollancz, 1971.

Cross, J. A.: *Sir Samuel Hoare*, London, Cape, 1977.

Dalton, Hugh: *The Fateful Years. Memoirs 1931–1945*, London, Muller, 1957.

Deakin, F. W. D.: *The Embattled Mountain*, London, OUP, 1971.

Deighton, Len: *Fighter*, London, Cape, 1977.

Dilks, David (ed.): *The Diaries of Sir Alexander Cadogan*, London, Cassell, 1971.

Douglas of Kirtleside, Marshal of the RAF the Lord: *Years of Command*, London, Collins, 1966.

Dowding, Air Chief Marshal the Lord: *Twelve Legions of Angels*, London, Jarrolds, 1946.

Ellis, Major L. F.: *The War in France and Flanders*, London, HMSO, 1953.

Falk, Stanley L.: *Seventy Days to Singapore*, London, Hale, 1975.

Foot, Michael: *Aneurin Bevan*, Vol. I, London, MacGibbon & Kee, 1962; Vol. II, London, Davis-Poynter, 1973.

Foot, Professor M. R. D.: *Resistance*, London, OUP, 1976.

Frankland, Dr Noble: *see under* Webster.

Gallico, Paul: *The Hurricane Story*, London, Michael Joseph, 1959.

Gamble, C. F. Snowden: *The Story of a North Sea Air Station*, Oxford, OUP, 1928.

Gibbs, Air Marshal Sir Gerald: *Survivor's Story*, London, Hutchinson, 1956.

Gibbs, Norman H.: *see under* Butler.

Gilbert, Martin: *The Roots of Appeasement*, London, Weidenfeld & Nicolson, 1963.

—— *Winston S. Churchill*, Volume V, London, Heinemann, 1976.

—— and Gott, Richard: *The Appeasers*, London, Weidenfeld & Nicolson, 1963.

Gretton, Vice-Admiral Sir Peter: *Crisis Convoy*, London, Peter Davies, 1974.

Grigg, P. J.: *Prejudice and Judgment*, London, Cape, 1948.

Grinnell-Milne, Duncan: *The Wind in the Wires*, 1933, revised edition London, Jarrolds, 1971.

Groves, Brigadier-General P. R. C.: *Behind the Smoke Screen*, London, Faber, 1934.

Guedalla, Philip: *Middle East 1940–1942. A Study in Air Power*, London, Hodder & Stoughton, 1944.

Harris, Marshal of the RAF Sir Arthur: *Bomber Offensive*, London, Collins, 1947.

Harrod, Roy: *The Prof*, London, Macmillan, 1959.

Harvey, Lord, ed. John Harvey: *The Diplomatic Diaries of Oliver Harvey 1937–1940*, London, Collins, 1970.

Harvard-Williams, Jeremy: *Night Intruder*, Newton Abbot, David & Charles, 1976.

Howard, Professor Michael: *The Mediterranean Strategy in the Second World War*, London, Weidenfeld & Nicolson, 1968.

—— *The Continental Commitment*, London, Temple Smith, 1972.

Hyde, H. Montgomery: *Baldwin*, London, Hart-Davis MacGibbon, 1973.

—— *Neville Chamberlain*, London, Weidenfeld & Nicolson, 1976.

—— *British Air Policy Between the Wars 1918–1939*, London, Heinemann, 1976.

Irving, David: *The Rise and Fall of the Luftwaffe. The Life of Erhard Milch*, London, Weidenfeld & Nicolson, 1973.

James, Robert Rhodes: *Churchill. A Study in Failure 1900–1939*, London, Weidenfeld & Nicolson, 1970.

—— *The British Revolution. British Politics 1880–1939*, Vol. II, *From Asquith to Chamberlain 1914–1939*, London, Hamish Hamilton, 1977.

James, Admiral Sir William: *The Eyes of the Navy. A Biographical Study of Admiral Sir Reginald Hall, KCMG, CB, LLD, DCL*, London, Methuen, 1956.

Jones, H. A.: *see under* Raleigh.

Jones, Thomas: *A Diary with Letters 1931–1950*, London, OUP, 1954.
——, ed. Keith Middlemas: *Whitehall Diary*, Volume I 1916–1925, Volume II 1926–1930, London, OUP, 1969.
Joubert, Air Marshal Sir Philip: *The Third Service*, London, Thames & Hudson, 1955.
—— *Birds and Fishes*, London, Hutchinson, 1960.
Kahn, David: *The Codebreakers*, London, Weidenfeld & Nicolson, 1965.
Keith, C. H.: *I Hold My Aim*, London, Allen & Unwin, 1946.
Kirby, Major-General S. W.: *Singapore: The Chain of Disaster*, London, Cassell, 1971.
Laffin, John: *Swifter Than Eagles. The Biography of Marshal of the RAF Sir John Salmond*, Edinburgh, William Blackwood, 1964.
Leasor, James: *Singapore*, London, Hodder & Stoughton, 1968.
Lewis, Cecil: *Sagittarius Rising*, London, Peter Davies, 1936.
Lloyd, Air Marshal Sir Hugh: *Briefed to Attack*, London, Hodder & Stoughton, 1949.
Londonderry, The Marquess of: *Wings of Destiny*, London, Macmillan, 1943.
Marder, Professor A. J.: *From the Dardanelles to Oran*, London, OUP, 1974.
Masterman, J. C.: *The Double-Cross System*, New Haven, Conn., Yale University Press, 1972.
McLachlan, Donald: *Room 39. Naval Intelligence in Action 1939–1945*, London, Weidenfeld & Nicolson, 1968.
Middlebrook, Martin: *The Nuremberg Raid*, London, Allen Lane, 1973.
Middlemas, Keith and Barnes, John: *Baldwin. A Biography*, London, Weidenfeld & Nicolson, 1969.
Ministry of Information: *Atlantic Bridge*, London, HMSO, 1945.
—— *Merchant Airmen*, London, HMSO, 1946.
Morpurgo, J. E.: *Barnes Wallis*, London, Longman, 1972.
Nicolson, Harold: *Diaries and Letters 1939–1945*, London, Collins, 1967.
Postan, Professor M. M.: *British War Production*, London, HMSO and Longman, 1952.
Price, Alfred: *Instruments of Darkness*, London, Kimber, 1967.
Raleigh, Sir Walter and Jones, H. A.: *The War in the Air 1914–1918*, Vol. I, Raleigh; Vols. II–VII, Jones: Oxford, Clarendon, 1922–1937.
Reader, W. J.: *Architect of Air Power. The Life of the First Viscount Weir*, London, Collins, 1968.
Richards, Denis and Saunders, Hilary St George: *The Royal Air Force 1939–1945*, Vol. 1, Richards; Vol. 2, Richards and Saunders; Vol. 3,

Saunders; London, HMSO, 1953–1954.

Roskill, Captain S. W.: *The War at Sea*, 3 volumes, London, HMSO, 1954–1961.

—— *Naval Policy Between the Wars*, 2 volumes, London, Collins, 1968, 1976.

—— *Hankey. Man of Secrets*, Vol. III, *1931–1963*, London, Collins, 1974.

Saunders, Hilary St George: '*Per Ardua*'. *The Rise of British Air Power 1911–1935*, London, OUP, 1944.

Sharp, C. and Bowyer, Michael J. F.: *Mosquito*, London, Faber, 1967.

Slessor, Marshal of the RAF Sir John: *Air Power and Armies*, London, OUP, 1936.

—— *The Central Blue*, London, Cassell, 1956.

—— *These Remain*, London, Michael Joseph, 1969.

Snow, C. P.: *Science and Government*, London, OUP, 1961.

—— *A Postscript to Science and Government*, London, OUP, 1962.

Speer, Dr Albert: *Inside the Third Reich*, London, Weidenfeld & Nicolson, 1970.

—— *Spandau, The Secret Diaries* (tr. R. and C. Winston), London, Collins, 1976.

Swinton, Lord: *I Remember*, London, Hutchinson, 1948.

—— *Sixty Years of Power*, London, Hutchinson, 1968.

Sykes, Major-General Sir Frederick: *From Many Angles. An Autobiography*, London, Harrap, 1942.

Taylor, Professor A. J. P.: *English History 1914–1945*, London, OUP, 1965.

Tedder, Marshal of the RAF the Lord: *With Prejudice*, London, Cassell, 1966.

Templewood, Viscount: *Empire of the Air*, London, Collins, 1957.

Thomson, Lord: *Air Facts and Problems*, London, Murray, 1927.

Tree, Ronald: *When the Moon was High. Memoirs of Peace and War 1897–1942*, London, Macmillan, 1975.

Waddington, Professor C. H.: *Operational Research in World War 2. Operational Research against the U-boat*, London, Paul Elek, 1973.

Walker, Percy B.: *Early Aviation at Farnborough. Balloons, Kites and Airships*, London, Macdonald, 1971.

Watson-Watt, Professor Sir Robert: *Three Steps to Victory*, London, Odhams, 1959.

Watt, Professor D. C.: *Personalities and Policies. Essay on Sir Warren*

Fisher and British Re-armament against Germany, London, Longman, 1965.

—— *Too Serious a Business. European Armed Forces and the Approach to the Second World War*, London, Temple Smith, 1975.

Watt, Sholto: *I'll Take the High Road*, Fredericton, New Brunswick, Brunswick Press, 1960.

Webster, Professor Sir Charles and Frankland, Dr Noble: *The Strategic Air Offensive against Germany 1939–1945* (4 volumes), London, HMSO, 1961.

Wheatley, Ronald: *Operation Sea Lion*, London, OUP, 1958.

Wilmot, Chester: *The Struggle for Europe*, London, Collins, 1952.

Winterbotham, Group Captain F. W.: *Secret and Personal*, London, Kimber, 1969.

—— *The Ultra Secret*, London, Weidenfeld & Nicolson, 1974.

Wohlstetter, Roberta: *Pearl Harbor, Warning and Decision*, Stanford, Calif., Stanford University Press, 1962.

Wood, Derek and Dempster, Derek: *The Narrow Margin*, London, Hutchinson, 1961.

Wright, Robert: *Dowding and the Battle of Britain*, London, Macdonald, 1969.

Index

Index

Baldwin of Bewdsey, Earl—*cont.*
deputation to, 95; and parity, 116;
mentioned, 125, 303
Balfour of Inchrye, Lord, 181
separate air service, 22; and fleet Air
Arm, 42
Balfour of Inchyre, Lord, 181
Balkan Air Force, 223–4
Ball-bearings, 279–80
Balloons: factory at Farnborough, 6;
barrage balloons, 64–5, 192, 201;
balloon squadrons, 78
Baltic States, 135
Bandon, ACM Earl, 313
Barratt, ACM Sir A. S., 121, 130, 132
'Battleaxe', 210
Battle of Britain, 136–47 *passim*, 292
Battle for Europe, 232–5
Battle of France, 126–34 *passim*
Beamish, Gp Capt F. V., 166
Beams: radio beam *Knickebein*, 193–4.
See also Radar
Beatty, Adm of the Fleet Earl, 18, 36
Beaverbrook, Lord: and aircraft pro-
duction, 74, 77; Minister of Aircraft
Production, 126; effect of on aircraft
production, 137–8; proposes
transfer of Coastal Command
to Navy, 172; mentioned 29, 67,
91, 181, 216
Bergen, 123
Berlin, 266, 276, 287
Bertrand, Col G., 188
Bevan, Aneurin, 48, 185, 304
Bevin, Ernest, 185
Big Bertha, 197
Billotte, Gen G. H. G., 128
Binney, Vice-Adm Sir T. H., 168
Bismarck, 158, 162, 164
Blackett, Prof P. M. S.: and Com-
mittee for the Scientific Survey of
Air Defence, 60; and bombsights,
68, 259; and attack on U-boats,
156, 158; views on strategic
bombing, 292–5
Blériot, Louis, 5
Bletchley Park, 189–90
Blitz, 140–1

Blomberg, F-M W. von, 110
Blount, AV-M C. H. B., 120
Bluie West, 178
'Bodyguard', 230
'Bolo House', *see* Hotel Cecil
Bomber Command: re-armament
1935–1939, 35–9, 65–9; role of from
September 1939, 119; breaches
Dortmund-Ems and Mittelland
canals, 150; operations against
enemy shipping in co-operation with
Coastal Command, 162–71 *passim*;
attacks on Peenemünde and St-Leu-
d'Esserent, 199, 202; attacks on
Northern Italy, 202, 204; 254–97
passim
Bombing: for police purposes, 42;
defeats, triumphs, morality of, 292–
297
Bombs, 68, 197, 258–9, 306
Bombsights, 68, 259
Boot, Dr H., 62
Bose, Subhas Chandra, 249
Bottomley, ACM Sir N., 283
Bowhill, ACM Sir F. W., 176
Boyd, AM O. T., 311
Boyd, Wing Cdr R. F., 166, 311
Brancker, Maj-Gen W. S., 29
Brand, AV-M Sir Q., 144
Bremen, 274
Bridges, Lord, 101, 181
British Air Forces in France, 120
British Overseas Airways, 176. *See also*
Imperial Airways
Broadhurst, ACM Sir H., 313
Brooke, Gen Sir Alan, *see* Alanbrooke,
F-M Viscount
Brookes, A. J., 169
Brown, Sir A. W., 11
Broz, Josip, *see* Tito, Marshal
Bucknill, Mr Justice, 168
Bullock, Sir C. L., 89, 90
Burma, 249–53 *passim*
Butler, Lord, 56
Butt Report, 268

Camm, Sir Sydney, 63
Campbell, FO K., VC, 164